The John Tradescants

By the same author

The Florilegium of Alexander Marshal at Windsor Castle

The John Tradescants
Gardeners to the Rose and Lily Queen

PRUDENCE LEITH-ROSS

PETER OWEN • LONDON AND CHESTER SPRINGS

ISBN 0 7206 1246 2

PETER OWEN PUBLISHERS
73 Kenway Road, London SW5 0RE

Peter Owen books are distributed in the USA by
Dufour Editions Inc., Chester Springs, PA 19425-0007

First published 1984
© Prudence Leith-Ross 1984
Revised edition published 2006

Printed and bound by
Excel Print Media Pte Ltd, Singapore

Contents

Illustrations

Preface

Until forty years ago the story of the Tradescants, father and son, was known almost solely by specialists – and then only by those aspects of their extraordinarily wide-ranging careers that concerned the individual researcher, depending on whether he or she was a botanist tracing the Tradescants' plant introductions or a keeper at the Ashmolean Museum in Oxford investigating the origins of the museum's collection. Then in 1964 the late Mea Allan published *The Tradescants*, an eminently readable account of their lives and work shedding light on hitherto unexplored areas of the Tradescants' careers and bringing their name to the attention of a wider public. Her book, which was soon out of print, did, however, leave much material still to be uncovered; more serious, perhaps, deeper research revealed that some of her assertions and conclusions were not supported by the available evidence

In 1977 the Tradescants finally began to receive the recognition that is their due. In that year, under the chairmanship of the late Mrs J.E. Nicholson, the Tradescant Trust was founded in order to save the church of St Mary-at-Lambeth from demolition and to establish there the first Museum of Garden History. Its Victorian structure, with the fourteenth-century tower, that great landmark on the Thames adjacent to Lambeth Palace, had been left to fall into decay, with the Tradescants' curious tomb still standing in the churchyard. Restoration work began in 1979, and four years later the first permanent exhibition about the Tradescants was opened. The work of the trust, now called the Museum of Garden History and covering a much wider field, led to renewed interest in these two remarkable men and to a demand for further information about their lives and work.

This interest continues today – hence this revised edition of their biography.

Prudence Leith-Ross
2005

Acknowledgements

First, I should like to thank Mrs J.E. Nicholson, Chairman of the Tradescant Trust, without whose encouragement this book would never have been attempted.

I should also like to thank the Marquess and Marchioness of Salisbury for allowing me to study and quote from the manuscripts at Hatfield House and their librarian, Mr R. Harcourt Williams, for his help in turning up so many references; and also Lord Delamere for permitting me to examine and quote from Samuel Hartlib's unpublished manuscript *Ephemerides*, deposited in the library of the University of Sheffield, and Mrs G.H. Turnbull for granting me access to her late husband's transcript thereof.

It would have been quite impossible to attempt to identify so many of the plants listed by the Tradescants without the help of Dr John Harvey, and I am extremely grateful to him for all his advice in this respect, for information abour dates of plant introductions and particularly for his generosity in allowing me to publish his modern botanical names for the 1656 plant list as printed in the *Musaeum Tradescantianum*. I should also like to thank Dr W.T. Steam for checking the plant lists and the chapter on plant introductions, Dr David Willis of the New University of Ulster for information about the Narcissus section, Mr David Field for identifying Alexander Marshal's *Clematis virginiana* and Mr Alan Mitchell, Mr Brian Halliwell and Mr J.K. Burras for other botanical information.

I must also express my gratitude to the Director and staff of the Ashmolean Museum, particularly Mr Arthur MacGregor and Mr Gerald Taylor for information about items in the collection and Miss April London for assistance in identifying some of the benefactors to the Tradescant collection.

I must thank Viscount Massereene and Ferrard for letting me inspect such papers as remain at Chilham Castle; Mrs C.H. Hanbury for showing me the house and garden at Burley-on-the-Hill; Mr Paul Pollak of the King's School, Canterbury; Miss Sandra Raphael for kindly checking that there were no references to the Tradescants in John Evelyn's unpublished manuscript *Elysium Britannicum;* and all those descendants and connections of the benefactors whom I approached for information about their forebears.

I have received so much advice and information from so many people that it is impossible to mention them all individually. I must, however, single out the following: Mr David Sturdy for much help and advice, particularly in interpreting seventeenth-century Latin deeds, Miss Linda Moon for translating the two Danish references, Mr A.F. Allen, Dr Peter Bergstrom of the

Colonial Williamsburg Foundation, Dr Helen Brock, the Rev. Dr Edward Brooks, Mr J. Carley, Mr R.O. Dennys, Dr A. de la Mare, Miss Mary Edmond, Dr Helen Forde, Dr David Houston, Mr David Howarth, Mr J. Hull, Mr P.H. Hulton, Dr C.H. Josten, Mr Peter Northeast, Mr R.F. Overnell, Mr Neil Pryor, Dr W.F. Ryan, Mr F.N. Steiner of the Worshipful Company of Gardeners, Sir John Summerson, Mr Richard Thompson of the Worshipful Company of Coopers, and Mr Martin Welch.

I should also like to record my thanks to the librarians and archivists at the Royal Library, Windsor, the Bodleian Library, the British Library and British Museum Manuscript Room, the Guildhall Library, the Library of the Royal Botanic Gardens, Kew, the National Library of Wales, the Minet Library, Lambeth, Canterbury Cathedral Archives and Library, Lambeth Palace Library, the General and Botanical Libraries at the British Museum (Natural History), the Library of the Royal College of Physicians, the Libraries of Magdalen College, Oxford, and Magdalene College, Cambridge, the library of the University of Sheffield, the Lindley and Wisley Libraries of the Royal Horticultural Society the Public Record Office and the County Record Offices of Cumbria, Essex, Hertford, Kent, Leicestershire, Norfolk, Northamptonshire, Staffordshire, Suffolk, Surrey and East and West Sussex; M. J.P. Samoyault of the Musée National du Château du Fontainebleau; Mr Ian Friel of the National Maritime Museum and Mrs Avril Lansdell of Weybridge Museum.

The material from Crown Copyright records in the Public Record Office appears by permission of the Controller of H.M. Stationery Office. The extract from Lord Danby's letter and *Plantarum in Horto*, John Tradescant's plant list of 1634, are reproduced by kind permission of the President and Fellows of Magdalen College, Oxford. The British Library and the Curators of the Bodleian Library have kindly given permission for quotation of extracts from manuscripts in their possession, and the Worshipful Company of Coopers and Worshipful Company of Gardeners kindly gave permission to quote from their records.

Lastly, I should like to thank my editor, Dan Franklin, for all his help in putting my manuscript together.

P.L.-R., 1984

Author's Note

Throughout this book dating conforms to the modern style, that is, the year is taken to begin on 1 January rather than on 25 March. In most quotations the more familiar £ sign has been used to denote the pound sterling.

Know, stranger, ere thou pass, beneath this stone
Lye John Tradescant, grandsire, father, son,
The last dy'd in his spring, the other two
Liv'd till they had travell'd Orb and Nature through,
As by their choice Collections may appear,
Of what is rare, in land, in sea, in air,
Whilst they (as Homer's Iliad in a nut)
A world of wonders in one closet shut,
These famous Antiquarians that had been
Both Gardiners to the Rose and Lily Queen,
Transplanted now themselves, sleep here & when
Angels shall with their trumpets waken men,
And fire shall purge the world, these three shall rise
And change this Garden then for Paradise.

Epitaph on the Tradescants' tomb
in the churchyard of St Mary-at-Lambeth

Introduction

The elder John Tradescant (*c.* 1570–1638) and his son John (1608–62) were gardeners, collectors of curiosities and importers of exotic plants. They were responsible for introducing many new plants into Britain from abroad, both those found on their own extensive travels and others supplied to them by friends who had ventured overseas. Both Tradescants supervised some of the great gardens of their day, and their own botanic garden at South Lambeth, from which plants were disseminated far and wide, became the centre of horticultural interest in Britain. Inside their Lambeth house they opened The Ark, the first museum in the country which the public could visit, a permanent exhibition that attracted the curious and the scholarly alike. In the range of their interests and in their expertise, both Tradescants were unique and were justly famous among their contemporaries. If one were seeking a modern analogy one might say that these two men were responsible for establishing and maintaining the seventeenth-century equivalents of the Royal Botanic Gardens at Kew and a museum such as the Victoria and Albert.

In their interests, father and son reflected the spirit of their age. At home, the garden was beginning to occupy the place within the concerns of the English gentleman that it has held ever since: an object of delight, devotion and, on occasion, intense rivalry. With trade developing throughout the world, new varieties of plants were being brought into Britain and wealthy gentlemen competed to grow them in their gardens. And of course this interest in the novel and curious was not confined to plants. As trading factories became established in places that a century before had been little more than the stuff of rumour or legend, all manner of strange and unusual objects flowed into Britain, to be gazed at by sensation-seekers or studied seriously by those with a more scholarly turn of mind. To be called a 'curious' or 'ingenious' man was, in the seventeenth century, a mark of considerable respect. It indicated someone with a scientific mind, an interest in the unusual and a thirst for knowledge. Both terms suited the Tradescants well.

The new plants and objects were inevitably accompanied by curious and fantastic tales, often so well embroidered as to have become pure fantasy. There was, for instance, the 'Tartary Lamb' or 'Borametz'. This plant was supposed to resemble a lamb, attached by its navel to a stem three feet high and grown from a seed similar to that of a melon but 'lesse and longer'.[1] In 1629 John Parkinson, the King's herbalist and a close friend of the elder Tradescant, went so far as to illustrate it in the frontispiece of his otherwise scholarly and important botanical book *Paradisi in Sole Paradisus Terrestris.*

(Reflecting the prevailing interest in curious objects and ingenious inventions was a craze for anagrams and puns; Parkinson's title is a pun on his own name: 'The Earthly Paradise of Park-in-Sun'.) Even in 1656 the Tradescant museum boasted 'a very small part' of borametz skin and a 'coat lyned' with it. Unicorns, of course, were said to roam wild on distant shores. Specimens of their horns were much prized and could be found both at Windsor and in the Tower of London, where there was also a gown 'lined with the skin or fur of a unicorn'. The fur was 'said to be a long, shaggy, uncouth lining, but because it is found nowhere else, it is very highly esteemed'.[2] Finally, as late as 1678, no less august and scientific a body than the Royal Society published an eyewitness account of Barnacle Geese emerging from shells attached to a piece of driftwood on a Scottish island. It was recorded that these shells had 'within them little Birds perfectly shap'd'.[3]

With so many rarities both 'natural' and 'artificial' – as man-made objects were then described – arriving in the country, it was not surprising that imaginations were carried away in the prevailing mood of enthusiastic wonder and that almost anything came to seem possible. Looking back from the world of today, it is difficult to imagine the intense interest and excitement that derived from so many new experiences. The arrival of the first moon-rocks might perhaps make a suitable comparison: only the moon-rocks seem dull indeed when compared with the colourful birds, strange animals and vast shells that were brought back from those overseas voyages.

People in a position to do so, like the wealthy politician Sir Walter Cope, began to acquire 'Cabinets of Rarities', so called because these miscellaneous collections were carefully stored in wooden cabinets with drawers. Such hoards were said to 'enriche the minde'[4] and were tucked away for private contemplation and brought out only to share with a few privileged friends. Collecting became a mania: others acquired fine pictures to hang in their galleries, while mechanical devices – in particular those involving the elusive and intriguing concept of perpetual motion – caused intense interest.

As only the rich could afford them, such collections became a status symbol, but their poorer fellows were not starved of wonders. In Shakespeare's *The Tempest*, published in 1610, Trinculo remarks:

> A strange fish! Were I in England now (as once I was), and had but this fish painted, not a holiday fool there but would give a piece of silver; there would this monster make a man; any strange beast there makes a man: when they will not give a doit to relieve a lame beggar, they will lay out ten to see a dead Indian.

Then, as today, a visit to London would include a trip to see the tombs in Westminster Abbey and the armoury and royal menagerie at the Tower, but visitors of all classes also flocked to the shows put on at inns or at St

Bartholomew's Fair. John Evelyn evidently did not consider it beneath his dignity to stare at the 'hairy maid',[5] while Samuel Pepys regularly met acquaintances at the Fair – although on one occasion it did trouble him 'to sit among such nasty company' to see the dancing monkeys.[6] Sir Daniel Fleming happily paid out for the sight of a dromedary and to see 'the Turk'[7] – perhaps the rope-dancer of that name whom Evelyn was to see two years later.

Some idea of the variety of entertainment available can be gleaned from a poem by Henry Farley published in 1621:

> To see a strange out-landish Fowle
> A quaint Baboon, an Ape, an Owle,
> A dancing Beare, a Gyants bone,
> A foolish Ingin move alone,
> A Morris-dance, a Puppit play,
> Mad Tom to sing a Roundelay,
> A woman dancing on a Rope,
> Bull-baiting also at the Hope;
> A Rimers Jests, a Juglers cheats,
> A Tumbler shewing cunning feats,
> Or Players acting on the Stage,
> There goes the Bounty of our Age;
>> But unto any pious motion,
>> There's little coine, and lesse devotion.[8]

Ten years later London had a new attraction, Tradescant's Ark, where 'a Man might in one daye behold and collecte into one place more Curiosities then hee should see if hee spent all his life in Travell'.[9]

Meanwhile the landed gentry, with time and money on their hands, endeavoured to outdo one another in their building achievements. For almost the first time they started to cultivate gardens, not just for culinary and medicinal purposes as they had done in the past but purely for pleasure – to look at and enjoy, and to walk in 'for refreshment'. To stock these gardens they sought new varieties from abroad and engaged gardeners to tend and care for them. No expense was spared, for the gardens were exposed to view even more than the houses, and the beauty of a gentleman's garden was one measure of his wealth and quality.

'God Almighty first planted a garden: and, indeed, it is the purest of human pleasures,' wrote Francis Bacon in his famous essay.[10] He went on to describe the perfect garden, which, although a figment of his imagination, must have been based on those he had seen. He wanted flowers for every season of the year and listed what he would expect to see in bloom each month. Only after July did he get stuck and have to resort to various varieties of fruit because, with the exception of monkshood, poppies, late roses and 'holly-oaks', no autumn-flowering plants were grown at that time. Perhaps this explains why fruit and flowers were so often grown together in the same beds.

'Nothing is more pleasant to the eye than green grass kept finely shorn,' Bacon pronounced, and when it is remembered that such lawns had to be cut by hand with a scythe the cause for admiration can be doubly appreciated. On either side Bacon wanted 'a covert alley, upon carpenter's work, about twelve foot in height by which you may go in shade'.

Bacon disapproved of garden knots made with 'divers coloured earths', a practice often resorted to at the time as a substitute for plants because it was considered to have the merit of providing perpetual colour. Topiary he dismissed as only 'for children', but a thirty-foot mount, fountains and a banqueting house were all considered essential.

Sir Henry Wotton, for many years Ambassador to Venice, wanted an irregular garden to contrast with the regularity of the building or at least one 'cast with a very wilde Regularitie'. He had seen a garden 'into which the first accesse was a high walke like a Terrace, from whence might he taken a general view of the whole Plott below; but rather in a delightfull confusion, then with any Plain Distinction of the Pieces. From this the beholder descending many Steps, was afterwards conveyed againe, by several Mountings and Valings, to various entertainments of his Sent; and Sight: which I shall not neede to describe (for that were poeticall) let me onely note this, that every one of these Diversities, was as if hee had been Magically transported into a new Garden.'[11]

An element of surprise was to be found in all the best gardens of the time, with the plot divided up into a series of 'rooms'. By the Tradescants' time, knots, always based on a square, had progressed from simple patterns to immensely intricate designs and were edged with low-growing evergreens, such as box, thyme or hyssop, that were comparatively easy to keep clipped. The open knot was often filled with sand or the coloured earth so much despised by Bacon, the closed with flowers of uniform colour.

Although Stephen Blake, when he published *The Compleat Gardiners Practice* in 1664, was still illustrating designs for knots, one of which bore the inscription

> Heere I have made the true Lovers Knott
> To try it in Mariage was never my Lott

the embroidered parterre was soon to become paramount. Geometrical designs gave way to feathery scrolls in leaf- or shell-like shapes.

Fruit trees in plashed or pleached alleys surrounded the plots, and there were shady walks in leafy tunnels. A gazebo, raised terrace or artificial mound enabled one to look down on a carpet of knots or parterres below and perhaps also to catch a glimpse of the countryside beyond.

This then was the scene into which the elder Tradescant stepped and left his mark as a plantsman and cultivator of exotics. Perhaps it was to compensate for the fact that he had no sense of smell that he constantly sought out the strange and the rare, the biggest and the best, for a sweet-scented rose or fragrant honeysuckle could make no impression on him. The younger Tradescant followed in his father's footsteps but, probably because of the more stringent times in which he lived, grew more mundane but useful species alongside the curiosities.

The equipment of the seventeenth-century gardener differed from that of his modern counterpart only in its sophistication. To preserve their rare introductions from frost, the Tradescants would simply have covered them with straw. The really delicate exotics, such as the citrus trees, were planted in hooped wooden tubs with lugs on them so that poles could be inserted for easy carrying. In this way they could be moved by two men without risk of damage, and as frosts became imminent they were put into shelter. Orange-houses at this time were seldom more than wooden sheds with windows and perhaps a stove.

For watering there were watering-pots, similar in shape to the cans of today, and butts that were trundled about on wheels. In more sophisticated gardens elaborate pumps were used to squirt water like a modern hose; as early as 1577 Thomas Hyll described 'great Squirts of Tinne': the thrusting-down of the pump requiring 'mightier strength' than the drawing-up, causing the water to 'flee forthe of the pipe holes . . . in the forme of raine'.[12]

To scare away birds, Gervase Markham recommended a young boy with a bow and arrows: if he ran up and down 'making a great noise and acclamation' this would be the 'best and safest meanes to prevent this evil'.[13] As an effective deterrent against thieves, Ralph Austen proposed 'a lusty Mastiffe or two'.[14]

By the middle of the century John Evelyn was advising the use of a lattice to ensure regular planting and suggested carrying a fully furnished four-poster bed into the garden to 'draw over and preserve the Choysest flowers'. In Evelyn's view, the best rollers for gravel walks were those 'of the hardest Marble' such as could be 'procured from the ruines of many places in *Smyrna* when old *Colomns* of demolish'd Antiquities are being sawd off'. These, he declared, 'may be procur'd by the friendship of some Merchant trading into the Levant'.[15]

During their working lives both the Tradescants witnessed many changes in garden fashions, not least those made possible by the advances in engineering which led to all kinds of elaborate waterworks, such as those constructed at Hatfield House. Hillsides were levelled into descending terraces, and gardens began to spread out on a much grander scale to encompass the landscape. There were orchards, vineyards and 'wildernesses', which, contrary to their name, were carefully ordered plantations of trees crossed by radiating walks.

Such changes in garden design were gradual. Nothing happened overnight, and many gardens must have remained exactly as they had been in Tudor times. A further change was occurring in the theory and literature of gardening, the seventeenth century seeing the publication of a number of important books on botany and horticulture, but again the advance was gradual. Astrology was still an important factor to be considered in horticulture, and, although he was becoming disillusioned with some aspects of it, when William Coles published *The Art of Simpling* in 1656 he, in common with most other contemporary gardeners, still firmly believed in the influence of the sun and the moon.

In 1629 John Parkinson published the first book to be devoted entirely to pleasant flowers as distinct from useful and medicinal plants. Parkinson was a shrewd observer of the botanical scene and a writer with a delightful prose style; his *Paradisus* describes nearly one thousand flowers, of which more than three-quarters are illustrated. On the strength of this work Charles I appointed him Botanicus Regius Primarius.

Born in 1567, Parkinson trained as an apothecary, holding the royal appointment to James I and helping to found the Society of Apothecaries in 1617. Three years later he became Warden of the Society, but in 1622 he retired to devote himself to the study of plants, which from then until his death in 1650 became his sole and consuming interest. His own garden in Long Acre was well stocked with exotics, and he was responsible for many introductions, often employing paid collectors to send him plants from abroad. Always effusive in his affection for John Tradescant senior, Parkinson often refers to the generosity of his 'great friend' in passing on plants.

Parkinson's other great work, the *Theatrum Botanicum*, published in 1640, is basically a herbal. It covers about 3,800 plants, of which more than two-thirds are illustrated, all grouped under their medicinal properties. The few for which he could find no use are listed as 'The Unordered Tribe'.

At the end of the previous century the barber-surgeon John Gerard had also published a *Herbal*. Born in Cheshire in 1545, he travelled to Scandinavia, Russia and possibly also to the Mediterranean before returning to London to become apprenticed. He was admitted to the freedom of the Barber-Surgeons' Company in 1569.

Renowned as a skilful herbalist, Gerard also supervised the gardens of Lord Burghley, both in the Strand and at Theobalds, Burghley's palatial new residence in Hertfordshire. Gerard also devoted much of his time to his own Holborn garden which became famous for exotics and which must have been the focus of horticultural interest in Britain at the turn of the century. In 1596 he published a list of the plants growing in this garden and a year later brought out his *Herbal*, which he dedicated to Burghley. This was basically a translation of Dodoens's *Pemptades* in rearranged form and with additional information as to where in England various plants could be found, but it contained many errors.

In 1604 he was granted a lease on a garden adjoining Somerset House by Queen Anne of Denmark, the wife of James I, but in the following year he passed it on to Lord Burghley's second son, Robert Cecil, the first Earl of Salisbury. Gerard died in 1612, five years after being appointed Master of the Barber-Surgeons' Company.

Probably the best herbalist of the age was the apothecary Thomas Johnson, who was born at Selby in Yorkshire about 1600. By 1626 he was in business on Snow Hill where he also had a physic garden. Accompanied by a group of interested colleagues and friends, he made several botanizing expeditions to various parts of England and Wales. He published accounts of these expeditions, but he is best remembered for his 1633 revised edition of Gerard's 1597 *Herbal*. In addition to correcting many of Gerard's mistakes, he added more than 800 new plant species and about 700 illustrations. 'Gerard emaculate', as Johnson's edition became known, proved so popular that it was reprinted three years later without alteration.

Johnson visited the Tradescants' South Lambeth garden in July 1632 and almost certainly on other occasions, too. During the civil war he served as a Lieutenant-Colonel in the Royalist army. Probably while at Oxford he was made a Bachelor of Physic in 1642 and in the following year MD. He died in 1644, a fortnight after being wounded at the siege of Basing House.

The works of Parkinson, Gerard and Johnson will be referred to often in the pages that follow. So, too, will the Tradescants' own plant lists. The elder Tradescant made two that have survived, the first being a list of the plants that he received from abroad between the years 1629 and 1633, which he recorded in the back of his copy of *Paradisus*. (This list is reproduced in Appendix I.) In 1634 he published his own plant catalogue under the title *Plantarum in Horto Iohannem Tradescanti nascentium Catalogus* (see Appendix II). It contains more than 750 plants and a wide variety of fruit trees, showing remarkable diversification for the period. In 1656 John Tradescant junior published a much more substantial volume called *Musaeum Tradescantianum* (*see* Appendix III). It catalogues in considerable detail both the contents of the museum and, using Latin terminology with the English equivalents, all the plants then growing in his garden. These included some that he had collected during his journeys to Virginia.

A number of the plants listed are named after the two Morin brothers, eminent Paris nurserymen dealing mainly in bulbs. René, the elder, also specialized in cyclamen. Pierre became the more famous; 'from an ordinary Gardner', in the words of John Evelyn, he 'arriv'd to be one of the most skilful and Curious Persons of France'. His garden, 'of an exact Oval figure planted with Cypresse', contained 'Tulips, Anemonies, Ranunculus's, Crocus's &c', which 'were held for the rarest in the World'.

The coat of arms used by the younger John Tradescant

Chapter 1

Tradescant's Early Life

Despite the elder John Tradescant's fame in his own lifetime both as a plantsman and a collector, his origins have remained obscure. One theory is that the Tradescants came originally from Holland, the evidence being a description of John Tradescant senior as 'a Dutchman' *in Athenae Oxonienses* by the seventeenth-century historian Anthony Wood.[1] Wood was a friend of Elias Ashmole, who became closely involved in the affairs of the younger John Tradescant, and such a comment from an informed contemporary cannot be dismissed out of hand.

Nevertheless, no other hard evidence can be found to support this theory. Lists of aliens do not include the name Tradescant in any of its various forms, nor is it known in either Holland or Belgium, although the name 'Traskine' is still current in the south of France. Early references to the name are often written 'Tredeskyn' or 'Tradescon', which might indicate an attempt to spell it phonetically with a French pronunciation, later becoming Anglicized as Tradescant, always with the emphasis on the second syllable.

If Tradescant was a Dutchman then one possibility is that he found his way to England under the auspices of the Dutch Ambassador, Sir Noel Caron, who served in London between 1590 and 1624; the painter and architect Balthazar Gerbier arrived in England by this route. Certainly Sir Noel's garden at South Lambeth was famous. In 1606, when sending a present of fruit to Robert Cecil, first Earl of Salisbury, Caron 'thanks God he has found such a fertile place for his garden, where everything grows in abundance'.[2] He does not name his gardener, but, had it been Tradescant (from wherever he came), Caron would have been well placed to recommend him to Cecil when the latter decided to plant out the garden at Hatfield House. It might also explain why Tradescant later chose Lambeth as the site of his own garden.

Further, very circumstantial evidence is that the elder Tradescant was able to find his way around in Holland with apparent ease, while in Paris he took along an acquaintance to act as a guide.

It is much more likely, however, that Tradescant's antecedents came from

21

Suffolk. A search of surviving parish records, subsidy returns and wills shows that there were Tradescants in Suffolk from at least the mid sixteenth century.

Indeed, although it is impossible to be certain owing to the many variants in spelling that were the norm in the sixteenth century and earlier, they were probably there before that. In 1382 the rector of Kirkley was a John Tradesham.[3] The printed subsidy return for 1524 shows a William Treylnseant (probably a mistranscription of 'Treyluscant') living at Wenhaston; he must have had some standing in the village as he later acted as executor to the vicar, William Hobson.[4] William Treluskant (as it is spelt in his will) died in 1536; the will shows that he had two sons, Richard and Thomas.[5] Richard remained at Wenhaston, appearing in the subsidy returns for 1547 and 1568, and no doubt fathered the William Tradeskante who featured in those from 1581 to 1598 and died in 1609.[6] He is described in his will as 'Willm Tradescant alias Luske'.

Thomas probably moved to the nearby village of Henstead where, in a deed of 1567, there is mention of a 'Thomas Traluscant alias Tradescant'.[7] The Henstead parish records show that in 1543 he married Elyner Durrant and by her fathered a large family, most of whom died almost as soon as they were born. Among the survivors were Thomas, born in 1552, Jone in the following year and William in 1563.

According to the will of Elyner's father Benedict Durrant, there had been two elder sons called Thomas and Nicholas, both born before 1551.[8] Unfortunately some of the early pages of Henstead parish register are damaged and their baptisms cannot be traced. Nicholas died in 1566, when his burial is recorded, and it seems likely that Thomas died before 1552 when the second Thomas was born.

After Elyner's death in 1564, Thomas married Johanne Settaway of Gisleham, the daughter of Thomas and Agnes Settaway. In quick succession she bore two sons, John in 1565 (who lived for less than a month) and Nicholas the following year. They were both baptized at Henstead, and it must have been soon afterwards that Thomas and his wife moved to the village of Corton on the Suffolk coast, about four miles north of Lowestoft; in a deed drawn up after his death he is described as 'of Corton'.[9]

His son Thomas made his will in 1577, some six years before he died. In it he is described as a 'single man' of Somerleyton,[10] but he is probably the same Thomas Tradescant who is called 'yeoman of London' in a slightly later deed.[11] He left legacies to his three brothers William, Steven and either Thomas or John, as well as to his sister Jone. While the official transcript of this will gives the last brother's name as Thomas, in the original, which is written in an untidy hand, it can be read as Jhon, a common spelling at that time. (Although there is a contraction on top to indicate that letters have been omitted, the scribe was fairly free with these embellishments and also put one over the name Stanton, which is clearly written out in full.)

Christian names did recur with great regularity in the same families, but it seems too much of a coincidence that there could have been another family with the unusual surname of Tradescant living at the same time with these three identical names; a search of innumerable parish registers and subsidy returns for a wide area of Suffolk has failed to reveal any more Tradescants. This suggests that, after leaving Henstead, Thomas fathered two more children with the names of Steven and Thomas or John. Unfortunately it has not been possible to trace their baptisms as the Corton parish register does not start until 1579.

Moreover, the will of the 'single man' Thomas Tradescant also mentions his 'father in law' William Stanton. In 1573 a marriage took place in Norwich between a Johanne Tradeston and a William Stanton, both of Corton, and in using this phrase Thomas probably meant his stepmother's second husband. The Stanton family held land in Somerleyton, where they flourished. One, another William, was Chief Constable for thirty-two years, to which position his son succeeded. It may be purely coincidence that Somerleyton had two imposing gardens by the mid seventeenth century.

The surprising discrepancy in Thomas's will is the omission of Nicholas from the beneficiaries. When it was made he would have been thirteen years old and, as the oldest son of his father's second marriage, in line to inherit his maternal grandfather's lands at Gisleham after his widow's death in 1591.[12] The fact that there are no Tradescants listed in the subsidy returns for Henstead in 1580, when Nicholas would have been only fourteen, but that his name appears in those for 1592 and 1598 suggests that he also inherited land there from his father, perhaps after the death of his elder half-brother, the single Thomas of Somerleyton, which could well have been tied up separately from his will. Moreover, the fact that Thomas leaves 'all ye rest of my goods not bequeathed' to his stepmother's new husband might indicate that the other beneficiaries were still quite young.

Finally, mention must be made of two other Tradescants. In his will, made in 1661, the younger John Tradescant left legacies, 'in remembrance of my love', to his two 'namesakes', Robert and Thomas Tradescant of Walberswick, but the sum involved does not suggest that they were particularly close. His widow Hester, in her will, called them her husband's 'kinsmen' but appears to have lost touch with them. Although it seems likely that they were related, they are not mentioned in the will of John Tradescant senior, which suggests that any connection was distant and perhaps they only came to know John junior after the South Lambeth family became famous. If the suggested family tree (see pp. 324–5) is correct they would have been distant cousins.

In view of the complexity of some of the genealogical details given above, a short summary might be useful. The name Tradescant appears to have evolved from that of Treluscant, and it seems probable that the elder John

Tradescant was born on the Suffolk coast at Corton about the year 1570, his parents being Thomas Tradescant (formerly of Henstead) and his second wife Johanne (*née* Settaway).

Nothing is known of the elder John Tradescant's education and upbringing. From the various documents in his hand that survive, it is obvious that he had been taught to read and write, but it is unlikely that he attended a grammar school as he does not appear to have received a classical education. While familiar with the Latin names of plants, he did not spell them according to correct, standardized Latin but used any phonetic form that sounded right, as was then correct practice when writing English. Had he been brought up in Corton he would have become familiar with boats and the sea from an early age, which would account for the knowledge of maritime affairs displayed later in his Russian diary.

The first known fact about John senior is his marriage at Meopham in Kent in 1607 to Elizabeth Day. There were two girls of this name in the village, both with fathers called James. The elder, the daughter of a farmer, was baptized in 1573, and on the grounds that only one child seems to have been born as a result of the marriage it has been suggested by Mea Allan that this was John's bride. Had Tradescant married the younger Elizabeth, she writes, 'it is likely that they would have had more children'.[13]

In fact it was the Elizabeth Day baptized on 22 August 1586 whom Tradescant married. Her 'borrowers' or godparents were Dirreck Harman, Janikin Jessop and Janikin Garrat of London. Elizabeth was the daughter of the late vicar of Meopham, James Day, who had been ordained at Fulham by the Bishop of London in 1564 and who is thought to have come originally from Langley in Hertfordshire.[14] James Day, together with his children Samuel and Sara, had died of the plague in 1593, perhaps after a visit to London, as there are no other deaths from the disease recorded in the parish register for that year. Elizabeth, who was only six years old when this tragedy struck the family, remained in the village with her mother, Gertrude. Within three years Gertrude Day had remarried, but her husband, John Forward, died almost immediately, in 1597. That same year she married again, becoming Gertrude Wilcock, probably the wife of the Richard Wilcockes who was buried at Meopham in 1606. Finally, two years later, she contracted a fourth marriage, to George Lance. Her last three husbands all came from local families, the names recurring in the parish register and among the list of borrowers.

We know that Tradescant's bride was this Elizabeth Day because her sister Dorcas, some six years older, married as her second husband Alexander Norman, whom Tradescant referred to as his brother-in-law. Dorcas's first husband, Leonard Chambers, whom she married at the church of St

Katherine by the Tower, was a cooper in East Smithfield. He died in 1620, and at the beginning of the next year Dorcas married Alexander Norman at St Botolphs-without-Aldgate. He was the son of John Norman, a husbandman of Ho(l)mer in Herefordshire, and had completed his seven-year apprenticeship as a cooper two years earlier.[15] Alexander Norman not only took on Leonard Chambers's widow but also his cooper's intabulation mark,[16] his apprentices[17] and presumably his business, too.

Although Tradescant married a Meopham girl there is no evidence that he ever lived in the village himself. His name does not occur among the long list of borrowers in the parish records, nor in any of the Kent Lieutenancy papers for the period that have been searched. It seems much more likely that he met his bride elsewhere, possibly in London when she was visiting her sister, and that she returned to her mother for the birth of her son, another John, on 4 August of the following year. It was common practice to return home for the birth and baptism of the eldest child, and the fact that the younger John was born in August, always a dangerous time for the plague in London, might have been an added incentive in view of the losses the family had already sustained from the dread disease.

On the strength of a pair of mulberry trees (possibly dating from the early 1600s) and some possible Tradescant flowers growing in the garden, it has been suggested (by Dr C.H. Golding Bird and Mea Allan) that Tradescant lived in Pitfield Cottage on Meopham Green. It is a delightful story which it would be nice to perpetuate, but unfortunately the evidence does not support it. Mulberries were planted all over England in pairs as the result of James I's attempt to found a silk industry, and the pair at Meopham probably date from his edict of 1607.

It has also been suggested that Tradescant could have met his bride at Meopham while working near by, either at Shorne or at Cobham Hall. Shorne was acquired by Robert Cecil and, so the theory has it, he might have taken over Tradescant with the garden. But Shorne's gardens were never noteworthy, and Cecil first leased the property in 1609 (before receiving it as a perk in 1611), two years after Tradescant's marriage. It is not even known whether Cecil ever visited the place.

Cobham Hall's gardens were renowned, but they were laid out and planted in the 1590s, and, had Tradescant worked there, he is hardly likely to have been courting a little girl of ten years old. In 1603 Lord Cobham was impeached and was languishing in the Tower, after which little work seems to have been done on the gardens, although his wife continued to live in the Hall.

The fact is that we do not know where John Tradescant was employed before 1610, when he went to work at Hatfield for Robert Cecil. What we can be certain of is that he must have already made his name, for the first Earl of Salisbury employed only the best. There are, however, various possibilities. One is that he was working for Sir Henry Fanshawe, the Remembrancer of the Exchequer, in his garden at Ware, Hertfordshire, which was famous for fruit and was extensively redesigned in 1606.[18] Another is that Tradescant was employed at Theobalds, the Hertfordshire palace built by Robert Cecil's father, Lord Burghley, which was also renowned for its splendid gardens, but such papers as do survive do not mention Tradescant's name. There is, however, a connection, albeit faint, between Tradescant and Theobalds at this period. Lord Burghley's gardener was the barber-surgeon John Gerard, whose *Herbal* published in 1597 describes the Painted Sage. In repeating this description in the revised edition of 1633, Thomas Johnson adds: 'The fine or elegant painted Sage was first found in a countrey garden by Mr John Tradescant, and by him imparted to other lovers of plants.'[19] This indicates that Gerard received the plant that he grew in his own celebrated Holborn garden from Tradescant before 1597.

All that we can say for certain is that by 1609 Tradescant was already travelling on behalf of an eminent employer and that he had probably been doing so for some years. In November of that year he wrote to William Trumbull, then British Resident in Brussels:

My humble duty remembered – Good Mr Trumbull.
I humbly thank your Worship for all your Cortisies but your good Will and labours hath not efected what you desired to dooe for they have put me upon the Rack. I have given for every hundred an angell in one ofis beside many other pedy offisis that hath had halfe a crowne apeese for the share soe the whole hathe cost me 40s besids 24s the pasag to flusshing. They saye that is no pasport because the other had on before. They say that two pasports canot be in on, and beside that they say that he had had the Last yeare halfe his Supplements and this yeare he hath had the full sume of all and more. Therfor I have gotten this muche that if he hathe a newe pase this year that I shall have my mony againe, and if it com to perfecion that eyther your self or Thomas Strong an Irishe man in the Curt Riders Street may Reseve it for me, but I feare it will not be Done Soe I Rest yours ever to Dooe you servis.

Next to the Signe of the Rose in the above said place. Remember Mr Lassells.

John Tradescant

I also Disir your Worship to asist the berer herof for another pase if it ma be eslye don.[20]

The letter provides frustratingly little information besides revealing that bureaucracy was obviously as aggravating in the seventeenth century as it is today. We can, however, deduce that Tradescant must already have been moving in court circles, as Mr Lassells, to whom he wishes to be remembered, was Edmond Lascelles who, having spent a fortune as a Groom of the Privy Chamber, had gone to Antwerp to join the army of the Marquis of Brandenburg. The letter is endorsed as having been sent from London, but there is no record of a 'Curt Riders Street' there. The first word, however, might have been intended to be 'Cnit', to represent Knightrider Street, which lay south of St Paul's, parallel with the river and Thames Street, part of which later became Old Fish Street and where, in about 1660, there is known to have been a public house called The Rose.

Chapter 2

Plantsman at Hatfield

On 1 January 1610 John Tradescant went to work for Robert Cecil, first Earl of Salisbury, at Hatfield House in Hertfordshire. Tradescant's wages were not paid until the following November when he received £37 10s. 'for 3/4 of a year ending at Michaelmas for keeping the gardens there'.[1] His salary was thus fifty pounds a year, a very substantial wage for a gardener. The fact that he received no payment before this indicates that he must already have been of reasonable means to support himself and his family for nine months.

It was a time of intense activity at Hatfield. Three years earlier England's Secretary of State had accepted this royal palace and sixteen other manors in exchange for Theobalds, the palatial residence that he had inherited from his father.[2] James I had become enamoured with the style and comfort of Theobalds while enjoying the generous hospitality of his host. Cecil had in any event found it too large,[3] and no doubt the sale of the other manors that came to him with Hatfield at least helped towards the cost of rebuilding.

Theobalds must have been a splendidly ostentatious building. The hall ceiling was decorated with the twelve signs of the zodiac, showing at night the 'stars proper to each', while by day the sun performed 'its course'; on each side of the hall stood six trees with 'the natural bark so artfully joined with birds' nests and leaves as well as fruit upon them' that 'when the steward of the house opened the windows, which looked upon the beautiful pleasure garden, birds flew into the hall, perched themselves upon the trees, and began to sing'.[4]

By comparison, the old Tudor palace of Hatfield was obviously out of date and unfashionable. The Earl of Salisbury decided that it had to be rebuilt. He started on this task at once, choosing for his site the rise of a hill to the southeast and leaving only one wing of the old house standing. Building was his hobby. He was already involved in large-scale reconstruction work on his properties at Cranborne in Dorset and in London. Nevertheless everything at Hatfield had to be of the best – as befitted the greatest statesman of the age.

Although Jacobean, Hatfield House was built to the 'E' design so popular in Elizabethan times. The white stonework dressing, central clock tower and open colonnade stand out in stark contrast to the red brick walls, bearing some Renaissance influence and reminiscent in style of Cecil's father's great edifice Theobalds.

Robert Liming was responsible for the design, with the first Earl involved at every stage of the planning; at one point Inigo Jones seems to have been called in to give advice on the south front and the clock tower. The organization of a steady flow of materials was a massive task. Stone came from Caen and blue slate from Plymouth; the paving was of Purbeck stone. The white marble for the three main fireplaces was shipped all the way from Italy. Bricks were fired locally, the walls of the old palace being used in the garden and for levelling the courts, but nails were sent from Sussex and the lead for roofing was mined in Derbyshire.

The house was much too large for the family's needs, a major part being set aside as state rooms for the royal visit that the first Earl never lived to enjoy. The decorations were carried out by the best craftsmen of the day, whether English, French, Dutch or Venetian.

Much of the interior of the house has been changed in the intervening years, and a fire destroyed most of the west wing in 1835, but the Marble Hall, two storeys high, and the Grand Staircase remain as masterpieces of the period.

The Earl of Salisbury also took a keen personal interest in the gardens that surrounded his houses and is known to have been consulted for his ideas on the subject by no less an authority than Francis Bacon.[5] By 1610 work was sufficiently advanced at Hatfield for the gardens to be laid out. In January of that year the carpenters were already 'in hand with the framing of the walkes in the west garden'.[6] Mountain Jennings, who had accompanied his employer from Theobalds, was the gardener in charge.[7] The whole place bustled with activity both inside and out, as is shown by the ever-mounting pile of bills for the ensuing year.

Labourers were paid for 'the digginge and carryinge of earth and gravell' for the walks; there were 'workes done aboute the vineyard' where the paths were of turf; others were kept busy in 'the dell' and on 'the iland' which were being set 'with whitethorn and sweetbriars'. Indeed, planting was going on apace in every direction and labourers 'carried water' to assist survival.[8]

Tradescant seems to have taken over the kitchen garden, where weeders were already busy, as he puts in a bill for £2 1s. 4d. for 'compass' (compost) to feed the soil.[9] Roots, artichokes, cabbages 'and all other herbs necessary for the kitchen' were already growing there;[10] 'the Herb mans bill' for the following year shows that these included spinach, asparagus, rosemary, lettuce, radishes, purslane, tarragon, rocket, bays, parsley, 'rosemary gold flowers', carrots, onions and 'corn salat'.[11]

In the autumn of 1610 Tradescant wrote to the British Resident in Brussels, William Trumbull, to order plants for the Hatfield garden. The letter is endorsed 21 October 1610 and reads:

Right Worshippfull and my honorable good frend, I have no good thing to send y^r Worshipe but onlye my servise ever indepted to y^r Worshipe, since I last wase with y^r Worshipe it hathe plessed my Lord tresorur to give me enterteynment and he Spake to me to know wheare the Rarest thing wear then I tould him of Brussell then my Lord said Sirra Remember me and at Miccalmas ye shall goe over now since it hathe plesed his Lordshipe to Remember y^r Worshipe being theare then he said he thought ye wold Do^e somunthe if I would writ for those things that I thought weare Strang the things I most desire is that peer the Kichin gardner would Send me of all Sorts of Viens that he hathe especialye of those Sorts that most cumest Ripe that is the blewe muskadell the Russet grape a greattest quantity of those but of aull other sorts what he hathe and a Rose of that sort that he gave me on the last yeare and of the great portingall quince trees all the things that he sendethe over may be sent in a baskit and if y^r Worship can get sum two or three of small grafted orang trees to send them over my Lord I thinke will send over p^t [payment] for to bye them withe for the flowers m^r John Joket can furnishe ye withe and Round about the Baskit that comethe over that ther maye be Roots of the best Sorts of gilliflowers theye may be young plants the better to Carye and he that bringeth them must have leave of the Vats in the Ship on gilliflower they saye is Rare they Call the Infanto and What other Sorts he knowethe that be Strang allso I desire him that he will send me Somm muske mellon seed of that sort that he Calleth his Wintter muske mellon and as for the flower Roots they maye be put into a Basket or a Box withe Dri mose or Dri Sand sealed uppe.

It enclosed a long list of plants. This is reproduced here with their modern botanical names in brackets underneath.

Mr John Joket	The names of the flowers be thes
for flowers	The Duble hippatiq red whit and purple (*Hepatica nobilis* Miller 'Flore Pleno')
	The martygon pomponye (*Lilium pomponium* L.)
I pray let every	Lilly montayne tottus albus (*Lilium martagon* L. *album*)

severall plant have	Colchecum Duble and beyzantine (*Colchicum autumnale* L. 'Flore Pleno' and *Colchicum byzantinum* Ker-Gawler)
his name	Junkellis Duble yell and junkellis totus albus major (*Narcissus jonquilla* L. *flore pleno* and an unidentified *Narcissus*)
And every severall	Junkillis totus albus minus junkillis amplo Calece (unidentified *Narcissus* and *Narcissus* x *odorus* L.)
Vine his name	phalangeum alebrogecum (*Paradisea Liliastrum* Bertol)
	Renunkelus tripolatanus totus albus (*Ranunculus asiaticus* L. cv)
	Renunkelus Rouge Duble (*Ranunculus asiaticus* L. cv)
	Narssissus Calsedonica major (*Narcissus tazetta* L. ssp *lacticolor plenus*)
Two things ye hast	Narssissus Tertius mathiolye (*Pancratium illyricum* L.)
Can best furnishe y^e	Narssissus quartus mathiolye (*Ornithogalum nutans* L.)
withe withe the Rosa Sine	Pulsatilla Danyca (*Pulsatilla vernalis* (L.) Miller)
Spina and the whit	Also peer the Archdukes man to send me a plant of his specled Anemone
Clematus	Iris anglicus tottus albus (*Iris xiphioides* Ehrh. var.)
	Iris bulboza tottus albus (*Iris xiphium* L.)
	Crocus meziacus Crocus Argentum Crocus maior Autumnalis (*Crocus flavus* Weston, *Crocus biflorus* Miller, *Crocus nudiflorus* Sm.) Hiasintus pereneanno All Sorts (*Brimeura amethystina* (L.) Chouard)
	The Duble yello Rose at the posts or boye van brussell *Rosa hemisphaerica* J. Herrm
Peer the archdukes	also that pere will send a plant 2 or 3 of the Laurus Serus and a plant of Laurus stinnos (*Prunus laurocerasus* L. and *Viburnum tinus* L.)
kichin gardner for	and of the Whit Clematis (*Clematis flammula* L.)
Vins and trees and Rosses	the Rosa Semper Virente

(*Rosa sempervirens* L.)

The Rosa Sina Spina
(possibly a variety or hybrid of *Rosa Gallica* L.)

I praye if Mr Joket hath and the Rosa icanadine per gave me on the last yeare
but it is dead
(*Rosa* x *alba* 'Incarnata')

any strang sorts of The Russet Vien good store bothe Cuttings and
any a seede that is Rare Roots and all other Sorts whatsoever he can furnishe me
he will send me Somme withe for Lord maketh a Vinyard
at Hatfield and hathe the french men to make it therfor if it
be possible to let me have what y^r w^p can
procure for to equall them I never sawe better then I
have seen at the archduks mans Kichin gardin
this hoping of y^r Worshipe I sease
y^r Worshipe ever to Comand
till he is John
Tradeskent garner
To the Lord Tresurer[12]

Evidently the Earl of Salisbury expected Trumbull to order the plants listed and arrange for their dispatch to Hatfield. On 30 October Tradescant had been given an advance of £10 'by yr Lordshipps command to send over into Flanders to by vynes',[13] and there is a further payment in the accounts of £6 9s. 'for trees which came from Brussells'.[14] Assuming that all the plants listed arrived in 1610, the new introductions included the double *Hepatica nobilis*, although there seems to be some doubt as to whether the white double, often written of, ever existed. Parkinson, in 1629, described its deep blue and purple flowers like 'small buttons' and 'as double as a flower can be'. In 1597 Gerard had the single varieties but described the double flower as 'a stranger to England'. Other new arrivals were the pure white St Bruno's lily, *Paradisea liliastrum*, previously first listed as being grown by the London merchant John de Franquevil in 1617; *Pancratium illyricum*, the sea daffodil, previously thought to have been first grown by Parkinson in 1629, who had received seed 'from the liberality of Mr. Doctor Flud, one of the Physitions of the Colledge in London, who gathered them in the University garden at Pisa'; the little Pyrenean hyacinth, *Brimeura amethystina*, more sky blue than amethyst, also previously attributed to Parkinson in the same year, and *Prunus laurocerasus*, collected again by Tradescant the following year as 'larus serus', the cherry laurel.

The 'Narcissuss tertius' and 'quartus' of 'mathiolye' refers to a flora by Pier Andrea Mattioli (1500–1577), the eminent Italian physician and botanist, called *Commentarii in libros sex Pedacii Dioscoridis de materia medica*. It was first published in Italian in 1544 and subsequently in other languages with illustrations. Although the plants were generally known by these names at that time, it is possible that Tradescant owned a copy of this book, perhaps that of 1565, which is the best illustrated. The vines bought at this time were in addition to the 30,000 that had been given by Mme de la Boderie, the French Ambassador's wife.[15] The vineyard at Hatfield was to become famous. When the diarist John Evelyn visited it in 1642 he described the garden and vineyard as 'the most considerable Rarity besides the house' and 'rarely well water'd and planted',[16] while twenty years later Thomas Fuller found it difficult to restrain his enthusiasm for the place.[17] Two Frenchmen were engaged to tend it, and, like some other seventeenth-century vineyards, it was probably laid out geometrically with the beds of vines edged with hedges of privet or sweet briar.

On 10 November Tradescant was sent down to Cranborne in Dorset when he was paid £2 2s. 10d. for planting trees there.[18] He had probably already paid a visit in September when Thomas Hooper, who seems to have been acting as agent, reported that, because the house was not yet roofed or plastered, 'ther is yet lytle done to purpose' in the gardens, 'onlie the court or the foresyde of the house beutified and the wales set round with fruite trees fit for the same'.

A hundred thousand bricks had been fired ready for garden walling. Some of these were to be used to enclose the orchard, which was next to the priory. Hooper also reported that 'the gardiner doth desyer to have a brick wall from the eastend of the newe buildinge to range towards the priorie which he holdeth to be the fittest place for apricocke and such lyke'. He had requested that this 'maie be done withall convenient speed that he maie sett them in convenient tyme, and also the better to fashion his plott'.[19] It was probably these apricots and 'such lyke' that Tradescant went to plant.

In the following year Tradescant was back at Hatfield, where he had 'taken order for the planting of a hedg in the bottome of the North walke'. Two divisions were to be put over the cross walk, with trellis gates to keep out the deer 'till the hedg be growne and seates sett up in the halfe rounds to sit in'. He had also 'staked out the two triangle walkes that goeth from the house, one towards the parsonage, and the other answerable to it', where trees were being planted, and he was to 'take order for the setting of trees and shrubs in the valleyes which will doe very well'.[20]

He was soon off on his travels to fulfil these orders. Of this journey his detailed bills survive, and so we can travel with him step by step. On 25 September 1611 he was given an advance of six pounds,[21] and after three days in London he packed his 'clok bag' and took the normal passage by water to Gravesend. He spent the night there before embarking for Flushing but was held up in Ramsgate for four days 'by contrary wind'. Once across the Channel he went on to Middelburg and thence to Rotterdam and Delft, always seeking suitable plants to take back with him to Hatfield and buying baskets in which to pack them.[22] His further expenses were covered by bills of exchange amounting to sixty pounds which had been arranged by the city merchant Peter Vanlore.

In 1634 Sir William Brereton travelled some of the same route, and from his account of his journey we can gain an impression of the places Tradescant visited. From Rotterdam, where he remarked upon the windmills on the top of high houses, describing the malt grinder that he visited as 'a pretty nimble stone', Brereton, with three others, hired 'a scute' for the two-hour journey to Delft. 'This was drawn by a good strong horse whereupon a little boy rid. He trotted altogether, a cord fastened to the top of the mast of the boat, which also fastened to the horse.'[23] But Tradescant, like the naturalist John Ray who left an account of his journey in 1673, is more likely to have taken the passage boat which went off 'every hour of the day at the ringing of a bell' and which would also have been horse-drawn.[24]

In Delft, where Brereton admired the fair, 'spacious market place' and the tame storks and shovelers that abounded, Tradescant visited a nurseryman called Dirryk Hevesson from whom he bought a variety of fruit trees. His bill reads as follows:[25]

Of the Rathe Ripe Cheryes 3 trees	0	: 9:	0
for two trees Called the Vulgars Cheryes	0	: 3:	0
for the Rathe Ripe portingall quince on tree	0	: 6:	0
for the lions quince tree	0	: 3:	0
for the portingall quince trees	0	: 16:	0
for two great medlar trees	0	: 4:	0
for the Scent aple tree on	0	: 2:	6
for the dubble gilldiling aple tree on	0	: 2:	6
for the eyght aple tree on	0	: 1:	6
for the peare Called the thomas peare on	0	: 2:	6
for the begine peare on	0	: 2:	6
for the Whit Currant plants 30	0	: 3:	0
for on Rathe Ripe Chery tree	0	: 3:	0
for two great medlar trees of naples	0	: 5:	0
for the Sceveling aple tree on	0	: 1:	6

The 'Rathe Ripe' cherry was probably the 'Early Flanders Cherry' which John Parkinson described as 'more rathe or early ripe'[26] than the Flanders, the word 'rathe' meaning to bloom or ripen early. The quinces originated from Lyons and Portugal respectively, and the former was a new variety, the latter having been ordered the previous year when it would have been an introduction, too. They are among six varieties of quince listed by Parkinson in 1629. The 'two great medlar trees of naples', a description found in all contemporary herbals, were in fact the Azarole (*Crataegus azarolus* L.).

From Delft Tradescant went on to the Hague, where the Prince of Orange kept a fine, spacious garden much admired for its covered walks. Like Brereton's some years later, this journey would have been by boat before continuing on to Leiden in a wagon. Sir William tells us that the ride took about three hours, for the most part through 'barren land'. The route was bounded by 'deep sands, which have been wrought and laid there by the sea' so that the shore on the left hand 'seems to be much above you . . . like high hills', making the ground that the wagon passes along look 'much higher than the country below' and yet 'seems a valley'.

At Leiden was the famous university physic garden, which Tradescant would surely have contrived to visit. Sir William describes how the lecturer, a doctor of physic, took a whole bed 'four yards long and one broad' and discoursed 'of the nature and quality of every herb and plant growing therein'. And, like both Brereton and Ray, Tradescant must have gazed in wonder at the famous museum collection in the Anatomy School.

It was in Leiden that he was able to indulge his fancy for the 'strang and rare', buying 'Roots of flowers and Roasses and Shrubs' so described and also bringing back several varieties of 'gilliflowers' (carnations). He made his purchase from a nurseryman called Falkener.[27]

Tradescant then took passage for Haarlem. Sir William made this journey, too, travelling on the passage boat which passed through various 'Meares', one of which he describes as 'a mighty, vast, spacious thing', adding: 'It being a side wind, sometimes the boat rowled so much on one side, that it went within less than a quarter of a yard of the water, the sail almost leaning into the water.' In Haarlem Tradescant added eight hundred tulip bulbs to his hamper. They cost him ten shillings the hundred. (The 'Tulipomania' that became the rage in Holland in the 1630s, when vast sums exchanged hands for unusual varieties, was yet to come.) He also bought another dozen great blackcurrants, a vine, two baskets, one of them with a hook by which to hang it, and two scythes.

From a second Haarlem nurseryman, Cornellis Helin, he acquired:[28]

Rathe Ripe Cherry trees 32 at 4s the peece	6: 8: 0
on littil peare tree kalled the Spanieshe peare	0: 2: 0
for on aple quince tree	0: 3: 0
for flowers Called anemones	0: 5: 0
for 16 Province Rosses	0: 8: 0
for one great Cherye Called the Rathe Ripe Cherye	0: 3: 0
bought of the master of the here speld 200 lim trees	13: 0: 0
for tuo mulberry trees	0: 6: 0
for six messeryer trees	0: 3: 0
for the great Red Currants 6 plants	0: 1: 0
for two arborvita trees	0: 1: 0

The flowers of the Province Rose were described in *The Flower Garden Displayed* (1732) as 'the most double of any we have'. A 'flesh' rose, shaded with crimson, similar in colour to the damask rose, it flowered freely with clusters of two or three blooms together. Messeryer trees were the February-flowering *Daphne mezereum* L., while the Great Red Currant was probably an introduction of the large Dutch currant considered by Johnson 'twice as big' as any other.[29] The arborvita trees were the tree of life (*Thuja occidentalis* L.), introduced into France from Canada probably in 1536 and, judging by the price, no longer rare. On the same bill Tradescant lists two purchases made from another Haarlem nurseryman, Cornellis Cornellison: 'fortye frittelaries at 3 pence the peece' and 'Junkillis amplo Calice 40 at 3 pence the peece'. The latter were the larger campernelle jonquil, which Parkinson illustrated and called the 'yellow junquilla with a great cuppe'.[30]

His next stops were at Amsterdam, Utrecht and Vianen. He does not seem to have had much luck in any of these towns as his only acquisition was another basket. From Vianen he returned to Rotterdam by more or less the same route.

He put in expenses for 'supper and bed' along the way, which usually cost him 1s. 6d. John Ray, when writing of his later travels, grumbled about the surliness of the Dutch innkeepers, the lack of good English puddings and the 'inconveniently short and narrow' beds. He tells us that the Dutch men and women 'are almost always eating as they travel, whether it be by boat coach or wagon'; even the wagoners baited 'themselves and their horses four or five times' a day. He seemed surprised to find every inn ready with a meal of thin slices of beef or cheese laid on top of bread and butter, to be washed down with strong beer: 'Thick beer they call it and well they may.' One 'great dish' he found 'all over these countreys' was 'Boil'd Spinage minc'd and buttered (sometimes also with currans added)'. The only thing that really seemed to please Ray were the pickled herrings, which he considered cured and prepared 'better than we do in England'.

While shopping for the Earl of Salisbury in Holland, Tradescant also made some purchases for one of his employer's friends, the wealthy politician Sir Walter Cope, builder of Cope Castle in Kensington, the remaining part of which is now known as Holland House. Tradescant bought thirty-eight pounds' worth of trees for him.[31]

Cope was also the owner of a celebrated cabinet of rarities with which Tradescant was almost certainly familiar. The prolific letter-writer John Chamberlain recorded in 1602 that Sir Walter was on such good terms with Cecil that the latter did him 'a very extraordinarie favor' by admitting him 'a partner in his entertainment to the Quene', permitting him 'to present her with some toyes in his house'.[32] 'Toyes' in this instance can be interpreted as curiosities.

From Rotterdam Tradescant travelled on to Antwerp. The boat must have called in at 'The Brill', now Brielle, as he charges up eight shillings for freight paid to Sir Edward Conway.[33] Sir Edward was Governor there, and he presumably arranged for the trees and plants that Tradescant had bought in Holland to be dispatched direct to London.

A week later, stepping ashore in Antwerp, Tradescant drew forty pounds from Peter Vanlore[34] before embarking on another boat for Brussels. There he bought more plants from several different nurserymen. The first was John Buret, obviously a specialist in fruit trees:[35]

Cheryes of the great Creeke 4 at 4s the peece	0: 16: 0
Cheryes of the long Speckled 8 at 4s the peece	1: 12: 0
Cheryes of the lat Ripe 2 at 5s the peece	0: 10: 0
Pears the gratiola 3 at 4s the peece	0: 12: 0
peare the portinggall 1 at 4s the peece	0: 4: 0
peare Dorns 2 at halfe a croune the peece	0: 5: 0
of the Rathe Ripe Cheryes 5 at halfe a croune the pece	0: 12: 6
on excedyng great Cherye Called the boores Cherye	0: 12: 0
on aprycoke tree Called the Whit aprycoke	0: 6: 0
also bought of the archedukes gardner Called Peere vyens	
ten Sorts	1: 0: 0
Larus Serus 6 plants at 2s the peece	0: 12: 0
on Chery tree called the archeduks cherye	0: 12: 0
on peache tree called the Spanishe peache	0: 5: 0
of tulipen Roots 500 at ten Shillings the hundred	2: 10: 0
On peare Called the pear of portinggall	0: 4: 0
bought of small wallnut trees 50 at 6 penc the pece	1: 5: 0
also bought of Mr John Jokket for the dubble Epatega the	
martygon pompone blanche the martygon pompony	
orang Coller and the Irys Calsedonye and the Irys	
Susyana	2: 0: 0
also bought at Ripper mount on hundred chery trees halfe	
Rathe Ripe and halfe Watterlosen	7: 10: 0

The great cherry called the 'boores Cherye' is significant. This is the variety that later became associated with Tradescant's name, although it was really the 'Bigarreau Gros Noir' of France or the 'Grosse Schwarze Knorpelkirsche' of Germany.[36] It was still called after Tradescant in 1823 when Brookshaw described it as 'a remarkably fleshy Cherry, of a rich flavour with a faint pleasant bitter taste; the stone is very small, and the shape of the fruit differs from that of all other Black Cherries'.[37] He added that it had a broad, coarsely serrated leaf and 'bears very freely'. Parkinson described it 'as a fair great berrie, deepe coloured, and a little pointed'.[38] The Iris are two types of 'Turkie Flowerdeluce',[39] as described by Parkinson, both needing perfect drainage, prolonged heat and undisturbed cultivation. Martygon pompoms are identifiable as *Lilium pomponium* L.

The white apricot had white flesh and a pale yellow skin, while the Archduke's cherry is still available today. It seems that it was difficult at that time to produce it true to type; Parkinson related that 'John Tradescantes Cherry is most usually sold by our Nursery Gardiners for the Archdukes cherrie, because they have more plenty thereof, and will better be increased.' He added that 'it is so faire and good a cherry that it may be obtruded without much discontent'.[40] The Archduke was Albert, Governor of the Spanish Netherlands, from whom Tradescant had obtained a passport at a cost of four shillings. His gardener, who supplied ten sorts of vine, was presumably called Pierre.

Perhaps it was on this occasion that Tradescant brought back from Brussels a strawberry that he 'in seven yeares could never see one berry ripe on all sides, but still the better part rotten, although it would every yeare flower abundantly, and beare very large leaves'.[41] He also met with the Chardon Artichoke near Brussels, as Parkinson recorded: 'John Tradescante assured mee, he saw three acres of Land about Brussels planted with this kinde, which the owner whited like Endive, and then sold them in the winter: Wee cannot yet finde the true manner of dressing them, that our Countrey may take delight therein.' Parkinson added that these were eaten raw 'with vinegar and oyle, pepper and salt, all of them, or some, as every one liketh for their delight'.[42]

Tradescant had now accumulated more stock that needed to be dispatched home with care and speed before he continued on his way to Paris. His baskets and padlocked hampers, all filled with precious plants, were entrusted to a shipper to be sent down-river to Flushing. In spite of paying ten shillings to have them freighted and tipping the fellow an additional florin, the shipper failed in his duty.[43] Again Tradescant must have invoked diplomatic assistance, for on 14 November 1611 Sir John Throckmorton wrote from Flushing to William Trumbull, British agent in Brussels, 'The trees and plants which you sent for the Lord Treasurer, being brought no further than Middelburg by the slothfulness of the shippers, I sent thither to receive them and shipped them into another boat that went for London next day.'[44] This time there was no delay, for on 15 November there is an entry in the Hatfield accounts recording payment of 42s. 'to a skipper for bringing of trees and roots from by yoandeseas'.[45]

Freed from the care of this burden, Tradescant took coach for Paris. The journey, which lasted eight and a half days, cost him £1 5s. 0d. and his food £1 2s. 0d. In Paris he made, or possibly renewed, acquaintance with the French King's head gardeners, Jean Robin and his son Vespasien. If this was their first meeting it was to prove a fruitful one, for thereafter the Tradescants and the Robins exchanged plants on a number of occasions. Although their system of nomenclature is not regarded as particularly scientific, the Robins were both skilful gardeners, cultivating a wide range of exotics and helping to spread them by sending plants not only to England but also to Basle and Rome.

Born in 1550, Jean Robin was an apothecary who had a famous garden at the western end of the Ile Notre Dame. According to Gerard, he dwelt 'at the signe of the black head, in the streete called Du bout du Monde, in English, The end of the world'.[46] Around 1586 Robin was appointed botanist to Henri III and took over the garden at the Louvre; he retained the post under both Henri IV and Louis XIII. In 1597 Jean Robin was commissioned to lay out a plot for growing simples for the use of the Faculty of Medicine. His *Catalogus stirpium*, issued in 1601, shows that he was growing a range of plants from a variety of far-flung places.

Vespasien Robin, born in 1579, assisted his father in the royal garden and took it over when the old man died in 1629 at the age of seventy-nine. Vespasien added many new plants from his collecting expeditions to Spain, Italy, the Pyrenees and even as far away as the Guinea coast. The Robins also cultivated plants brought back from Canada by the early French explorers. Many of these were passed on to John Tradescant senior and listed by him in 1634; he reciprocated with plants he received from Virginia, but these exchanges seem to have become less frequent in their sons' time.

The Robins' garden gave place to the Jardin Royal des Plantes Médicinales, eventually becoming the Jardin des Plantes. Authorized by royal decree in 1624, it was not opened to the public until eleven years later, by which time many of the Robins' plants had been transferred to it. Vespasien Robin was appointed lecturer and given living quarters in the garden, where he continued to live until his death in 1662.[47]

Perhaps through his visits to the Robins, the elder Tradescant was to become familiar with the French capital, but in 1611 he was obviously less sure of his ground. He sought out the company of 'my Lord Imbassettors gardner to goe withe me two and fro in Parrys to by my things'. The British ambassador then was Sir Thomas Edmondes, and his gardener received a French crown worth six shillings for his services. Tradescant must have remained there for well over a week as the cost of his food and lodging amounted to 28s.[48]

It was in Paris that he found the exotics that must have gladdened his heart:[49]

On pomgranet tree withe many other small trees at the root	0:	6:	0
On bundall of genista hispanyca	0:	2:	0
8 pots of orrang trees of on years grouthe grafted at 10s the pece	4:	0:	0
Syx other at 8s the pece grafted the tops on Cut of	2:	8:	0
Ollyander trees 6 at halfe a croune the peece	0:	15:	0
myrtill trees 7 at halfe a croune the peece	0:	17:	6

on fyg tree in a pot by it Selfe bearying 3 times a yeare	0:	2:	0
two fyg trees in an other baskit called the whit fygs withe			
manye other Rare Shrubs give me by master Robyns	0:	4:	0
Also bought in parrys and put into the Same boat of trees			
pears, plums and Cheryes 60–7[0] trees	6:	9:	0
Also of vyens called muscat two bundals of plants	0:	4:	0
Vyens Called lurdlet plants 15	0:	1:	0
on pot of gilliflowers Cost nothing	0:	0:	0
on great hamper of flowers and Seeds Cost	3:	0:	0
on packet of books 6 in number cost	0:	10:	0

'Genista hispanyca' is of course the Spanish broom with long spikes of yellow flowers (*Spartium junceum* L.).

This collection was put on board a boat by porters hired for the job at a cost of 3s., with the French King's gardeners giving a hand and being tipped the same amount. Then, while the boat wound its way down-river to Rouen, Tradescant pressed on by coach. He stayed for eleven and a half days in Rouen where he made yet more purchases.[50]

Cheryes called Biggandres at 2s the peece 24	2:	8:	0
[Sy]pris t[rees] at on Shilling the peece 200	10:	0:	0
Sypris t[rees] on littill bundall 6 trees	0:	1:	0
two Orang trees in pots on grafted	0:	10:	0
pear sekes trees 4 at 2s the peece	0:	8:	0
blak mulberry trees at 2s the peec 17	1:	14:	0
peache the troye 4 trees at 2s the peece	0:	8:	0
peache the alberges 4 trees at 2s the peece	0:	8:	0
peache the melecotton 4 trees at 2s the peece	0:	8:	0
peare trees 16 trees of 4 sorts at 2s the peece	1:	12:	0
on Chest of Shells with eyght boxes of Shells	12:	0:	0
Pomgranet trees 3 littill ons at 1s the pece	0:	3:	0
On basket of Shrubs given my by munser Lamont	0:	0:	0
on peache tre Called the muske peache	0:	2:	0
peache the pave 4 trees at 2s the tree	0:	8	0
on great buffells horne	0:	2:	6
for trees peaches mulberyes and Cheryes called biggerawes			
104 trees	10:	0:	0
for an artyfyshall byrd	0:	2:	6
for on pot of the dubble whit stok gilliflower and on pot of			
other gilliflowers	0:	3:	0
for on pot of mirtill trees 3 trees in it	0:	3:	0

The Troyes peach, as described by Parkinson, was a 'great whitish Peach, red on the outside, early ripe' and longer than it was round.[51] There were two types of Alberge peach, the yellow and the purple. The malacoton, according to Parkinson 'better relished then any of them', was a large peach with a thick, downy skin from which it took its name, while paves or pavies were those types of peach with flesh that adhered to the stone. Philip Miller recorded that pavies were 'much more esteem'd in France than the Peaches, though, in England, the latter are preferr'd' by many.[52]

The shells were destined to be laid in the bottom of the stream in the garden at Hatfield where they would shine and glisten in the sunlight beneath the flowing water. They were all in place by the following May when water was reported to be running over them in the little river in the east garden.[53]

His shopping in Rouen completed, Tradescant obviously grew impatient at the delay in the arrival of the precious cargo of exotics that had been so carefully laden on to the boat in Paris. He decided to dispatch a 'Duche man' to speed them on their way.[54] Meanwhile, concerned about the welfare of his more recent purchases, he tipped a boy a shilling to heel them into the ground at the house where he was lodging.[55] Eventually the *Robert Mot* appeared, porters were again engaged to load the new-found exotics and all were dispatched down the Seine and along the coast to Dieppe. Tradescant, having waved them off, hired a horse and rode on to await their arrival.

He remained in Dieppe for about a week, then took passage for Dover, probably on the same boat as there is no further charge for porters. This cost him twelve shillings, more than double his outward journey, so the price presumably included the cost of freight as well. From Dover the plants continued by water to London, after he had given 'the boys of the ship' a shilling 'to be Carfull of the trees'. He himself hired horses, riding to Canterbury where he spent the night before proceeding on to Gravesend next day. There he took the passage boat to London. When the plants eventually arrived in the capital they were transferred into two wherries, these light, shallow rowing-boats being hired to take them up the River Lea 'to the gardin' at Hatfield.[56]

Planting out and caring for these acquisitions, many of them requiring very specialized treatment, must have kept the gardeners at Hatfield busy for some time. Judging by the prices that had been paid, at a time when labourers earned a shilling a day and women weeders only half that amount, many of them were not readily available on the Continent and were obviously quite impossible to find in England. It is unlikely that Tradescant did any physical work himself. The fact that he could employ a boy to heel in plants he had purchased and engage porters to carry his 'clok bag' in Holland suggests that his gardening would by now have been only of a supervisory nature.

No sooner was he back than he started to busy himself at Salisbury House in the Strand, Cecil's London home, where the garden was being enlarged. He paid labourers to work there in January and February and submitted two bills for the purchase of sweet briars, osiers, roses, thorns, eglantines and poles, all of which suggest the construction of a pergola. He also seems to have crossed the Channel again, as he was paid twenty pounds 'for his charges in going overseas to by trees and in coming back again'.[57]

Perhaps it was on this occasion that Tradescant acquired 'a small Ozier from St Omers in Flanders, which makes incomparable Networks'.[58] The willow was said to grow there 'on Islands which floate up and downe' and to make fine baskets. Forty years later his son was still growing this plant, which was considered 'worth the procuring' by Samuel Hartlib.[59]

Meanwhile the carpenter at Salisbury House had set up 'railes and ballisters', and his bill shows that two staircases from the end walks led to this 'garden nowe finyishing'.[60]

There were also long and close walks, and an elaborate seventy-foot portico was designed but never built for the south end of the garden overlooking the Thames. However, two square garden houses are shown at the end in the river terrace in Holler's bird's-eye view of 1666.[61]

There are bills relating to the enlargement of this garden. A copy of one from Tradescant, now missing, dated January 1612, lists '20 standards of white roses at 2d., 800 sweet briar at 8d. the 100, 600 long briar at 1/6 the 100, 300 short thorn at 4d. the 100, 14 hundred of prime at 3d., 8 car loads to Red Cross St, my lodging in London 30 nights at 4d., 3000 osiers at 3d. the 100. 10 tubs for cherry trees, lilacs, white and yellow jessamines, clematis, "fladson" roses, murry roses, 310, 15s. 8 particoloured roses at 10d. wages 1/s & 2/s a day.'[62]

A surviving bill of 5 January 1612 also relates to the grounds of Salisbury House:[63]

l	*s*	*d*	
3	0	0	of the 5 li Reseved of mr Jams blakleche
0	1	6	for the fraught over of the pots and trees 3 li
0	2	0	the taking the trees over the ships 3 men 1s 6d
0	1	8	for the wharfyg 2s for the Carmans hire to bryng
0	5	0	them to salsbery house 1s 8d for Carag of the
-	1	0	pots to petycote Lane 31 pots for ten porters 5s
0	12	6	for taking them out of the shipe by porters on
2	15	9	shillyng for prymmyg and avryg 12s 6d also payd
0	0	8	to mr bell 55s 9d

The Sume is 4 li   3s   6d

7	0	1		2	15	9

6   19   3
also for on bushell of Charcole 8d
Summa Totallis vij li j d

'Primage' was an allowance to the master and crew for the loading and care of the cargo on board and 'average' was a customs duty on the freight.

And a second bill relating to the gardens of Salisbury House is dated 3 March 1612.[64] These purchases were to make the hedges.

Salsbery house	a bill for the gardyn for the monthe of februarye 1611 [1612]		
Item for long thorne on thousand Six hundred at 2s the hundred	2 li	12 s	0
for on thousand of Short thorne at five pence the hundred	0	4 s	2 d
long Eglantine Seven hundred at 18d the hundred	0	10 s	6 d
of Short brier Seven hundred at 8d the hundred	0	4 s	8 d
of prim 4 thousand Seven hundred at 3d the hundred	0	ii s	9 d
for fowre thousand osiers at 3d the hundred	0	10 s	0
four two thousand at 4d nayles and foure hundred	0	8 s	0
for hassle pols 3 hundred 6p^d the hundred	0	1 s	6 d
for 15 nyghts loging at a groat the nyght	0	5 s	0
	4	7 s	7 d

Tradescant adds a detailed account for the hire of nine gardeners and labourers, their wages ranging from one shilling to twenty pence per day, and the purchase of two brooms at a penny each, to add a further £6 0s. 8d. Another bill shows that Tradescant paid women weeders 6d a day.

'Prim' was another name for our native common privet (*Ligustrum vulgare* L.), rarely seen today, since the Japanese species, introduced in the last century, has taken its place. However, it was popular at that time for hedging, topiary and arbours. According to Parkinson, 'it is so apt, that no other can be like unto it, to be cut, lead, and drawne into what forme one will, either of beasts, birds, or men armed, or otherwise'.[65] 'Hassle' or hazel poles were flexible and probably to be used in making a covered walk or tunnel, with the osiers to bind the climbing plants. Thomas Hyll describes in *The Gardeners Labyrinth*, first published in 1577, with many subsequent editions, how these were constructed and, among other plants, recommended roses and privet to cover them.

A plan for the garden of Salisbury House, which was never implemented, shows a garden leading down to the river in four terraces and, on one level of these, two avenues could represent tunnels.[66]

By April 1612 Tradescant was back at Hatfield, where he submitted another bill for 'seedes and other necessaryes bought for the kitchin garden'. Costing forty shillings and a penny, his purchases were '24 earthen panns' and two 'water tubbs' for melons, as well as onion, spinach, sweet marjoram, buglas, borage and marigold seed. The bill also included two garden rakes, two pairs of shears and the cost of replacing the handles on three mattocks. Twelve bundles of small hazels 'to mend the hedges in the gardens' were also noted, as well as the inevitable 'donge' – five loads this time.[67]

A month later he put in another account for *Carduus benedictus*, the 'Blessed Thistle' then considered an antidote to the plague, radish seed, a basket of cucumber plants and '2 basketts to bring Doune Mellon plants in', both bought in London. He also included entries 'for my horse charges at London' and for a new scythe. The latter was to be used for the task described in the final sad entry: 'for mowing of the coorts and East gardyn against the funeral 4s'.[68]

Robert Cecil, the first Earl of Salisbury, was dead. He had died on 24 May 1612 on his way back from Bath, where, exhausted by the affairs of state, he had gone to take the waters. Failing to benefit as he had hoped, he embarked on the long, slow journey home by coach but died before he could reach London. His body was taken back to Hatfield, where he lies buried beneath a stone effigy in the church. Hatfield House, his greatest building achievement, stands today almost as he conceived it, but his life was cut short before he had a chance to enjoy the comfort it provided.

Tradescant continued to work at Hatfield for his son William, the second Earl. In October of that year he received one hundred pounds from Robert Liming, who was acting as clerk of the works and supervising all the building operations, 'in consideration of my pains about his Lordships worke at Hatfield'.[69] This payment appears to be in addition to his salary. Tradescant put in various small bills in 1613, including one for five pounds for buying another sixty trees 'to sett in the east garden'. These were plum and cherry trees for planting in 'the two upper quarters' there.[70] Another was for paying 'laborers for stakeinge and busheinge of trees in Potters Park'.[71] And in November he submitted 'a bill of laying out for trees and my owne Charges being last at London the 18 of October'. It came to 25s. 4d. and included:[72]

Imprimus: for on great Cherytree caled the Arche duks			
Rathe Ripe	0:	5:	0
It: for the yello nectaline tree	0:	2:	6
It: for the great blewe Cherye	0:	2:	6
It: for the Whit Chery	0:	2:	0

It: for the Whit primordin plum	0:	2:	0
for two Siethes at 3s 4d the peece	0:	6:	8
Also for mine oune Dyet in london 3 mealls	0:	1:	6
for my horse meat	0:	1:	8
for barberyes 40 plants	0:	1:	6

The leaves of 'barberyes' (*Berberis vulgaris* L.) were at that time used for making sauces for meat, and the bitter berries were pickled for decoration and flavouring. Surprisingly, Tradescant's diet cost less than that of his horse.

Early in 1614 he was summoned to Salisbury House to speak to Captain Brett, Lord Salisbury's Receiver-General of Revenue. He used the occasion to buy 'two Doussin great glasses to cover Muske mellon plants' and a peck of 'Rathe ripe pease' as well as onion and radish seed.[73]

The expenses paid to him on his trips to London indicate that he lived in accommodation at Hatfield during the years that he worked there. Certainly there were 'gardeners lodgings in the garden', as these were reglazed in 1610.[74] His shopping expeditions often included a variety of errands for his employer. On different occasions he was paid 41s. for 'two stills', 8s. for a cheese press[75] and 1s. 'that hee paid for setting a pare of soles upon your Lordships "pompes"'.[76]

The various payments of the salary paid to Tradescant indicate that he continued to work for the second Earl at Hatfield until at least the summer of 1614.[77]

Virtually nothing of the original gardens at Hatfield House remains today. In 1660 Hatfield was still among the most celebrated gardens in England, but by the end of the century the vineyard had disappeared and the rest was restyled as changes in fashion dictated, although the present east garden still retains some vestiges of the original terracing.

Some idea of the original plan for the east garden is shown in a rough sketch in the margin of a letter sent to Lord Salisbury by his secretary, Thomas Wilson, on 25 November 1611.

Saloman de Caux, the French engineer who was responsible for designing the royal gardens at Greenwich and Somerset House, was called in to plan the waterworks, and the sketch on p. 46 shows four fountains on three different levels, three of them forming the centre-pieces of hedged knots.[78] Gooseberries, raspberries, strawberries, roses and other flowers are recorded as all growing together in the lower part of the east garden.[79]

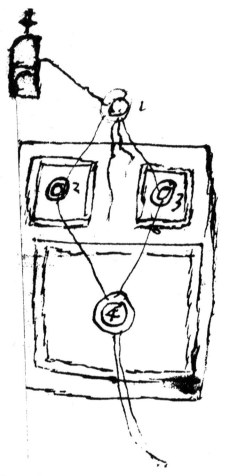

Thomas Wilson's sketch of the original plan for Hatfield's east garden

Thomas Wilson also enclosed a sketch of the island. This was in the shape of a diamond, surrounded and cut horizontally in two by water. It was divided into eight beds, all lined with trees and separated by walks; what was probably a banqueting house bridged the central stream, and there was a fashionable grotto.[80] The structure with the wheel was no doubt the 'force att the going out of the water from the Iland', which 'by the currant' was to 'dryve up water to the topp of the banck above the dell and soe descend into two fountaynes'.

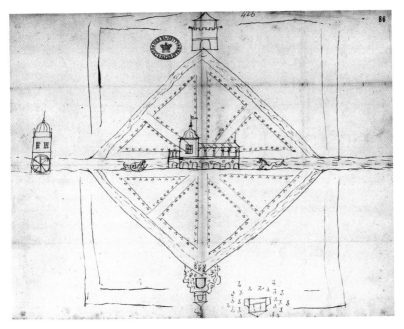

Sketch of the island at Hatfield

Otherwise little is known of the original design for the garden at Hatfield, although there is no doubt that it was plentifully stocked. Over and above Tradescant's purchases and Mme de la Boderie's vines there were 500 fruit trees from the French Queen;[81] Lady Tresham begged acceptance of 'half a hundred' trees from her orchard;[82] 400 sycamore trees were sent by Sir Edward Cecil from the Netherlands;[83] Sir John Tufton sent 453 cherry trees;[84] and 176 oaks and 500 mulberry trees were bought.

A description of a journey made to Hatfield House in 1663, although some years after Tradescant's time, gives a good description of the garden:[85]

It stands very advantageously, from which you have a Prospect of nothing but Woods and Meadows, Hills and Dales, which are very agreeable Objects that present themselves to us at all Sorts of Distances . . . a small River, which as it were forms the Compartiments of a large *Parterre*, and rises and secretly loses itself in an Hundred Places, and whose Banks are all Lined or Boarded. I never saw a more engaging Retreat than this . . . We Dined in a Hall that looked into a Greenplot with Two Fountains in it, and having Espaliers on the Sides, but a Balister before it, upon which there are Flower Pots and Statues: From this Parterre there is a way down by Two Pair of Stairs, of about Twelve or Fifteen Steps to another, and from the Second to the Third: From this Terrass you have a Prospect of the great Water Parterre I have spoke of, which forms a Fourth; there is a Meadow beyond it, where the Deer range up and down, and abbutting upon a Hill, whose Top ends in a Wood, and there bounds the Horizon to us. I ought not to forget the Vineyard, nor the several small Buildings on the side of it, some of which serve for a Retreat to several Sorts of Birds, which are very tame. There are also Arbours or Summer Houses, like *Turkish* Chiosks, upon some of the Eminences, which have a Gallery round, and are erected in the most Beautiful Places, in order to the Enjoying of the Diversified Prospects of this Charming Country: You have also in those Places, where the River enters into and comes out of the Parterre, open sort of Boxes, with Seats round, where you may see a vast Number of Fish pass to and fro in the Water, which is exceeding clear; and they seem to come in Shoals to enjoy all the Pleasures of the Place; and quitting their own Element by jumping sometimes out of the Water, this they do as it were to observe all the things I have describ'd to you.

As we have already noted, James I, in an effort to promote an English silk industry, had imported large numbers of mulberries and decreed that they were to be sold and planted in every county. Alas, this venture was doomed to failure because silkworms do not thrive on the black mulberry, which grows well in Britain, while the white mulberry, on which they do flourish, is much less happy in the English climate. Although the silkworms' preference was understood at the time, the surviving trees that are supposed to date back to this order all seem to be of the black variety. One, thought to have been planted by Tradescant, still stands in the garden at Hatfield. Of the many trees that have been attributed to him, this is one that could have some basis in fact.

Another reminder of Tradescant's presence can be found at the top of the Grand Staircase in Hatfield House. A newel-post, carved to represent a gardener of the period, is thought to portray Tradescant with some of the flowers and fruit that he brought back from Europe to stock the original garden.

While he was living at Hatfield, Tradescant took the opportunity to invest in various leases of arable land, amounting to more than twenty-seven acres. These consisted of seven acres three roods in Upper Aldwick, six acres in Stonecross field, four acres in Thistlefield, six acres in Flaxlands, four acres in Milkwellfield and one enclosed croft called Cock Croft containing by estimation half an acre – for all of which he paid £5 7s. annually.[86]

Although Cock Croft sounds to modern ears as though it was a farmhouse, it would have been, like the others, the name of a field. (The term then used for a building would in all probability have been a 'messuage'.) No doubt Tradescant needed a field for his own horse or horses. He also sold the surplus produce. In June 1612 he 'delyvered for the use of the Earl of Salisburye to his groomes' thirty-two trusses of hay at one shilling a truss.[87] In addition Tradescant had for a time the lease of thirty-two acres in Hatfield wood for which he paid £19 10s. annually, although on at least one occasion half this rent was abated on condition that the wood and timber was not 'etten rid of'.[88] This particular lease was to cause him some anxiety a few years later.

Chapter 3

The Old Monastery Garden

By 1615 Tradescant had moved on to Canterbury to work for Edward, Lord Wotton, who was then living at St Augustine's, a stone's throw from the Cathedral precincts.

We know from Parkinson[1] that he was there, and this timing for his change of employment is confirmed by a letter sent by Tradescant from Canterbury which is dated 23 July of that year. It was addressed to the Keeper of Salisbury House in the Strand, Mr John Glasse; to Mr Christopher Keighley, who was Receiver-General of Revenue to the second Earl of Salisbury; and to 'my ould frend and fellowe' Mr Ralphe Cox, Porter of Salisbury House, the designation then being more in the nature of door-keeper.

Tradescant entreated them as a favour to receive £9 10s. for his rent for Woodfields, which should have been paid by mid-summer and was overdue because others had let him down. Mr Clarke, his sub-tenant, had thirty-three pounds of his money, which he had been appointed to pay but had failed to do so. Tradescant had also appointed him to 'take upe' eighty pounds for him in the country there, 'but they all have mad bould to keepe my mony and not to pay it therfor if ye will be pleased to doe me this much favor as to reseve it or to send it to Mr Carter I shalbe much behouldint to you . . . I prayse God that I have not yet bin so hardlie pent but I Could have pay my Rent at the Day and I presume that if I had forfetid it my Lord woud not take the forfeture . . . ' 'I pray give this man apeece of paper of the Receipt of it,' he added and signed the letter 'with my best love'.[2]

At the dissolution of the monasteries, the King's House of St Augustine's became one of several royal posting-houses set up on the route between London and Dover for the use of the King and distinguished foreign visitors. It was a substantial building incorporating the abbot's lodgings and hall in a rearranged form. Subsequently it passed through various hands, being taken over by Lord Wotton in 1612.

Ironically, the previous owner had been Tradescant's former employer, Robert Cecil, who had heaped destruction upon the ruins by carting off the stones to build Britain's Burse, his shopping precinct in the Strand. In September 1608 it was reported that the inner part of the gate, which would yield '60 or 70 loads of stone', had been taken down, but the writer was refraining from meddling with the outer part until further instructions were received, because 'the townsmen keep so much ado'.[3] The local citizens must have won the day, for the outer gate was spared, along with the Ethelbert Tower, which finally fell in 1822.

Much of the abbey ruins, now excavated and exposed, would then have been covered with soil and planted into an elaborately laid-out garden with knots and mazes; an exquisite chequered Tudor wall (which still stands) must surely have provided the blackcloth for some of Tradescant's more colourful exotics. A plan of this garden made in about 1642 survives.

There is also a full description of it as it was in 1635, made by a military surveyor. Although Tradescant had left some years before, Lady Wotton was still living there and it had probably changed little in the intervening years – except that the 'Sentinel' referred to at the end would not yet have been 'disarm'd':

> In this famous Place . . . I had . . . a full continiue view without, of all the Buildings and Towers; the faire gardens and Orchards, sweet walkes, Labirinthlike wildernesses and groves; rare Mounts and Fountaines; all which togeather take up the encompassing space and circuit of neere 20 or 30 Acres; In most part of which did those rare demolish'd Buildings sometimes appeare in much Glory and Splendor.
>
> That which remaines as sad Reliques of this goodly Monastery, and which are yet standing, is King Ethelberts Tower, St Augustine's Gate, the spacious and stately great Hall, the Ruines of the Abbey Church and Chappells, the round Archt Kitchin with 8 Chimneys in it and Cellars adjoining: most of the goodly Stones belonging to these sumptuous Edifices are changed to a new Habitation besides other that were caryed away and plac'd in great Mansions of this Kingdome, the which will fully testify what the pristine beauty and magnificence of this place hath beene, and whiche (doubtlesse) had been the stateliest and richest Structure of the Nation.
>
> But doe not thinke that I weary you with my Relation, since the honest Head Gardiner was not att all weary'd to march with me those long walkes, to wheele into those pretty countriv'd wooddy Mazes; to climb and scale those high Mounts, which I will only give a touch off, for thus I found them.
>
> In the middst of this delicate Garden and Paradice with the Orchard of delicate Fruites, there is one sweet and delightfull walke of 40 Rod in length, beset and shaddow'd, and on both sides guarded with Lyme Trees; And in the middle of that sweet Garden, of fragrant, and delicious

Flowers, close to the new Mansion Abbey, is a neete and curiously contriv'd Fountaine of pure cleere water, knee deep and 4. square, and in the midst a little green Island and Charon in his Boat; upon the Banke lyes Snakes, Scorpions and strange Fishes, which spout forth water about the Ferriman's eares and his Dog's, which is convey'd away by the turning of a Cocke. About it stands Sentinells the watry Ninmphs, on every Quarter, yet one of them lamely with but one arme, the other being disarm'd by the Royall steddy hand of our gracious Soveraigne at his Marriage of his Royall Spouse in this City.[4]

Within a few years of Tradescant's arrival the garden became renowned for its melons. A letter preserved in the State Papers, addressed to Lord Zouche, then Lord Warden of the Cinque Ports, from Sir Henry Mainwaring, who was overseeing his gardens, describes how 'This last week having some leisure I went on Saturday to Canterbury to see my Lord Wotton's garden and to confer with his gardener for I do much desire that your Lordship should eat a muske melon of your own in Dover Castle this year.'[5]

Tradescant had probably learned the art of melon-growing from the Earl of Essex's gardener. There are two similar manuscripts in the Bodleian Library written in the same hand. The shorter is described as 'A breefe note of the setting and planting of the Melon seed from my Lord of Essex gardener', while to the other has been added a title that is almost certainly in Tradescant's hand: 'The Melonniere: or the order to dresse and plant the Melon seedes'.

The melons were to be grown in a sunny and sheltered 'knotte'. The secret lay in sheep's 'doung' – that of goats and cows being considered too strong. The plot had to be divided into four, three parts of which were left to rest, while the fourth was planted. The dung had to be carefully applied, well before use, so that the fruit was not 'taynted'. Once in fruit the melons had to 'be warely kept from catts who love them greatly' and had to be 'gathered in the mornings before summer risinge when they smell pleasantly at the butt end'.[6]

John Parkinson was another visitor. He first saw there, in the care of his 'very loving and kinde friende John Tradescante',[7] an unusual type of male mandrake with folded greyish-green leaves (possibly *Mandragora autumnalis* Bertol.) growing alongside the more common variety (*Mandragora officinarum* L.). 'But', he added, 'what fruit it bore could not be assured having never borne any as they said.'[8]

Also growing at St Augustine's was the 'Indian Moly', a member of the garlic family and a variety of *Allium magicum* L., which had been sent from Turkey. 'It grew also with John Tradescante at Canterbury,' Parkinson recorded. He 'sent me the head of bulbes to see, and afterwards a roote, to plant in my Garden'.[9] This plant was not new, however; it had been growing with Gerard in 1597.

While Tradescant nurtured the plants in his garden, his thoughts ranged further afield. The great topic of the day was the New World, in particular the new colony of Virginia.

The first settlers had arrived in Virginia in 1607, establishing Jamestown as a fortified trading post on a low-lying, swampy island. It was hardly an ideal site, and conditions were hard: many of the early colonists died from disease or starvation. There were also the Indians. For some reason the Indian tribes had been expected to co-operate with the white men who arrived to take over their land. Not surprisingly, few did so and there were many massacres.

Despite, or perhaps because of, the hardships of life in the colony, the Virginia Company mounted a vigorous publicity campaign. Innumerable broadsheets and pamphlets were published painting conditions in Virginia in the most glowing terms, in the hope of luring settlers across the Atlantic. There seemed to be nothing that did not, or would not, grow there; the sea teemed with fish and in the forests lived abundant wildlife. And, of course, they hoped to find gold.

Both individuals and city companies were encouraged to subscribe to the Virginia Company in order to populate this prosperous land. Unfortunately, the settlers who were attracted by the publicity were not always of the most suitable kind. Some preferred to starve rather than sully their hands with labour, and there was little incentive for even the Company's hired men to exert themselves.

Tradescant had two friends with first-hand experience of Virginia, Captain John Smith and Captain Sam Argall. Both were colourful, adventurous characters, and Tradescant must have listened spellbound to their tales.

John Smith had spent some years soldiering in the Low Countries and in Hungary, where, after performing seemingly miraculous feats, he was captured, enslaved and sent to Tartary. There, after a severe beating-up, he killed his cruel master, stole his clothes and horse and escaped. After travelling all round Europe, he returned to England.

In 1606, seeking further adventure, Smith sailed for Virginia, where he served a term as Governor. An able man, who learned to deal with the Indians better than most of his fellow settlers, always treating them with firmness but never with cruelty, he was captured on one of his trading expeditions and taken before the great Indian chief Powhatan. The chief decreed that Smith should have his brains beaten out. He was saved, however, by Powhatan's young daughter, Pocahontas, who, having pleaded in vain for his life, rushed to his rescue by putting her head beside his and thus preventing the executioners from doing their job. It was the start of a lasting friendship between the English colonist – who was afterwards released – and the Indian child.

In 1610 Smith suffered a terrible accident when his powder bag exploded on his lap. Lucky to survive, he sailed for home. He never returned to Virginia but spent the rest of his life promoting the colony. He had successfully mapped Chesapeake Bay and, with Christopher Newport, who was then Governor, had helped to persuade the reluctant Powhatan to be 'crowned' in the name of the King. To celebrate the occasion Powhatan was presented with various pieces of furniture and apparel. In exchange he proffered his moccasins and mantle, probably the deerskin 'habit' that later found its way into the Tradescant collection.

Sam Argall also had an adventurous career. A skilful navigator, he pioneered the fast northerly route to Virginia. He made this passage several times in nine weeks and could have lopped off two more had he not been becalmed.

Argall first came to notice in 1609, off Jamestown, when, in charge of a small barque, he was sent to trade and fish for sturgeon to help feed the early settlers. He was back again in the following year, this time helping to replace the stock the colonists had eaten during the previous winter. In 1612 he returned again and, while exploring the trading possibilities along the Potomac River, seized the opportunity to abduct Princess Pocahontas in order to gain the release of some English hostages, an act which achieved its object and brought about a temporary peace.

In 1613 conditions improved in Virginia when John Rolfe crossed tobacco seed from the West Indies with a local strain to produce the crop that was to capture the English market. It was not the gold that the colonists had been ordered to find and wasted much time searching for, but it was eventually to bring Virginia great prosperity.

Rolfe met Pocahontas while she was being held prisoner at Henrico, fifty-five miles up-river from Jamestown. In 1614 he married her, after she had been baptized into the Christian faith. This brought about a more lasting peace between the Indians and the settlers.

In 1616, Rolfe brought Pocahontas and their son Thomas on a visit to England. She was well received and was the object of enormous interest, but her health suffered from the change in climate. She died at Gravesend, where she was buried, on her reluctant way home.

A month before this sad event, on 12 February 1617, Captain Argall and his associates were allowed Bills of Adventure by the Virginia Company for the transport of twenty-four persons at their charge. An 'adventurer' was someone who 'adventured' his money but did not go to the colony in person, thus distinguishing him from the 'planter', who did.

Argall was being sent out to Virginia as Deputy Governor and Admiral of the adjacent seas. Among his fellow adventurers was John Tradescant, who bought two £12 10s. shares. In doing so he was in good Kentish company, for the other partners in this venture were Sir William Lovelace, MP for Canterbury; his daughter Mabell, Lady Cullamore; Sir Anthony Aucher, a former Sheriff of the county; and Sam Argall's elder brother John. Between them they subscribed £300.[10] As they were entitled to transport one person for each £12 10s. invested, this meant that they could send twenty-four people to start a plantation of 2,400 acres. It was standard practice at that time for settlers to arrive in Virginia at the expense of individual adventurers; as tenants on half-shares, the settlers had equal rights with their patrons.

Argall established his colony in the area west of Jamestown. The settlement seems to have prospered, for two years later it is listed among the populated areas of the colony and was one of only eleven communities to send representatives to the first Assembly in 1619.

Like most of his contemporaries Argall did what he could to improve his own lot while carrying out his official responsibilities. To advance his settlement, 300 acres of afforested land were cleared at a cost of £600 and a house built on it, all of which he hoped to recoup. Evidently the land and accommodation were good, for the settlement was reputed to reap better crops and lose fewer men than most others.

Argall Town, however, did not endure to become a settled community. In 1619, when Argall's successor, Yeardley, arrived with instructions to set up a plantation for the Governor's own use (in order to relieve the Company of the costs of maintaining him), it became 'Governor's land'. The plantation was to be on land formerly held by the Paspaheg Indians, and the inhabitants of Argall Town, which by 1621 was being described as a 'subberb of James Citie', were given permission to remove themselves as free men. What recompense the adventurers received is not documented.[11] As Argall was removed for alleged tyrannical conduct it seems unlikely that they got any. In the end, however, Argall survived these charges of maladministration and was afterwards knighted.

Although peace had come to the colony in 1614 after the marriage of Pocahontas to John Rolfe, it lasted for less than a decade. In 1622 there was another massacre and the white settlers took their revenge, finally subduing the Indian tribes and pushing them further and further west.

While Tradescant was leaning on his spade in the old monastery garden with his thoughts upon Virginia, his son was having a classical education drummed into him at the nearby King's School. The school buildings stood then, as they do today, in the shadow of Canterbury Cathedral.

The younger Tradescant was enrolled as a scholar some time between Michaelmas and Christmas 1619. He was then eleven years old. He left four years later, having signed for his allowance each quarter in a neat, clear hand. In order to become a scholar, he would have already received some preliminary education, at least in reading and writing. In addition, every boy admitted to the school had to know by heart the Lord's Prayer, the *Angelus*, the Apostles' Creed and the Ten Commandments.

The King's School Statutes of 1541 allowed for the endowment of fifty scholars each year. Elections (examinations) took place in November, and pupils usually entered the classroom in the following January. The normal attendance was for four years, and each scholar received a total of four pounds annually, £1 8s. 4d. of this being the actual scholarship, the remainder a food and clothing allowance. Scholars were expected to parade in purple gowns and on Sundays in surplices, which had to be 'so timely washd and dried in the week' that they were ready for wear. Any boy arriving without this apparel was automatically regarded as absent.

The number of commoners who attended is not recorded, but both masters, the headmaster and the lower master, are known to have supplemented their incomes by taking additional pupils, probably as many again and mostly boarders from outside the town.

The King's School, Canterbury, claims to be the oldest educational establishment in England, and some of the buildings standing today were already old by Tradescant's time. The large, bare-boarded schoolroom was housed in the Almonry, long since vanished from Mint Yard. It was furnished with wooden benches and long, narrow tables at which the boys sat to write. The younger Tradescant's headmaster was John Ludd, a former scholar of the school and of Cambridge, who had previously been Lower Master. He had been appointed two years before Tradescant arrived and was to devote his life to the job.

The curriculum consisted of Latin and more Latin, a few of the brighter boys progressing on to Greek and Hebrew as well. Grammar, spelling and possibly some mathematics and astronomy were also included, as were singing and music, for one of the Almonry rooms housed an organ. The whole school was examined weekly by the headmaster, with promotion between forms possible three times a year.

There are records of prizes in races against other schools and, as these took place on downs which later became a racecourse, it has been suggested that some at least may have been mounted. The Statutes firmly stipulate: 'And they shall not practise any games which are not of a gentlemanly appearance and free from all lowness.' Certainly an ability to ride was a necessary accomplishment for any gentleman in the seventeenth century.

Boys usually entered the school between the ages of nine and fifteen, and there were five or six forms. Those reaching the fourth form came under the direction of the headmaster and by that time were expected to have a thorough command of Latin, 'so that no noun or verb may be found anywhere which they do not know how to inflect in every detail', while in the form above they were to practise making verses, polishing speeches and to become 'versed in translating the most chaste Poets and the best Historians'. Indeed the final command in the Statutes was 'that whatever they are doing in earnest or in play, they shall never use any language but Latin or Greek'. Even if this last rule was not always obeyed it must have been a tough regime. The boys' day was a long one, beginning with the Lower Master offering prayers at 6 a.m. There was another service at 5 p.m., but even when this was over they were not finished. For the next hour they had to repeat lessons to 'their fellow pupils who have become ripe in learning', which indicates that some form of monitoring system was already in operation.

Perhaps even more can be gleaned from the regular plays the boys were encouraged to put on and which were duly recorded. These contain constant references to the bitter cold of the classroom, which lacked even a fireplace, and to corporal punishment. 'The ink freezes on one boy's inkhorn, the very brains freeze in the head of another,' reads one of them. A day boy has been drenched by 'slops thrown from windows overhead' as he was rushing to early prayers on a dark winter's morning; another has 'received a black eye from bumping into the unseen Cathedral'; while one master is described as 'a shrewd Tanner of boys' fleshy parts'.

The organ obviously came into its own on these occasions, for the stage directions of one drama command: 'Enter Guy Fawkes booted and spurred, the barrels of Gunpowder are brought in while ye Musick plays.'

Some dialogues show boys preparing for their chosen careers. 'A clergyman will preach the parish asleep once a week for thirty pounds a year', and a future physician will be 'a learned tormentor, a lingering executioner'.

The Statutes had further evolved by 1665, when it was decreed that 'to prevent the breaking of windows . . . the boyes be not suffered to hurle, fling or sling stones', that 'their demeanour . . . be civil without bellowing, hooting or any other unseemly noise'; and to 'prevent ye boyes loytering and idleing under a pretence of going to the Forrains notice be taken by the Schoolmʳ or Usher what boyes go forth for easement, that so they may see to their return in convenient time'.

The tolling of 'Bell Harry' was the call for Sunday prayers, when 'sermon notes in writing' had to be made 'to prevent gazing, slooping and the like irreverent carriage'. After Sunday-evening prayers all boys had to 'repair to the schoole and be there catechised'.

But there were some lighter moments. In the week before Lent there were disputations between selected scholars and commoners. The rest of the school listened and voted two victors, who were crowned with laurel wreaths and entitled to special privileges. These seem to have included the chance to compose original Latin verse which could bring a reprieve to any comrade due for a caning in Lent or even obtain a half-holiday, either for a selected few or, if of sufficient merit, for the whole school. On Christmas Day the headmaster's chair was decorated with bays and the schoolroom festooned in greenery.[12]

When he left the King's School at the end of 1623, John Tradescant was obviously well grounded in Latin, the universal language of botanists.

Chapter 4

The Earliest Russian Flora

In 1618 the elder John Tradescant was involved in a new adventure. At nearby Chilham Sir Dudley Digges had been busy erecting a fine house near the site of the old castle. The inscription over the door tells visitors that it was completed in the year 1616. The terracing of the garden is considered to be contemporary with the house, and it is thought possible that some of the trees, such as the vast Holm Oak on the lawn, could also date from this period.

It has been suggested that Tradescant laid out the original gardens, but, while this is possible, no documents to prove it can be traced. However, the fact that Digges' name is linked with that of Tradescant in his next venture may add authority to the idea.

Born in 1583, Sir Dudley Digges had spent some years travelling abroad after graduating from Oxford in 1601. Interested in the expansion of trade, he had become an early shareholder in the East India Company and in 1612 joined the North West Passage Company as a founder member, after a suitable route to the East had supposedly been discovered. In 1618 Sir Dudley was dispatched to Archangel, then called Muscovy, on what John Tradescant describes as 'A Viag of Ambusad'.[1] The Russian Tsar, Michael Fedorovich, at war with Poland, had sent over ambassadors to negotiate a loan. James I, having ordered the Muscovy and East India Companies to furnish the money, sent Digges, who was a member of both, to arrange terms.

He sailed on 3 June with £20,000 and a company of forty-one men. Among them was John Tradescant. The Russian ambassadors sailed home alongside in another ship. It was hoped that Digges would be able to negotiate the right of free transit for English merchandise to and from Persia through Russia and perhaps also establish a direct trade route to China.

The mission, however, proved a failure. For some reason Digges retreated hastily when he was less than half-way to Moscow, sending on only part of the money with a few of his retinue. It was a surprising decision as, although Russia was in chaos, Digges himself was in no personal danger. Possibly he realized that Russia was in no state to warrant such an investment and decided that it was pointless to continue.

Digges left Archangel on 2 September, but Tradescant had sailed home a month earlier. Clearly he had gone along for the botanizing and had already achieved all that he could hope to do in that respect. Moreover, he would obviously have wanted to get his collection of plants home as quickly as possible.

Tradescant kept a full and complete diary of this trip, which is reproduced below. The original manuscript was discovered in the Bodleian Library by Dr Joseph von Hamel in 1814.

Tradescant's journal is in two parts. In the first he records the major events of the voyage; in the second, headed 'Things by me observed', he describes events ashore and lists his botanical discoveries. The original manuscript is divided into paragraphs but has virtually no punctuation; some has been added to make it more readable. The original spelling has been retained, however, and it should be borne in mind that it was not then standardized – a word could be spelt phonetically in any way that sounded correct.

'A viag of Ambusad undertaken by the Right Honnerabl Sr Dudlie Digees in the year 1618, being atended on withe 6 genttillmen whiche beare the nam of the Kings Genttillmen, whose name be heere notted – on Mr Nowell, brother to the Lord Nowell, Mr Thomas Finche, Mr Woodward, Mr Cooke, Mr Fante & Mr Henry Wyeld, withe every on of them ther man. Other folloers – on Briggas, Interpreter; Mr Jams, an Oxford man, his Chaplin; on Mr Leake, his Secretary; with 3 Scots, on Captain Gilbert and his son, with on Car; also Mr Mathew De Questers son of Filpot Lane in London. The rest his own retennat sume 13, whearof note on Jonns an Coplie, Wustershir men; Mr Swanli of Limhouse, Master of the good shipe called the Dianna of Newcastell; Mr Nelson, part ownner of Newecastell.

'The 3 of June 1618 being Wednesday we wayed ancor at Gravesend and fell doune to Tilbery Hope. The Thursday after we, after diner, wayed and went to lee withe a calme wind, the wind being West. On Friday being the 5 date we ancored short of the Spits. But the wind changing and blowing hard we wayed and put roomer [tacked] for Quinborrow [Queenborough], whear we lay 2 nights and on day withe a conttrary wind. On Monday, being the 8 of June, at 4 of the clock in the morning we wayed ancor withe a Southwest wind whiche conttinewed 48 howers but sumwhat calm. On Wednesday morning the wind changed to the West Norwest and so conttinewed over blowing till Satterday the 12 of Jun, the wind conttrary, whear all our landmen fell sick, and my Lord himselfe for 4 daies very sick. On Satterday to wars night the wind sumwhat seased. On Sunday the 14 daye ther cam up with us a man of war of Encusan, on of the Stats men of war, which halling us gave eche other the curtisi of the sea and so parted, wee standing in for the land. On Sunday nyght mad the l[a]nd of the Bishopbrick of Durram. On Monday and Mund night we tyded up with the shore and Tusday all day, to recover the Tinmouthe haven to releve our sick men withe freshe vittells from Newcastell, the wind all this while beinge just in our teethe. I must not omit the great fleet of Hollonders that lay at ancor in the sea, which wear to our thinking wear 100 and 50 sayls, all fishing for cod and somer herring.

'On Sunday being the 14 day we had sight of toune 7 leags to the Southe of Newecastell. Munday and Tewesday we beate up and doune to recover Newcastell, but could not. On Wednesday being the 17th day my [Lord] caused the boat to [be] hoysed out to set his people on shore and my selfe and on other to goe to Newchatell for make provissions of beef and muttons withe many other nesesaryes, wheare I bought ii salmons for 5s. the cupple and sum for 4s. the cupple, whiche at London would have bin worth 2 $^{li.}$10$^{s.}$ the cuple. Also we went to suppe at the best ordinary in the toune with many dishes. Our win being payd for cam but to 8d. the peece, whiche in London I think 2s. the peece would have hardli mached it. On Thursday we returned to the shipe with sume 17 $^{lis.}$ worthe of provission, the wind then being fayre. But withein an houre after the wind changed and cam full in our teethe, that on the next morning the wind being so full in our teethe we determined with the counsell of our Vise-admirall to put into the harber. But my Lord and myself most against it, we continewed without. On Friday in the afternoone the wind cam to the East and be Northe, so we claud it of to sea and avoyded the former feare. Sir Georg Selbe sent to my Lord Imbassator for a present 2 salmons and on hogshead of beeare. The Mayre of Newcastell the day before sent him on samone, using his genttillmen withe much curtisie, being ashore at Shialds 6 mylls short of Newcastell, his Lordship keeping abord all the while.

'On Thursday being the 19 of June about 4 of the clock in the afternoone we weyied ancor before Tinmouthe Castell, the wind being West and by Southe, but slack, whiche we pased that night. But on Fryday the wind scantted [veered ahead] to the Nor west, wheare we laye Northeast away withe a leeward way, the wind increasing and changing mor Northe. The Satterday the wind began to rise, on Sunday to encreas, being full in our teethe. Munday and Tewsday still the storme conttinewing till Thursday morning. In all this whill we weare constrayned to [go] under our two coorses. On Wednesday the wind changed West. In whiche 4 dayes my Lord Ambassittor was exstreem sick, in so much that all they in the ship mad question of his life, partli by sea sickness and partli by over muche coller, that he was purswaded to to be set on land or not to live. Being just 40 leags from the Northern part of Scotland and 40 from the coast of Norway, and in 58 and better in the lattatud, the wind then changed to the West, whiche Scotland we could not recover, the[n] to the Southeast Bar Elsenoor, whiche was the next plase, which wase 110 leages from us, the wind still coming more calme and more larg [free], that we perswaded him to hould on his coorce. And on Thursday his lordship, after the calme, reseved sume meate, which in 4 dayes before he hade refused. On the Friday morning being the 26 of June he had a littill sleepe, the Great God be blessed for it.

'Even beyond our hops the wind and sea was calme and fair whiche before that time had bine still cros. Now on Tewsday and Wednesday we had sight of 4 sayll to windward of us, to the Eastward of us, and on the morow we lost them not speaking withe them. On Wednesday we had sight of on sayll to the westward, standing our corse, but spake not withe hir. Nowe on this present Friday the 26 the wind is fayr and our sick people well recovered. God conttinew them bothe, healthe and wind. Now being in 60 degrees, by the reason of my Lords sicknes I wached and had no night. This was the first plas whear darknes seases for the night. Thear you mought have wrought or wrot at midnight. The satterday the wind fayr but dead; came Sunday and Munday, being the 28 and 29 of Jun, the wind scant but a fine gall at the East and by Northe.

'On Saynt Peetter's day on the morning my Lord sent the Russian Imbassator fresh vytalls: on quarter of mutton, half a littill porker, and 3 live pullet, ther Lent being but then ended. Also at New Castell my Lord sent hime two small salmons and 9 gallons of Carnary Sack. The curtiseys hathe pased a yet witheout requittall.

'Also on Munday nyght the cam a strang bird abord our shipe, which was taken alive and put to my costody, but dyed within two dayes after being 60 leags from the shore, whos like I yet never sawe, whos case I have reserved. This was in 66 degrees in the latitud. On Tewsday night the wind cam fayer, being the first of Jully, in 67 or a littill short, whear the sune did showe sume small part of hir boddy all the night. At 65 we layd the light of the moone being so far to the Sutheward of us.

'On Friday the 3 of July a man of Mr Decrass cam abord of us to take counsell about sending away the pinnas for Greenland, the year being so far spent. As they thought the Russes being landed, the time of the yeare would be too far spent, whear it was decreed that that shee should goe on of hir intended vyage. This mans name was Mr Spyke who was made welcom according to the maner of the seae. My Lord sent back withe him two bottells of his wine, on of sack and on of clarret, even present fit for suche people, yet two great as the time required by reson of our long voyag. Now from Munday the 29 of June to Friday night the 3 of July the wind hathe bin very fayre at the Southe and Southewest, whiche God continnewe, we lying our coorce Northeast.

'On Satterday the 4 of July the pinnas partted withe us, we then standing our coorse East and East and by Southe, the pinnas standing away from us Northe and by East. That night at 12 of the clocke we sawe the sune shine about an howr hyghe just Northe, whiche we had not seene 4 dayes befor nor in two dayes after, being ever an extreem fogge.

'On the Sunday the 5 of Jully we saw many whalls, sum hard by the shipe. On the Munday morning being an exstreeme fogg our Master thought he had sene land, whiche mad hime alter a poynt or two of his compas to the North. This [thus] have we been witheout the light of sune 5 dayes, being in the heyght of the Cape, whiche as we think we wer 72 and better to the Northe.

'On Munday morning we had sight of the Northe Cape, whiche is all covered withe snow, whear we felt the ayre very could, the land being highe land, all ilands, withe many bayes amongst the lande.

'On the Tewsday morning very early we came upe with on of the King of Denmarks men of war, who demanded of us to com abord to show oure pase, but we ansered that our boat was stowed, we could not; besides we had an lnglishe Ambassator abord, whiche he presentlie desisted from his demand. Our consort also told him in lik sort that he had a Rus Ambasitor abord. Also in his company we found the Companyes other shipe who had bin from hir port from Hamborow 3 weeks withe other two in his company, allso two Hollanders, who he caussed ther boats to com abord. We at that time had bin out of Ingland 5 weeks lacking a daye. This man of war laye to waft or watter the fishermen that fishe upon that coast of Wardhouse [Vardöhuus], wheare the King hathe a castell withe great comand of Lapland, wheare many Danes live withe the Laps which, if I mought have the wholl kingdom to be bound to live ther, I had rather be a porter in London, for the snow is never of the ground wholly, but liethe in great packes conttinnewally. Ther is no shadowe for the sun shinethe ther continnewally when it is no foggs whiche most tims it is. The Kings man of war gave us a peece or gune, whiche we ansered withe another; and our Vise admirall gave him 3. And so for that time partted, being now short of Wardhouse 3 leags, standing our coorse Southeast, the wind at the West, being Inglishe and strangers 7 sayls bound for Archangell.

'Now from the time befor named on the eleventh of July we have had a fayer wind, sumetimes going Sutheaste and sumtimes Suthe and su[m]times Suthewest, all being our corse. This eleventh day we had a small boat of that cunttrie of the Cros Iland that brought his bote laden withe salmons 3 dayes salted. My Lord bought on for 4s. 0d. mony, a very great on. Now after wee wer so far as Cross Iland the snowe began to abate and the natur of the coaste to change from russet to a greener coller, the inland being full of shruby trees, and further of of we moughte perseve great woods, but all this way no kind of grayne. Nowe to speake of the boate and the men. The men on of them was a man about 50 yeares withe on eye, hard favored. The yonger man was about 25 years, well favored and well limbed, and bothe clad in lether, withe the skins of sheepe withe the firs syde inwards, bothe having crusifixes about the necks very arttifityally mad. I have seene manie in lngland of ther profetion worse fationed. Ther boat was small, very neatly mad, lik to the manner of Holland scuts.

'On Sunday being the 13 of Jully the wind being conttrary, being sume 6 leags short of Foxnose, we had sighte of a great whight fishe tw[i]se so great as a porpos, being all over as white as snowe, whiche they say is a great destroyer of the salmons.

'On the Munday the 13 of Jully, ther were many small birds cam abord the shipe, being sume 3 leags from the shore. I have thre of ther skins whiche were caut by my self and the rest of the company. They did muche resemble the maner of our Inglishe linnets but far lesser.

'On Tuesday the 14 of Jully wee cam to the bar, wheare we spent on daye because it was calme. On the Wednesdaye we went over the bar having but on foot watter mor thin the shipe drew.

'On the Thursday the 16 day we came into the harbor but before we cam halfe the way the souldgers cam to sallut their owne ambassators, but not us. But in the halfe way pasag in the river the Grand Prestave sallutted my Lord withe mani boats full of souldgers, who himselfe was entterteyned in the cabbin withe a banket of sweetemeats, the agent and the rest of the Inglishe marchants having had the like entterteynment just before his coming. Whear at his departur we gave 3 peeses of ordnance, and he us his small shot, whiche was but poorlie performed, ther peeces being hardli so good as our callivers, neyther had the soulgers any expertnes like to thees in thees parts. Farther at our first entterance over the bar intto the river we reseved from the agent on good bullock, 2 sheep, 10 hens, 2 fesants, 6 pattriges, non lik the Inglishe. That night came abord of our ship a boat of Sammoyets, a misserable people of small grouth. In my judgment is that people whom the fixtion is fayned of that should have no heads, for they have short necks and commonly wear ther clothes over head and shoulders. They use boues and arrowes. The men and women be hardli knowne on from the other because they all wear clothes like mene and be all clad in skins of beasts packed very curouslie together, stokins and all. They kill most of the Lothi deer that the hids be brought. The[y] be extreme beggars not to be denied.

'Farther that night we wayed anccor by reson of the two fluds. The first is but 2 howres and then a swift ebe; and then, presentlie after two howers, a long flud like ours. In that place wheare we anccored I desired to have the boat to goe on shore whiche was hard by, wher, when we wear land, we found many sorts of beryes, on sort lik our strawberyes but of another fation of leaf. I have brought sume of them hom to show withe suche variettie of moss and shrubs, all bearing frute, suche as I have never seene the like. Also at our first landing we found a peece of a snacke skin. Also in that same place we sprung 5 foulls suche as all those in the place whear we landed hardlie knewe, the ould ons were great to the bignes of a fesant, the wings whit, the bodies green, the tayll blewe or dove coller. I would have given 5s. for on of ther skins. Now Thursday night we mord our shipe befor the Inglishe house. On Friday we went on shore withe all the showe we could make, being ffeched withe the Prestave and the rest of his band. The houses that wer taken up for my Lords lod[g]ing were 3 severall mene, 2 Duche and on Wilkinson a Inglishe mane. They be all built of wholl trees layd on on the top of the other, very strong withe fayr roomes, packed betwin the hollowes with wood moss. Havying but poor bedsteds, content to lay our bodi on the ground.

'On Munday I had on of the Emperors boats to cari me from iland to iland to see what things growe upon them, whear I found single rosses wondros sweet withe many other things which I meane to bringe withe me, wheare I observed the basness of the people. For we had a comander withe us who was glad to be partaker of coorce cates, as we thear could get, whiche was sower creame and otmeall pasties very poorli mad, whiche to them was a great bankit.

'The 5 of August 1618 we set sayll for Ingland from the poynt a myll from the toune. That night we cam to an ancor under Rose Iland, wheare I [and] divers [others] went on shore, whear ther was a littill souldgers house poorly garded withe sum 10 men, whear we bought gras for our live sheepe, whear I gathered of all suche things as I could find thear growing, whiche wear 4 sorts of berries, whiche I brought awaye withe me of every sortt. This iland is lowe land all over but wheare the house stands, and that place is a long banke of drie white sand, the land being eyther woods or meddow, bur seldom eyther mowne or fed.

'The 6 of August we weyed ancor, the wind being fayer, and went. For the bar is but 11 foot watter and our shipe drew 10 and a halfe, the tide being then neape, whear we cam on and sat 6 or 8 howers to oure great grefe, a flawe [sudden gust of wind] presentli rising, whiche if it had continewed the shipe must needs have perished. But, thanks be to God, the next tyd we cam of without any harme. The next day we wear becalmed. The 8 day in the morning we mad Cros Iland, the wind being fayre but small and much raine, insomuche that all the decks wear leake, whiche for my own part I felt for it rayned doune thourow all my clothes and beds to the spoyll of them all. The 8 day at night we met withe on of the Stats men of war that the Russian Ambassator cam home in of Cape Grace. From the 8 to the 10 conttrary winds. From the 10 to the 13 extrem fogs, so that in 4 or 5 dayes we went but 10 leags ahead. Of Cape Gallant we met withe the race of a tyde; the fog being extreme we wear afrayd of being brought upon a rock. But thanks be to God it proved better.

'The 14 daye being Fridaye, dead calme, we mad a sayll whiche we thought had bin but a Dingo bote, whiche when we wear com up withe hir it was a great Flemin, but could not speake withe hir. That daye we sawe mani whalls, whear the owner of [the] ship sawe on chased withe a thresher and called me to see it, but they rose no more. The next day being Satterday wee had a great storme, the wind being at East. On Sunday towards night the storme seased and the wind changed West. That night we mad the Northe Cape. On Munday it was calme withe much fog, [to] whiche that place is muche subject.

In the night the wind ros. On Tuesdaye the wind blew hard all day at the Northe and by West, so that the Master feared the making the way good, we going und[er] bothe oure corses withe raine and snow.

'On Tuesday the 18 of August we laye West and [West] and by Northe, the wind being scant. On Wednesday we went roomer 25 leags. On Thursday we stood our coorce. On Friday and Satterday we had a fayre wind. On Satterday at noone the Maste[r] obse[r]ved and found his heyght to be 68 to the Northe and in the Bay of Ros. On the Friday night we had 3 howers night, whiche we had not had since the going outward from the heyght 66, which was all day 8 weeks together withe us.

'On Sunday, Mu[n]day, Tusdaday the wind contrary. On Wednesday we had sight of a saylle. On Thursday we mad hir mor perfectly cloce by a wind, the win[d] being for the most part sowethe. We mad two saylls, but lost them presently by reson of a fogg. On Friday morning being the 23 of August the wind cam fayre to the Northeast and continnewed so 5 waches. That night it changed, wheare they observed and found themselves in 64. On Satterday midnight the wind changed East and so continewed all that day wit a great storme. At night it changed. On Munday the last of August we observed and found them in the lattitude of 62 degrees, the wind directly against them.

'On Tusday and Wednesday sutherly winds contrary. On Thursday the Southe and by East very vyolently, that the storme was great 18 howers against us, that we wear constrained to trie withe oure main coorce shiping sum seaes. On Thursday night the wind calmed. On Friday it veered westerly. Then we stood our coorse. But it presently chan[g]ed. Now all this whill we had much rayne. On Satterday being the 5 of September we observed and found our ellivation to be 61 so that in on 6 dayes we got on degree. Now in this time of fowlle wether we had twice sight of a Flemen but never spake withe hire by resin of conttrary winds and over blowing.

'On Satterday at nyght towards the morning we had an exstreem gall of wind at the Southe withe muche rayne and continewed all Sunday, but not so voyolently. Now on Sunday morning being the 6 of September we had sight of two sayles of Flemens to leeward, but did not speake withe them. Just at twellfe of the clok, the sun shining thowroue the cloud had a great sircle aboute hir, even as hathe the moone in raynie time. Also before the sune was a dogg lik the shining of an other sun. Also for sum two howrs we had scoll of grampuses swiming by the shipe syde, all at on tyme. God send good sucses. The wind being at the Southwest, whiche God send to chang, for in 6 dayes we gained but on degree, our course being from Northe to Southe. On Sunday night, the wind being Southe and Southe and by West, it having blown hard all day, towards night we had sight of a Hollonder that gave us chace, but our Master would not speak withe him. That night and Mu[n]day we had a marvelus great storme that put us to leeward by our Tuesdayes acount in observation 16 leags only. In trying under our main saylle we had sight of two saylls mor on Sunday, but our Master would neyther speak withe any nor let any speake with him, becas he thinking they cam awai after him it his disgrace. This Tuesday, still the galle continnewing, but yet a littill better, the wind being Southewest and Southe West and by West, we lying sumtime Southe and sumetime Southesowest, but with mor temperat wether. On Wednesday the 9 of September we had muche rayne and calme, the wind continnewing Southe.

'On Thursday mornyng being x of September, thanks be to God, the wind cam to West Norwest. That same day at noone we observed and found ourselvs to be in 60 on minne[t] to the Sutheward. On Fryday the 11 of September we observed and found to be in 59, the wind being East and by Southe, sotherly, fayer and drie wether. On Sunday, being the 13 of September, I withe on o[ther] were walking on the wast of the shipe, I descryed lande, whiche was present[ly] approved by the wholle company, which land was to the southward of Baffam Ness, part of the cuntrie of Scotland. Oure Master imajened it to be the Frithe, but could no mor tell than any other. This [thus] in on just monthe we had bine witheout sight of land. For the Sunday monthe befor wee had syght of the Northe Cape of the land called the Asumtion. The wind then coming fayre to the Northeast but ever calme when it was faier and still overblowing against us.

'On Sunday nyght, being the 13 of September, having mad the land, the wind being scant, we stood of to seae, whiche nyght the wind rose very tempesteously, continewing all that day withe the best part of the Tewsday. On Tusday nyght the wind cam mor large. On Wednesday the 16 of August [September] we observed and found our selves to be in 54 and 28 minnets to the Northward. Having the wind at the Southe West, Westerly, we changing our tack to the Northe west and by West. I know no reson for it. But as I conseved upon the other tack to mak Flamborrow Head, the better to fall withe the coast of Norfolke whiche is lowe land.

'On Friday 12 of the clok, after oure standing to the Northeward, we mad Flambrow Head, the 18 of August [September], standing our course Sothsowest for Yarmouthe, the wind being for the most part Norwest and Northe and Northe and by East, whiche wind we had not had in 3 weeks before. On Satterday the 19 of August [September] the wind was fayer so that that night we recovered Yarmouthe Road whear we ancored and dyned in the toune.

'On Sunday after dinner we weyed ancor and that night, the wind being fayer, we recovered Alboroug. The next morning being Mundaye we weyed and that daye cam to Gravesend. On Tewsday the 22 of August [September] we landed at Saynt Katharins neer London whear, God be thanked, we ended our viage having no on man sick, God be thanked.

'Things by me observed.

'Imprimis for the sowing of rye the[y] sewe in Jully, ther wheat in June. Theese two grayens growe sume 13 monthes before they be reaped by reson of the snow falling in August or September, and so liethe till the May after.

'Ther harvest is in August and the begining of September. Ther barly oats and pease they sowe in May the last, and comonly reaped the first of August or the last of July.

'I have bin showed oats whyte, very good, whiche wer sowne and mowne and reapet thrashed in 6 weeks.

'For ther howses they be made all of long peeces of fire [fir], being half cut away on the insyd. They be glased withe glas called slude. Ther ruffes be flat almost and cut bordes of a hand full thick layd longwayes doune the ruffe. They have the rinds of birche trees under the bords, which be as broad a yearing calfe or broader and 3 yards long, whiche they lay the edges on ove[r] another and doo defend the wet and rayne and snowe.

'Now for ther warmthe they have stooves wherain they heate ther meat, whiche is so well don that it givethe great content to all strangers.

'For beds I have seene none of the Ruses, but think for the most part they sleepe upon bedsteads, and most of ther beding is beare skins and other skins. The Inglishe and Leefelanders, I have seene ther beds like to thees borded beds in Ingland of a mean fation.

'For ther meat and bread, it is resonable god. They have bothe wheat and rie bread and as full as good as most plases of Ingland dooe afford, only they never bake it well and have many foollishe fatyons for ther form of ther loafe. Sum littill ons so littill as on may well eat a loafe a[t] two mouthe full; other great onse, but muche shaped like a horse shooe, but that they be round and a horse shooe is open in the on end.

'Also they have a broune kind of rye bread whiche is bothe fine and good. I have seene at the Inglishe house and also in the Duche houses, Leeflanders so good bread as I have yet never seene the like in this cunttrie.

'For ther drinks they be meads made of hony and watter and also beere. But ther Ruse beere is wonderfull base of an ill tast. But ther best meade is excelent drinke, mad of ther hony, whiche is the best honny of the world. I have drunke suche beere brewed by a Ruse in the Inglishe house, bothe for strengthe and for good tast as I have never betterd it in Ingland.

'For the mutton and beefe it was bothe small and lean, ther sheepe muche lik to ther Northfolk sheepe; ther beefes like runts of 4 marks price; ther hens and cokes small and no capons. Ther pidggs they spend wonderfull small, the hogs short, well trused swine. Ther bacon tasts muche after oylle because of the muche fishe ther hogs eate.

'Ther land, so muche as I have seene, is for ther earable, fine gentill land of light mould like Norfolke land, without stones. Ther maner of plowes like owre but not so neat, muche lik to Essex ploughes withe wheells but the wheells very evill made.

'The carts be littill ons, long narrow ons, muche like them of Stafordshir. The Wheells be lowe, mad of two peeces of slit fir timber, being thik wheare the excelltre [axle-tree] goeth thorow, and so deminnishe les till they com to the rime, and follow the cattle withe muche labor. For ther horses they be well shaped, short knyt, well joynted. Only ther Tarter horses be longe, muche like to the Barbery horses, but of the best use of any in the knowne world. For, as I have heard Captaine Gilbert report, that hathe long lived theare, he had on whiche he hathe rod a wholl day together and at night hathe given him a littill provender and the next day hathe don the like and so for many dayes, and yet he confessethe that he hathe not knowne seldom on of tire.

'For ther streets they be paved whithe goodli timber trees cleft in the midell. For they have not the use of sawing in the land espetiali in that part whear I was, neyther the use of planing withe the plane, but onlie withe a shave, or as sume parts of this kingdom callethe it, a draing knife. And yet yu shall see things don beyond any mans judgment onli withe a hatchet and a chisell and a draing knife and withe muche speed. But that I think is by reson of the softnes of ther woods. The yards of ther howses be all paved withe timber and devided betwin neybor and neybor withe palli[s]adowes of yong timber of 12 or 13 foot highe, the timber being so big, as from post to post they put through a long peece which cume throw a mortis.

'Also the cunttrie howses be bult liketo those of the townes and pallisadeed, whiche be don all in on forme, having ther yard rounded withe cowhouses and plases for shepe and horse, being all open to the yardsyd, muche like cloysters heer in Ingland. Ther ploughes and carts amongst ther cattell to make partission an[d] over liethe the hay. For the most part they b[e] quadrand and on corner is the dw[e]lling-howse and on syd the barn whiche is comonly the front.

'Farther it is to be observed that all thees cuntrie howses stand on littill hills, whiche hathe bin raysed by art at the first; and also without the pallisado or fence of inclosure, ther stands the bodyes of timber trees sume 7 or 8 foot highe, and from the inclosure sum 16 foot, and on from an other 7 or 8 foot, whiche they say is to defend the isse whiche at the first thawing, if it be withe rayne, makethe a very great flud. Ther lyethe by the rivers syd many great stones, some of halfe a cart load and mor, whiche I demanded on to aske how they cam thear, the land being witheout, being moorishe toward the watters syd. And they tould our interpreter that they wer brought ought out of the land by the isse.

'Now for thos trees and woods and that I have seene. In the cunttrie, as 5 parts is woods and unprofitable grounds, I have seene 4 sorts of fir trees an birche trees of a great bignes, whiche in the spring tyme they make insistion for the juce to drinke, whiche they say is a fine coolle kind of drink, whiche lastethe the most part of May and the beginning of June. Also they have littill treese that they make hoops of, whiche the Inglishe saye they be wilde cheryes, but I canot beleeve it is of that kind. But is lik a chery in leafe and bearethe a bery les than our Searvis bery, sumwhat blackishe, but was not ripe at my being theare. The wood is wondros pliant and if a twig chance to tuche the ground it will take roote, as I have seene in many places. I took up of them in July an brought them over a plant or two, whiche I hope will growe, for all the unfit season of the yeare they be very willing to grow. Now for the abu[n]dance of hoopes that ther is mad, I may imagin, for owr coopers, for ther great caske of caveare, and the Flemins, Hollonders and Hamburgers and Russes, spend suche abundance. Yet our people bring them away for the hooping of the cask in Greenland, and by the report of the coopers, they be the best hoops in the world, for they say in a wholl day they break not on.

'I have also seene shrubs of divers kinds.

'As Ribes, or, as we call them, currants, whit, red and black, far greatter than ever I have seen in this cuntrie.

'Also roses, single, in a great abundance, in my estemation 4 or 5 acars together. They be single and muche like oure sinoment [cinnamon] rose; and who have the sence of smelling say they be marvelus sweete. I hop they will bothe growe and beare heere for amongst many that I brought hom withe the roses upon them, yet sume on may grow.

'For p[l]ants: helebros albus, enoug to load a shipe, whiche the Ruses call camaritza.

'Also angellica, great stor; and lisimachia, penttafyllon maior, geranium flore serulie, saxifrag, sorrell half the heyght of a man.

'Also rosasollis I found theare.

'3 or 4 sorts of whorts, red ons and two sorts of blewe ons. And also on sort of plant bearing his frut like hedge mercury, which made a very fine showe, having 3 leaves on the tope of every stake, having in every leafe a berry about the bignes of a hawe, all the 3 berryes growing close together, of a finener bright red than a hawe, whiche I took up many roots. Yet am afraid that non held becase, at our being on ground, we staved most of oure frese watter and so wear faint to watter withe salt watter, but was mad beleeve it was freshe, whiche that plant having but a long whit thin root, littill biger then a small couche gras. And the Boys in the ship, befor I per[r]seved it, eat of the berries, except sume of them com up amongst the earthe by chance. I found this plant to growe in Rose Iland. Thear I found pinks growing natturall of the best sort we have heere in Ingland, withe the eges of the leaves deeplie cut or jaged very finely. I also sawe straberyes to be sould, but could never get of the plants, but the beryes wear 3 times at my Lords table. But they wer in nothing differing from ours, but only les, whiche mad me that I did not so muche seek after them. But for the curants and all other things that I found, being they wear so muche biger than ours was, as I could gather, by the vygor of the somer, which is so quick that when a thinge is in blosom it never felle the could tyll it is a perfect frute. Also I found a bery growing lowe at my first landing whic, in bery, was muche lik a strabery but of an amber coller. The people eate it fo[r] a medsin against the skurvi. The leaves be much lik our avince and of suche a greene. I dried sume of the beryes to get seede whearof of I have sent par[t] to Robiens of Parris.

'All thes things I have seene, but by report They have most sorts of trees that we have in England up in the contrie, bothe oake, elme and ashe, aple, peare and cheryes, but the frut les and not so plesant. This have bin tould me and amongst the rest of a plant that growethe upon the Volga, whiche they call Gods tree, whose leaves be muche lik to fennell. But the[y] report it is pasing sweet and of great vertues. Also I have bin tould that thear growethe in the land bothe tylipes and narsisus. By a Brabander I was tould it thoug, by his name, I should rather think him a Hollander. His name is Jonson and hathe a house at Archangell. He may be eyther, for he always dru[n]ke once in the day.

'Now for ther navegablenes: it is of 3 sorts. They use great lyters or barges or keches, for they be sume of them that will cary 3 or 4 score tuns or loads. They goe withe crose saylls and the masts made all of on peece like Gravesend Barge; and, at the uper end, they have cote thorowe a thin bord of 3 quarters of a yard long sume shape or liknes, sume to a foulle and sume to a dragon or any other thing that ther fancy leads them two. And at the end of the wood worke they have fastned sume linen or thin stuffe, comonly fringed, and most of them have eyther hanks, bells or horsbells hanging theron that maks a noyse withe the winde. For ther hulls of theese vessells they be without naylls of iron or trunells of wood, for they be sowne together withe rinds of trees and calked in the seames withe fine mosse and rosinned and tared, but dresed rosen coller. Ther fation muche like as if on would tak two litters and clap on upon an other, none being open aloft, but they go in on the syd where they tak the loading in. The top or upper part is under the planks lined withe the rind of birche trees to defen[d] watter. Theese great vessells they call loddes. They sayll all or els set them of withe long polls. The ruder of on of theese is sumtims 10 foot long behind the vessell and of a great thiknes and breathe, gyded by a long tiller within bord. I have seene at the lancheing of on of thees 3[0] men prising withe leavers to get them of and making a noyse as if all the wholl toune had bin together by the ears. And for ther labor I durst have bin on of the 6 Inglishe that should have done more than those 30. Nowe they ly on ground at every port they com to.

'They comonli never goe without a faire wind, espetyally the Laps or Laplanders, for if the Inglish se them coming they still curse them knowing the wind will chang and be in ther poops.

'They have also a littill second kind of boate sumwhat les than our wheryes in the river of Thames, whiche they call Dingo boats. They will carry sume 8 or 9 persons. Thees most of the Mossicks be furnished withe to bring the hogs and sheepe and fishe and hense and wild foulle to market, whiche they have in great abundance. This boat is mad of 4 or 3 deall bords finely cleft and then hewed, but is for depthe comonly never but two bords, on above an other, sowne together withe rinds of trees. They be very light so that two mene will take on of them and cary them from highwatter mark to lowe eyther way as it pleasethe them. They sume time will rowe in on of theese boats 3 payre of s[c]ulls, the sculls being about 5 or 6 foot long, the blad being the longest part but not as ours be in Ingland, but be round almost halfe the way, and the other end dothe bear his breadthe equall to the end. The[y] go very swift, on of the rowers sitting rit behind the other and keep stroke, bu[t] if on sturs they be redy to tumble over by reson of the narrownenes of them.

'They have yet a third kind [of] boat that be mad all of on tree of an increddable bredthe and bignes, for many of thees boat be 25 or 30 foote long and longer, sume 7 foote broad. The keells of these boat be almost round, luttill tapard. They heyten the syds of the[m] withe strong hewed deall plancks and bayll theme all over from end to end withe hoops of this fornamed wild cherry tree, as the Inglishe calls it, and cover it withe birche rinds and sumtims withe sealls skins, having of those abundance. For withe those boats they hunt and persue them and fishe for them, for they cache abundance, whiche may appeere by the great store of oylle that they ther make, wh[i]che the Hollonders ther by, whiche stinkethe so filthily that it is redy to poyson all those that go by. But being deprived of that sence it ofended me not. The skins I have seene theme lye by, blowne out like a blader, the heare syd inward. I think it was to get the grease out or oyle that would spoyle the skine, for in ther taning of them they be very curfull to get the oyle cleere oute, for they mak great store of sellers of bottells for to keep hot watters. They sell most of them to the Duch and the Duche paints them within and puts the iron worke to them and bring them ther owne againe to sell.

'They have yet a forthe kind of boats or litters whiche be flat bottomed of wonderfull bignes for bredthe. They be fationed alnomost ovall. They be littill above 3 foot deepe, but be mad of suche strengthe that I have never sene biger timber in any shipe for the myty knees and jyces whiche ly crose. On of theese will load the best shipe that ther was in the harbour at twice going abord. The name I have forgotten. The[y] [are] open and subject to wet, otherwis they weare good for the East Indian Company.

'They have yet a fift sort, suche as the great persons of the land have to pas up and doune the river. They be of divers bigneses, sume greatter, sum lesser. They be mad of two sort. The on have a fine littill borded house in the poope or after part. Thees be of the leser sort. The greater sort have houses in the midell, prettili bult with pr[e]tti windowes in them. So bothe sorts have. But the state of [them] is, when any on great person is in them, they must then be covered, all that part that is lik a house, withe eyther red, blewe or greene, but the greattest all red, whiche I judge is of greatest state.'

As the only surviving manuscript composed by the elder Tradescant this Russian diary is obviously of enormous interest, not least because of what it reveals about Tradescant himself. He was obviously a practical man who could turn his hand to almost anything, and he also had an eye for detail. He was a skilled seafarer and navigator and was generally knowledgeable about boats, although his familiarity with agricultural matters suggests that his roots lay in the soil. Finally there is the fascinating revelation that the great gardener possessed no sense of smell. This fact is presented so casually that Tradescant had obviously come to terms with the disability, but it might perhaps go some way towards explaining his constant pursuit of the strange and rare.

Tradescant begins his diary by listing some of his fellow passengers on the *Diana*. Of these, 'Mr Jams' was in fact Richard James, a nephew of Bodley's first librarian, who remained in Russia for two years; Captain David Gilbert seems to have been a surprising choice, as he had only just been released from detention in Russia but was nevertheless going back with his son Thomas to offer their services to the Tsar. Captain Robert Carr commanded a company of British cavalry in Russia and was later to be the sole survivor of a battle against an overwhelming number of Poles. Tradescant's list omits the name of Giles Hobbs, a messenger whom Digges is known to have taken and dispatched on to Persia. He is presumably included among Digges' retinue.

In 1845, thirty years after his discovery of the manuscript, von Hamel published an account of his find in which he identified the other leading members of the expedition as Arthur Nowell, Thomas Woodward, Adam Cooke, Joseph Fante, Thomas Leak, George Brigges, Jessy de Quester, Adam Jones, Thomas Wakefield, John Adams, Thomas Crisp, Leonard Hugh and John Coplie. He also pinpointed 'Fox Nose' as a promontory on the eastern shore of the White Sea, while the islands that Tradescant explored were in the delta of the River Dvina, north-west of Archangel. The *Diana* left the port by the Pudoshem mouth, having entered by the Beresov mouth.[2]

The phrase 'Helebros albus, enoug to load a shipe' is of particular significance in that it first enabled von Hamel to identify the manuscript as coming from the hand of John Tradescant. It is almost identical to a phrase used by Parkinson when reporting that the 'White Ellebor' was found in Russia 'by my very good friend, John Tradescante . . . as hee said, a good ship might be loaden with the rootes hereof, which he saw in an Iland there'.[3] The plant is in fact the false helleborine (*Veratrum album* L.); in Russian it is called *Tschemeritza*, meaning 'gnat plant', because it was once considered effective against those irritating insects. It was a plant well known to Tradescant as it had been growing in England since at least 1548 when Turner recorded it at Syon Park.

The roses 'wondros sweet' that Tradescant brought back must have thrived, as his son was still growing a Rosa Moscovita or Moscovie Rose in

1656. Parkinson called it 'Rosa sylvestris Russica, the wild bryer of Muscovia',[4] and it has been identified as *Rosa acicularis* Lindl.[5] This was an introduction.

Nearly all the other plants that Tradescant records are British natives, although he was obviously not familiar with either the cloudberry (*Rubus chamaemorus* L.), the plant with amber strawberry-like fruit and leaves that he compares to avens or geum, or the bird cherry (*Prunus padus* L.), which was the source of the pliant wood.

The four sorts of fir tree he mentions are likely to have been the Scots pine (*Pinus sylvestris* L.), the Siberian spruce (*Picea obovata* Ledeb.), the Siberian fir (*Abies sibirica* Ledeb.) and the Siberian larch (*Larix sibirica* Ledeb.). Of these, the last three would have been new to him, but, if he did bring them home, there is no evidence that he was able to establish any of them. None are included in either of the Tradescants' published plant lists. In fact they do not thrive in England as their early growth makes them susceptible to late spring frosts.

The 'red whorts' are believed to have been the cowberry (*Vaccinium vitisidaea* L.) and the cranberry (*Oxycoccus palustris* Pers.); and the 'blue' the bilberry and bog bilberry (*Vaccinium myrtillus* L. and *V. uliginosum* L.), all native.

'Gods Tree' is a literal translation of *Boshige derewo*, the Russian name for southernwood (*Artemisia abrotanum* L.), which was already long established in England and very common. Gerard described several varieties of jagged pinks (*Dianthus superbus* L.) growing in 1597, and the plant 'like hedge mercury' may have been the British native *Cornus suecica* L. 'Rosasollis' is another British native, probably *Drosera rotundifolia* L.

The 'geranium flore serulie' must surely be Parkinson's 'Purple Cranesbill of Muscovy' which he calls 'Geranium Moscoviticum purpureum' and describes how it was 'brought to us by Mr John Tradescant'.[6] But by 1656 this was recognized as the same as our native *Geranium pratense* L. when it was catalogued as 'Geranium Batracoides flore caeruleo'.

'Sorrel half the heyght of a man' has been claimed by Mea Allan to be the sorrel tree (*Andromeda arborea* L.), but this was a much later introduction from North America. Tradescant's plant was probably just our common sorrel (*Rumex acetosa* L.), which can grow to a metre in height.

Unfortunately Tradescant does not mention the souvenirs that he brought home. These almost certainly included the items of Russian clothing listed in the *Musaeum Tradescantianum*:

A Russian vest
Boots from Muscovy
        Russian
Shooes to walk on Snow without sinking

Russian stockens without heels
Shooes from Russia shod with Iron

but it would have been a great stroke of luck if he had managed to lay his
hands upon the 'Duke of Muscovy's vest wrought with gold upon the breast
and armes' at that time. It was probably a later addition. The Ark also
exhibited 'Knives from Muscovy'.

One item in the *Musaeum Tradescantianum* that almost certainly did come
from this trip is misleadingly catalogued as 'Beads strung upon stiffe wyers,
and set in four-square frames wherewith the Indians cast account'. It is in
fact an abacus, now regarded as the oldest surviving Russian *schety*. (There is
no evidence that the Indians ever used such equipment, and it was probably
given this attribution because its origin had been forgotten.) Not then
known in Western Europe, the abacus was the calculating machine of its day,
and Tradescant would have found it a fascinating piece of equipment. Made
to be worn, perhaps slung from a belt, this one is considered to have been a
simplified version designed for money transactions and had probably been
well used by the time he acquired it. Dr W.R. Ryan suggests that its presence
in the famous museum may have been the inspiration for later English bead
calculators.[7]

Chapter 5

Off to Quell the Barbary Pirates

'The Argier Apricocke is a smaller fruit than any of the other, and yellow, but as sweete and delicate as any of them, having a blackish stone within it, little bigger then a Lacure Cherry stone: this with many other sorts John Tradescante brought with him returning from the Argier voyage, wither hee went voluntary with the Fleete, that went against the Pyrates in the yeare 1620.'

So wrote John Parkinson nine years later,[1] leaving a clue as to why Tradescant embarked on his next adventure.

The Barbary pirates had for some years been harassing British trading vessels in the Mediterranean and indeed to an even greater extent much nearer home. Cargoes were taken as prizes, crews sold into slavery and ships confiscated. In 1617 a pirate ship was captured in the Thames, and it was not uncommon for villages on the British coast to be raided and their inhabitants taken into slavery. Algiers, the town that harboured the pirates, had the reputation of being more or less impregnable.

In 1620 an expedition was dispatched under Sir Robert Mansell, who was given strict instructions to proceed diplomatically and not to attempt any hostile action against Algiers itself. War with Spain was a distinct possibility and James I saw no point in upsetting so formidable an enemy of that country as were the Algerians.

Having presented the Grand Signior with a letter from the King, Sir Robert was to demand the surrender of captured ships, the return of goods seized as prizes and the release of English captives. If these conditions were met then he could try his hand at setting fire to the pirate fleet. His instructions strictly forbade him from going east of Cape Spartivento, on the southern tip of Sardinia, unless the weather or a chase made it necessary.[2]

The main fleet arrived in the Mediterranean in the autumn of 1620. John Tradescant sailed in the *Mercury*, under Captain Phineas Pett, master shipwright to the Navy. The *Mercury* was one of two pinnaces sent out with supplies, the other being the *Spy*, and they did not join the fleet until the following year. By that time negotiations had been tried and discarded.

Tradescant was one of fourteen 'gentlemen collected' and with six others, two of whom were also 'gentlemen', formed the team that comprised 'shott 7'. The *Mercury* was of 240 tons burden. She had a crew of sixty-five men and carried twenty pieces of brass ordnance.

The two pinnaces made their rendezvous at Malaga in February and then sailed to join the rest of the fleet at Gibraltar. From there the *Mercury*, accompanying two naval vessels – the *Lion*, Mansell's flagship, and the *Constant Reformation* – and the merchantman *Barbary*, sailed in a hard gale for Tetuan, on the Moroccan coast, where the *Mercury* spent just twenty-four hours before they all returned to Malaga to take in wine, wood and water. Two weeks later they put in to Alicante and by the end of April arrived at Formentera, putting in on the northern coast opposite Ibiza.

There are several accounts of the expedition. One relates that 'Uppon the illand of Firmentera there is noe inhabitance but affoordeth wood in greate aboundance, very easey to be gotten for yt groweth downe to the sea shore of which the whole ffleete tooke in great store. There is uppon this illand wild hogge and wild asses.'

The next stop was Majorca to take in water. 'Mayourk is a faire cittie well fortified full of tradesmen. It affordeth all maner of victualls in plenty. And at easey rates, the people very loveinge and curteous.' Their chief merchandise was 'oyle, wood and cheese, whereof the country affordeth plenty'.

Well victualled, the British fleet was ready to sail for Algiers by mid-May. On arrival the pinnaces plied up and down to stop the movement of pirate ships while the 'Kings ships' anchored 'about halfe a league' off shore. The pinnaces then proceeded to their anchorage outside the main fleet, which lay between them and the town.

Two small vessels had been bought for firing purposes, the idea being to tow them into the harbour alight and full of 'fireworks' in order to set fire to the pirate ships anchored within the mole. Three attempts having been frustrated by calm, they made their attack on the fourth night when the wind seemed suitable. But, as the boats went in, the wind suddenly dropped and, as it was a bright, moonlit night, the plan was discovered. Despite this, the attack continued as best it could under fire from 'the Turks ordnance' which 'played continually upon them'. Little damage was inflicted and those involved were lucky to escape with only few casualties.

Nothing more was to be achieved by staying. The fleet sailed away. The British vessels picked up a few captives from the water as they endeavoured to escape and caught the odd pirate ship, but otherwise the mission was a total failure. As it had been carefully planned and rehearsed, bad luck seems to have been at least partly involved. The fleet then went by way of Alicante and Malaga to Cadiz. Here some of the ships received orders to return home immediately and the others, including the *Mercury*, followed soon after.[3]

The stops on the Spanish coast and the two islands must have allowed Tradescant plenty of opportunities for botanizing. Indeed Formentera sounds like a plant-hunter's paradise. It was there that he found a 'rough starry headed Trefoil', as Johnson recorded,[4] no doubt the 'Trifolium Barbaricum stellat. Tradesc.' in the 1634 list (*Trifolium stellatum* L.). Tradescant must surely also have contrived to get ashore at Tetuan. His impatience to take advantage of any such opportunity is evident from his Russian diary. Moreover, his assurance to Parkinson 'that hee saw many acres of ground in Barbary spread over' with the Corn Flagge or Gladiolus[5] would seem to confirm this, as he had no other opportunity to set foot on the Algerian shore. (Any suggestion that he could have journeyed to the eastern Mediterranean at this time is most unlikely in view of Mansell's strict adherence to his orders. In fact it is quite possible that Tradescant, who would have been anxious to get his collection back home as quickly as possible, managed to transfer to one of the ships that were recalled immediately, which included not only naval vessels and the pinnace *Restore* but also three merchantmen.)

Besides the plants mentioned by Parkinson and Johnson, Tradescant probably gathered many more. These may have included *Pistacia terebinthus*, four of the *Cistus* and two of the *Smilax*, all listed for the first time in 1634 and not recorded as having been received in the previous five years, and perhaps the sweet yellow rest harrow (*Ononis speciosa* Lag.). All are native to the western Mediterranean area.

Tradescant is also known to have brought back with him some 'small' and 'greater or double blossomed wilde' pomegranate trees, as Parkinson, who paid another visit to Canterbury after Tradescant's return, recorded that 'the Wilde I thinke was never seene in England, before John Tradescante my very loving good friend brought it from the parts beyond the Seas, and planted it in his Lords Garden at Canterbury'.[6]

Parkinson carefully distinguished between the 'wilde' pomegranate and the 'tame or manured kindes . . . with us preserved and housed with great care: and the wilde kinde with much more'. Cultivated pomegranates had been known in England since medieval times and they had of course been on Tradescant's shopping list for Hatfield. But the double wild variety (*Punica granatum* L. var. *flore pleno*), although it never bore fruit, was considered 'farre more beautifull', being more double than the Province Rose and 'of an excellent bright crimson colour, tending to a silken carnation'.[7] In fact Gerard had recorded it flowering in English gardens in 1597, but as it was apparently unknown to Parkinson it must have been extremely rare if it had not died out altogether.

Always observant, Tradescant also told his friend about the long, flat Spanish onions, so sweet that they were 'eaten by many like an apple', although the ordinary variety were consumed there in greater quantity.[8]

Tradescant was still at Canterbury in the summer of 1623; a letter addressed to him 'at my Lord Wotton's house' is listed as among those sent over from Virginia on the *Abigail* on 23 June. This list was apparently compiled by Sir Nathaniel Rich, a prominent member of the Company involved in a dispute between two factions, who was bent on showing that in private correspondence conditions in the colony were admitted to be miserable, despite all official reports to the contrary.[9] Many of the intercepted letters are summarized but not the one addressed to Tradescant. Presumably this was because the writer did not have any complaints.

It came from the pen of that much travelled poet George Sandys. After an extended journey to Italy and the Middle East he had already given Tradescant some Egyptian scarabs and other souvenirs, which were destined to find their way into the museum collection. Sandys was sent out to Virginia as Treasurer in 1621 where he also seems to have acquired a plantation. His main claim to fame lies in his verse translation of Ovid's *Metamorphoses*, which, after completion in Virginia, was duly published.

With mutual interests in travel, the curious and natural history, he and Tradescant obviously had much in common. No doubt the letter described the flora of the New World and perhaps told of specimens he was collecting to bring back or send home to his friend.

Chapter 6

The Duke's Right-Hand Man

It must have been soon after Sandys's letter was written that Tradescant moved from Canterbury to a new post. He was summoned to work for the King's favourite, George Villiers, first Duke of Buckingham. Born in 1592, Villiers was tall and handsome. As a youth he had been sent to France to acquire the courtly accomplishments of riding, dancing and duelling, at which he excelled. Soon after his return in 1614 he caught the eye of King James and began his meteoric climb to fame.

From the position of a humble cup-bearer, Villiers rose to eminence with incredible rapidity, purely on account of his physical attributes. One honour and office after another was heaped upon him by the King. Within two years he became a Viscount, held the Order of the Garter and was appointed Master of the Horse. In 1617 he was made an Earl and in the following year a Marquis. By the age of twenty-six he had become the most powerful man at Court. His beauty apart, however, he must have been able to exert considerable charm in order to captivate two such entirely different characters as the dissolute James and his politically unimaginative son Charles.

Tolerating no rivals, Buckingham worked himself into a position of absolute power. While he was busy feathering his own nest, he was also in a position to bestow privileges on those whom he favoured. He held innumerable posts and profitable monopolies himself, and he installed many of his relatives in various prestigious positions. That he could choose whom he wanted to work for him, and was also able to improve their lot if he so wished, goes without question; he now sought out the travelling plantsman who had put the garden of St Augustine's on the map.

In 1622 Buckingham had bought Wallingford House near the Tilt Yard in Whitehall, which stood on the site of the present Admiralty building and in which he seems to have lived. He also acquired York House on the Embankment, where he entertained on a lavish scale and kept most of his art treasures. He already owned Burley-on-the-Hill in Rutland, but, wanting a new country house nearer to London, in the same year added New Hall, near Chelmsford in Essex, to his estates. It was considered a bargain at £20,000.[1] New Hall had been built by Henry VIII as a summer residence. In 1573 it was granted to Thomas Radcliffe, Earl of Sussex, and largely remodelled. A two-storey building of red brick, the south front was embellished with bay windows with panelled mullions. The gate-house, great hall and unusually wide staircase were all regarded as particularly fine. The house also contained a chapel with a beautiful stained-glass window. Erected after the dissolution of the monasteries, it depicts the scene of the crucifixion. Originally intended for Henry VII, who is shown with his Queen, Elizabeth of York, in the sidelights, he died before it could be completed. Above the King is St George and a white rose within a red one; over the Queen is St Catherine and a green pomegranate on a gold field, the arms of Granada, to denote descent from the Spanish royal family. It remained at New Hall until the civil war, when it was hastily taken down and buried to preserve it from Puritanical destruction. In due course it was sold and put up in the church of St Margaret's, Westminster, in 1758.

John Evelyn visited New Hall in 1656 and wrote admiringly of the grounds: the 'Garden a faire plot, & the whole seate well accommodated with water; but above all the Sweete & faire avenue planted with stately Lime-trees in 4 rowes for neere a mile in length: It has 3 descents which is the onely fault, & may be reformed. There is another faire walk of the same at the Mall & Wildernesse, with a Tenis-Court, & a pleasant Terrace towards the Park, which was well stored with deere, & ponds.'[2]

New Hall obviously made a lasting impression on Evelyn, for some years later he noted: 'How goodly a sight were it if most of the Demesnes of our Country Gentlemen were crown'd and incircl'd with such stately rows of Limes, Firs, Elms and other ample, shady and venerable Trees as adorn New-Hall.'[3]

The Tudor house, now a girls' boarding-school, has been extensively altered and rebuilt, although the façade must be much as it originally looked. Even today the double tree-lined drive leading up to the house, although obviously newly planted, conveys a little of the effect.

That Buckingham himself took an informed interest in his properties is evidenced by a letter to James I, whom he addressed as usual as 'Dear Dad and Gossip', meaning sponsor. 'Now for my own park,' he wrote. 'I have found this morning another fine wood that must in with the rest, and two hundred acres of meadowland, with broome closes and plentiful springs running through them, so that I hope Newhall Park shall be nothing inferior to Burlie. My stags are all lusty and my calf bold, and others are so too. My Spanish colts are fat, and so is my jovial filly.' He signed himself, as always, 'Your Majesty's most humble slave and dog Steenie'.[4]

King James had given directions for 'one thousand timber trees of Oake' to be transplanted to New Hall from various of his woods in Kent. But because these were 'not sufficient by reason of the smallenes of them in bulke', Charles I added another five hundred to the gift when he came to the throne.[5] The Earl of Northumberland sent two thousand walnut trees, and elms were also planted.[6] The direction of their planting was almost certainly the responsibility of John Tradescant.

We do not know exactly when Tradescant entered Buckingham's service, but the first entry concerning him in the account-book for 1622–7 kept by Sir Sackville Crowe, who was acting as Buckingham's treasurer, is dated 1624. In the spring of that year the sum of £124 14s. was 'Paide to John Tradescant by his Lordships order for his journey into the Lowe Countries for his charges and Trees bought for his Lordship there'.[7] These trees may well have included the limes for the famous avenue at New Hall.

Buckingham seems to have had a particular love of trees. In the autumn of 1621 Thomas, Earl of Kellie, beseeched his cousin, John, Earl of Mar, to send Buckingham a batch of fir trees because the Duke was 'desirous to have firre trees planted aboute his house at Burleigh on the Hille'. Mar was asked to 'provyde soe mutche firr seed as you can and with all speid that can be, and that you haistin it awaye' and was ordered by the King to 'send one to Burleigh with 4 or 5 thousand of them, with the like instructions of time, place and maner of setting and preserving them'.[8]

Burley-on-the-Hill was burned down by the Parliamentarians during the civil war. Evelyn wrote in 1654 that it was 'worthily reckon'd among the noblest seates in England, situate on the brow of an hill, built a la modern neere a Park Waled in, & a fine Wood at the descent'.[9] The biographer Thomas Fuller admired another aspect. 'Buckingham's house', he wrote, 'was superior to all for the stable; where horses (if their pabulum so plenty as their stabulum stately) were the best accommodated in England.'[10]

No picture of the original house survives, and all the papers were destroyed in a fire earlier in the twentieth century, but there is a copy of a plan of the garden showing a double avenue of trees leading up to the main gateway into the forecourt, three rows of terracing to the south overlooking the park, with a mount and bowling green to the west.[11]

These, then, comprised the gardens for which Tradescant would have taken over responsibility when he entered the Duke's service. But Tradescant was no ordinary gardening adviser. He also fulfilled many other roles for his new employer.

In 1625 the Duke was appointed to go to Paris to bring back the French princess, Henrietta Maria, as the bride of Charles I. In the original plan for the wedding Buckingham was to have acted as proxy bridegroom for the actual ceremony, and for months he had prepared his elaborate 'equippage'. 'A splendid train for France,' it was called, and so it undoubtedly would have been.[12]

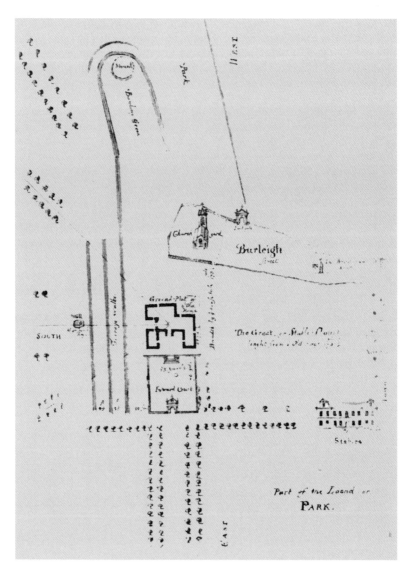

Ground plan of Burley-on-the-Hill

Hoping to cut a dash at the French court with his dazzling appearance, the Duke had had made '27 ritch suits imbrodered and laced with silk and silver plusches besides, one ritch white satten uncut velvet suite sett all over both suite and cloak with Diamonds, the value whereof is thought to be fourscore thousand pounds besids a feather made with great Diamonds with sword, Girdle, hatband and spurs with Diamonds which suite his grace Intends to Enter into Paris with. The other ritch suite is of Purple Satten Imbroidred all over with ritch orient pearle, the Cloak made after the Spanish fashion with all things suitable.' The value of this suit, designed to be worn at the wedding ceremony, was £20,000, while the one set with diamonds was described as being of white and 'watchett', which is sky blue. His other suits were reputed to be 'all ritch as Invention can frame or Art fashion'.[13]

The Duke's grand train was to number about six hundred, with even the grooms receiving one new suit apiece and the footmen three. Obviously everyone taking part would have been suitably attired.

Buckingham's departure for Paris had to be postponed, however, when James I became seriously ill; the favourite dared not leave his side. The King died on 27 March, but his embalmed body was not buried until 7 May, the elaborate and costly funeral requiring long preparation. In the meantime the delicate arrangements for the papal dispensation allowing a Catholic princess to marry a Protestant king had at last been finalized and, as Louis XIII, Henrietta Maria's brother, had promised to have the marriage solemnized within thirty-one days, it was decided that the ceremony should go ahead with the Duc de Chevreuse fulfilling the role of proxy bridegroom in Buckingham's place.

After the celebrations were over it was planned that the Queen should travel towards Boulogne, accompanied by members of her immediate family, while the Duke of Buckingham would cross the Channel in command of a welcoming fleet and journey overland to meet her at Amiens.

When it came to the point, Buckingham, fearing that in his absence he might lose his powerful position at the side of the new king, was reluctant to go. Nevertheless three days after the funeral he was on his way, the 'splendid train' which had been planned reduced to a mere handful of attendants.

On reaching Amiens, however, Buckingham found that the fifteen-year-old bride had not even left Paris, where her brother Louis XIII was ill. So he decided that there was nothing for it but to travel on to the capital.

'He left in disgust and so suddenly, that his commissions were sent after him,' reported the Venetian Ambassador to England.[14] His clothes followed, too. M. de Rusdorff, the representative of the Elector Palatine in London, wrote: 'Il a envoyé par deça un gentilhomme pour lui apporter ses nouvaux riches habits afin qu'il se puisse montrer en ses vanités' ('He has sent in addition a gentleman to bring him his new rich clothes so that he may show himself in all his vanities').[15]

This gentleman was John Tradescant. In Buckingham's account-book, under the heading 'The Disbursements of His Lps privat Purse in his Lps Journey to Fraunce beginning the xth May 1625', is the following entry: 'Paide to John Tradescant for his journey to Paris with my Lords stuff and Trunkes &c by waie of Imprest £20.'[16]

Tradescant evidently acted as baggage-master under Sir Sackville Crowe, being entrusted with the care of the Duke's elaborate wardrobe. But once these duties were fulfilled he returned to his real business, taking the opportunity to buy another one hundred pounds' worth of trees and plants while in Paris. He also renewed acquaintance with his old friends, the Robins, for there is an entry in the accounts which shows that the French King's gardeners were tipped twenty pounds for 'divers plantts' which were then presented to 'his Grace by John Tradescant'.[17] He had probably taken out some choice seedlings to the Robins in exchange and had perhaps received an equally handsome tip from the French King.

Charles went to meet his bride at Dover. He seems to have taken the normal route, completing the first stage of the journey, to Canterbury, in one day. He went by water to Gravesend and then on by coach, crossing the Medway by the old stone bridge with its eleven arches which had been built in 1387. Bells rang in celebration in church towers as he passed.

He took Henrietta Maria to Canterbury by coach, being duly cheered along the route. 'All the ways [were] strewed with green rushes, roses, and the choicest flowers that could be gotten, and the trees laden with people of all sorts who gave them a continual welcome.'[18] They spent the night at St Augustine's, explored the garden and relieved 'the sentinel' of an arm and then moved on to Cobham Hall before progressing up-river to London.

The Rose and Lily Queen – as Henrietta Maria became known, because she combined the rose of England with the heraldic lily of France – was hopelessly unprepared for the task that lay ahead of her. She arrived unable to speak one word of English and surrounded by her own entourage, which included a cluster of Catholic priests, who were enough to cause suspicion in themselves. Buckingham regarded her as a threat to his influence over the King, and it was not until after his assassination, by which time the bulk of her French courtiers had been sent home, that she and Charles settled down to their devotedly happy marriage.

Meanwhile the park and gardens at New Hall were beginning to take shape, and, with the other gardens in good running order, Tradescant had time to spare for other matters. Buckingham was gradually building up a picture gallery of enviable proportions and was importing classical statuary and other treasures to furnish his various residences. Balthazar Gerbier, a painter and architect with sound taste who had been supervising the work at New Hall, was sent to the Continent to seek out suitable works of art.

On 17 November 1624 Gerbier wrote from Boulogne insisting that he had 'not passed one hour without searching after some rarity'. The Duke had obviously chided Tradescant for starting his correspondence with an apology, for in the same letter Gerbier wrote: 'However I will not do as John Tradescant, who asks pardon at the beginning; for as your Excellency well replied to him at Newhall, that, for him who has an evil purpose to offend, asking pardon first is not enough.'[19]

In the pursuit of rarities Gerbier was not alone. Buckingham wanted to build up a Closet of Rarities to be filled with the strange and rare. It was something after Tradescant's own heart. Indeed, he may well have been the instigator of the idea. He must have been familiar with such collections on the Continent, had probably admired Sir Walter Cope's and any small show that London had to offer on the same lines and was almost certainly already collecting on his own account. Now here was his great opportunity, for he was to be appointed keeper.

In the summer of 1625 Tradescant wrote to Edward Nicholas, then Secretary to the Navy:

Noble Sir,
I Have Bin Comanded by My Lord to let yr worshipe understand that it is H[is] Graces Pleasure that ye should In His Name Deall withe All Marchants from All Places But Espetially the Virgine & Bermewde & Newfound Land men that when they into those parts that they will take Care to furnishe His Grace with All Maner of Beasts & fowels & Birds Alyve. Or If Not Withe Heads Horns Beaks Clawes Skins fethers flyes or seeds plants trees or shrubs. Also from Gine or Binne or Senego turkye. Espetially to Sir Thomas Rowe who is Leger At Constantinoble. Also to Captain Northe to ther New Plantation towards the Amasonians withe all these fore Resyted Rarityes & Also from the East Indes withe Shells Stones Bones Egge Shells with What Cannot Com Alive. My Lord Having Heard of the Dewke of Sheveres [Chevreuse] & partlie seene of His strang fowlls. Also from Hollond of Storks A payer or two of young ons withe Divers kinds of Ruffes whiche they theare Call Campanies. This having mad Bould to present my Lords Comand I Desire ye furtherance yr asured servant to be Comanded till He is

Newhall this 31
day July 1625.   John Tradescant

A detailed postscript was appended to the letter:

To the merchants of the Ginne Company & the Gouldcost, Mr humfrie Slainy, Captaine Crispe & Mr Clobery & Mr Johne Wood Capemarchant. The things desyred from those parts Be theese
Imprimis on Elephants head withe the teeth in it very larg

On River horsses head of the Bigest that Canbe Gotten
On Seacowes head the Bigest that Canbe gotten
On seabulles head withe hornes
Of all there strang sorts of fowelles & Birds skines & Beakes, leggs &
    phetheres that be Rare or Not knowne to us
Of All sorts of strang fishes skines of those parts
The Greatest sorts of Shell fishes Shelles of Great flying fishes & Sucking
    fishes withe what els strang
Of the habits, weapons & Instruments of ther Ivory Long fluts.
Of All sorts of Serpents & Snakes skines & Espetially of that sort that
    hathe a Combe on his head lyke A Cock.
Of All sorts of ther fruts Dried As ther tree Beanes, Littil Red & Black in
    ther Cods withe what flower & seed Canbe gotten the flowers layd Betwin
    paper leaves In a Book Dried.
Of all sorts of Shining Stones of Any Strang Shapes. Any thing that is
    strang.[20]

The list was fully comprehensive. Edward Nicholas received it the same
day and noted in the margin: 'Letters to be written to the marchants of
Gynny according to this now delivered to me by Mr Carey.' No doubt, as
his letters were received, the merchants, captains and ambassadors hastened
to pander to the Duke's latest whim, knowing that it was in their own
interest to do so. The strange and the rare must have poured in to
Tradescant's welcoming arms, as, for those on the spot, it was not difficult to
pick up such souvenirs, dead or alive. This is shown by the story of one
London merchant who wrote to his factor overseas desiring that he 'send
him 2 or 3 Apes'; he forgot the 'r', and the letter read '203 Apes'. Eighty
were dispatched at once, with the rest promised on the next ship.[21]

While the Duke obviously had first pick, Tradescant was in a good
position to carry off the duplicates. Indeed in the climate of the times he
would have been foolish not to have done so: it was very much a case of
everyone for themselves.

The men Tradescant mentioned in his letter were all famous in their day.
Sir Thomas Roe was the British Ambassador to Turkey; from Constantinople
he sent a stream of rarities to Buckingham, to William Laud, Archbishop of
Canterbury; and to other great men who had become infected with the craze
for collecting. More details on his career are given in Chapter 17.

Captain Roger North had sailed with Sir Walter Raleigh to Guiana in 1617,
when he commanded one of five ships to explore the Orinoco River. Two
years later North petitioned for letters patent to establish the King's right to
the coast and country adjoining the Amazon and to found a plantation and
settlement there with the object of trading with the native population. James
granted the request, nominating North as Governor, but delayed the project

1. Portrait, probably posthumous, of the elder John Tradescant, attributed to Cornelius de Neve. The surround was possibly painted by Alexander Marshal.

2. Portrait of the younger John Tradescant, attributed to Thomas de Critz

3. A map of the garden at St Augustine's Abbey, *c.* 1642

4. The warrant for the elder John Tradescant's employment at Oatlands Palace in 1630

after intervention from the Spanish Ambassador, Gondomar. North, having obtained a pass from Buckingham, became restless and sailed on his way. The King promptly issued a proclamation ordering him to return, and, as soon as the news reached him, he did so. Back in England he was sent to the Tower, and his ship and rich cargo were confiscated. After some months Buckingham intervened on his behalf and he was released, his ship and cargo restored to him and he was granted the immunities that he had originally been promised.

Humphrey Slaney, William Cloberry, Nicholas Crisp and John Wood were successful businessmen dominant in the affairs of the Guinea Company. 'Gynney and Binney' had become identified with the coast between Senegal and Sierra Leone, although in 1631 the company acquired exclusive trading rights along the whole African coast right down to the Cape of Good Hope.[22] Slaney, a London haberdasher, was a merchant with wide commercial interests, his chief concern being the redwood trade in the Sherbro River area of Sierra Leone where he built up a prosperous business. Cloberry and Wood had started as his apprentices; they devoted their lives to the development of the redwood trade on the Sherbro and Sierra Leone Rivers. John Wood is probably the benefactor of that name listed in the *Musaeum Tradescantianum*. Crisp's main interest was the gold trade. Together these men laid the foundations of African commerce and at one time claimed to have as many as sixteen trading factories in Guinea.

Buckingham granted Tradescant at least one other position. It was that of yeoman garnetter at the Whitehall granary. The only record of this is in the petition of a James Heydon who, having lost that office to Tradescant and claiming also to have lost money in picking up various bits of old ordnance that had been granted to him instead, now sought 'the benefit of the custom on the importation of herrings', which he alleged was being evaded.

'For as much as your Majestie heretofore was graciously pleased to bestow on your petitioner ye garnetters place at Whitehall . . . which the Duke of Buckingham afterwards conferred upon John Tradescan then his servant,' Heydon's petition began. In due course his request for the revenue from the herring custom was granted.[23]

There is little information available about the position of garnetter or even about the granary itself, which must have been situated somewhere in the area of the new palace. There is one payment in the works accounts to the bricklayer, John Benson, 'for rippinge lathinge and tyleinge both the sides of the greate wheat granary two sheddes' which 'in measure' contained more than eighty-eight rodds. As a rodd is equal to five and a half yards and in this case was probably used as a square measure, it must have been quite a sizeable building.[24]

The position appears to have been taken over by Tradescant's friend William Ward, for in 1629 he, as yeoman garnetter, together with the Sergeants of His Majesty's Bakehouse, was called upon to try to sell some

'Sussex wheate in His Majesties Granary at Whitehall the which by lying next the bottome of the shipp and there taking wett is founde to be altogether unfitt for the service of His Majesties house, by the view of His Majesties Officers of the Greencloth'.[25] The wheat was duly sold to a London merchant.

This shows that the position was no sinecure, and so perhaps Tradescant gave it up because it took up too much of his time. Alternatively, Buckingham may have given it to him as a perk to dispose of as he wished.

In the autumn of 1625 the Duke of Buckingham went to the Low Countries on diplomatic business and to try to raise money by pawning the Crown Jewels. As always there was money enough for his own personal expenditure, and Tradescant, who accompanied his employer, spent another £150 on trees. There is a further entry in the accounts for £100 spent in France by 'the gardener', so it is possible that he also took a trip to Paris at this time.[26]

Tradescant's next overseas adventure occurred two years later when he enrolled as an engineer on the Duke's ill-fated expedition to relieve the Huguenot stronghold of La Rochelle. La Rochelle was the chief Protestant town in France and an important port on the Atlantic coast, its wealth deriving from the salt and wine trades. The town's independence posed a threat to Richelieu's policy of political unity, and he was determined to take it by siege.

Tradescant was one of several men enrolled who were described as in 'The Dukes alone keep' and so probably sailed with him in his flagship the *Triumph*. The full reference in an anonymous account of the expedition reads: 'John Tradescant the Dukes gardiner now an Ingineere and best of all this true and most deservinge'.

It does not sound as though Tradescant would have had much difficulty in shining among the rest of the Duke's retinue. His fellow engineers included Rudde-Keene, 'a Cheefe-Ingeneere never but a simple ourseer of pioners before', and Audly-Rowe, 'a prime Ingeneere, but soe unknowen a one, as he cast up the trench the wronge waye'. Others in the party included a young knight who had 'lost his estate foolishly'; a well-known pirate; two 'saved from hanging' by the Duke; Bartlett, a 'violent Papist'; and Dawson, 'so infamous for swearing' that it was said he would get a 'serjant majorshipp by it'. There was also the Duke's 'Major Domo', an Italian called Francisco.[27] Most of the English army were of similar quality, having been press-ganged into service.

The fleet assembled at Portsmouth on 13 June but, because of contrary wind, did not sail until the 27th. There were ninety-odd sail in the fleet, about half of them being men-of-war. Supplies were already depleted because the men had been living off their victuals for some time previously. The Duke himself, however, was well catered for. In May it was reported that there was 'a great collier-ship pressed to be for the grace's living store of provision, and many carpenters at work making stalls for four fat oxen, two milch cows, two goats and coops for poultry and fowl'.[28] One can only hope that Tradescant came in for a share of it, for the troops were appallingly ill provisioned, thanks to Buckingham and his 'Bottomless Bagge', as Sir James, the corrupt Admiralty official responsible for supplies, became known.

The fleet arrived at the Ile de Rhé, just off the French coast opposite La Rochelle, on 11 July. It is a low-lying island, eighteen miles long, its width varying between one hundred yards and three miles. Troops began to disembark the following day. But, having failed to take the normal precaution of holding back foreign shipping before leaving Portsmouth and by wasting time in chasing privateers on the way, news of the fleet's arrival had preceded it. Even as the troops attempted to disembark they were set upon by French cavalry who charged them and put them to rout. Eventually the French were pushed back, withdrawing to the safety of the fortress of St Martin, but it was 'an honour dearly purchased' and the attack was not followed up.

Moreover, the British found no support even from the Rochellois, for whose relief they had come. The French Protestants sent messages to say that they wanted to harvest their corn and wine and see the invading forces in possession of the island before committing themselves to giving assistance. Meanwhile they were content to profiteer on such much-needed provisions as they had to spare.

Entrenchments were begun at once. 'The trenches go on as fast as the hardness of this stony ground will permit,' Buckingham wrote on 28 July. It was of 'such a continued and hard kind of rock, as the pick axe will hardly fasten in it, which takes off all possibility of making of mines,' he added, begging for more good engineers to be sent out with 'shovels and pick-axes, and those somewhat shorter than the former, which their length makes something unwieldy'.[29] His request for engineers was echoed by Henry de Vic, who recorded that they had 'hardly amongst us one that can lay a battery, work in a mine, or make a trench'.

The months dragged by as Buckingham dithered, trying to make up his mind what to do. Attempts to take the port of St Martin by siege failed, as French supply-boats slipped through in one way or another, The weather was against the British. The trenches filled with water. Provisions ran out and the troops were left with meat 'which stunck' and only water to drink, the 'wine in the iland being spent'. Promised supplies failed to arrive. Then the soldiers began to sicken and by the beginning of October 'dyed apace'.[30] 'Pity our misery,' wrote William Bold, the Duchess's steward who also seemed to be part of Buckingham's force, again singling out Tradescant as one of their best engineers.[31]

Eventually, against all advice, Buckingham decided to make an assault on the citadel. The enemy were waiting for him, and the attack failed dismally. The fort of St Martin was far too well defended, and the British scaling ladders proved too short for the height of the walls.

At last the Duke was persuaded to retreat, but by this time the enemy were hard on his heels. Furthermore, he picked quite the worst possible place at which to re-embark his men. To reach the ships they had to cross the 'Loys bridge', a long, narrow, wooden bridge connecting what is practically a small island to the rest of the Isle of Rhé. Today it is called Loix and the present road is well raised and lined on either side with salt pans, just as it was then. It proved the perfect trap.

Here, 'before two Regiments had passed', the French attacked the British cavalry 'in the Rear and put them to Rout'; they then 'had the Execution of five whole Regiments, which they put all to the sword, except for 20 Officers and 100 Common Soldiers prisoners and those that were drowned which were many'.[32]

Out of 7,833 men, only 2,989 returned.[33] Tradescant must have counted himself lucky to be among them. No wonder that Rhé became known as 'the Isle of Rue'.

The fleet reached Plymouth by 12 November, with the men not only disgraced in defeat but starving and riddled with disease, from which many more were to die. Buckingham was welcomed by the King, but the disastrous expedition had sealed his unpopularity in the country as a whole. In the months that followed public feeling against the King's favourite was to mount in intensity.

Tradescant's stay on the ill-fated island had not been entirely unrewarded. According to Johnson, he brought back with him the 'Broad Leafed Sea Wormwood'[34] (*Artemisia maritima* L.), and Parkinson tells of him returning with the 'Greatest Sea Stocke Gillowflower' (*Matthiola sinuata* L.).[35] Both these are British natives, and it is doubtful if Tradescant's specimens varied from them specifically.

Also tucked into his pocket must have been the 'copper Lettercase an inch long, taken in the Isle of Ree with a Letter in it, which was swallowed by a Woman, and found', as it is so eloquently described in the 1656 catalogue.

After the traumas of the expedition Tradescant must have stepped ashore with relief. But as always he kept his eyes open and picked up the Plymouth strawberry (*Fragaria vesca* L. var. '*Muricata*'), a variety which is a botanical freak. It is like an ordinary wild strawberry until it blossoms, when the carpels develop into small folded leaves, the central portion of red flesh being studded with leaves with a double ruff of leaflets round the base which are the sepals and petals. It is Thomas Johnson who tells us of Tradescant's find 'in a womans garden at Plimouth, whose daughter had gathered and set the roots in her garden in stead of the common Straw-berry: but she finding the fruit not to answer her expectation, intended to throw it away: which labor he spared her, in taking it and bestowing it among the lovers of such varieties'.[36] Johnson called it the 'Prickely Strawberry', and it can still be found in botanic gardens.

By the following summer Buckingham was preparing for another expedition to relieve La Rochelle. He was never to depart. On 23 August Buckingham was assassinated at Portsmouth by a young naval lieutenant, John Felton. There is no doubt that the culprit had a personal grudge against the Duke, but the motives for his deadly attack with a cheap dagger seem to have sprung more from patriotism than self-interest. He genuinely believed that he was ridding the country of a tyrant, and there were many who agreed with him. The Duke's unpopularity had for long made his family fear for his safety, and the crowds that turned out to line Felton's route to the Tower made it almost a victory procession. For all Buckingham's personal charm and bravery, which were considerable, the people were glad to be rid of a man who exemplified court patronage at its worst. After pleading guilty at his trial, Felton was hanged at Tyburn.

Tradescant must have mourned his employer. The Duke had helped him climb several rungs of the proverbial ladder, and, as a loyal employee who had come under his hypnotic spell, he must have felt Buckingham's untimely death as a severe blow.

Tradescant's life now takes such a dramatic change that it is tempting to suggest that this was brought about by his inheriting the Duke's collection of rarities. The latter had amassed so many valuable and beautiful possessions that his Cabinet of Rarities would have been of comparatively little significance. Only the previous year he had purchased Rubens's magnificent art collection for £10,000. His distraught widow was left with four houses stuffed with treasures, and Buckingham had, after all, left instructions in his will that she should look after his servants.[37]

Unfortunately the facts do not support such a theory. In 1649 a book entitled *Les Antiquitez* was published in France; it included a list of famous European collections. In London, the Cabinet of the Duke of Buckingham was considered the only collection worthy of note, besides that of the Tradescants.[38] This indicates that it passed to Buckingham's son who after his father's death had been raised in the royal nursery and then sent to Cambridge. His estates had been sequestered at the beginning of the civil war but, in consideration of his youth, were returned to him in 1647. A year later they were sequestered again because of his political activities, and he went into exile in Holland.

So despite the fact that the young Duke was not even in London when this list was published, his collection was. As the list was compiled in central France it may have been slightly out of date; nevertheless it could not have been twenty years behind the times, as in 1629 Tradescant's collection was not established.

Chapter 7

The Ark

Whatever the circumstances that brought it about, Tradescant was now financially independent and in a position to establish his own botanic garden and museum. It must have been soon after Buckingham's death that he took a lease on a house and garden in South Lambeth.

When he acquired it, Tradescant's house was probably still a half-timbered Elizabethan farmhouse built end-on to the road and some way back from it. For some reason, possibly involving inheritance, it had been divided into two. At around the time that the elder Tradescant acquired his lease a new brick wing was added – probably purpose-built for him – parallel to the street, with four grand Venetian windows, no doubt the work of a local builder with a pattern book and a smattering of classical building knowledge. Such ornamentation suggests that the windows would have been surmounted by a suitably imposing roof with perhaps two fancy Dutch gables, although there is no surviving evidence of this. One wall of the house was embellished with the Tradescants' coat of arms.

Tradescant's house stood on the site of the present 113, 115, 117 and 119 South Lambeth Road. A ditch alongside the road was crossed by a bridge through an arch of whalebones into the tiny front garden. The main garden ran back from the house to the east and extended for more than 300 feet. At the end nearest the house, the garden was only forty feet wide, but it broadened out to a width of more than 150 feet and comprised nearly an acre. It occupied most of the present Meadow Place.

Tradescant's lease also included a large orchard of about two acres, running southwards from this main garden, at the back of the adjoining property. Beyond that, extending towards the main road on the far side of the adjoining property was a field of about an acre and a quarter. These together stood on much of the present Tradescant and Walberswick Roads. He also leased a further twenty-one acres in the form of four scattered fields.[1]

The exact date when Tradescant acquired his Lambeth house is not traceable. The records relating to the Collections for the Poor Accounts are

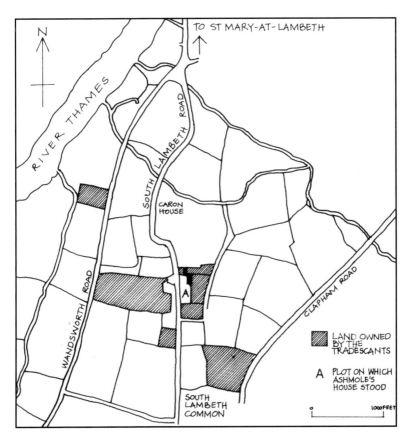

Vauxhall and South Lambeth
(adapted by John Drake for the Tradescant Trust from a map drawn by
Thomas Hill in 1681, reproduced in *The Survey of London*

missing between 1624 and 1632. There is no mention of Tradescant's name at the earlier date, but from 1632 onwards he regularly paid 8s. 8d.[2] Nor are the subsidy returns much help in solving the problem. He had not arrived by 1628. The next date for which records for the area survive is 1640, when the property was in the hands of the younger Tradescant, who from that time onwards paid 16s. on an assessment of £3.[3]

The most likely date for the establishment of the Tradescant home and business in Lambeth is 1629, as it was in that year that the elder Tradescant began to record in the back of his copy of Parkinson's *Paradisus* all the new acquisitions received at his garden.

The property, both house and grounds, was leased from a Mr Thomas Bartholomew.[4] According to the Rev. James Granger, vicar of Shiplake, writing in 1774, it had been taken over from a James Roelans: 'The late Mr James West told Mr Bull, that one of the family of Roelans, of which there are four or five prints by Hollar, lived a long while in Lambeth, in the house that afterwards belonged to John Tradescant, to whom he sold it.'[5]

Hollar's engraving of James Roelans is ornamented with fruit and flowers to denote his love of gardening, in much the same style as the well-known portrait of the elder Tradescant in the Ashmolean Museum. There is therefore a strong possibility that there was a connection between the two. Certainly the contemporary botanist John Goodyer, whose own work was strictly scientific and who must have known Tradescant, believed that there was: inserted into his copy of the *Musaeum Tradescantianum*, still preserved with his copious notes and papers at Magdalen College, Oxford, are copies of three of Hollar's portraits of the Roelans family. Finally, while there is nothing in either the subsidy or poor rate returns to substantiate the fact, it seems more than likely that Tradescant would have chosen to take over an already well-established garden.

A return of aliens for Spitalfield and Petticoat Lane shows a James Rowland in 1621, who may well be the same person. The Lambeth property had been acquired in 1618 by the Dutch Ambassador to England, Sir Noel Caron, a native of Bruges, with whom the Roelans family could have had a connection as Hollar engraved their portraits in Antwerp in 1648.

In 1592 Tradescant's property, together with that which adjoined it, was described as a messuage, barn, orchard and garden. Only later was it divided into two. Sir Noel died in 1624 and, because as an alien his will had been declared invalid, the half of the property later acquired by Tradescant – together with Caron's own imposing mansion, a stately home that had taken eight years to build and which possessed a fine garden and extensive park – reverted to the Dean and Chapter of Canterbury as Lord of the Manor of Vauxhall.

Tradescant's house must have been larger than it looks in later illustrations because it was assessed for eleven hearths in 1664 when the Hearth Tax was first implemented.[6] Moreover, the Tradescants kept several servants; the deaths of four, one woman and three men, are recorded between 1634 and 1655,[7] and they can hardly have been unlucky enough to lose their entire staff. Altogether the Tradescant family held leases on four houses in Vauxhall and South Lambeth; the other three, with twenty-one hearths, were empty in 1644.

In the seventeenth century, Lambeth, although only just across the river from Westminster, remained largely rural. Life centred around the church, whose wardens were responsible for such administrative problems as the relief of the poor, the upkeep of the highways and almshouses and the extermination of vermin. The collection of rent from two small tenements outside the churchyard and the acre of osier land referred to in the church-wardens' accounts as 'the chyrch hoopys' but better known as Pedlar's Acre, also fell on them, while the crier's wages, coroners' fees, transportation charges for pressed men to get to their place of muster and even the cost of fire-fighting equipment were further liabilities on parish funds.

The church of St Mary's was approached by a little bridge over a ditch and in and around the churchyard stood a group of fine elms. Opposite was the Swan Inn, dispensing hospitality as it had done since at least 1463.

But the dominating building was the Archbishop's Palace, much enlarged during the previous century and improved again during the tenure of Archbishop Laud. One source of income for the incumbent of Lambeth Palace, until the Commonwealth when it was sold into private hands, was the horse-ferry which plyed busily to and fro across the river where Lambeth Bridge stands today.

Other parts of Lambeth were more populated, but in South Lambeth there were only fourteen families in 1625; twenty-five years later the number paying the parish poor rate had increased to twenty-three.

One or more rooms in Tradescant's house contained his growing collection of rarities, and soon the entire building became known as 'Tradescant's Ark'. There are many contemporary references to this famous museum. The poet Thomas Powell was obviously struck by the intricate carvings. At the end of a poem about 'the patient stone Cut into various forms' he added that 'John Tradeskins Ark in Lambeth, can afford many more instances of this nature.'[8] John Cleveland referred to 'natures whimsey, one that out-vyes Tredeskin and his ark of Novelties';[9] Robert Herrick admired 'Tradescant's curious shels';[10] while John Oldham wrote:

> Then I Tradescant's Rarities out-do,
> Sands Water-works, and German Clockwork too,
> Or any choice Device at Barthol'mew.[11]

However, it was not just the curious who were attracted to the museum.

The far-sighted schoolmaster, Charles Hoole, whose ideas on education were remarkably advanced for his time, recommended that every child should be taken to it on an annual visit: 'But in London (which of all places I know in England, is best for the full improvement of children in their education, because of the variety of objects which daily present themselves to them, or may easily be seen once a year, by walking to Mr John Tradescants . . .).'[12]

The more scholarly also found it useful in their search for knowledge. Thomas Johnson, in his revised edition of Gerard's *Herbal*, illustrated 'Indian Morrice Bells' that could be seen with Mr John Tradescant at South Lambeth. He explained that these were the shells of a poisonous fruit from the West Indies, 'especially in some of the Islands of the Canibals', from which the kernel had been removed and small stones inserted instead. They 'tye them upon strings . . . which they dry in the Sunne, and after tye them about their legs, as we do bells, to set forth their dances . . . Which ratling sound doth much delight them, because it setteth forth the distinction of sounds, for they tune them and mix them with great ones and little ones, in such sort as we doe chimes or bells.'[13]

The ornithologist Francis Willughby and the naturalist John Ray, who translated Willughby's great work on birds from Latin into English, both used the museum for identification purposes. There they viewed the dodo, the penguin, the 'Brazilian Merula or blackbird' and the 'Indian Mockbird'. Of the last, Ray wrote: 'We saw this bird dried in Tradescant's Cabinet. It is of the bigness of a common Lark, hath a streight sharp Bill, a long Tail: And is all over of a blue colour. Upon second thoughts, however Tradescant might put the Epithete of Indian upon this bird, I judge it to he no other than the Caruleus or Blue ouzel of Bellonius.'[14]

It is from a contemporary book called *The Transproser Rehears'd* that we learn that the Tradescants had a keeper for the collection: 'As for conceipt page 6 he leads us into a Printing-House, and describes it in the same style as the Man who shows John Tradescants Rarities (which is extraordinary fine for those who have never seen such a Sight).'[15]

And from the way that the printing house is described it is quite clear that the rarities were shown with great drama and effect. 'The Man who shows John Tradescants Rarities' obviously liked to make the most of his material while his audience listened open-mouthed and spellbound. And why not? Such outlandish things were not to be met with elsewhere.

We know, from entries in family account-books of the period, that there was an entrance charge for viewing the collections. Unfortunately, it is not possible to tell from such accounts whether the Tradescants were also selling plants and keeping a nursery garden. The various small sums are usually entered as 'spent in going to John Tradescants', and while in some cases these obviously included the cost of the ferry crossing from Westminster to Lambeth, or some other transport charge, there is reason to believe that purchases of plants were also included. The Tradescants certainly had enough land for a nursery garden, and various entries in the contemporary herbals add weight to the idea.

In his description of 'The Plum Tree' John Parkinson states: 'and of all which sorts, the choysest for goodnesse, and rarest for knowledge, are to be had of my very good friend Master John Tradescante, who hath wonderfully laboured to obtaine all the rarest fruits he can hear off in any place of Christendome, Turky, yea or the whole world; as also with Master John Millen, dwelling in Olde streete, who from John Tradescante and all others that have good fruit, hath stored himselfe with the best only, and he can sufficiently furnish any'.[16] Millen was a nurseryman who specialized in fruit trees.

Thomas Johnson frequently brackets Tradescant's name with that of another nurseryman, Ralph Tuggie, as for instance in the remark: 'There are kept in the Gardens of Mr Tradescant, Mr Tuggye, and others, Two Starrewoorts.'[17] Ralph Tuggie's family business in the parish of St Margaret's, Westminster, was famous for carnations, colchicums, auriculas and 'gillie flowers'.

The first Lord Hatton, busy stocking the garden of Kirby Hall in the late 1650s, made a note to ask a contact in London 'if he have procured the plants from John Tradescant he undertooke to gett & have sent them to Kirby. To desire him to gett from thence the sweet leafed Maple & the large leafed Laurus tinus. To mind him of the White Mulberry trees he promised me & desire to helpe me to 6 ordinary mulberry trees – 200 Apples 200 Peares 100 Cherries 100 Plumms 100 for Peaches & Nectorins.' Beside the latter is added 'A larger proportion of stocks then last yeare.'[18]

Sir Daniel Fleming, antiquary and Member of Parliament, was obviously fascinated by The Ark, and he it is who provides the best clue as to what sum was paid as an entrance fee. For one visit, on 2 May 1662, he made the following entries in his accounts:[19]

It[em] spent at Jo. a Tradeskins	00.02.06.
It[em] given for ye sight there unto 4	00.02.00.
It[em] for a Boat thither & back again	00.02.00.
It[em] for a coach from Whitehall	00.01.00.

This makes it clear that for four people to have a 'sight' of the collection the charge was two shillings – or sixpence each. Unfortunately Sir Daniel does not record on what he spent the 2s. 6d., but it can probably be assumed that it was for plants. Had it been a tip to the keeper it would almost certainly have been so described, as the other items are well detailed.

On an earlier visit he had spent 'in going unto Tradeskins 00. 04. 06.'; the next entry underneath reads 'spent more 00. 00. 02.', as if some minor exotic had caught his eye on the way out and he had rushed back to purchase it. On yet another occasion he spent 4s. 6d. 'in goeing to Westm: & Jo Tradeskins'. Although these accounts refer to a period some thirty years after the museum first opened, the price probably remained the same from the beginning.

Sir Edward Dering was another eminent visitor with antiquarian tastes who evidently enjoyed the place. He went in 1649 and again the following year, at which time he was living at Lambeth, paying 2s. 6d. and 2s. respectively.[20] His accounts at this time are full of purchases of various seasonal fruits and, although he does not specify where they were bought, it is tempting to imagine that these, too, might have come from the Tradescants' garden.

The fame of the collection spread to the Continent, and when, in distant Castres in southern Tarn, the French collector Pierre Borel published a list of the principal cabinets in Europe, one of the two entries for London was 'Jean Tredesquin à la Maison des oiseux'.[21] There is no other reference to the museum being called 'the House of Birds', and, although, as we have seen, it certainly contained various stuffed birds, one can only speculate on the reasons for it.

An overseas visitor in September 1661 describes calling at the museum of 'John the Diskin where one can see in a large long room a collection of rare antique curiosities, costumes of various nations and strange weapons, also fishes, plants, horns, shells, and many other things'.[22]

Evidently, the Tradescants' name lived on in association with 'collectables'. Sir Andrew Balfour, an Edinburgh doctor who had spent fifteen years travelling abroad, when writing to a friend in 1668 described how, in a field near Vendôme, he had 'often seen very large green *Lizards*, which because it is a beautiful creature and not found with us, I must intreat you where ever you find of them to cause preserve 1 or 2, to add to my *Tradescants*. I know now which will be the best way of preserving them.' And to the same friend when in Carcassonne, which he commended for the making of boxwood combs, he entreated him to bestow 'foure or five crowns' for him 'because of the carving' to add to 'my *Tradescants*'.[23]

Two much earlier visitors were Lord Cranborne and 'Mr Robert', sons of the second Earl of Salisbury, who spent nine shillings in 'going by water and for seeing John Tradeskins Antiquities' in 1634.[24]

It was in that year that Tradescant printed his garden catalogue, *Plantarum in Horto* of which the only surviving copy appears to be that of the botanist John Goodyer at Magdalen College, Oxford. A small pamphlet of fifteen pages, it lists, more or less alphabetically and in Latin, the names of more than 750 plants. At the end of the booklet is 'A Catalogue of Fruits' which includes forty-eight varieties of apple, forty-five pears, thirty-three plums, fifteen cherries, six apricots, four nectarines, twelve peaches and six vines. The collection of plants noted is a remarkable one for the period.

Because the title page contains an uncorrected typographical error – Tradescant's name being put as 'Johannem' instead of 'Johannis' – it has been suggested that the surviving copy is only a proof; indeed the entire pamphlet is full of similarly uncorrected errors. However, the list was certainly published because Georg Christoph Stirn, one of the many foreign tourists who flocked to South Lambeth, remarked that there were 'in the garden all kinds of foreign plants, which are to be found in a special little book which Mr Tradescant has had printed about them'.[25] Samuel Hartlib also noted its publication: 'A Catalogue of Herbes etc. in John Traduskens garden produit 1634'.[26]

Chapter 8

Royal Appointment

On 20 August 1630 John Tradescant was appointed Keeper of the Gardens, Vines and Silkworms at Oatlands Palace. It must have been his proudest moment. The warrant for his appointment reads:

> Charles by the grace of god King of England Scotland ffrance and Ireland defender of the faith. To the Treasurer and Under Treasurer of our Exchecquer for the tyme being, greeting. Whereas we are pleased to allowe unto our trustie and welbeloved John Tradescant Keeper of our gardens Vines and Silke-wormes at Oatlands in our Countie of Surrey the some of one hundred pounds by the yere as well for the charges both of workemanship and materialls, in digging dressing weeding supporting and keeping our vines and vineyard there, and other works and charges incident to the keeping of our said gardens and vineyards and the walks thereunto belonging as also for feeding heeding and keeping of our Silke wormes there as formerly we were pleased to allow unto John Bonnall deceased late keeper of our said gardens Vines and Silkewormes at Oatlands aforesaid; we will and command you of our Treasure from tyme to tyme remaining in the receipt of our said Exchecquer to pay or cause to be paid unto the said John Tradescant or his assignes the said allowance of one hundred pounds by the yere in full satisfaction of and for all manner of charges and expenses in and about the premisses; the first payment thereof to beginne from the feast of Thanunciacion of the blessed Virgin Mary last past, before the date hereof, and to be continued unto him or his said assignes quarterly by even porcons from tyme to tyme at the fower usuall feasts of the yere during our pleasure. And these our treasurers shalbe your sufficient Warrant and Discharge in this behalfe. Given under our Privie Seale at our Pallace of Westminster the twentith day of August in the sixth year of our raigne.[1]

The Feast of the Annunciation, or Lady Day, falls on 25 March and, as payments were backdated to this time, Tradescant had presumably already taken up his duties. One hundred pounds a year was a vast salary at that time, but the warrant makes the reasons for it clear. He had to meet all the expenses of upkeep, both labour and materials. It was, in fact, a contract to maintain the palace gardens.

Appointments were usually held during pleasure, during good behaviour or during life, and they ranked in ascending order of security.

The warrant clearly states that Tradescant was to be paid quarterly, but in fact he regularly picked up 'the some of £50 parcell of his allowance' twice a year, after it became due on Lady Day and at Michaelmas, which falls on 29 September.[2] No doubt this suited his convenience. The clerk who issued the money took 6s. 8d. each time as his perks.[3] This was standard practice, for the job was otherwise unpaid.

It is unlikely that Tradescant actually lived at Oatlands, although he would have paid regular visits to supervise the staff that he employed there. We know that he was allocated quarters in one of the buildings that comprised the Palace complex, as in 1636 two carpenters were paid for 'cutting a doreway and pinning in a new dorecase att John Tredeskins lodging'.[4]

It is possible that his rooms were in the silkworm house that had been erected by Queen Anne of Denmark, the wife of James I, in 1616. Unfortunately no picture or description of the building survives, but it was designed by Inigo Jones as a two-storey building comprising four small rooms downstairs and one large room of 400 square feet above, perhaps ten feet by forty. It had wainscoting of 'ovall and arched panells', a 'wrought freeze' and a portal which, in an afterthought, was 'made alike on both sides'.

The building had eight large and ten small 'lights' with an enlarged west window that probably incorporated the Queen's coat of arms 'paynted in glass'. Two chimneys surmounted the roof, which was tiled, crested and gabled. One room boasted 'a carved mantle' and three had paved floors.[5] William Portington, the carpenter, must have been particularly busy as one 'whole chamber' was shelved for the silkworms;[6] his bill amounted to twenty-eight pounds, so it was perhaps the large room upstairs.

At the same time the vineyard and the long privy walk adjoining were enclosed by eleven-foot walls with interconnecting gates, and Inigo Jones's 'greate gate' was set up between the vineyard and the park.

Oatlands had originally been built by Henry VIII as a glorified hunting lodge. It stood on a rise overlooking the Thames between Walton and Weybridge. The red-brick buildings extended over fourteen acres, and the estate had been granted to Henrietta Maria as part of her jointure.

Within a short time of Tradescant taking up his appointment the Queen wrote to her mother, Marie de Medici, saying: 'as I am sending this man into France to get some fruit-trees and some flowers, I most humbly entreat your majesty to be pleased to assist him with your power, if by chance anyone should do him wrong and hinder him'.[7] Unfortunately 'this man's' name is not given, but it is possible that it was Tradescant taking another trip to the Continent to stock the palace gardens. The Parliamentary Survey of 1650 describes Oatlands as a 'Capital Messuage and Royal Mansion House' and records 'five severall gardens lyeing round the foresaid first mentioned buildings commonly called and known by the names of the greate garden the Long garden the Kings privy garden the Queens privy garden and the new garden all which may be made very usefull and proffitable to the whole house if ordered and preserved as they ought to be'.

The survey of Oatlands is not nearly so detailed as are those of some of the other royal palaces, and the value of the garden is lumped together with that of the house, the resale price of the materials being put at £4,023 18s. But it does record 162 wall fruit trees and 314 other fruit trees growing there; 'one faire and handsome Cisterne or fountaine' in the Great Garden; and 'a Close Walke of one hundred yards in length arched and very neatly ordered' in the Long Garden.[8]

A gateway surmounted by a twenty-four-foot 'dial' led into the Great Court, which was turfed. There were two other courtyards, the Middle Court and the Innermost Court, the former also being 'green', while the latter was 'paved with rough freestone'.

The Inner Courtyard was embellished with an even larger and more elaborate 'dial' illustrating 'the seven planetts and twelve signes', all gilded, while the 'outwarde creste' contained 'a concave deciphering the fower quarters of the yeare, with shippes hills dales etc'.[9]

By the time of Tradescant's arrival water had already been laid on to a cistern in the kitchen garden and 'cockes' had been set up in the privy garden and vineyard, which was entered through a pair of 'folding gates'.[10]

Tradescant was to supervise many improvements in his time there. In 1632 an arbour was added to 'the little garden next the vyneyard'. Two carpenters were involved in making the frame, which extended for 263 feet with a width and height of fourteen feet. It incorporated twenty-six ten-foot bays or recesses, and this garden was further embellished with a six-foot fence of pales 'with round topps'.[11]

In the autumn of the following year Tradescant was instructed to lay out a new bowling green for which he was paid an additional £100, which again included both workmanship and materials. It must have replaced the bowling green put down in the outer court in 1613. The warrant reads:

Charles r. To the Treasurer and under Treasurer of the Exchequer for the time being greeting. Our will and pleasure is and we doe hereby will and command you out of our Treasure remaining in the Receipt of our Exchequer to pay or cause to be paid unto our Servant John Tradescant Keeper of our Gardens at Oatelands the sume of one hundred pounds by

way of imprest and upon Accompte for the making of a Bowling greene at
Oatelands and for workmanshipp and materialls for the same according to
our direccon and Command. And these our treasurers shall be your
sufficient warrant and discharge in this behalf. Given under our privy seele
at our Pallace of Westminster the three and twentieth day of September
in the nynth yeare of our Raigne.[12]

Shortly afterwards the bricklayer brought 'upp with Bricks a new wall in
the Parke . . . with Butresses to inclose an orrenge Garden there'. This was
off the privy garden and a new 'dorecase and doore' was set into the
intervening wall. Part was walled off for the bowling green which was set
about with 'Posts pailes and Railes' forming fifty-two ten-foot bays.
Tradescant acquired a new roller for it in the same year.[13] The warrant that
gave the instructions for it reads:

Charles by the grace of God King of England Scotland ffrance and Ireland
defender of the ffaith. To the Treasurer and Under Treasurer of our
Exchequer for the time being, greeting. Whereas we have directed the
inclosing of a peece of ground with a Brick wall containing five and twenty
roods or thereabouts adjoining to our gardens at Oatlands intended for
the keeping of orange trees in winter and making of a shedd in length
about two hundred threescore and two foote with a Colehouse adjoyning
thereunto. As also for the inclosing of a peece of ground for a Bowling
greene there, with rayles posts lattices and Painters worke and which by
an Estimate made by the Surveyor of our workes will amount to the some
of foure hundred and fifty pounds or thereabouts besides the somme of
One hundred pounds already allowed unto John Tradescant for the said
Bowling greene. Our will and pleasure therefore is and wee doe hereby
will and command you out of our treasure remayning in the Receipt of our
Said Exchequer to pay or cause to be paid unto Henry Wicke, paymaster
of our Workes, the said some of foure hundred and fiftie pounds, by way
of imprest and upon accompt for the service aforesaid. And these our
treasurers shalbe your sufficient warrant and discharge in this behalf.
Given under our Privie Seale at our Pallace of Westminster the last day of
September in the ninth yeare of our raigne.[14]

There is one more payment. This time it is for sixty pounds and it was made
by the Queen's treasurer, Sir Richard Wynne: 'John Tradescan her Majesties
Gardiner by Warrant dated the vijth of December 1636 which Her Majesty
was pleased to allowe unto him towards the chardge of some alteracons to be
made in her Majesties gardens at Oatelands.'[15] Unfortunately it has not been
possible to trace the warrant which would indicate what this payment covered.
But there must have been additional work done in the vineyard that year after

bricklayers had taken down a brick wall and carried away the rubbish.[16]

During these years at Oatlands Tradescant was of course still running his own garden and museum, which were becoming increasingly popular. In 1633 there may have been a new attraction: the banana. Tradescant's friend, Thomas Johnson, received from Bermuda a plant with unripe green fruit. 'This stalke with the fruit thereon I hanged up in my shop, where it became ripe about the beginning of May, and lasted until June: the pulp or meat was very soft and tender, and it did eate somewhat like a Muske-Melon,' Johnson declared.[17] It must have caused considerable interest hanging in the apothecary's shop on Snow Hill and, from whomever it was acquired, Tradescant evidently found a means of preserving one, as a banana is listed in the *Musaeum Tradescantianum*.

With his new post, Tradescant was collecting not only for himself but also for the King. On 27 November 1633 a letter from the Secretary of State, Francis Windebank, was read to the Court of the East India Company. It signified 'His Majesties pleasure, that the Company should write for such varieties as are expressed in a paper thereinclosed, and being returned to deliver them to John Tradescant to be reserved by him for His Majesties Service'. The Court ordered 'the same' to be sent 'by their next shippe to their severall ffactories that such things as may be had may be returned for England according to His Majesties pleasure'.[18] Unfortunately the paper enclosed does not survive, but it looks as though Tradescant was by this time in charge of the King's Cabinet of Rarities.

It has often been suggested that the King and Queen were entertained at South Lambeth, and, while there is no evidence to prove it, a visit in the autumn of 1635 seems likely. For at that time Tradescant received several items of royal clothing of historical interest, sent to him on the King's instructions.

On 13 November 1635 there was 'A warrant to Wm Smithsby Keeper of Hampton Court Wardrobe to deliver unto John Tredeskyn King Henry the Eight his Capp, his hawking Bagg and Spurres'. Six weeks later another warrant to Smithsby ordered him 'to deliver to John Tradescant King Henry the Eight his cap, his stirrups Henry the 7th his gloves and combcase'.[19]

The museum catalogue lists 'Henry the 8 his Stirrups, Haukes-hoods, Gloves' and 'Henry 8, hawking-glove, hawks-hood, dogs-coller', all of which still survive. Most of these were duplicates as similar items were sold during the Commonwealth.[20] Tradescant also acquired Edward the Confessor's 'knit-gloves' and Anne Boleyn's embroidered 'night-vayle' and 'silke knit-gloves', but no record of their transfer from the royal wardrobe can be traced.

In 1636 Tradescant's name became associated with an Oxford garden. In 1621 Henry Lord Danvers, Earl of Danby, had given five acres of land on the banks of the Cherwell, near Magdalen College, for the establishment of a botanic garden. He had erected houses with stoves for the over-wintering of delicate plants, enclosed the garden with a wall fourteen feet high and engaged the services of Nicholas Stone to construct the gate-house. He had also raised the level of the soil to avoid flooding from the river in winter. This was to be a physic garden, growing simples for the use of the faculty of medicine.

Lord Danby, whose brother Sir John Danvers's famous Chelsea garden lay upstream and across the river from Lambeth, then came 'to some reasonable good terms of agreement with John Tradescant' who was 'designed for ye gardener, viz, for a yearly stipend of £50 to be by ye yeare or thereabouts'. On 1 November 1636 Tradescant was the 'bearer' of a letter sent by Lord Danby from his Oxfordshire residence, Cornebury Park, to Dr Frewen, President of Magdalen College. It states that 'Mr John Tredeskine is willinge to persever in his worke with some assurance of Estate, & I alsoe must add divers thinges for the furnishinge of that worke.'[21] It seems likely that Tradescant was appointed to supervise the garden in the same way as he was already doing at Oatlands, but as it was smaller and primarily designed for the cultivation of medicinal plants his expenses would have been less. It is possible, too, that the garden at Cornebury Park was also receiving attention; Nicholas Stone had recently completed a new south-west wing there for Lord Danby.

Tradescant held the post at Oxford for little more than a year. The account of the garden's founding continues: 'Not long after, viz, in ye year 1638, about Easter, ye said John Tradescan died.'[22]

Although Tradescant supervised the Oxford Physic Garden for only this short time, he took on at least one employee to work under him. This was fifty-year-old Thomas Bayler who, as a privileged craftsman, matriculated on 18 April 1637, when he was described as 'Serviens mri Johis Tredescant Universit oxo hortcul', meaning: servant of Master John Tradescant, gardener to Oxford University.[23] This refutes the suggestion that he never took up the appointment.[24]

After Tradescant's death the contract was given to the eccentric German, Jacob Bobart, who always worked alongside the goat he kept as a companion. By 1648 he had built up a fine collection of no less than 1,600 plants, with two yews, clipped to look like giants, standing guard over the entrance and becoming famous as the butt of university wits. It seems likely that a number of these plants emanated from South Lambeth and that Tradescant was responsible for the original lay-out of the Oxford Physic Garden. Later it was extensively redesigned by Bobart, possibly during the Commonwealth, the walls of the garden having been a strongpoint in the Royalist defence of Oxford.

Chapter 9

A Burial and a Marriage

John Tradescant was survived by his son, John junior, and his grandchildren Frances and John III. His wife, Elizabeth, *née* Day, is not mentioned in his will and had evidently died before him. Despite checking through innumerable parish records for the burial of Elizabeth Tradescant, it has not been possible to find the date or place of her death. Clearly she must have died before the move to South Lambeth or else she would have been buried in the family tomb.

John the younger left school in the year 1623 and presumably started work at once with his father, as nothing more is known of him until his wedding day on 29 February 1628 at the City church of St Gregory by St Paul. He was nineteen years of age, and his bride was called Jane Hurte.[1] The marriage took place by licence of the faculties, but unfortunately the licence is no longer in existence so that nothing is known of her parentage. She could perhaps have been the daughter of the William Hurt who supplied the Ordnance with 'cases and funnells of plate for cartouches' (or cartridges as they would be called today) and was also responsible for mending 'cristoll branches and building two parrot cages' for the Queen.[2]

The Tradescants' daughter, Frances, must have been born soon afterwards, probably at the end of that year; their son, another John, was baptized in the Lambeth church of St Mary's on 4 November 1633.[3] Poor Jane did not live to enjoy her children for long. She died when her son was only one year and seven months old and was buried on 1 June 1635. There is an entry for twelve shillings against her name in the churchwardens' accounts of St Mary-at-Lambeth under the heading 'Extraordinary receipts for buryalls'.[4] This high charge doubtless included the construction of the family vault as she was the first to be buried in it.

On 19 December 1634 the younger Tradescant was admitted and sworn a freeman of the Worshipful Company of Gardeners on payment of 2s. 6d. and the promise of ten shillings more. The oath of the Company, that he would have sworn, reads as follows:

You shall swear that you shall be true to our Sovereign Lord the King that now is and to his heirs and successors; and to the Master and Wardens of the Mystery of Gardeners of the City of London, and their Successors you shall be obedient; their counsel lawful and honest you shall keep secret; and all the Laws, Ordinances and Statutes made by the Master, Wardens and Assistants of the said Mystery, touching you yourself, you shall observe, fulfil and keep; So help you God, and by the contents of this Book. God save the King.

Few of the Company's records survive, but those that do indicate that John junior was not a particularly active member, paying his dues of sixpence a quarter spasmodically and on one occasion, in 1657, remitting 8s. 6d. in one payment, having run up arrears for no less than seventeen quarters. In this instance, however, there must have been good reason for his absence, as the fine to which he would otherwise have been liable does not appear to have been incurred.

There were then, as today, four ways of becoming a freeman of a City company. First, by presentation in reward for services rendered, for which no financial consideration is involved. Second, by patrimony at the age of twenty-one for any son born to a freeman of the company. (Daughters can now also benefit from this method of entry, but this is a recent innovation.) Third, by servitude, after an apprenticeship of between four and seven years; and, last, by redemption, which is to say on payment of a set fee.

John junior was twenty-six years old when he was admitted. There is no evidence that he had made any outstanding contribution to gardening by this age, nor is there any record that his father was ever a freeman of the Company, so it is unlikely that he gained admittance by either of the first two methods. Moreover, had he served an apprenticeship after leaving school he would almost certainly have been made free at a younger age. Thus it would seem that he became a freeman by redemption, buying his admittance for the sum of 12s. 6d.

The Gardeners' Company had been incorporated by Letters Patent from James I on 18 September 1605. It covered those living within six miles of the City of London using the 'trade, craft or mystery of gardening, planting, grafting, setting, sowing, cutting, arboring, rocking, mounting, covering, fencing and removing of plants, herbs, seeds, fruits, trees, stocks, sets, and of contriving the conveyances to the same belonging'. There was obviously much to be learned during the statutory years of apprenticeship.

The meetings of the Gardeners' Company were held in the Common Hall of the Company of Free Masons, which was situated near the Guildhall. They took place at 8 a.m. in summer and an hour later in winter. After the completion of business, members adjourned to a local inn to pass the rest of the day in 'convivial intercourse'. Judging by some bills from a later period, this was helped along with generous hospitality.[5]

John Tradescant senior was buried on 17 April 1638. The 'great bell' of St Mary's tolled at his funeral and the parish 'blackcloath' was brought out to cover his hearse. Both these services contributed to the parish income and in Tradescant's case, with the charge for 'breaking the grounde', cost 5s. 4d. St Mary's was the Tradescants' church, and both father and son were active in its support and upkeep. In 1637 the elder Tradescant had contributed 3s. 4d. towards the building of a new brick wall at the west end of the churchyard and for the repair of 'other ruines and decayes in and about the church'.[6]

Tradescant had many friends, and the cortège at his funeral must have included a long and distinguished line of mourners to grieve his passing. Not least among those who would miss his expertise and his good company must surely have been John Parkinson, soon to be appointed herbalist to the King, who always referred to Tradescant with such affection. 'My very good friend', 'my very loving and kinde friend' and 'my especiall good friend' were phrases he had used.[7]

The church would have been hung with garlands of cypress and perhaps of rosemary and bay, too, these last two being used more by the 'Commons' and less popular at funerals of 'the gentiler sort'.[8]

The rector, Daniel Featley, would have taken the service. He was a strong upholder of the English Church, always careful to tread a narrow path between Romanists and Protestant sectaries, and was said to be a 'stupendous disputant' because he never lost his temper and enjoyed 'his adversaries frets'.[9]

But there was one member of the family who was not present. It was Tradescant's only son John. For Parkinson tells us of a 'Forraine or strange Maidenhaire' which 'Mr John Tradescant the younger brought out of Virginia presently upon the death of his father'.[10]

John can have had no inkling that his father's life was so near its end when he set out or surely he would never have embarked on so long and hazardous a journey. He had gone to Virginia 'to gather up all raritye of flowers, plants, shells &c'[11] and was almost certainly there at the King's request because this is recorded in the State Papers.

He was probably well on his way home by the date of the funeral. The journey must have seemed insufferably long, with the boat alternately becalmed under hot, windless skies while he endeavoured to eke out the always limited stock of fresh water in an effort to keep his plants alive or tossed by heavy seas while he tried to protect his precious cargo from the salty spray. Even the fastest journeys took two months, and many were nearer three.

On his return, Tradescant would have had to busy himself immediately

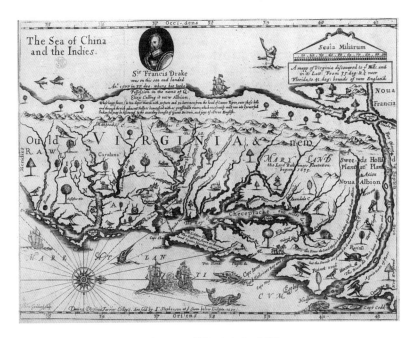

A map of Virginia in 1651

putting his father's affairs in order, seeing to the South Lambeth garden and museum and riding off post-haste to Oatlands to check that all had passed well there during the spring. He had evidently spent some months at the Queen's Court canvassing for his father's post.

John Morris, Master of the Watermills (his father having constructed watermills near London Bridge which provided much of the city's water), mentions this in correspondence undertaken in Latin with Johannes de Laet in Holland. De Laet was a director of the Dutch East India Company, with whom Morris was also exchanging plants. Morris confirms that Tradescant was in Virginia 'under the auspices of the King' and tells his friend that Tradescant 'brought back a couple of hundred plants hitherto unknown to our world'. A year later, a list of these was circulating among interested botanists, having been compiled with help and advice from John Parkinson after a thorough inspection of the actual plants and a collection of dried material that Tradescant had also assembled. Morris further reported that there were 'many seeds which do not yet show of what species they are likely to be'.

Although he obviously admired the younger Tradescant's skill, describing him as a man 'most experienced in gardening matters' who delighted in 'exotic plants', and bracketing his name with those of Johnson and Parkinson as 'those three great men of our native botanists', there was evidently a personality clash between Morris and Tradescant. Morris called the latter 'unschooled and clearly uncivilised', complaining that he had 'not a single streak of his father's vigour' because it took so long to 'squeeze out' of him a catalogue of his Virginian plants. Morris was also upset when 'several anemones of different colours', which, with their 'marker sticks', had been reserved for him by Tradescant, had been 'disturbed by the carelessness of the workmen or the weeding-girls'. Despite his complaints, Morris was constantly bothering Tradescant for plants and seeking his advice; only once in the correspondence does he acknowledge that Tradescant had 'generously offered' help over some botanical problem.[12]

The elder John Tradescant's will, which was proved on 2 May, about a fortnight after his death, reads as follows:

In the name of God, Amen, I John Treadeskant of South Lambeth in ye County of Surrey Gardener being sicklie in bodie but perfect in mynde – thanks be to God – therefore do this eight day of January Anno Domini 1637 make and ordaine my last Will and Testament in maner following viz: Renouncing hereby all former Wills. First I doe render my Soule to ye Almightie And my body to ye earth to be buried in that parish where it shall please God to call me out of this world. Item I give to my only sonne John Treadeskant my Lease in South Lambeth aforesaid and my Lease in Woodham Water in ye County of Essex. Item I give to my grandchildren John and ffrances Treadeskant my lease of twoe howses whereof one is in Long acre and ye other in ye Covent garden in ye County of Midd the profitte of that Lease to be equallie devided between them after our Ladieday now next comeing. Item I give to my said grandchildren the Some of One hundred and ffiftie poundes which is in the hands of ye right honourable the Lord Goring and ye some of Seventeen poundes which is in ye hands of my brother in law Alexander Norman. The same and severall Somes of money to be equally divided betwixt my said grandchildren And if either of my said grandchildren happen to dye before their age of one and twentie yeare or daie of marriage then my will is that ye survivor of them shall have and enjoy that pt^e of my said estate which I have hereby given to ye other. Item I give and bequeath all ye rest and residue of my goods and chattells whatsoever (not hereby before bequeathed to my said sonne) with this proviso – That if hee shall desire to pt^e with or sell my Cabinett that hee shall first offer ye same to ye Prince And I doe hereby make and appoint my said brother in lawe and Mr William Ward Executors of this my last will and Testament And I doe hereby desire my trustie and welbeloved friend John Whistler Esquire to be Overseer of this my last will and Testam[t]. In wittnes whereof I have hereunto sett my hand and seal the daie and yeare abovewritten. John Treadescant Signed sealed and published in ye presence of John Lardner, Arnall Cornellis, Edward Morgan.[13]

Although the will is dated January 1637, it was in fact made in 1638, three months before Tradescant died. At that time the new year started on 25 March. The several leases mentioned appear to have been held purely for investment purposes, as there is no evidence that Tradescant ever lived at any of them. While it would seem likely that he acquired the Woodham Walter lease through the Duke of Buckingham when he was working at New Hall, Buckingham in fact never held this manor. Woodham Walter remained in the hands of the Radcliffe, Earls of Sussex from whom the Duke had purchased New Hall.

Tradescant's executors were his brother-in-law Alexander Norman, who had married his wife's sister Dorcas, and William Ward, who had taken over his position as yeoman garnetter of the Whitehall granary. Ward had been steward at New Hall, where Buckingham had acquired him along with the house; he was also a churchwarden at Boreham, where he owned land, a messuage and a farm. A keen gardener, he grew there a 'very beautifull and rare' White Tamarisk.[14] Although he retired back to Essex, where he died in 1652, he still occupied quarters at York House, Buckingham's house on the Embankment.[15]

These two executors picked up Tradescant's final payment for the royal garden on Monday, 24 December 1638. The entry in the accounts reads: 'By order dated 16th day of June 1638 to Alexander Norman and Willm Ward executors to John Tradescant late Keeper to His Majesties gardens at Oatlands the some of £50 parcell of his allowance of £100 per annum for keeping the vyne and vyneyards gardens etc there payable quarterly and due for halfe a year ended at our lady day last 1638.'[16]

Of the witnesses, John Lardner was a near neighbour in South Lambeth.[17] Edward Morgan kept the Westminster Medical Garden, which was situated between the west cloister of the Abbey and Dean's Yard. A Welshman, Evelyn described him as 'a very skillfull botanist'.[18] Arnall Cornellis was perhaps the son of the Dutch miller of that name registered as an alien in the parish of St Olave's, Southwark, at the end of the previous century.

Mea Allen suggests that the money held by Lord Goring was unpaid salary due to Tradescant for work done at Oatlands, but in fact he collected his wages regularly throughout the time that he held the royal appointment. In any case, Lord Goring did not become Comptroller of the Queen's Household until the following year. At the time of Tradescant's death he was Master of the Horse to the Queen. It is tempting to speculate that the money owing to Tradescant may have been for improvements to the garden at Danny, Lord Goring's Sussex home.

Tradescant, it will be noted, sealed his will. Yet he was not entitled to use arms. Between 1530 and the late 1680s there was a system for the compulsory registration of arms, but some people evidently managed to slip through the net. The more eminent a person was, the fewer questions were asked about their right to use them. A search of the Official Registers at the College of Arms has revealed no entry that relates to either the elder or the younger Tradescant. Nor can any coat of arms resembling that used by the Tradescants be traced. They were not alone in using arms in that way; plenty of others, some of much higher standing, did the same.[19]

In fact both father and son used arms blatantly. They both sealed their wills, as did Hester, the younger Tradescant's second wife. They erected their coat of arms for all to see on their house at South Lambeth,[20] and it was sculpted on their tomb. Moreover, in 1656, when the *Musaeum Tradescantianum* was published, it took pride of place on the first page. Obviously their social standing had become such – they were frequently described as 'gent' – that nobody bothered to question their use of arms, taking it for granted that it was their entitlement. (Robert Tradescant of Walberswick was less fortunate when he applied for arms in 1661. He was disclaimed as an 'ignoble person' forbidden to continue using arms as he was 'no gent'.)[21]

It was in the autumn following his return from Virginia that the younger Tradescant remarried. He took as his wife Hester Pooks of St Bride's parish, but they chose St Nicholas Cole Abbey, another City church, for the ceremony on 1 October 1638. The marriage licence, describing the bride as a twenty-five-year-old spinster, had been issued by the Bishop of London two days earlier.[22] Hester Pooks was related to the artistic de Critz and de Neve families who, between them, contributed most of the Tradescant portraits now in the Ashmolean Museum.

The younger Tradescant continued his father's interest in parish affairs. In 1639 he made a voluntary contribution towards furnishing 'the Communion Table with a decent guilt cup and twoe silver flagons'. Later he served, with two others, as a surveyor of the highways. The highways were maintained by communal labour. There was no money contribution, but fines were imposed on those parishioners who neglected their duty. Bridges for whom no one was directly responsible also came under their jurisdiction. Tradescant also served a term of duty as one of four collectors for the poor, responsible for the collection and distribution of the parish poor rate.[23]

Chapter 10

In Place of His Father

John took over his father's position at Oatlands immediately. Although the warrant for his appointment is dated 12 November 1639, payment is backdated to follow on from that made to his father's executors after his death. This was his due as he would have been paying for the upkeep of the garden during that time.

The warrant reads: 'A like payment of an allowance of £100 per annum unto John Tradescant Keeper of His Majesties gardens at Oatlands payable quarterly from Midsomer 1638 during his Majesties pleasure, in the place of John Tradescant his father deceased, subscribed by order from Mr Secret. Windebanke and by him procured.'[1]

In the following year there must have been great excitement at Oatlands when a 'snowe well' with a thatched roof was constructed in the park. Sixteen feet in diameter and thirty feet deep, it was entirely bricked and drained out into the valley.

In the same year the painter George Portman was paid 'for paintinge uppon the walls in the open gallery in the privy Garden . . . viij of the Queens Ma^te housses in Landskipp in oyle and underneath a leaninge place aboute threefoote high painted with devisions of marble and the Ceeleinge with cloudes and sky coulor'. This gallery was eighty feet long, twelve feet broad and ten and a half feet high.[2]

The wall was designed by Inigo Jones, Surveyor of the King's Works. His original plan had a narrow decorative border with blank rectangular compartments for the paintings. But the drawing has been inscribed by Jones 'for the painting in oyle of the open wale wit landscapes in the garden at Oatlands 1637 to bee a landscap only and no compartments', which indicates that the design was not accepted and that he had to make another.[3]

Sir Thomas Herbert, who accompanied the King on his last visit to Oatlands in August 1647, left a more detailed description. 'Upon the Plaister'd Wall in the Stone-Gallery respecting the Gardens', he wrote, 'were very curiously pourtray'd that Royal Edifice (with Pontefract Castle,

Havering, Eltham, Nonsuch, and some other Palaces assigned to her Majesty) in like manner as you see at Fontainbleau, of several stately Houses of the French Kings.'[4] In fact the Fontainebleau Galerie des Cerfs, on which it was based, still stands. It portrays fifteen royal houses in line, separated only by their forests, and was sometimes used as a banqueting hall.[5]

That Tradescant was regarded as a highly trusted royal servant is shown by a letter written some years later by Elias Ashmole. Endeavouring to authenticate Tradescant's claim that a piece of wood was from the 'true cross', a popular relic, Ashmole described how Queen Henrietta Maria, before going abroad, had 'caused a slender piece of this wood (above half a Foot long) to be delivered to him to keep till she sent for it'. The relic had been brought out of the great wardrobe by command of the King and was traditionally said to have been given by King John of France to Edward III.

'Afterwards when the said Queen was in France, she sent to Mr Tradescant for this Wood thither; but before he delivered it, he deteyned the abovementioned small piece, which casually had been broken from it, and gave me a little part thereof, when I made the foresaid catalogue.' Such, at least, is Ashmole's account of this fortuitous incident.[6]

Parkinson tells a different story: 'Yet I have seene with Master Tradescant the elder before he dyed, a great peece of true Lignum Aloes, and of the best sort, as bigge and as long as a mans legge, without any knot therein, which as he said our King Charles gave him with his own hands, but was here kept before, and accounted by many, as a great religious rellicke, even to be a piece of the wood of that Crosse, whereon our Saviour was crucified, and therefore was fetched away againe from his Sonne, to be kept as a monument or rellicke still.' 'Assuredly,' Parkinson adds somewhat scathingly, 'if all those peeces of wood, that are . . . said to be parts of that Crosse, were all set together, they would goe neere to make . . . many cart loads full.'[7]

In 1640 Oatlands was the scene of a happy event when Queen Henrietta Maria gave birth to her fourth son there. The silver font was sent down for the baptism of Henry, Duke of Gloucester. But the palace was not to be the place of many more happy occasions. Clouds of trouble and uncertainty had been looming on the horizon for several years. With Charles's belief in royal absolutism, his inability to handle Parliament and his failure to realize the depth of feeling against his policies, both political and religious, they were now building up into a veritable storm. In November of the same year the Long Parliament was called and promptly began to assert its rights and to attack the King's advisers, notably the Earl of Strafford and Archbishop Laud. Despite his problems, Charles remembered his 'distressed Protestant subjects in Ireland' and ordered a collection towards their relief to be made before June 1642; Tradescant contributed 2s.[8]

Throughout 1641 Charles made concessions, unable to decide how to proceed. In May he signed the warrant for Strafford's execution, at the same time agreeing that Parliament could not be dissolved without its own consent. By the end of the year, however, he switched to the attack, giving orders that five members of the House of Commons should be impeached for treason. The five men escaped down the river and Charles had lost the support of the city. A battle of manifestoes between King and Parliament followed, but when the latter passed ordinances placing military forces under its control, a measure that Charles had resisted, civil war became inevitable, as it meant that Parliament must defeat the King on the field or submit to high treason.

In January 1642 the King left London, and in February he sent Henrietta Maria to Holland for her own safety and to try to pawn the crown jewels in order to buy arms. With her she took all but the two eldest of their children. By May he was established at York, preparing for war, while Parliament had set up a Committee of Safety to defend the kingdom against the King. On 22 August the royal standard was formally raised in Nottingham and the civil war began.

It is difficult to generalize about how the two sides lined up, as even individual families were divided in their loyalties, one brother fighting for Parliament, another for the King. On the whole, however, the North and West and Wales were Royalist, while the South and East supported Parliament. Parliament held London and most of the ports and with them the Navy; it also held the purse-strings, as it was in a position to levy customs duties at the ports and to borrow from the London financiers. Charles still had the support of the aristocracy in the areas under his control but was perennially short of money. The Oxford colleges melted down their silver to help his cause.

The first pitched battle, which was indecisive, was fought at Edgehill on 23 October 1642. Tradescant either saw what was coming and did not like it or, as a royal servant, found it expedient to leave. In any event he opted to get out of the country. Once again he headed for Virginia. This time he took passage under an immigrant called Bertram Hobert, who, by paying for the transportation of thirteen persons, became entitled to 650 acres of land. To stimulate emigration and settlement the Virginia Company had decreed that any person paying his own fare to Virginia should be granted fifty acres for his own personal adventure, with a further fifty acres for each additional person he transported. This became known as 'headrights', the right of fifty acres for each 'head'.

Hobert's land was to be 'on the North side of Charles River, in Peanpetanke Creek, near land of Mr. Vaus, etc. and East into the great creek from the Oystershell banck'.

The thirteen people he transported were: himself twice; Sarah, his wife; Francis Pepper; Francis, a Negro; Thomas Austin, his wife and two children; John Tradescant; John Eyres; Edward Goldborne and Thomas Bawcocke. The entry in the Patent Book is dated 10 October 1642, just two weeks before the battle of Edgehill.

Hobert had already been out to Virginia, no doubt to explore the possibilities of settlement for his family and to select the site of his land. This is why he was now claiming for himself twice over. Land upon 'headright' did not have to be claimed immediately. Nor should it be assumed that the people transported were necessarily immigrants. Even men of prominence in the colony, taking one or more voyages home and out again, appear as 'headrights' for their friends, who were willing to pay the cost of their passage in order to get the grant of land. This is what happened in Tradescant's case, and there was no rule against it. Contrary to popular opinion, the younger Tradescant never owned land in Virginia.[9]

What was frowned upon was when 'headrights' were claimed twice over for the same person. Ships' masters, for instance, found it expedient to submit their passenger lists for headrights when the same passengers had made individual claims for land after paying their own fares. Although claimants were supposed to present receipts to show that passage money had been paid, the lax administration allowed many double claims to go through. Such grants of land were then sold and the proceeds pocketed.

Hobert returned to England several times to bring out more emigrants and acquire more land. He was an alien, and in 1660, after his death, his son-in-law petitioned for the land that had been granted to him to be divided between his children according to his will instead of escheating to the Crown as was normal practice in the case of aliens.[10]

There is no record of Tradescant's voyage. It can only be hoped that his passage was not as bad as one made by a Colonel Norwood in 1649. He had agreed passage with the master of the *Virginia Merchant* for six pounds. Storms and mountainous seas left them with broken masts and only the mizzen still standing and with a gaping hole which let water into the hold, ruining the food supplies. Men fell overboard right and left, with everyone expecting the same fate. Rations were cut to half a 'bisket cake' a day, and even rats exchanged hands for sixteen shillings each. It was three and a half months before they made land.[11]

Nor is it known what cargo his ship carried. The *Tristram and Jane* had gone to Virginia some years earlier with butts of sack and caskes of 'strong waters' as well as sugar, 'candy oyle' (probably a kind of syrup), quince marmalade and other conserves, shelled almonds, raisins, clothing, fowling pieces (shotguns), nails, vinegar, candles, oatmeal, peas, cheese and a pair of scales. She also carried seventy-six passengers. Her return cargo was tobacco, 31,800 pounds of it worth fourpence a pound.[12]

And what was to be found in Virginia on arrival? Everyone was struck by the beauty and vastness of the primeval forest that grew right down to the shore. 'All the country is overshadowed with trees,' wrote William Strachey in about 1612. 'Woods yt hath, great, beautifull, fruictfull, pleasant, and profitable, the grounds, cleane under them, at least passeable both for horse and foote.'[13]

Visitors were struck by the vast height of the trees. The elder Tradescant's friend, Captain John Smith, described oaks 'with 20 yards of usable timber'.[14]

'Nor is the present wildernesse of it without a particular beauty, being all over a naturall Grove of Oakes, Pines, Cedars, Cipresse, Mulberry, Chestnut, Laurell, Sassafras, Cherry, Plum-trees and Vines, all of so delectable an aspect, that the melanchollyest eye in the World cannot look upon it without contentment, nor content himselfe without admiration,' wrote E.W. Gent in 1650. There were 'large and delicious' strawberries growing beneath the trees and many other varieties of fruit in abundance. The rivers teemed with fish, and there were deer in plenty and wild turkeys weighing up to fifty pounds.[15]

Who could fail to be attracted to the place? Certainly not Tradescant, this time on a botanizing expedition for himself. There is no record of how long he stayed or where he went in this fertile land, but it seems likely that he would have returned early in the following spring to plant the seeds and roots he brought back, in order to give them the best chance of survival.

That both Tradescants were born with green fingers cannot be doubted, but even so it seems little short of miraculous that they were able to transport plants over such long distances through uncertain weather and still get them to thrive. If the elder Tradescant had problems in bringing home plants from the Continent, they can have been as nothing compared with those that confronted his son.

Sir Thomas Hanmer's *Garden Book*, written in 1659, describes 'How to Packe up Rootes and Send them to Remote Places'. 'The fibrous sorts must bee made up alone by themselves, with moist mosse or grasse about them tyed fast, which is better than earth, which will dry and fall away, unles the voyage bee short, but all the other kinds must bee packt up dry without earth in papers, and soe boxt up that they shake not, nor have any havy thing to presse them hard together, and thus they may bee convey'd safely very farr.'[16]

John Evelyn also left a clue as to how some of the difficulties were overcome. In 1686 he wrote to Samuel Pepys at the Admiralty giving instructions to a sea captain who had offered to bring him plants from New England.

'The seedes', he advised, 'are best preserv'd in papers: their names written on them and put in a box. The Nutts in Barills of dry sand: each kind wrapd in papers written on.

'The trees in Barills their rootes wraped about mosse: The smaller the plants and trees are, the better; or they will do well packed up in matts; but the Barill is best, & a small vessell will containe enough of all kinds labells of paper tyed to every sort with ye name.'[17]

Were they, perhaps, drawing on Tradescant's experience? Those voyages across the Atlantic must have taken a minimum of two months and very often extended to three or more, with lengthy calms under hot skies and frightening storms when waves swamped the decks. Fresh water was always in short supply. Anything kept on deck or in a damp hold would have been in danger from the salty spray, so detrimental to living plants.

Barrels for transportation would have been made in Virginia, where there was wood in abundance, but Tradescant would have had to carry out with him any paper with which to wrap and label his plants and seeds.

If he had tried to bring back animal specimens, preserved in rum, for The Ark, he would have faced a different problem. These frequently 'fell prey to sailors' who, it seems, had no objection 'to a snake or opossum in their illicit grog'.[18]

Finally, if his precious cargo had survived the weather and the attentions of the crew, there was the ever-present danger of pirates and privateers.

Tradescant was presumably home long before his daughter's wedding, which took place on 28 January 1645, although it is his wife's name that appears on the marriage allegation. This was obtained the day before and reads: 'Alexander Norman, of St Botolph, Aldgate, Citizen and Cooper of London, widower, 56, & Frances Tradescant, dau. of John Tradescant, of S. Lambeth, Gent, who consents, about 19, his consent attested by his wife Hester Tradescant, at Little St Bartholomew, or St Mary Magdelen, Old Fish Street.'[19]

In the event they chose 'Little St Bartholomew', the hospital church of St Bartholomew the Less. Its parishioners were then, as today, made up of the patients and staff of the hospital. At that time the church was a Royalist stronghold in the midst of a Puritan city, still somehow managing to provide traditional services. The parish records show that these were much in demand, with the number of marriages taking place under its roof increasing from about twenty-five to nearly three hundred a year.

Frances Tradescant cannot have been as old as nineteen years. Her parents were not married until February 1628, and, had she been born at the end of that year, she would have been just seventeen. Her husband, more than twice her age, was in fact her great-uncle. Alexander Norman's first wife, as we have seen, was Dorcas Chambers, *née* Day, the sister of Frances's grandmother Elizabeth. Unlikely though this marriage seems, the groom is clearly the same Alexander Norman. However, it is possible he was slightly younger than the age on the marriage allegation, as this would have made him twenty-two years old when he started his seven-year apprenticeship as a cooper in 1611. Most boys taken on were aged between fourteen and sixteen years, but only three years after completing his time he married the forty-one-year-old Dorcas.

By June 1624 Alexander Norman had become Cooper to the Ordnance. His 'allowance' was three pounds a quarter and was the same amount as that paid to the other artificers 'dailie attendant and emploied in the said office'. In addition there are numerous bills for 'casques, hoopes and cooperage by him made and done and brought into His Majesties stoares and there emploied about powder matches and other necessaries'. These show that he was paid for cooperage over and above his quarterly allowance.[20]

The Ordnance was at that time situated in the Minories, near the Tower of London, on the site of an old convent or, to give it its full title, the Abbey of the minoresses of St Mary of the Order of St Clare. The site had been held by the Crown since 1563, the church of the dissolved abbey becoming Holy Trinity Minories and the great mansion house being turned into the principal storehouse for the Ordnance. Other buildings were converted into workshops and residences.

Frances went to live in the Tower Hill precinct of St Botolph, Aldgate, where her husband paid an annual rent of six pounds for a house.[21]

Alexander Norman made every type of barrel for the Ordnance – grandbarrels, budgebarrels, casks for musket shot and double-casked barrels for powder. Budgebarrels were smaller than ordinary powder barrels and had leather tops which could easily be opened and closed; they were carried next to the cannon in action.

In the last quarter of 1627, the year that the elder Tradescant went to the Isle of Rhé, he was busy supplying additional cooperage. Even in November he was paid for sending 120 barrels of powder in double caskes 'on horseback to Plymouth', but unless the bill was post-dated these must have arrived too late.

Alexander Norman's barrels found their way into various forts around the country, on to pinnaces, frigates and other naval vessels, as well as to the army in Ireland. He supervised the packing of the barrels before they left for action, employing additional labour for this job. To give just one example, in 1631 four men were employed for four days at 1s. 8d. a day per man for 'casquing upp of ye Burreshott in His Majesties Stoares'.[22]

On 1 December 1641 he received payment from Sir John Heydon, Lieutenant-General of the Ordnance. It was for the charge of 'hyring teames to carry muniton to Westchester [Chester] viz ffor double casque for powder, and shott, and for driffat hoopes to packe upp Match, by him provided and brought into His Majesties stoares, and afterwards sent for Ireland'. Alexander Norman receipted this bill in his own hand.[23]

In the following year Sir John Heydon left his house in the Minories and went to join the King at York. London was in the hands of Parliament. Alexander Norman remained at his job. His allowance continued to be paid regularly until June 1649, when there is a gap in payments to all artificers for three and a half years, which must have made their lives difficult. They were paid in the end but not until December 1652. There are no entries recorded in his or any other artificer's name thereafter.[24]

Alexander Norman was active in the Cooper's Company during most of his life. He paid his tenpence quarterage as a 'householder' regularly until the end of 1651, and, as he took on his last apprentice in Michaelmas 1653, he must have continued his payments although these are not recorded. He joined the livery in 1631, was elected and sworn Younger Warden in 1647 but unusually did not go on to serve as Upper Warden and Master, although he was twice nominated for the former office.[25]

His cooperage must have been large because he took on many apprentices, often having five or six at the same time in different stages of training. Most signed on for seven or eight years, but one was apprenticed for nine years for 'all sorts lasts'.[26] He evidently kept in touch with his family in Herefordshire, as several of his apprentices came from that county. One, Paul Norman, whom he took on in 1627, the son of John Norman of Hereford, a shoemaker, was probably a relation.

Alexander Norman was buried at St Botolph's, Aldgate, on 2 September 1657. He did not leave a will, but Frances was granted letters of administration on the 15th. He and Frances do not appear to have had any children. There is no record of any baptism in the parish records of St Botolph's and, had any children survived, they would undoubtedly have been mentioned in the wills of her father and stepmother.

What happened to Frances after her husband's death remains a mystery. The Hearth Tax returns of 1666 show an empty house in Windmill Court in the Ward of Faringdon Within in the name of a 'widow Norman', and a Frances Norman married William Ranes at St James, Clerkenwell, on 17 May 1667. But, as Hester made her will in September of that year and Frances is not mentioned in it, she had almost certainly died.

The cooper's intabulation mark
of Alexander Norman

Chapter 11

Adapting to the Times

How long the younger Tradescant was able to continue working at Oatlands is not known, for apart from the original entry in the State Papers which records that he had taken over from his father no payments made to him can be traced. Early in the civil war Prince Rupert made the palace his headquarters, and the King was taken there as a prisoner in 1647.

In the vestry of Meopham parish church there hangs a document which shows that on 12 April 1648 Tradescant claimed forty pounds under an 'Ordinance of both Howses of Parliament' dated 21 September 1643 'for Worke to be don for amending the Walks in the Vineyard Garden & for Worke to be don to the Gardens at Oatelands, & for repairing the Bowling Greene there'.

The receipt, which Tradescant signed, shows that he was given only half the money 'in part' payment, but he may well have received the other half at another date. Another copy of this document, possibly Tradescant's own, can be found enclosed in the 'Book of Benefactors' to the Ashmolean Museum.

The ordinance referred to ordered all revenue due to the Crown to be seized and handed over to Thomas Faulconbridge, who was to act as Receiver-General and was also empowered to pay from this money such debts as were due.

The gardens at Oatlands were certainly kept up until the Parliamentary Survey of 1650, after which the buildings were dismantled for the resale value of the materials and this once great palace disappeared as though it had never been. Many of the bricks were sold to line the lock walls of the Wey canal, while the orange trees, 'about three score' in number, fetched twenty pounds.[1] An excavation at the site uncovered a seventeenth-century melon glass, perhaps once used by the gardeners to the Rose and Lily Queen.

Tradescant obviously had to fall back on his other source of income, the South Lambeth garden and museum. On 14 September 1647 a foreign visitor called Rasmus Bartholin wrote to the famous Danish collector Ole Worm:

There is however one thing that I must not fail to mention, and that is Mr Tredoscus' collection of artefacts, which I have viewed with particular care and admiration; it would however have moved me to even greater admiration if I had not been convinced that your very well equipped collection is many parasangs ahead of his, although I did not have your museum catalogue at hand, and I have not ever succeeded in obtaining a view of the latest edition of it. I cannot deny however that he possesses excellent objects in the way of natural curiosities, brought back from India. He has promised to have an inventory of them printed.[2]

Two years later, however, it seems that Tradescant was thinking of selling The Ark. In 1649 the Puritan educationalist and natural philosopher Samuel Hartlib, whose great interest lay in husbandry and the general spreading of knowledge and ideas, jotted down in his *Ephemerides*, a sort of diary documenting the people he met and the ideas and information that they passed on to him, that 'John Tradusken if hee might have a hundred lib. per annum offers to part with all his Rarities'.

The collection, he suggested, might be added to the University of Cambridge, by which means they might 'outstrip Oxford in their bookish-library'. He had been told by Dr Robert Child that Tradescant offered to sell the rarities for one hundred pounds a year, when they were really worth more than a thousand. He added: 'But then the advantage is that his son being brought up to looke to the Botanical Garden and plants the charge of keeping one of purpose to attend those businesses is clearly saved.' By this Hartlib presumably meant that, as Tradescant's son was more interested in the garden and had been brought up to supervise it, by disposing of the museum collection for an annuity of one hundred pounds Tradescant would be saved the cost of employing a keeper. Presumably the sum of a hundred pounds represented his profit from visitors less the cost of the keeper.

Samuel Hartlib was an admirer of Tradescant, whom, he recorded, 'daily raiseth new and curious things'. In pointing out that plants brought to England from hot countries 'do flourish with us', he cited as an example 'the great Spanish Cane (much used by Weavers and Vintners)' that John Tradescant 'brought from the Western-Isle, and it flourisheth well in his garden, and groweth great and well'.[3] In fact the Spanish cane (*Arundo donax* L.) was first received by the elder Tradescant as *Herunde hispanica* in 1632. Evidently his son picked up another in the Azores on one of his trips home from Virginia.

Hartlib's informant, Robert Child, came from a wealthy Kent family. Although he had qualified as a doctor, he was more interested in the spread of scientific knowledge. He had lived in Massachusetts for some years, not practising medicine but studying the environment and prospecting for raw materials.

In the same year, 1649, it was reported that the eminent Hatton Garden doctor George Bate was offering to endow a garden for the College of Physicians, either at the Tradescants' or at the Earl of Arundel's.[4] The College of Physicians, although soon to acquire a museum through William Harvey, had yet to establish a physic garden for its own purposes. Despite the fact that there is no record of any formal agreement, perhaps some sort of arrangement did come out of this idea, as the 1656 list includes many more medicinal plants than the elder Tradescant had been growing in 1634. It could also explain why the *Musaeum Tradescantianum*, when eventually published, was dedicated to the College of Physicians.

The Puritan thinkers were happy to absorb any co-operative ex-Royalist with knowledge and expertise, their considerations being purely practical (George Bate, for instance, treated in turn as his patients Charles I, Cromwell and Charles II). Tradescant obviously fell into this category. He was valuable to them because they were particularly concerned with the cultivation and spread of useful plants and were desperately anxious – and in fact did much – to improve the hitherto often poor standards of horticulture and agriculture in the country. Perhaps this explains why Tradescant grew, besides medicinal plants, many food plants such as beans, peas, root vegetables, oats, barley and wheat. It was probably a case of having to adjust to the times, as the younger Tradescant was obviously just as interested in the exotics as his father had been and still grew these alongside the more mundane species. To many it must have been the broad range represented in his garden that made the collection so interesting.

That Tradescant had long since been absorbed into this elite circle is shown by a letter written by Robert Child on 1 March 1645 to his friend John Winthrop junior 'at his house in New England': 'I received likewise some seeds which I have delivered to the Gardiner of Yorke garden and Mr Tredeschan, who are very thankfull to you for them, and have returned diverse sorts which you shall Receive by the hands of Mr Willoughby. I have sent you 5 or six sorts of vines in a Caske marked, with some prun grafts, some pyrocanthus trees, and very many sor[ts] of our Common plants, and seeds. I desire you that they may be carefully planted with all Expedition, and I am confident in 3 yeares wine may be made as good as any in France . . .'[5]

Winthrop was later to become the first Governor of Connecticut and probably did more than anyone else in those early days of settlement to take scientific knowledge to the New World.

By 1646, however, it seems that Tradescant had found a new interest, as a merchant. John Morris, lamenting that with the deaths of Johnson and Parkinson the 'crop of Botanists' had 'become so thin', reported that 'Tradescant himself almost lives in banishment from the art, so far has he virtually given up these studies and now maintains trade with the Canary Islands.'[6] Contemporary London merchants were exporting 'Hides, Ginger,

Tobacco, Cochenil, and other India goods' to the Canary Islands under licence.[7] Perhaps Tradescant was involved in this trade, but, if so, the venture was short-lived, as three years later Morris once again sent his gardener to consult with Tradescant about a 'sea cabbage' and was acknowledging him in a letter as one of 'our three great men most experienced in plant affairs', this time bracketing his name with those of Edward Morgan and an unidentified botanist called Blackburn.

Tradescant received another foreign visitor in 1652. This time it was Willum Worm, the son of the eminent collector, who was on a visit to England. On 26 June his father, Ole Worm, wrote disparagingly: 'You have met various scholars, but do not write how they have received you. About Tradescant I have previously heard that he was an Idiot. You neglect Arundel's marbles.'[8]

In that same year Tradescant's only son, John the third, died. It is not known from what cause. His death occurred on 11 September 1652, and he was buried four days later in the same tomb as his mother and grandfather.[9]

A year later Tradescant was again on his way to Virginia. This time it was a William Lea who paid his passage in order to claim land. On 6 February 1654 he was granted 500 acres in Charles City County, 'on South side of the James River & West side of an Indian Swamp called Ohoreek'. Altogether he transported ten persons. They were John Trediskin, John Aires, Bertrum Obert, Thomas Austen, his wife, John Austin, Richard Austin, Edward Golbourn, Jane Glinn and himself. It is surprising to find the recurrence of so many of the same names from Tradescant's previous journey. Despite the variations in spelling, all except for Jane Glinn, whose first trip it was, are obviously old friends who had been home on a visit. This time (H)obert, instead of acquiring more land for himself, has his passage paid by William Lea.[10]

Again we do not know how long Tradescant stayed in Virginia. He was probably there for the winter of 1653–4, Lea not claiming his land until February of that year. However, in view of the fact that he did not pay his dues to the Gardeners' Company for four years, it is possible that his visit was slightly more prolonged.

Chapter 12

Enter Ashmole

John Tradescant first met Elias Ashmole on 15 June 1650. The latter records the event in his autobiographical notes with these words: 'My selfe, wife & Dr Wharton, went to visit Mr John Tradescant at South Lambeth.'[1] It was an auspicious day for him.

Ashmole was the son of a Lichfield saddler. He was educated at the local grammar school and as a chorister of the cathedral. In 1633 he moved to London and embarked on the legal training that was later to stand him in good stead, for he eventually became an able solicitor. He was admitted to Clement's Inn in 1641. In 1644 he studied for a time at Brasenose College, Oxford, and, like many others, claimed to have developed a lasting attachment to the university. At Oxford he studied natural philosophy, mathematics, astronomy and astrology. Astrology was then both fashionable and legitimate, a worthy subject of study in universities. Together with alchemy, it was to have an enormous influence on Ashmole's life. Rarely thereafter did he take any step without first asking a 'horary question', examining his horoscope to discover the answers to even the most mundane of the problems that confronted him in his daily life.

Oxford was, of course, the headquarters of the King, and during the civil war Ashmole supported the Royalist cause. Through friends he was granted several minor appointments in Lichfield and Worcester. When these towns surrendered in the summer of 1646 he was, however, allowed to go free after giving the standard undertaking never again to bear arms against Parliament.

It was not until 1648 that Ashmole started 'simpling', but from that time onwards he took a keen interest in botany, visiting the Oxford botanic garden the following year and John Goodyer's garden at Petersfield in 1651.

From humble beginnings, Elias Ashmole was to rise to fame and wealth. An ambitious social climber, he was prepared to go to extreme lengths to gain his ends. He was undoubtedly clever, with wide-ranging interests, and he fulfilled all his official positions with efficiency and integrity. Although an astute lawyer, his great strength lay in historical research and his history of

The Institution, Laws & Ceremonies of the Most Noble Order of the Garter (1672) and his *Theatrum Chemicum Britannicum* (1652), a collection of old English alchemical writings, are still regarded as classics.

An early, if not a particularly active, member of the Royal Society, Ashmole was fascinated by scientific discovery; he little realized that the experimentation he so applauded would ring the death knell on his two fanatical obsessions, alchemy and astrology.

Anthony Wood described him as 'the greatest virtuoso and curioso that ever was known', but his posthumous fame rests on the foundation of the Ashmolean Museum at Oxford, a distinction which, as we shall see, perhaps really should have gone to another.

Ashmole married three times. His first wife, Eleanor Manwaring, died in 1641. After a lengthy courtship and several dalliances he married his second wife, Mary, Lady Manwaring, the daughter of Sir William Forster, in November 1649. Apparently not related to Ashmole's first wife, she was already thrice widowed and, having been born in 1597, was nearly twenty years older than her fourth husband. She was also rich.

Three years previously, Ashmole's horoscope had predicted that he would 'labour for a fortune with a wife and get it'.[2] The prediction seems to have come true. On 16 June 1647 he recorded that 'It pleased God to put me in mind that I was now placed in the Condition I alwaies desired, which was, that I might be enabled to live to my selfe & Studies, without being forced to take paines for a livelyhood in the world.'[3] He was probably already receiving an allowance from his future wife for acting as her legal adviser in successful lawsuits against her first husband's family.

This was no doubt one cause of her family's disapproval of the match, which was such that Humphrey Stafford, one of her sons by her first marriage, tried to murder Ashmole while he lay ill in bed.

Ashmole survived, married his rich wife and buried himself in the alchemical studies that were to produce the *Theatrum*. By 1652, however, a shadow had fallen over the marriage; in January Ashmole noted that he was 'astranged' from his wife and he had to effect a reconciliation. Mary Ashmole may simply have been lonely, for on 11 May 1652 her husband asked the horary question 'Whether my wife shall have any disgrace by going to Mr Tradescants to live / Proposed by her'.[4] While, with Ashmole's leanings towards the occult, the horary question was inevitable, the wording of it shows his lack of respect for the eminent botanist and collector whom he later claimed as a friend.

Nothing is known of how Mary Ashmole became friendly with the Tradescants – and particularly, one presumes, with Hester Tradescant – but evidently the answer to the horary question was satisfactory, as a few days later she seems to have moved in at South Lambeth. On 28 May Ashmole recorded the words: 'I & my wife Tabled this Summer at Mr Tredescants.'[5]

Although Ashmole was renting a house at Blackfriars at the time, the idea of gaining access to the Tradescants' garden and collection cannot have been unattractive to him. His own magpie instincts had yet to be aroused, but there was plenty to interest him in the famous Ark, and the garden provided endless scope for furthering his botanical knowledge.

On 2 August Ashmole took Tradescant 'to heare the Witchis tryed' at Maidstone Assizes.[6] The Kent summer sessions in that year dealt with various people accused of bewitching children, adults, pigs, sheep, mares and grain. Six women were ordered to be hanged, and others of both sexes were gaoled.[7]

Ashmole seems to have left his wife at South Lambeth while he went on a three-month journey into the country in mid-August, so that Mary Ashmole was presumably there when the Tradescants suffered the tragic loss of their son. Ashmole was back in London at the beginning of November, but three weeks later Mrs Ashmole again returned to the Tradescants 'to stay some tyme there'. With them she watched a comet in the sky on the night of 21 December, and Ashmole records that she left the Tradescants' house on 17 January 1653.[8] However, as Dorothy Manwaring, the sister of Ashmole's first wife, is recorded as having come 'to live with my wife' between 18 December and 16 January, these visits to the Tradescants were presumably only short ones.[9]

We can never know for certain why the Tradescants permitted the Ashmoles to 'table' at South Lambeth, a move that was to have fateful consequences, but Ashmole (if he had not already done so) was quick to consolidate the relationship by offering, together with Dr Thomas Wharton, to assist Tradescant in cataloguing the museum collection. In his address 'To the Ingenious Reader' that prefaces the *Musaeum Tradescantianum*, Tradescant records that 'About three yeares agoe, (by the perswasion of some friends) I was resolved to take a Catalogue' of the famous collection and of the plants growing in the garden. The argument used by these 'friends' was that the rarities 'being more for variety than any one place known in Europe could afford', such a catalogue would be both 'an honour to our Nation' and of benefit to enquiring visitors.

With the assistance of his 'two worthy friends', Dr Wharton and Ashmole, and after a great deal of work, a draft was made which was left in his hands to check. But the death of his only son, the doctor's long illness and Ashmole's 'unhappy Law-suits' caused this first draft to lie neglected for a year. Then the work was further delayed because Tradescant's 'kinde friend' Wenceslaus Hollar was too busy to finish the illustrations.

The *Musaeum Tradescantianum* was eventually published in 1656. For some reason Ashmole offered to pay for its publication, which immediately put Tradescant in his debt. As he must have been well able to have stood the cost himself, it is difficult to imagine the reasons that persuaded him to accept this offer. With the education that he had received he must have been well capable of compiling the catalogue on his own but presumably accepted help in order to speed up the lengthy process of listing and identifying the mass of objects in the collection. He must have known far more about them than either of his collaborators, neither of whom are likely to have ever even met his father, although both are listed as benefactors. Ashmole is specifically cited as having given a bird 'taken upon the Thames', and Wharton is probably the more reticent 'T.W.' noted as the donor of a fossil and some 'Catt' and fish relics.

The book was dedicated to the President and members of the College of Physicians for whom, as we have seen, Tradescant was possibly cultivating medicinal plants. Sir Edward Alston was president in that year, having just taken over from Sir Francis Prujean, an eminent physician who had his own laboratory, a 'workhouse for turning & other Mechanics' and a collection of pictures.[10] Alston had been selected on the recommendation of Dr William Harvey, famous for his discovery of the circulation of the blood, who had declined the appointment because of failing health, having founded the College's own museum two years earlier. Harvey had been educated at the King's School, Canterbury, but well before Tradescant's time.

Dr Thomas Wharton, still remembered for his research on glands (the duct conveying saliva to the mouth being named after him), had been a fellow of the College for six years. Much later, with a large and important London practice, he was to enhance his reputation even further by being one of the very few doctors to remain in London to treat the victims of the Great Plague. He shared Ashmole's interest in astrology and consulted him frequently on horary questions relating to his practice and his personal life.

The introductory verses for the *Musaeum Tradescantianum* were written by Walter Stonehouse, who described himself as 'worst of poets'. He also compiled suitable anagrams: John Tradescant became 'Cannot hide Arts', while his own name, Gaulturus Stonehouse, was appropriately transposed to 'Theologus servus natus'. In 1631 Stonehouse had been appointed Rector of Darfield in Yorkshire, where he collected coins and medals and established a famous garden. It consisted of five beds laid out in knots, a saffron garth and many fruit trees. Altogether he listed 866 plants growing there. A friend of Parkinson, he had taken part in a botanizing expedition to north Wales organized by the apothecary Thomas Johnson in 1639, and, as his plants included many from overseas, with fourteen species from Virginia, it is probable that these were acquired from the Tradescants.

In 1648 he was ejected from his living and put in prison by the Parliamentary Commissioners. When he was freed he went again to visit his garden and added a sad little note in Latin to his plant list: 'Alas! but few are there today, and I have no hope of founding a new colony.'[11] He is then thought to have settled in London, no doubt becoming a regular visitor to South Lambeth, as he must have come to know the Tradescants well.

Having written the eulogistic verses, he died the year before they were published, leaving many botanical notes. In addition to the two printed verses, his original manuscript shows that he contemplated a third, possibly to commemorate John Tradescant III, which is crossed out.[12]

The *Musaeum Tradescantianum* was illustrated with portraits of the two Tradescants made by the Czech émigré Wenceslaus Hollar, who had been brought to England under the patronage of the Earl of Arundel in 1637. In London he became acquainted with Ashmole, who seems to have helped to find him commissions. As a Royalist sympathizer Hollar had to leave the country for some years, returning in 1652. Exploited by his publishers, he toiled for long hours with deteriorating eyesight, dying penniless but leaving for posterity not only a mass of portraits but also immortal views of London that recorded many buildings subsequently destroyed in the Great Fire. Evidently he became a lifelong friend of the Tradescants,

The catalogue was a success when it was published, probably on 1 May, the date it was acquired by George Thomason;[13] it is thought to have cost 1s. 10d.[14] Like the elder Tradescant's catalogue it contains many uncorrected errors, particularly in the plant section where lines have been omitted, and English equivalents do not always agree with the Latin. This suggests that Tradescant left the task of proof-reading to his clerk.

Four years later, with Charles II restored to the throne, a new edition was rushed out. The only difference is in the dedication. The page with that to the College of Physicians has been hastily cut out about a quarter of an inch from the central stitching, leaving part of the original text still showing, and a new page has been inserted.

No sooner was the King back on his throne when his father's Master of the Revels, Sir Henry Herbert, tried to regain his old powers. As a Royalist he had suffered by having his estates sequestered, and his job had been suspended during the Commonwealth when revels were discouraged, so his income had been severely depleted.

During Charles I's reign he had been responsible not only for arranging extravagant court dramas but for issuing licences for every other kind of public entertainment throughout the land. These ranged from live animal shows of an elephant, a beaver, a 'possum' and dromedaries, to vaulters, tumblers, conjurers and those who showed waxworks. All these and many more had been required to pay him a fee for the privilege of a licence to perform.[15] On the face of it, it seems rather surprising that the Tradescants had managed to escape his clutches.

Now that people were going to be allowed to enjoy themselves again, Herbert saw a golden opportunity to regain both his lost power and his income. The popular museum must have seemed an obvious target. He wrote to Mr Ralph Nutting, Officer to His Majesty's Office of the Revels:

TO THE

SACRED MAJESTY

OF

Charles the II.

By the Grace of God

KING of *England*, *Scotland*,
France and *Ireland*, Defender of
the Faith, &c.

JOHN TRADESCANT,

His Majefties moft obedient
and moft Loyal Subject,

IN ALL HUMILITY
Offereth thefe Collections.

Dedication page of the second edition
of the *Musaeum Tradescantianum*

'Whereas information is given me that John Tradeskyn does make shew of several strange creatures without authority from his Majesties Office of the Revells. These are therefore in His Majesties name to will and require you to bring before me the said John Tradeskyn to answer for the said contempt, and this shallbe your sufficient warrant. Dated at the office of the Revells this 4th day of May 1661.'[16]

The museum was certainly open in the previous month when, on a sight-seeing visit to London, Brampton Gurdon, the son of a Norfolk MP, had on his itinerary not only 'John Tradeskin's rarities' but also the 'Floating Bowling Alley' and the 'Swimming Bath at Westminster'.[17] But when he received Herbert's summons Tradescant appealed to the King for his support and in the meantime closed The Ark, an event noted by the poet and miniaturist Thomas Flatman:

> Thus John Tradeskin starves our greedy eyes,
> By boxing up his new-found Rarities;[18]

These lines are included in a poem written in answer 'To Mr Sam Austin of Wadham Col. Oxon on his most unintelligible Poems', the latter referring to Austin's *Panegyric on the Restoration*, which had just been published.

The King dealt with the matter effectively. In the following month he issued his command, although the actual date has been left blank.

Complaint being made unto us by John Tredeskyn that he hath been lately served by a Warrant from Sir Henry Herbert for a contemptuous practice as is pretended, in taking the confidences to shew his rarities to the invading of the rights which do belong to the Master of ye Revells. And wee being satisfied, that the fact, in itself, is not onely of very harmless import, & not to be found prejudicial to any person; but that it hath been practiced, is continued, uninterruptedly, by him & his Father, with the Allowance or Good Liking (at least) of our Progenitors, for many years past. Our expresse pleasure & Comand is, that the said Tredeskyn bee suffered, freely & quietly to proceed, as formerly, in entertaining & receiving all persons, whose Curiosity shall invite them to the delight of seeing his rare & ingenious Coleccions of Art & Nature: and to this purpose that the said warrant be recalled and noe proceeding had against him for or by occasion of the same. And hereof all Persons whome it doeth or may concerne are to take notice and to conform themselves. And this shalbee sufficient Warrant on this behalf. Given at our Court at Whitehall the   of June 1661.[19]

Meanwhile on 7 May Tradescant had been warned to appear as a witness to 'certify the truth . . . concerning a ryott latelye committed . . . against the public peace'. He was to testify about the stopping-up of a highway. The hearing took place at '2 of the clocke in the afternoon' at the Queen's Arms Tavern in Southwark.

Five months later he was summoned to appear at Surrey Quarter Sessions. His offence, with eighteen others, was that of having wilfully 'refused to pay their assessment for poor relief there, to the grave damage of all parishioners and inhabitants, in evil example and against the peace'. But it proved to be a mistake and, with most of the others, he was exonerated. In the same month he was called upon for jury service.[20]

While Tradescant went back and forth from the courts, Ashmole had been launched on the career of historian which was to prove his forte. Charles II, with whom he had rapidly ingratiated himself, granted him the office of Windsor Herald in June 1660. In the following year he also became a member of the Royal Society.

Chapter 13

The Deed of Gift

By 1659 the Tradescants were beginning to concern themselves with the future of their collection. Evidently the question of to whom it should be entrusted after they were gone was a topic of much discussion. John's beloved only son was dead. The elder Tradescant had suggested that the collection should be offered to the Prince, but he was still banished from the land with little evidence of an imminent return. Besides, the Tradescants wanted to ensure that the collection was preserved for posterity, and they realized that it would not be safe to leave it to any individual from whom it might be too easily extracted or 'imbezzled'.

The idea of donating the rarities to a university must already have occurred to them, as two years earlier Hartlib had noted that 'John Tradescant has no roomes for his Rarities but Oxford hath roome enough.'[1]

Ashmole had been casting covetous eyes in their direction for some time. He longed to possess the famous rarities. He had carefully ingratiated himself into the Tradescants' favour by helping to prepare the museum catalogue, for which he afterwards tried to take full credit. Moreover he had insisted on paying for its publication, which debt they duly acknowledged. No doubt Elias Ashmole could be excellent company when he wanted. Pepys found him diverting, describing him as 'a very ingenious gentleman',[2] although Evelyn rather dismissed him as being addicted to astrology, 'though I believe not learned; but very Industrious'.[3] Industrious he certainly was, and his industry at South Lambeth was about to produce its rewards.

Ashmole's autobiographical notes, which are in the style of a diary and often referred to as such, were written when he was sixty-one, nearly twenty years after the events that concern us here.[4] They record that on 12 December 1659 'Mr Tredescant & his wife told me they had been long considering upon whome to bestow their Closet of Rarities when they dyed, & at last had resolved to give it unto me.' Two days later 'they gave their Scrivenor instructions to draw a deed of Guift of the said Closet to me'. This deed was duly sealed and delivered on the 16th.[5]

Ashmole was later to claim that the deed, leaving the collection to him after the death of whichever Tradescant lived the longer, having been drawn up, signed and sealed, was delivered to him before witnesses together with a Queen Elizabeth milled shilling as a token of the entire Cabinet. Hester Tradescant, having also signed the deed, then asked to keep it, and Ashmole gave it to her.

Hester never disputed that the deed of gift had been signed and sealed. Rather she claimed that, on the evening of 16 December, her husband had arrived home 'distempered', meaning that he was intoxicated. He had brought back four strangers with him, none of whom she knew, and when some writing was produced they both inadvisedly signed it without first reading the document. When she saw the milled shilling exchanging hands she was afraid that the fact that she had signed the deed as a witness might be prejudicial to her own interests. And when she read the document she told her husband 'that she thought he would not have suffered himself to be so much abused and threw the said writing to him'.

At this, as she recalled events, Ashmole said: 'I pray you take it and consider thereof and if you like it not I will not have it for a world.'[6]

Ashmole, the crafty solicitor, knew that he was quite safe in so doing. A deed of gift had been signed in front of witnesses. It contained no clause of revocation. Whatever happened, the rarities must by law in the due course of time become his.

Next morning Hester confronted her husband with the deed that he had sealed the previous evening and asked him whether he realized what was written in it. They had intended to leave the rarities to Ashmole in trust for a university, as they both recognized the importance of saving the collection for future generations and had agreed that it should not be left in private hands.

When they carefully read through the deed they found that, contrary to their intentions, the collection was to go to Ashmole without restriction. There and then they decided to cut off the seal and obliterate the signatures in the belief that this would automatically cancel the deed of gift. They discussed whether or not to burn it but in the end decided to keep it as proof of how badly Ashmole had treated them. Indeed John was so annoyed at the way he had been taken advantage of that he declared to his wife that Ashmole 'should never have a groat of his'.[7]

Ashmole, however, had other ideas.

On 22 April 1662 John Tradescant died. He was buried in the family tomb three days later.[8] His last will, made a full year before he died, makes his final wishes in regard to the collection absolutely clear. It reads:

The last will and testament of me John Tredescant. In the name of God, Amen. The fourth day of April in the yeare of our Lord God one thousand six hundred sixtie-one, I, John Tredescant of South Lambeth in the Countie of Surrey, Gardiner, being at this present of perfect health, minde, and memorie, thanks be therefore given to Almightie God, and calling to minde the uncertaintie of death, and being desirous whilst I am in a Capacity to settle and dispose of such things as God of his goodnesse hath bestowed upon me, doe make and declare this my last Will and Testament as followeth. First and principally I commend and yield my soule into the hands of Almighty God my Creator, and my bodie to the Earth to be decently (according to the quality wherein I have lived) interred as neere as can be to my late deceased Father John Tredescant, and my sonne who lye buried in the parish Churchyard of Lambeth aforesaid, at the discretion of my Executrix hereafter named; hoping by and through the merits, death, and passion of my onely Saviour and Redeemer Jesus Christ to have full remission of all my Sinnes, and to see my God in the Land of the Living; and for my temporall Estate I doe will, bequeath and dispose thereof as followeth. That is to saie, I will that all such debts as shall be by me justly due and owing to anie person or persons whatsoever at the time of my decease (if anie such be) shall be truly paid and satisfied, and after my Funeral charges shall be defrayed, for the doeing whereof I appoint the summe of twenty pounds or thereabouts shall be expended by my Executrix but not more. Item, I give and bequeath upon the condition hereafter mentioned to my daughter Frances Norman the summe of ten pounds of Lawfull money of England, which I will shall be paid unto her within six moneths after my decease, and likewise I do forgive her the sum of fourscore pounds or thereabouts, Principall Money, besides the Interest thereof which I long since lent her late deceased husband Alexander Norman. Provided that shee and her husband, if she shall be then againe married, give my Executrix a generall release for the same. Item, I give and bequeath to my two namesakes Robert Tredescant and Thomas Tredescant, of Walberswick in the Countie of Suffolk, to eache of them the summe of five shillings apiece in remembrance of my love, and to every childe or children of them the said Robert and Thomas that shall be living at the time of my decease the summe of two shillings and sixpence apiece. Item, I give to Mris Marie Edmonds, the daughter of my loving Friend Edward Harper, the summe of one hundred pounds, to be paid unto her after my wife's decease; and in case she die before my said wife, my will is and I doe hereby give and bequeath the said summe of one hundred pounds, after my wife's decease, to my Foure God-children, vizt. Hester, John, Leonard, and Elizabeth Edmonds, sonnes and daughters of the said Mris Mary Edmonds Equally to be divided amongst them, share and share alike . . . Item, I doe hereby give, will, devise and bequeath to my Cosin Katherine King, widdow, after the decease of my wife, the Little House commonly called the Welshmans house situate in South Lambeth aforesaid together with that Little Piece of Ground now enclosed thereunto adjoyning; and to her heirs and assignes for ever. Item, I give, devize, and bequeath my Closet of Rarities to my dearly beloved wife Hester Tredescant during her naturall Life, and after decease I give and bequeath the same to the Universities of Oxford or Cambridge, to which of them shee shall think fitt at her decease. As for such other of my friends and kindred as I should nominate for Rings and small tokens of my Love, I leave that to the Care of my said wife to bestow how manie and to whome shee shall think deserving. The rest and Residue of all my Estate Reall and personall wheresoever and whatsoever, I wholly give, devize, and bequeath to my deare and loving wife Hester Tredescant, and to her heires and assignes for ever. And I do hereby nominate, ordaine, constitute and appoint my said Loving Wife Hester Tredescant full and sole Executrix of this my last will and Testament; and I doe desire Dr Nurse and Mr Mark Cottle to be Overseers of this my last Will and Testament, and I give to each of them fortie shillings apiece. Lastly, I do hereby revoke all Wills by me formerly made, and will that this onely shall stand and be my last will and Testament, and no other. In Witnesse whereof I the said John Tredescant to this my present last will and testament have set my hand and seale the daie and [year] above written.

John Tredescant.

Signed, sealed, published, and declared by the said John Tredescant the Testator, as and for his last Will and Testament, in the presence of John Scaldwell, Foulk Bignall, Robert Thompson, Junris, Ric. Newcourt, Junr, Richard Hoare, Notary Publique.[9]

Hester was granted probate on 5 May 1662. Of the witnesses, John Scaldwell and Foulk Bignall were both near neighbours involved in parish affairs.[10] Mark Cottle, one of the overseers, was Registrar of the Prerogative Court of Canterbury, and Dr Thomas Nurse had a thriving practice in Westminster. Mary Edmonds was the widow of a South Lambeth victualler called Robert Edmonds, who had died in 1655.

The will shows that Tradescant had now decided to leave the rarities to his wife for her lifetime and then to either Oxford or Cambridge University as she thought fit. He had taken the precaution of making his will while he was still 'in perfect health', something of a novelty in the seventeenth century when most signatories described themselves as 'sick in body', convinced that it tempted providence not to leave such affairs until the last moment. Tradescant obviously believed that these, his final wishes in regard to the collection, would be carried out.

Ashmole wasted no time. Within a month of John Tradescant's death he preferred a Bill in Chancery 'against Mrs Tredescant, for the Rarities her Husband had setled on me'.[11]

In his Bill of Complaint Ashmole, after taking full credit for the compilation of the *Musaeum Tradescantianum* and pointing out the debt that the Tradescants were under because he had paid for its publication, claimed that John Tradescant had ordered his scrivenor to draw up a deed granting the rarities to him. These were to be held in trust by whichever Tradescant was the longer lived, who was to preserve them 'without spoil', and within six months of receiving them after their deaths he was to make a payment of £100 to Mary Edmonds or, if she was already dead, to her four children.

Ashmole admitted that he could not remember the exact wording of the deed as he was no longer in possession of it, having entrusted it to Hester, but claimed that it had been delivered to him, together with the shilling, in the presence of several witnesses, including Hester who had herself been a signatory to it.

He claimed that, since her husband's death, Hester had 'possessed herselfe' of the collection, which was rightly his; and that 'endeavouringe to defeate and defraude' him she 'giveth out in speeches' that many items had been 'passed away' by her husband in his lifetime, that the collection had been altered and changed since the compilation of the catalogue and that those items newly acquired were not included in the deed, all of which he disputed.

He also alleged that Hester claimed to have burned the deed, declaring that he should never have the rarities as she would otherwise dispose of them, thus avoiding the 'intention of the said John Tradescant who was so careful that your orator should enjoy the same'. Moreover she now denied that her husband had ever made the deed of gift and refused to give particulars of the collection, thus preventing him from having any relief at Common Law.

Ashmole also claimed that Tradescant 'in some writing purporting his last will which he signed not long after the making of the said deed' – presumably an earlier will – had 'excepted his Closet of Rarities'. Ashmole confirmed that he was willing to allow Hester to continue to keep the rarities during her lifetime, 'preserving the same from spoil', and that he would make the payment to Mary Edmonds. Finally he asked for a writ of subpoena to direct Hester to answer these charges.

In her answer to this Bill of Complaint Hester acknowledged Ashmole's assistance in compiling the catalogue and agreed that it had been printed at his expense, but she denied that she had ever told him that her husband was resolved to bestow the Closet of Rarities upon him or that there had been any mention of financial consideration to Mary Edmonds.

She described the events as they have already been related, with her husband coming home 'distempered' with four strangers and how next morning they had cancelled the deed by 'cutting out the seal and razing out his name and the endorsement'. She claimed that Ashmole had never demanded the deed during her husband's lifetime, nor did he 'make any complaint for the want thereof. Nor pretend any title thereby', but now took advantage of her 'weakness'.

She said that her husband had made a previous will bequeathing the collection to 'the Kings most excellent Majesty', but because some 'private person might begg the same of his Majesty so as they should not be preserved to posterity he did alter that will and made another will as well'. This left the 'Closett' to her during her natural life; after her death it was to go to the University of Oxford or Cambridge as she thought fit.

Furthermore, as there had been no financial consideration, 'nothing did or could pass' by the said deed, which was only in the nature of a conveyance of a personal estate after two lives. She considered that the deed had been revoked by her husband's will and stated that she was now resolved to leave the collection to Oxford University and intended to preserve it 'with all care and diligence'. She denied endeavouring 'to defeate or defraude the complainant', desiring only that her 'late husbands will may be performed'. She agreed that her husband had parted with some of the catalogued rarities, acquiring others instead, but contested that she was in any way bound to disclose particulars of these changes as the defendant had no claim to them.

Moreover she denied affirming that she would 'grant away all her personall estate in her life time' but intended carrying out her husband's will and prayed to be 'honourably dismissed' with 'reasonable costs and charges'.[12]

It was two years before the case was heard. On 18 May 1664 Ashmole recorded, 'My Cause came to hearing in the Chancery against Mrs Tradescant.'[13]

Appearing for Ashmole were Sir John Glynne and Sir John Maynard, both King's Sergeants and the two most able advocates of the day. Hester's counsel went by the names of Gillingham and Keeke Eydon.

Ashmole produced as his witnesses Sara Barker, Edward Harman, Thomas Bowyer (who was probably related to Ashmole as this was his mother's maiden name), Dr William Curren, the physician, alchemist and mineralogist, and Elizabeth Dugdale, who was later to become his third wife.

Hester's witnesses were her cousins Katherine King, who lived in 'the Welshman's house' near by, Katherine's half-brother, the painter Cornelius de Neve, Mary Edmonds, to whom the payment was allegedly destined and obviously a great family friend, Richard Grimes, Mary Whetstone and the engraver Wenceslaus Hollar. Hester was also able to count on the notary public, Richard Hoare, who seems to have become a staunch friend of the family, and her old friend and neighbour, Foulk Bignall.

The case came up before the Lord Chancellor, the Earl of Clarendon. After hearing a summary of the evidence from both sides, during which Mr Gillingham claimed that 'the pretended deed' was 'gained by a surprise and afterwards cancelled' and Sir John Glynne retorted that Hester's answer was 'scandalous all over', Clarendon declared in favour of Ashmole.[14]

He found that 'the deed was fairly gained and well executed with the defendants consent and was made upon good and valuable consideracon and with intention to be irrevokable'. He decreed that the rarities now belonged to Ashmole and that there was no need, as had been suggested, to make the University of Oxford a party to the suit.

Although the case was much concerned with the 'valuable' (that is, financial) consideration to Mary Edmonds, Hester was correct in stating that there had been none. During the hearing it was claimed that 'it was not thought fitt to clogge the deed with the payment of the said £100 to Mrs Edmonds or her children to the end that the same might the better appeare to bee a free and generous gift'.

It was 'thereupon ordered and decreed' that Ashmole should 'have and enjoy all and singular these Bookes, Coynes, Medalls, Stones, Pictures, Mechanicks, Antiquities and all and every other the Raryties and Curiosities of what sort or kind soever whither naturall or artificiall and whatsoever was graunted by the said Deed as itt now stands good in court which were in the said John Tradescants said Closet or in or about his said house att South Lambeth the said 16th day of December 1659 when the said Deed was executed'.

The list could hardly have been more comprehensive and, by including the words 'in or about his said house', must also have included everything in the garden. Even though Hester was to retain the rarities for her lifetime, her hands were now completely tied. Indeed, there was worse to come.

In order to preserve the collection from 'spoil and embezzilment', a commission consisting of Sir Edward Bysshe, Clarenceux King of Arms, and William Dugdale, Norroy King of Arms, was appointed to 'repaire to Mistress Tradescants house' and to see that a 'catalogue of all the said Rarities whither naturall or artificiall be taken and made and to certify the particulars that are wantinge if any bee'. Both men were friends of Ashmole, the Windsor Herald. Dugdale was to become his father-in-law.

Hester was ordered to be examined on oath 'for the better discovering of the said particulars', and if anything was 'wanting or imbezzilled' she was to restore the same 'within the said Closett' and was to give such security for them as Sir William Glascocke, a Master in Chancery, should allow.'[15]

The judgement was clearly contrary to Tradescant's last wishes, but a deed of gift, even today, is irrevocable unless it contains a specific clause of revocation. Ashmole was absolutely within his legal rights. Whether he was morally right is another matter.

One of Hester's first tasks after her husband's death, long before this case was heard, had been to arrange for the erection of a tombstone over his grave. She had to apply for permission which was duly granted:

We whose names are hereafter written parishioners of the Parish of Lambeth in the County of Surrey do hereby give our free consent, yt Mrs Tredeskin wid. of Mr John Tredeskin late of Lambeth deceased shall erect a Tombstone in ye Church Yard of Lambeth aforesd over ye Place where her husband lyeth interred, And ye sd Mrs Tredeskin giving Security to pay to ye Church wardens of Lambeth £50 to 60 Kept as a stocke for ye use of ye poor of ye Parish as the Minister, Church Wardens and Parishioners shall think fit witness our hands this 12 May 1662.[16]

Fifteen parishioners signed in support.

Appropriately, Hester had the tomb sculpted in a strikingly novel design. The south end shows the Tradescant coat of arms, three fleurs-de-lys on a bend wavy, as it appeared in the *Musaeum Tradescantianum*, being impaled with a lion passant. As impaled arms are regarded as belonging to husband and wife, the lion was presumably Hester's. Opposite, on the other short end, were reproduced a hydra and a skull, with various trees curving round the corners. The east and west sides were decorated with shells, a crocodile, pyramids and broken columns.

It must have been considered a curious work of art even at the time. Drawings of the design were evidently put on sale, as Samuel Pepys made a note to get hold of a copy from the shoemaker turned book collector John Bagford, who bought books and prints on commission for his customers.[17] Pepys was successful and his copy is now with his other ephemera in the library of Magdalene College, Cambridge. It was from this reproduction of the original design that the tomb was able to be repaired to its original form by public subscription in 1773 and again in 1852.

Chapter 14

Hester Acquires a New Neighbour

Despite their acrimonious dispute in the lawcourts Hester Tradescant and Ashmole seem to have remained on reasonably good terms for the next few years. They were years when life itself became even more precarious than usual. 1665 brought the Great Plague, when people died like flies and London church registers needed additional pages to record the names of all the dead in 'these sad tymes'.

In 1666 came the Great Fire. This time there was little danger to life, but the flames engulfed thousands of buildings. Ashmole's valuable library, housed in his rooms in the Middle Temple, lay in peril as the flames flickered towards them. He was sufficiently quick off the mark to hire a boat and fill it twice over with books and manuscripts. He was lucky to find one available, as everyone else had the same idea.

It was to Hester that he took them. And, incredibly, she gave them house room in her South Lambeth home. Ashmole does not appear to have pressed for the two Kings of Arms to get to work, and perhaps she hoped that they might be further delayed or even put off altogether by this act of kindness. She must have realized the importance of the book collection and, despite their differences, came to Ashmole's rescue at a time of real need. She obviously appreciated rare and beautiful things. In fact one has the impression that she loved and valued the collection of rarities far more than her husband had done.

The buildings of the Middle Temple miraculously survived the fire, and the books and manuscripts were returned there about six weeks later. Ashmole recorded that on 11 October 'my first Boat-full of Bookes, which were carried to Mrs Tredescants: 3 Sept: were brought back to the Temple'. The rest followed a week later.[1]

In that same month Hester was summoned before the Surrey Quarter Sessions at Reigate for refusing 'to watch by night or to send a suitable man to do so'.[2] It was probably a mistake made in all the confusion and turmoil of the fire as, unlike some of the others summoned at the same time, there is no record that she was fined for the offence.

Meanwhile Ashmole's appointment as Windsor Herald was keeping him busy. He became immersed in ceremonial, a subject on which he became an authority, and his duties included attendance at various processions including the elaborate funerals of members of the aristocracy. He made 'visitations' to various counties to check whether those using arms were actually entitled to do so. And he had a new post: he had been appointed Comptroller of the Excise.

Despite his many responsibilities, he found time to take his brother-in-law, Henry Newcome, Rector of Gawsworth, Cheshire, to Lambeth when the latter was visiting London. On 1 May 1667 they 'saw the great rarities in John Tredeskin's study'.[3] No doubt Ashmole made full use of the occasion to check that everything was in its place.

In that same month Hester sold a few items to another great collector, William Courteen (who also used the name Charleton). Courteen's famous museum was eventually to go by way of Hans Sloane to the British Museum. Because Courteen's father had retired to Italy, he had lived most of his life abroad and in fact did not come back to reside in England permanently until 1684. Hence it is not surprising to find him keeping accounts in a mixture of Italian and English, as the following excerpts, which in the original are interspersed with others, show:[4]

		s	d
May 1667			
Tredescant			
1 rostro d'un uccello		10	0
2 uuovi del soland goose		5	0
June 1667			
Tredescant			
Sponge		1	0
Barbadoes cotton		1	0
Cristallo che rapresenta il diamante del Duca di Toscana pd		5	0
1 cosa d'Ilnorio d. dal sorella		10	0
1 pittura in Ambra dal sorella data		10	0
carta d'India gialla		1	0
carta d'India rossa		1	0
characteri Indiani		1	0
Dalla sig^{ra}			
Tredescant			
Piume di fenice		10	0
Dall sig^{ra}			
Tredescant			
Testa d'un uccello di virginia		2	0

Virginia woodpecker v.c di questi 3 colori bianco rosso e nero	2	0
Jet box with small sheers	5	0
July		
Ring tailes egge	0	6
Sparrow hawkes egge	0	0
Linnetts egge	0	0
7 bre		
La testa d'un Heron with its top	2	6
1 Ostreea impetrita	0	0

Hester was, of course, forbidden to sell objects from the collection, and Ashmole would have been appalled had he ever got to hear of these items being disposed of. But, as Katherine King and Sarah de Critz, Hester's cousins, later made clear, she continued to collect on her own account after her husband's death and these sales were probably duplicates from this collection. Even a 'Soland goose' or gannet's egg cannot have been a particularly rare item, and she seems to have given away some of the more common birds' eggs and an oyster shell. Moreover, two of the items are recorded as coming from 'the sister', perhaps meaning one of Hester's cousins. Courteen may already have contributed to the collection as a benefactor, and it is possible that Hester acquired items from him in exchange at this time, too. And, of course, had she wanted to do Ashmole out of his inheritance, there were far more valuable things that she could have sold.

Hester must have become seriously ill that autumn, as she made her will on 9 September 1667 when she described herself as 'weak in body but of good sound and perfect mind and memory'. She recovered, however, and lived on for another eleven years.

The following April Ashmole's second wife, the former Lady Manwaring, from whom he seems to have been estranged for some years, died. Nothing is known of her whereabouts after the Restoration, but perhaps she still paid visits to Hester. Seven months later Ashmole married for the third time. His bride was Elizabeth Dugdale, daughter of his old friend and fellow herald William Dugdale.

On 15 April 1669 Ashmole went again to South Lambeth. Judging by the company he was keeping this visit was more in the nature of a garden inspection than to take stock of the collection. His companion was 'Mr Rose the Kings Gardner' and the two men 'went to Mrs Tradescants & thence to Capt. Forsters at South Lambeth, where I first was acquainted with him'.[5]

John Rose was an eminent nurseryman who specialized in the best varieties of grape vine. Having studied under Le Notre in France, he was now keeper of the royal garden in St James's Park, where he was growing orange trees and 'greens',[6] meaning tender plants requiring the protection of a greenhouse.

Captain Foster's garden also became famous. 'Captain Foster's garden at Lambeth has many curiosities in it,' a visitor noted in 1691. 'His greenhouse is full of fresh and flourishing plants, and before it is the finest striped holly hedge that perhaps is in England. He has many myrtles, not the greatest, but of the most fanciful shapes that are any where else. He has a framed walk of timber covered with vines, which, with others, running on most of his walls without prejudice to his lower trees, yield him a deal of wine. Of flowers he has good choice; and his Virginia and other birds in a great variety, with his glass hive, add much to the pleasure of his garden.'[7] He was a nurseryman selling specialities such as orange trees and by 1682 was marketing 'bastard trees' producing fruit that was 'part orange part lemmon'.[8]

This is the only visit to Mrs Tradescant that Ashmole mentions in his diary. But, as he did not bother to put down the occasion when he took his brother-in-law, there were probably many others that went unrecorded. In any event, relations between him and Hester seem to have continued relatively smoothly until 1674 when, on 15 September, he asked yet another horary question: 'Whether best to buy the house of Mrs Blackamore'.[9]

Hester must have been horrified. This house was not simply next door to her own but literally adjoined it. Without actually moving in with her Ashmole could not possibly get nearer the coveted collection. From his windows he would be able to see every caller arrive and depart and no doubt would be continually visiting himself. Moreover, with the museum still open to the public there would be nothing she could do to stop him.

The answer to the horary question must have been in the affirmative, as on 2 October at 11.30 a.m. 'I & my wife first entred my House at South Lambeth', although they did not apparently move in 'to lye' there until the following spring.

Three days later Ashmole records: 'This night Mrs Tredescant was in danger of being robbed, but most strangely prevented.'[10] His meaning is obscure, but no doubt this gave him yet another excuse to descend on the museum and check that nothing was missing. And it was only now, ten years after the order was made, that Hester was served with a writ of execution of the decree.[11] She was faced with the prospect of Ashmole's two friends and fellow heralds, one of them his father-in-law, coming into her house and going through the collection item by item.

Hester was obviously upset. She felt that Ashmole was breathing down her neck, waiting to snatch away the rarities as soon as the breath was out of her body. Furthermore, she was indiscreet enough to say so.

Ashmole's harassment became more than she could bear. She told him to take the collection away immediately Although an impulsive gesture, it was a natural reaction. Ashmole tried to persuade her to keep it. She had, after all, been granted legal custody of the rarities for her lifetime. Besides, his house was not yet ready to accommodate them. But Hester would have none of it.

Impetuously, even though her friends tried to remonstrate with her, she told him that she would 'throw them into the Streete' if he did not take them.

On 26 November, according to Ashmole's diary, 'Mrs Tredescant being willing to deliver up the Rarities to me, I carried severall of them to my House'; and again, on 1 December, 'I began to remove the Rest of the Rarities to my house at South Lambeth.'[12] His house, known as Turret House, had a fine attic, and eventually he decided to put them up there. Despite her frustration, Hester even helped to move some of the cherished objects herself.

Once the winter was over, preparations at Ashmole's house started in earnest. He added an extension which included 'a noble room' with a chimney adorned with his arms impaling those of his third wife. Other additions were brick walls at the back and at the front towards the highway and later 'my back buildings'. There must have been constant activity and noise over the next couple of years.

Hester had obviously never forgiven Ashmole for the way in which he had taken advantage of her husband. The lonely widow of about sixty-three, impetuous, indiscreet and prone to exaggerate her feelings about her overbearing neighbour, began to make public accusations: that he had stolen The Ark, that he was plotting against her. It was too much for Ashmole. He drew up and forced her to sign a 'submission':[13]

Bee it knowne unto all persons that I Hester Tredescant of South Lambeth in the County of Surry widdow doe acknowledge & confess in the presence of Mr Justice Dawling and other the Witnesses hereunder subscribed, that I have very much wronged Elias Ashmole of the same place Esq: by several fals, scandalous, & defamatory Speeches Reports, & otherwise, tending to the diminution and blemishing of his reputation & good name, more especially in these particulars following.

First, I have reported to severall persons, that the said Elias Ashmole had made a dore out of his Garden into my Orchard, by which he might come into my house as soone as the breath was out of my Body, & take away my Goods; when as in truth there was not, nor yet is, any such dore made by him.

Secondly that he had taken away 250 foot of my Ground, when he built his Garden wall; whereas his said Wall was set in the place where an old pale stood immediately before he built his Wall, & was lyned out in the presence of my cosen Blake the Plummer, whom my landlord Mr Bartholomew had impowered on his behalfe so to doe.

Thirdly I have reported to severall persons, as well Strangers as others of my Acquaintance, that the said Mr Ashmole had forced me to deliver up to him my Closet of Rarities, and that if I had not done he would have cut my throat. And in the presence of divers Neighbours I falsely charged the said Mr Ashmole; that he had robd me of my Closet of Rarities, &

cheated me of my estate; When as in truth I prest him to receive the said Rarities & when he intreated me to keepe them, and not only used many Arguments to perswade me to it, but set on other my friends and neighbours to perswade me likewise, I would not hearken to their advise, but forced him to take them away, threatning, that if he did not, I would throw them into the Streete; and he having at last consented to receive them, I voluntarily helped to remove some of them my selfe.

Fourthly I reported that I had made him promise me to bestow the said Rarities on the University of Oxford; and that I would force him to send them thither; when as I never moved the said Mr Ashmole to any such thing, when I delivered them to him, or at any tyme since.

Fiftly that I caused a great heape of earth & rubbish to be laid against his Garden-wall, so high, that on the sixt day of August last in the night, by the helpe thereof, it is strongly presumed that Theives got over the same & robd the said Mr Ashmole of 32 Cocks & Hens; and notwithstanding he admonished me to take it away, I told him it should lie there in spight of his Teeth; & soe it continued untaken away above six weekes after he was so robbed, whereby he lay in continuall feare of having his house broken open every night.

All which, and many other like false & scandalous Reports and Words, as I have unadvisedly & rashly spoken against him, without any Provocation of his in words or deedes; so am I really & heartily sorry that I have so greatly wronged him therein; and have in the presence of the said Mr Justice Dawling, and the subscribed Witnesses, acknowledged the said Wrongs and Injuries so done unto the said Mr Ashmole, and asked him publique forgiveness for the same; and doe hereby voluntarily & freely promise the said Mr Ashmole that no manner of Rubbish or Earth shalbe layd against his said garden wall, and that henceforth I will not say or doe anything against him or his wife, that may tend to the damage reproach or disreputation of them or either of them. In witness whereof, I have hereunto set my hand the first day of September 1676.

Ester Treduscant.

Subscribed in the presence of

Jo. Dawlinge
Tho. Bedford
Rich. Rendall
Tho. de Critz
Tho. Murrey
Gartrud Slaugh
K. King
Geo. Worye

The wording of the document, like the handwriting, is Ashmole's, and it is surprising that Hester's relatives persuaded her to sign it. One presumes that Ashmole must have threatened her with further legal action if she refused.

While Ashmole obviously had cause for complaint, Hester's actions and charges against him were perhaps not as serious, or indeed as irrational, as they sound. The '250 ft' of ground was the length of the back garden where Ashmole's wall had been built, so she was only accusing him of taking a foot along its length. This was probably the amount of ground messed up by those constructing it, as it is difficult to dig the foundations of a wall without a certain amount of inconvenience to those on both sides.

The 'greate heape of earth' had probably lain for six days rather than six weeks, the 'sixt day of August' being only three weeks before the date of the document. And one wonders why Ashmole should have been the one 'in continual fear of having his house broken open every night' when Hester, the elderly widow, who had already suffered one burglary, does not seem to have been bothered by the thought of intruders. Presumably the pile lay on Hester's side of the wall, so that any thieves using it to gain access into Ashmole's garden would have first had to have passed through her own.

Undoubtedly Hester felt cheated out of the collection by the legal judgement that had been made ten years previously and, had any strangers turned up to view The Ark not realizing that it was now closed to the public, she might well have said she had been 'forced' to deliver up the rarities rather than submit to the commission.

About eighteen months later Ashmole recorded drily: '4 April 1678 11 H:30 A.M. my wife told me Mrs: Tredescant was found drowned in her Pond. She was drowned the day before about noone as appeared by some Circumstances.' Two days later, at eight in the evening, Hester was buried in the family vault in Lambeth churchyard, as had been her wish.[14]

Whether her death was suicide or an accident is not known. The only evidence – coroner's records for the period no longer surviving – is that she was buried in sacred ground. Nothing is known about the pond as it is not marked on any map of the area, but presumably the authorities decided that she could have slipped and fallen in by accident.

Probate of the will that she had made eleven years earlier was granted on 16 May.[15] The will shows that Hester certainly had plenty of friends. Having already disposed of her lands, tenements and real estate by deed tripartite to her two kinswomen, Sara de Critz and Katherine King, who were also made residual legatees and executors of her will, she left token bequests to Thomas and Robert Tradescant and their children, describing them as her late husband's 'kinsmen . . . sometime of Walderswick'.

She made further bequests to 'Ester Sumpford', her children and grandchildren. Hester Samford was a relation who has sometimes been confused with Hester Tradescant because they bore the same names. In fact

Hester Samford was considerably older, having been born about 1596; she married a James Stanford, Stanforth or Samford in 1618. She was the granddaughter of John Pookes, the tailor of Valenciennes who, with his wife Hester Oblaert of Bruges, had settled in the Precinct of St Martin-le-Grand towards the end of the previous century, being the daughter of their eldest son, a merchant also called John.

Hester's kinsman, the painter Cornelius de Neve, also received a legacy. He was another grandchild of the tailor from Valenciennes by his daughter Sarah, whose second husband was the Sarjeant-Painter John de Critz. De Critz must have been well known to the Tradescants, as he had worked for Robert Cecil at Hatfield and had done decorative work at the royal palace of Oatlands. Thus Cornelius de Neve, as he shared the same mother, was a half-brother of Sara de Critz and her sister Katherine King. (The Sarjeant-Painter, John de Critz, had previously fathered seven children by his first wife. Three of them, John, Thomas and Emanuel, became painters, and Thomas and Emanuel, born in 1607 and 1608 respectively, are now regarded as responsible for most of the Tradescant portraits.[16] By the time Hester made her will all three were already dead.)

Hester left further small bequests to her 'goddaughter Murray and her children that I christned', to her 'Goddaughter Ester Grace', to 'Mistress Weyman', Joane Christmas and Grace and Elizabeth Hall. Nor was 'Goodwife Nightingale', who, with her husband William, had been a near neighbour for more than forty years, forgotten.

Hester duly remembered the 'poor of Lambeth' and also left legacies to the notary public Richard Hoare and his wife Charity; he was to receive 'forty shillings to buy him a ring', while she was left 'tenn pounds to buy her a peice of plate'. Her 'good ffriends Mark Cottle Esquire', the Registrar of the Prerogative Court of Canterbury, who now lived at Greenwich in a house built by Erasmus Snelling with four acres of splendid gardens, and 'Mr Thomas Southwood, gent' were appointed overseers of the will. Both received a legacy, as did the former's wife, Elizabeth Cottle, 'to buy them rings in remembrance of me'. The will was witnessed by Joane Christmas, Reu(ben) Parker and Richard Hoare.

Chapter 15

'My Rarities'

With Hester gone Ashmole moved quickly. On 22 April 1678 he 'removed the Pictures from Mr Tredescants House, to myne'.[1] These must have been the Tradescant family portraits which were not included in the museum catalogue, as he would already have had those listed there, such as the portrait of 'Old Parr' (see Chapter 16).

On 18 June he made the payment of £100 to Mary Edmonds and obtained a release from her and her second husband, Mathew Leigh or Lea.[2] One of Robert Edmonds's debtors, a brewer called Edward Searle, endeavoured to obtain sixty pounds of this money from Ashmole, claiming that he was still unpaid for deliveries of beer made to the victualler more than twenty years earlier,[3] but the case was dismissed.

In the following March Ashmole achieved his final ambition: he obtained a lease on the Tradescants' house and garden from their landlord, Mr Bartholomew.[4] So now the exotics in the garden were his as well. He made a list of the 'Trees found in Mrs Tredescants Ground when it came into my possession' in the back of the Tradescants' own copy of Parkinson's *Paradisus*. As only thirty are included it is difficult to believe this was a complete record; there is no reason to believe that Hester had allowed the garden to decay to such an extent, although some losses had to be expected without her husband's magic touch. Indeed, as the swamp cypress (*Taxodium distichum* (L.) Rich.), which was in the garden at a later date, is not recorded, it can only be assumed that Ashmole's knowledge of 'simpling' did not extend to the recognition of rare trees.

That Hester kept the gardens open after her husband's death is confirmed by a rather surprising reference to them by an Italian visitor, Count Lorenzo Magalotti, who did not arrive in England until 1668: 'I giardini di Lambeth di Tra[descant] di là dal fiume ed altri in vicinanza della città servono tutto l'anno per spasseggi d'osterie e di bordelli' ('The Lambeth gardens belonging to Tradescant on the other side of the river and others in the vicinity of the city serve all the year round as public walks, taverns and bordellos').[5]

(On 29 May 1669 Magalotti, after visiting the 'hydraulic machine' at the Marquess of Worcester's Vauxhall works, accompanied Cosmo III, Grand Duke of Tuscany, to 'India House'. His account of the excursion suggests that this was The Ark.

'His highness went next to the India House, situated on this side of the water, which is full of rare and curious things, both animal and vegetable. Amongst other remarkable things may be seen the sycamore trees which grow in abundance in Egypt on the banks of the Nile, and in quality somewhat resemble our mulberry trees, nor is the appearance of the leaves widely different; but they neither produce flowers nor fruit. There are several species of birds, and amongst others those called Birds of Paradise, which have a long body covered with red and flesh-coloured feathers of the most lively tints, and a very long tail, which render them exquisitely beautiful to the eye; there are also nightingales from Virginia, a part of North America in the possession of the English, joining New France; they are equal in size to ours, and are clothed with feathers of a red colour, and their heads, like those of our larks, are ornamented with a tuft of very small feathers. Besides the birds there are different sorts of animals, terrestrial and aquatic, curious for the magnitude of their bodies and the symmetry of their parts; of this description is the serpent, whose size is most remarkable, being more than twelves cubits in length, and of proportionate thickness; it is covered with scales lying one over another, but closely set, thick, and firmly united, and as broad as a man's hand. No less curious was a fish, equal in size to a sea-calf, without scales, but covered with a rough and uneven skin, and having a long and deformed head, with a horrid-looking mouth, in which are two rows of teeth, both upper and under, in shape like those of a saw. His highness examined many other animals and curiosities which came from India, and are kept here to gratify the curiosity of the public.')[6]

Just over a year later Ashmole was once again embroiled in legal action over the rarities. This time he preferred a Bill in Chancery against Hester's heirs, Sarah de Critz and Katherine King.

In his Bill of Complaint to the Lord Chancellor, now Heneage, Lord Finch, which is dated 2 June 1679, he outlined the contents of his previous Bill which had led to him being granted the collection in 1664, when Sir Edward Bysshe and William Dugdale had been ordered to catalogue the rarities and examine Hester upon interrogation. He claimed that Hester was duly served with a writ of execution of the decree 'on or about the month of December 1674', after which she had voluntarily delivered 'diverse of the said rarityes . . . and promised a full and just performance of the said decree' so that Ashmole 'did forbare further to prosecute' it.

But now, before such examination had taken place, Hester had died 'possessed of all the said Rarityes' except those already delivered to him, having disposed of some and changed others. He claimed that Hester was 'possessed of a very great personal estate consisting of Moneyes, Plate, Jewells, Goods, Household stuffes, Bonds, Bills, Mortgages and other goods and chattles att the tyme of her death', before which date she had made a will making Katherine King and Sarah de Critz her executrixes and that they had now possessed themselves not only of all the rarities as yet undelivered but also of Hester's personal estate, which amounted 'to a very great value'.

Ashmole declared that he was now determined to bestow the rarities and antiquities, both those already delivered to him and those yet to be received, upon the University of Oxford, which was building a 'faire museum to preserve them in'. Ashmole had 'required' Sarah de Critz and Katherine King to deliver the residue of the rarities, but they, with their nephew Thomas de Critz and their sister Grace de Critz and others unknown, were endeavouring to defraud him. He admitted that they had lately delivered to him two cabinets, 'one of medals and the other of other rarityes', but claimed that the cabinet of medals should have contained 'diverse gold coynes and medalls both ancient and modern' to the value 'of above £200', whereas those received were 'worth not above £5'. They had also delivered 'a few pictures and books and some other things all of little value pretending that they had noe other', nor knew where they were. Ashmole claimed that they did know and asked that they he ordered to 'sett forth the particulars of them and to deliver or procure the same', otherwise it would be to his 'great wrong' and the disappointment of the University of Oxford.

He asked that these 'confederates' be questioned under oath and that anything missing should be made good out of Hester's personal estate, particulars of which they should be ordered to divulge. He also asked for writs of subpoena against the four defendants and their other 'confederates when they shall be discovered' that they might set forth 'a right and true particular' of all 'the rarityes and curiosities of what sort or kind soever' that 'the said John Tradescant was possessed of and whereon they or other or any of them were contained whether in cabinett, chest, box, drawer or otherwise'.

Sarah de Critz and Katherine King gave their answer on 17 June. They had heard that 'there might be' a deed of gift but they believed that it had been 'fraudulently obtained . . . in a surreptitious manner and when the said John Tradescant was in drincke' and that Hester had tried to have it 'overthrowne'. While they agreed that Hester had retained possession of the items in the collection until shortly before her death, it was their belief that she did not 'conceal or embezill' any particulars of them nor 'dispose of any', having, before she died, delivered to the complainant 'all such rarities as by the said pretended deed did belong to him', keeping only some items collected after the death of her husband to which Ashmole was not entitled.

They claimed that, since Hester's death, Ashmole had demanded 'delivery of several rarityes' in their possession and that they had delivered to him 'several things and rarityes for to buy their peace and quietnes which as they beleeve and are informed were not nor are not within the graunt of the said deed'. They added that they were 'rather induced to believe' this because Ashmole had declared 'that he had received more than hee did or could have expected to have received'. Moreover, 'having received and gott what he could, nowe for vexation and molestation of these defendants, who are women unable to struggle with him', he had exhibited this bill, despite the fact that they had offered to make an affidavit stating that they had delivered all the rarities to him, which had in fact been drawn up and was now in his hands.

They declared that they had heard only 'by hearsay' of Ashmole's intention of giving the collection to the University of Oxford and of the 'faire museum building' to be built to preserve them. They denied concealing any coins or medals or anything else that rightly belonged to Ashmole, having delivered all they 'cann comme by' and hoped that 'they need not render' any account of Hester's personal estate, as Ashmole had no claim on it, having already received everything granted to him under the deed of gift and much more to which he had no right, which they had done to their own detriment in order to prevent him bringing this charge.

They claimed that the only rarities now remaining in their custody were from Hester's collection acquired after her husband's death and were 'not of the value of £5', for which sum they were willing to sell them to him.

They declared that Ashmole had been 'so well satisfied' with what he had received that he had promised to give them a 'general release' which he had so far failed to deliver. They prayed to be honourably dismissed with their costs.[7]

There is no record that this case was ever heard. Katherine King died in 1684 and Sarah de Critz two years later.

Ashmole, of course, had had the bulk of the collection since 1674. From that time on they became 'my rarities', no longer available to an interested public but only to a few privileged friends and acquaintances.

Izaak Walton was lucky enough to see them and not surprisingly it was the fish that impressed him. He saw 'the Hog-fish, the Dog-fish, the Dolphin, the Coney-fish, the Parrot-fish, the Shark, the Poison-fish, Sword-fish, and not only other incredible fish; but you may there see the Salamander, several sorts of Barnacles, of Solan Geese, the Bird of Paradise, such sorts of Snakes, and such Bird's-nests, and of so various forms, and so wonderfully made, as may beget wonder and amusement in any beholder'.[8] The 'Hog-fish' was the spiny scorpion and the 'Coney-fish' a burbot.

Dr Robert Hooke, surveyor to the City, was made 'exceeding welcome' when he went with two friends on 28 April 1677. They found 'Dugdale' there and together 'saw Tradescants raritys in Garret'. Five years previously Dr Hooke had been fortunate enough to pick up a copy of 'Tradescants book for 6d'.[9]

Evelyn paid a visit a year later when he was shown a toad in amber. 'The prospect from a Turret is very fine, it being so neere Lond. & yet not discovering any house about the Country,' he recorded.[10]

Long before Ashmole gained possession of the collection there was talk of it going to Oxford. On 27 August 1670 Evelyn had noted, 'You heare they talke already of founding a Laboratorie, & have beg'd the Reliques of old Tradescant, to furnish a Repositary',[11] and Ashmole intimated his intention of bestowing the collection on the university three years before Hester's death.[12] In 1677 Anthony Wood recorded that Ashmole was to bestow all Tradescant's rarities as well as his own collections of coins, medals and manuscripts, the gift being conditional on a 'fabric' being built to receive them.[13] At the time it was considered 'the greatest university news'.[14]

In fact most of Ashmole's collections never reached Oxford as they were destroyed by a fire in the Middle Temple in 1679. Only his manuscripts and the more valuable gold coins escaped, as they were at his house in South Lambeth. It was a great loss, and he went to considerable expense to try to retrieve them from the ashes but to little avail. He managed to replace many of the books when he bought the library of his friend William Lilly, the famous astrologer, after his death in 1681.

The site chosen for this first Ashmolean Museum, now the Museum of the History of Science, was between the Sheldonian Theatre and Exeter College, whose 'bog house' was undermined and destroyed when the foundations were dug. The architect is considered to have been the master mason Thomas Wood, who with his brother Richard had been a journeyman to William Byrd. Previously he seems to have been involved mostly with marble work and paving.[15] The building, suitably embellished with carved panels of shells and fruit round the main window, housed three fifty-six-foot rooms, of which the basement was to be the 'elaboratory', the ground floor the school of natural history and the upstairs room the museum or 'knick-knackatory' as it was irreverently called.

By 1683 the repository was ready. On 15 February Ashmole recorded in his diary: 'I began to put up my Rarities into cases to send to Oxford', and on 14 March, 'The last load of my Rarities sent to the Barge. This afternoon I relapsed into the Gout.'[16]

While these entries suggest that Ashmole (who was always obsessed with his health) had done all the work himself, in fact the task fell to Dr Robert Plot, the first Keeper, who spent a month at South Lambeth packing the rarities into boxes which were then sent to Oxford by barge. He was back there to receive them a week later when they were taken to the museum in twelve cartloads. Although 'humbugging' Plot was reputed to have been a popular Oxford pastime, he had a distinguished career as natural philosopher, antiquarian and historian.[17]

Dr Plot spent the next two months arranging the exhibits ready for a ceremonial opening on 21 May, when they were viewed by the Duke and Duchess of York and their second daughter, the Lady Anne (later Queen Anne).

On 26 May 1683 Ashmole wrote to the Vice-Chancellor, Dr John Lloyd:[18]

Mr Vice Chancellor,
It has of a long time been my Desire to give some testimony of my Duty and filial Respect, to my honored Mother the University of Oxford, and when Mr Tradescants Collection of Rarities came to my hands, though I was tempted to part with them for a very considerable sum of money, and was also press't by honourable Persons to consigne them to another Society, I firmly resolv'd to deposite them no where but with You. I also intended when they were brought down, to have accompanyed them, & personally made a present of my Respects and them at Oxford but being detained by necessary occasions in this Place, I now addresse to you unto whose Care & Prudence the affaires of the University are happily committed, desiring you would be pleased in my name to signify to the University, that I present to them the aforesaid Collection, with the Reservation to Myselfe and the Persons appointed by Me, the Custody of them during my Life; as also the making such Regulations, and if God give Blessing, such further gifts and endowments as maybe ornamental & useful to that noble Society whose Splendor and Happiness is by no Person more ardently desir'd than by   Sir
              Your Most faithful Servant   E. Ashmole

This letter bears out all too clearly the reasons for the Tradescants' concern that the rarities 'coming into a private hand . . . might be too easily imbezzled and made away'. Nevertheless, their final wish for the collection to go to Oxford University was fulfilled, albeit that the honour and glory went to Ashmole. It has been suggested that he even tried to suppress the name of Tradescant; this is clearly not the case, although he probably did little to further it. All the family portraits were sent down with the original accessions, and at the time of its arrival in Oxford the collection was referred to as 'Tredeskyn's rarities'.

Ashmole subsequently recommended that the museum should have an annual visitation and named those who were to carry it out; in an attempt to ensure the collection's future preservation he also drew up a list of statutes, orders and rules.[19]

Alas, Oxford did not cherish the rarities as it should have. Many of the more perishable natural history specimens deteriorated over the years and were destroyed. Although it is often stated that the dodo was consigned to a bonfire in 1755, it merely suffered the same fate, deteriorating with time, the head and one leg now being carefully preserved.[20]

Items became dispersed, the books and manuscripts going to the Bodleian Library, the natural history specimens to the University Museum and the ethnological material to the Pitt Rivers. As the items that were moved were not properly recorded, they became mixed with later acquisitions. In many cases it has proved impossible to identify objects from the Tradescant collection in order to reassemble them, although a number were marked with ink inscriptions and at one time the natural history specimens were given small pendant iron labels with numbers scratched on them.

The rarities suffered from the neglect of some of their later keepers. A German visitor in 1710 complained of the poor arrangement and state of preservation of the specimens, which were 'full of dust and soot'. He added that the curator could rarely be found as he was 'always lounging about in the inns'.

In 1880 there was general consternation when a group of objects from the collection were found lying about in 'a sort of outhouse easily accessible to passers-by in the street'. These included engraved gems, globes of crystal, carvings and a silver hookah.[21] As recently as 1968 the standard of care of the natural history and geological collections was criticized by the Rosse Commission.[22]

Despite the transfer of so much material to other collections, the original museum was outgrown by 1894, when the remaining contents were moved with various other acquisitions to the present building. Although the Ashmolean Museum now has a room dedicated to the Tradescants containing all the surviving objects believed to derive from their collection, it is but a poor shadow of the original. Such items as do remain are in many cases the earliest known examples of their type.

In 1915 two more portraits arrived. They had been taken down from the panelling of Turret House in South Lambeth when it was pulled down in 1881 and are said to represent the elder Tradescant with his wife Elizabeth in a double portrait and Jane, the first wife of the younger Tradescant. But as Turret House, then thought to have been the home of the Tradescants, is now known to have been that of Ashmole, they are unlikely to represent the famous gardener and his family and they in no way compare with the other family portraits.[23]

In 1926 the Garden Clubs of Virginia presented a window in honour of the Tradescants, which was erected in the Old Ashmolean building. It represents the Tradescants' coat of arms surrounded by a wreath of *Tradescantia virginiana*.

Finally, one wonders whether all the Tradescants' rarities even reached Oxford. In view of the comments of the antiquary Ralph Thoresby who in

1712 visited the house in which Ashmole lived and saw there 'the remains of Mr Tradescant's rarities';[24] the books which must surely have found their way into the sale of Ashmole's library when it came under the hammer after his death; and the fact that a rare shell believed to be from the collection has turned up in the Hunterian Collection in Glasgow, it seems most unlikely.

What was the fate of the famous garden? Ashmole obviously tried to keep it up when it came into his hands a year after Hester's death. He gave several plants from it to the second Lord Hatton for the garden at Kirby Hall. These included seeds of Arbor Judae (*Cercis siliquastrum* L.), pyracantha (*P. coccinea* M.J. Roemer), the Spanish Broom (*Spartium junceum* L.) and Acacia Americana (*Robinia pseudacacia* L.); cuttings from the American plane (*Platanus occidentalis* L.); a root of Rhodia radix (*Rhodiola rosea* L.) in a pot and some pear grafts. But Hatton was unable to have cuttings from Ashmole's Oriental plane (*Platanus orientalis* L.) or his 'Lazerole' (*Crataegus azarolus* L.) as these were too decayed. [25]

Ashmole died in 1692 and the property passed to his widow, who soon afterwards married the 'lusty' stonemason John Reynolds.[26] She died in 1701, when the property passed to her husband who married another widow called Mildred Prowde.

John Aubrey visited the garden on his 'Perambulation of Surrey', probably soon after Ashmole's death. He noted that the Balm of Gilead tree (*Cedronella triphylla* L.) was growing there. The rich eccentric Edmund Wyld had had some layers which had grown well in his Bedfordshire garden at Houghton Conquest 'till in the hard Winter the mice killed it'. 'I do not heare of any other now in England,' he added. Wyld, whose large house in Bloomsbury was 'a sort of knick-knackatory', was generally knowledgeable on horticultural matters and was reputed to delight in sowing salads in the morning to be cut for dinner, sprouting them in an earthen porringer of prepared earth over a chafing dish of coals. One can imagine him entertaining Tradescant to a convivial meal and watching with fascination as the pin-sized plants appeared.

Aubrey claimed that few of Tradescant's rare plants were then remaining – 'only a very fair Horse-chesse-nutt tree, Some Pine-trees, and Sumach-trees, Phylerees, &c.' – and at the 'entrance into the gate over the bridge of the mote, are two vast Ribbes of a Whale'.[27] This was another rarity that obviously never reached Oxford, although the omission can hardly have been an oversight.

On 21 May 1749 Mr William Watson, a Fellow of the Royal Society, visited South Lambeth in the company of a Dr Mitchell. Four days later he addressed the Society, giving 'an account [of] how he visited the garden of the famous John Tradescant . . . now lying uncultivated; the house ruinous and uninhabited'. According to a report of Watson's talk in the *Stukely Papers*, he 'was agreeably surprised to find, after so long a neglect and utter disregard, many curious plants of Tradescant's growing among the weeds, and still struggling to maintain the honor of their planter . . . He found some trees, too, in the orchard, of great age and stature, two arbutuses, a rhus obseniorum, and some more.'[28]

Another account gives more details about these plants and trees:

We found there [Watson reported] the Borrago latifolia sempervirens of C.B. [Casper Bauhin], Polygonatum vulgare latifolium C.B., Aristolochia clematitis recta C.B. and Dracontium Dod. [R. Dodonaei]. There are yet remaining two trees of the arbutus, the largest he has seen; which, from their being so long used to our winters, did not suffer by the severe colds of 1729 and 1740, when most of their kind were killed throughout England. In the orchard there is a tree of the rhamnus catharticus, about 20 feet high, and near a foot in diameter, by much the greatest he ever saw.[29]

The plants listed are alkanet, Solomon's seal, birthwort, *Dracunculus vulgaris*, the strawberry tree and buckthorn. Yet another version of Watson's report adds: 'It is not unlikely that there may be several other plants yet remaining in the garden but flourishing at a different time of year.'[30]

By 1773 the historian Dr A.C. Ducarel was living in Tradescant's house, with a John Small Esq. as his neighbour in Ashmole's old home next door. Small had purchased it some twelve years before from the successor to Ashmole's heirs.

Ducarel bemoaned the fact that the garden had been for so long neglected. 'It were much to be wished', he wrote, 'that the lovers of botany had visited this once famous garden, before, or at least in, the beginning of the present century.'[31]

One tree, however, apparently continued to thrive against all odds. In 1743 Philip Miller described a 'Virginian Cypress tree, with leaves like the Acacia, which fall off in winter' – the swamp cypress (*Taxodium distichum* (L.) Rich.) – which was still surviving from Tradescant's Lambeth garden. He reported that it was 'upwards of Thirty Feet High, and of a considerable Bulk; which, tho' in a common Yard at present, where no Care is taken of it, but, on the contrary, many Hooks are drove into the Trunk, to fasten Cords thereto for Drying of Cloaths, yet the Tree is in great Health and Vigour'.

He also found there 'the one large Tree of the true Service in England'. It was nearly forty feet high and produced great quantities of fruit each year. He added that he had seen others, but 'these are small, when compared to that in John Tradescant's Garden'.[32] Although the elder Tradescant was growing the Service Tree (*Sorbus domestica* L.) in 1634 as 'Cormus' (the French name for it being 'Cormier'), the tree mentioned by Miller was probably a relic of Ashmole's planting after he had obtained one from Kirby Hall. Charles

Hatton had begged 'a couple of your Cormiers' from his brother for Ashmole in 1680 when he claimed 'there was none else in England'.[33]

In 1880 the famous garden was sold for redevelopment and in the following year the former home of the Tradescants, together with that of Ashmole, was demolished and sold as building materials. Now rows of terraced houses occupy the site of the garden created by 'that painfull industrious searcher, and lover of al natures varieties'.[34]

It is pleasing to report, however, that the name of Tradescant lives on in the Museum of Garden History now established in the redundant parish church of St Mary's at which both father and son were regular worshippers. The area of the churchyard near their tomb has been laid out as a memorial to the two great gardeners, planted only with those varieties that grew in their own garden at South Lambeth in 1656. The wrought-iron gates that led to Turret House which were rescued from the rubble – to find a place in a Surrey garden – were later acquired by the museum where they are on view.

Chapter 16

The Museum Collection

The Tradescant collection was far and away the largest and most comprehensive of its day in England. There was one other collection of natural curiosities, supposedly the result of thirty years' travel, of which a catalogue was printed in 1664. It belonged to Robert Hubert, alias Forges, and could be seen at a music-house near St Paul's. But the Tradescants' was the only collection in the country worthy of being called a museum, and it was open to the public long before Hubert's. Even at the end of the century Evelyn regarded it as the only English collection worth noting other than that of William Charleton (alias Courteen), and Charleton's was not established until 1684.[1]

The Ark consisted of an incredible variety of miscellaneous and incongruous objects, a typical 'Closet of Rarities' but on a vast scale. Dyers' materials and artists' colours stood alongside exotic birds and fine carvings. Tradescant himself was obviously interested in anything and everything and expected his visitors to share his curiosity. Most undoubtedly did so, and Hoole was obviously right in claiming that a visit had educational merit.

In the *Musaeum Tradescantianum* (which is reproduced in Appendix III) the contents were carefully sorted into fourteen classes, but the arrangement would hardly be described as scientific in the modern sense of the word. The coins were kept in a special cabinet. Other objects had their place in 'cabinett, chest, box, drawer' or other container[2] but perhaps not as haphazardly as this sounds. The whole collection was probably crammed into one large room, with many of the natural-history specimens, such as the blow-fish and the armadillo, suspended from the ceiling; they still retain the holes originally made for this purpose.

The best description of The Ark was left by a twenty-four-year-old German student called Georg Christoph Stirn. He arrived in England in July 1638 to do the usual tourist round and recorded in his diary:

> In the art museum of Mr John Tradescant the following things: first in the courtyard there lie two ribs of a whale, also a very ingenious little boat of

bark . . . In the museum itself we saw a salamander, a chameleon, a pelican, a remora, a lanhado from Africa, a white partridge, a goose which has grown in Scotland on a tree, a flying squirrel, another squirrel like a fish, all kinds of bright coloured birds from India, a number of things changed into stone, amongst others a piece of human flesh on a bone, gourds, olives, a piece of wood, an ape's head, a cheese, etc.; all kinds of shells, the hand of a mermaid, the hand of a mummy, a very natural wax hand under glass, all kinds of precious stones, coins, a picture wrought in feathers, a small piece of wood from the cross of Christ, pictures in perspective of Henry IV and Louis XIII of France, who are shown, as in nature, on a polished steel mirror, when this is held against the middle of the picture, a little box in which a landscape is seen in perspective, pictures from the church of S. Sophia in Constantinople copied by a Jew into a book, two cups of 'rinocerode' . . . a cup of an East Indian alcedo which is a kind of unicorn, many Turkish and other foreign shoes and boots, a sea parrot, a toad-fish, an elk's hoof with three claws, a bat as large as a pigeon, a human bone weighing 42 pounds, Indian arrows, an elephant's head, a tiger's head, poisoned arrows such as are used by the executioners in the West Indies – when a man is condemned to death, they lay open his back with them and he dies of it – an instrument used by the Jews in circumcision (with picture) some very light wood from Africa, the robe of the king of Virginia, a few goblets of agate, a girdle such as the Turks wear in Jerusalem, the passion of Christ carved very daintily on a plumstone, a large magnet stone, S. Francis in wax under glass as also of S. Jerome, the Pater Noster of Pope Gregory XV, pipes from the East and West Indies, a stone found in the West Indies in the water, whereon were graven, Jesus, Mary and Joseph, a beautiful present from the Duke of Buckingham, which was of gold and diamonds affixed to a feather by which the four elements were signified, Isidor's MS of de natura hominis, a scourge with which Charles V is said to have scourged himself, a hat band of snake bones.[3]

These were only a fraction of the items on view: an odd selection to take his fancy. A remora is a sucking-fish, which was believed to have been able to stop a ship under full sail if it attached itself to the hull, and the lanhado some sort of snake. The feather sounds as though it might have been the one worn by the Duke of Buckingham on his entry into Paris in 1625. Inevitably the barnacle goose and the unicorn are singled out, while an elk's hoof, apart from being of museum interest, was also said to provide a cure for epilepsy, the animal being able to cure even itself of the disease by putting the hoof of its left hind foot in its ear. The cups of 'rinocerode', one of which survives, were made of rhinoceros horn.

It was this account by Stirn that enabled a twelfth-century moralized bestiary to be pinned down to the Tradescant collection because included in it is the treatise *De Natura Hominis* by Isadore of Seville, which he records as having seen. The bestiary has an inscription on the first page which shows that it was given to Sir Peter Manwood in 1609, and, as he is listed among the museum benefactors, he presumably passed it on to Tradescant, although he died long before the museum opened.

It is a beautiful volume containing 105 leaves of twelfth-century text on vellum with numerous pictures of beasts, both real and imaginary, wonderfully illuminated in glowing colours against a background of gold. It must have been one of the gems of the collection.

The book of pictures from the Church of St Sophia is no longer in existence, but there is a manuscript in the Bodleian Library with a drawing of St George which is reputedly copied from it.[4] Like so many of the natural history specimens, most of the waxworks have failed to stand up to the ravages of time, although one depicting the Annunciation survives.

Another early visitor was a much travelled servant of the East India Company, Peter Mundy, who, having just arrived back in London, found his way to Lambeth in 1634. He left the following description of his visit:

> Wee spent that whole day in peruseinge, and that superficially, such as hee had gathered together, as beasts, fowle, fishes, serpents, wormes (reall, although dead and dryed), pretious stones and other Armes, Coines, shells, fethers, etts. of sundrey Nations, Countries, forme, Coullours; also diverse Curiosities in Carvinge, painteings, etts., as 80 faces carved on a Cherry stone, Pictures to be seene by a Celinder which otherwise appeare like confused blotts, Medalls of Sondrey sorts, etts. Moreover, a little garden with divers outlandish herbes and flowers, whereof some that I had not seene elsewhere but in India, being supplyed by Noblemen, Gentlemen, Sea Commaunders, etts. with such Toyes as they could bringe or procure from other parts.[5]

The cherry stone with '80 faces' has also disappeared, but there is a drawing of it, four times enlarged, in the Bodleian Library. Ashmole left an inscription stating that the stone had been 'cut by Capt. Burgh, & given by him to Mr John Tradescant, who preserved it amongst his Rarities'.[6] Surprisingly Nicholas Burgh is not listed among the benefactors in the *Musaeum Tradescantianum*. There is a portrait of him dressed as one of the Alms Knights of Windsor, attributed to Cornelius de Neve, in the Ashmolean Museum.

The pictures that both Stirn and Mundy refer to are anamorphic or polyoptic drawings so distorted that they can only be viewed when reflected in a carefully positioned cylindrical mirror.

John Evelyn considered that the chiefest rarities were 'the antient Roman, Indian & Other Nations Armour, shilds & weapons; Some habits also of curiously colourd & wrought feathers: Particulaly that of the Phoenix Wing, as tradition gos.'[7] '

It would be interesting to know from what bird these last were taken; 'dragons' eggs', which were also on view, are thought to have been those of the ostrich, and the 'Indian goose' was a penguin. The 'bird Rock . . . able to trusse an Elephant', of which Tradescant exhibited a claw, was probably the Elephant Bird of Madagascar, now extinct.

After visiting the collection the ornithologist Francis Willughby described the dodo among the dried birds he had seen there.[8] A live dodo was exhibited in London in 1638,[9] and it is thought that Tradescant acquired its 'case' when it died. The fact that there is no mention of the bird in either of these earlier accounts by Stirn and Mundy adds weight to the suggestion.

The *Musaeum Tradescantianum* contains several 'firsts'. 'Mazer wood' is in fact the first reference to gutta percha,[10] a milky fluid from certain Malayan trees, which softens in warm water and regains its hardness when cold again. It was regarded as a form of wood and was called 'mazer wood' because it was used to make mazers or drinking-bowls. Before the invention of plastic it was an important commodity.

All the surviving North American specimens are the earliest known of their type. The 'Match-coat from Canada' is a three-quarter-length closed shirt made of well-tanned caribou skin and decorated with dyed porcupine quills in geometric patterns and pendants of beaver claws. The term 'match-coat' is probably a corruption of 'match kore', a native Virginian word for a skin garment.

There are three clubs with round balls on the end, no doubt some of the 'Tamahacks'. They are made of highly polished wood, and two of them still show signs of decoration.

Powhatan's 'habit' consists of four deerskins joined together and decorated with small shells to form the outline of a human figure and a pair of animals with thirty-two spirals. It is one of the three types of garment described as being in common use by Captain John Smith in 1608, the others being made from fur and feathers. Tradescant had examples of these, too, but they have not survived.

There are a few other items in the collection which perhaps deserve some explanation. Choppens were high pattens, verging into stilts, sometimes eighteen inches high and rising in accordance with the wearer's rank; they were considered fashionable by Venetian ladies at that time. Shakespeare's Hamlet refers to them when he says 'your Ladyship is nearer heaven than when I saw you last, by the altitude of a chopine'. Some are still on display.

Tea was still an expensive luxury and not yet in common use; with tobacco leaves and cacao seed, it was among the curiosities to be seen at South Lambeth.

The 'Blood that rained in the Isle of Wight' is thought to have been either dust containing iron oxide that had had rain falling through it or possibly the meteoric red dust recorded in the *Chronicle of Bromton* as having fallen in the Isle of Wight in 1177.[11] Certainly Sir John Oglander, the Royalist MP for Yarmouth, who vouched for its authenticity, was the right person to do so, as he was considered the leading authority on the island's affairs.

Among the 'Variety of China dishes' may have been the three surviving pieces made in the style of Palissy, the Huguenot potter from Saintes who strove for years, by trial and error, to discover the secret of reproducing enamel ware. He received little sympathy from either his wretchedly deprived family or his friends as he made one costly mistake after another, always preferring to destroy an imperfect piece rather than sell it off cheaply. Success did come to him in the end, but it took many agonizing years, and when he eventually became prosperous and moved to Paris it was only to suffer for his faith. The surviving pieces have an elaborate design of classical figures in relief on the base. There was little Chinese porcelain imported at that time, and, compared with other contemporary pottery, Palissy's work must have been considered fine indeed.

'Old Parr', whose portrait is listed among the paintings, was Thomas Parr, a smallholder from Shropshire who claimed to be 152 years old when he died in 1635. Described as that 'Olde, old, very Olde Man',[12] he was discovered by the Earl of Arundel, who brought him to London in that year and presented him to the King. He could be seen on exhibition at the Queen's Head in the Strand. Alas, he did not live to enjoy his fame for long, the generous hospitality that he received proving too much for his constitution. He died two months later and was buried in Westminster Abbey. A copy of the Tradescants' portrait, which is considered to be in the school of Honthorst, is in the National Portrait Gallery.

'Little Jeffreyes Boots' and 'Masking-suit' belonged to Jeffry Hudson, the famous dwarf who was presented to the Queen after the Duke and Duchess of Buckingham served him up in a pie when she and Charles I were staying at Burley-on-the-Hill. He was only three years older than Buckingham's daughter, Mary Villiers, who must have found him an intriguing playmate. By the age of thirteen his height was only twenty-one inches, and it did not change until he was nearly forty, when he suddenly grew to three feet nine inches. Jeffry became a great favourite at court. He seems to have led an adventurous life, being captured by pirates at sea and fighting a duel on horseback in which he shot his opponent dead. He lived to be sixty-two years old.

One of the most intriguing entries in the catalogue is 'A Booke of Mr Tradescant's choicest Flowers and Plants, exquisitely limned in vellum, by Mr Alex: Marshall'. There still remains in the Bodleian Library a delightful volume known as 'Tradescant's Orchard', which is something of an enigma.

It contains sixty-five very lifelike watercolour illustrations of fruit, each with the exact date on which they should ripen; under the Amber plum are inscribed the words 'which J T as I take it brought out of France and groweth at Hatfield'.[13] On several pages are insects and birds, so amusingly contrived that they are almost caricatures. Despite the fact that these brilliantly coloured watercolours are on paper and not vellum, this volume seems to have become associated with the above entry in the museum catalogue. This is certainly a mistake. Although there are similarities in the glowing colours, the drawings – with the possible exception of that showing the gooseberry – do not compare with Marshal's other known botanical work.

It has been suggested that 'Tradescant's Orchard' was a guide to the garden at Hatfield, but few of the fruits depicted correspond with those listed in Tradescant's bills for that garden, although most of them were growing at South Lambeth. Indeed, if these attractive watercolours have anything to do with Marshal (whose date of birth is not known but who did not die until 1682 and who produced some of his best work in the years immediately preceding his death), he would have had to have been something of an infant prodigy to have completed 'Tradescant's Orchard' before 1615 when the elder John Tradescant moved on to Canterbury.

The index to the volume was compiled by Ashmole, but the captions under the illustrations are not in his or in either of the Tradescants' hands. Nor does the writing appear to match that of Marshal.

In the Royal Library at Windsor there are two beautiful volumes of Marshal's work, but again both are on paper. They are known to represent flowers, not from Tradescant's garden but from another of a slightly later date, that of Henry Compton, Bishop of London, at Fulham Palace, where Evelyn recorded seeing them in 1682.[14]

In the back of one of these volumes, however, are inserted four small pieces of vellum, each representing a different fruit 'exquisitely limned' and individually signed or monogrammed. Their origin is not known, but they could well have come from the book that was once in the Tradescant collection as they clearly do not belong with the rest. The fact that they represent fruit and not flowers is of no significance, as there was little discrimination between the two. They were grown together in the same beds, and Marshal would have included both.

Little is known of this seventeenth-century botanical artist. That he was already famous in his own time is shown by the entry in the *Musaeum Tradescantianum* and confirmed by a reference in Sir William Sanderson's *Graphice* (1658) which states that in England 'our modern masters' are 'comparable with any now beyond seas', citing Marshal specifically for 'flowers and fruits'.[15]

According to Dr William Freind, Dean of Canterbury, who claimed to be his great-nephew (Marshal having married Dorothea Smith, the sister of his father's mother), he had an independent fortune and painted merely for his own amusement. Freind added that he had a particular art of extracting colours out of the natural flowers, a secret that died with those to whom he imparted it.[16]

In 1667 Marshal wrote a letter from Castle Ashby to a Mr Povey in which he said: 'As for the colours I make out of flowers, or berries, or gums, or roots, they are more subtle, and have not so great a body, as minerals . . . The search of colours has cost me much time in finding out, and to know, which would hold colour in water, and mix well; else I had not used them in my book, and, am sure, will be as fresh a hundred years hence, as when you saw them last. The truth is, they are pretty secrets, but known, they are nothing.'[17]

It is perhaps from the Puritan intellectual Samuel Hartlib that we learn most about Marshal. Hartlib seems to have heard about him first in 1650 when he relates that Marshal was living at Ham with 'a whole chamber of insects which make a glorious representation. Hee is also very skilful in drawing painting and representing of anything. As John Tradesken hath a booke very lively representing most of the things hee hath.'

Hartlib met him four years later and afterwards recorded that Marshal was a merchant by profession, having lived for some years in France; that he was a great 'florist', importing plants from abroad and growing both licorice and rhubarb, keeping two gardens, one at the Earl of Northampton's, presumably Castle Ashby, and the other at Islington, where he was then 'lodging'.

Hartlib added that Marshal had birds 'of all manner of Colours and hath a peculiar Art of representing or preserving of their skinnes with their feathers, as likewise of all manner of Insects'. He noted that Marshal had been offered £500 for his 'pictuary of flowers'.[18] This was presumably the book of Tradescant's flowers rather than the volumes at Windsor, as Dr Compton was not appointed Bishop of London until 1675. Marshal stayed with Compton for some years before his death and is buried in Fulham Church.

Unfortunately the manuscripts and books sent to Oxford by Ashmole were not catalogued on arrival, and so it is not known whether Marshal's book of flowers ever reached the Ashmolean.

Another unsolved mystery is what happened to John Tradescant junior's books. With his many interests it is inconceivable that he did not have a library that included works of both botanical interest and travel. Furthermore his father is known to have inherited a quarter of the books belonging to his friend Captain John Smith[19] and, in view of this friendship, must surely also have had his own copies of Smith's works. But there are very few books in the Bodleian today which can be traced to Smith or to either of the Tradescants.

One that can is a political pamphlet printed in 1626, which has under the title the inscription 'This is John Tradescants booke bought in January 1626.' It is called 'An excellent and Material Discourse Proving by many and forceable reasons what great danger will hang over our heads of England and France and also divers other Kingdomes and Provinces of Europe if it shall happen that those of Germanie which are our friends be subdued and the King of Denmarke vanquished'.[20] It shows that he took an interest in the political scene.

Also in the Bodleian is a volume containing William Strachey's *History of Travaile into Virginia* in manuscript form, interspersed with engravings that have been roughly hand-coloured. It is bound with part of a copy of Richard Hakluyt's 1588 *Book of Virginia*. With them is a short dictionary of the Indian language with English equivalents in manuscript 'by which such as shall be Imployed thither may know the readyer how to confer, and how to truck and trade with the people'. This could be in the hand of the younger Tradescant.[21]

A folio volume containing 180 parchment leaves in a fifteenth-century text and having illuminated capitals is indexed as being John Hardying's *Chronicles of Britain in ballad*. A woodcut pasted into the front of this book is wrongly labelled as being of John Hardying when in fact it represents George the Pious, Prince of Anhalt.[22] This, too, is roughly coloured but using different shades to those in the Strachey mentioned above. However, there are thought to be similarities in the manuscript lettering used in both.

One book that probably belonged to the elder Tradescant is a volume containing designs for garden knots with a few dried petals left in between the pages. It opens with very simple, rather crude designs roughly coloured in reddish brown and green, presumably to represent low hedging and coloured earth. But as the pages are turned the designs become more elaborate, and towards the end there is a drawing of the royal coat of arms used up to the end of the reign of Queen Elizabeth in 1603.[23]

At the royal palace of Theobalds the King's arms were set out 'designed to perfection in mixed borders of mignonette and pinks'.[24] This was in 1618 when the Italian, Orazio Busino, chaplain to the Venetian Ambassador, recorded seeing them. If the arms were not changed when James I came to the throne then this might link the elder Tradescant with Theobalds. On the other hand, Mountain Jennings, who is known to have worked there both before and after it became a royal palace, may merely have passed on the design.

There are three volumes of dried flower collections among the Ashmole manuscripts. Two of these are attributed to Edward Morgan, Tradescant's friend who kept the medical garden at Westminster; the third is possibly connected with the Tradescants, although it is not in the hand of either of them and it is doubtful if the compiler was an experienced botanist. The first page contains a recipe for making a paste with which to affix the specimens to paper, written by Elias Ashmole; a paste, incidentally, that has proved effective through the years. The index and the names written under the flowers are in two different hands; the book contains a wide variety of mostly European plants and from the nomenclature used this volume is judged to be contemporary with the 1656 plant list. It could possibly be an early exercise of John III's.[25]

Finally, there is the elder John Tradescant's own copy of Parkinson's *Paradisus*, in the back of which are five pages of manuscript notes.[26] These are written in his own hand and record the new plants that were added to the garden between the book's publication in 1629 and his own list of 1634 (see Appendix I). They are recorded year by year together with the names of the people from whom some of the earlier plants were received. Ashmole added a list of 'Trees found in Mrs Tradescants Ground when it came into my possession' in 1679.

This book did not come to the museum through Ashmole. It was acquired by the Bodleian Library only by chance in 1917, when it was purchased from an antiquarian bookseller. The inscriptions show that it must have passed through Ashmole's hands even though it was a personal possession of the Tradescants and not part of the museum collection. Evidently Ashmole chose not to pass it on to Oxford with the other items and no doubt kept other books, too. He had an extensive library of his own and, while his will decreed that Oxford should receive 'all my printed bookes which at the time of my decease shall bee in the two uppermost Studies in my Turret at my house in South Lambeth', together with those 'in the Inward Closet within my lower Study over the Milke house',[27] there was obviously at least one other room full of books as, after his death, more than a thousand were sold at auction. These included not only the *Paradisus* but a copy of Johnson's revised edition of Gerard's *Herbal*, works by George Sandys and Captain John Smith, books and maps on early travels, some even in duplicate, as well as historical and religious tracts. It seems likely that Tradescant's books were among them.

The supposition that Ashmole held back a number of items he had acquired from Hester Tradescant is confirmed by Ralph Thoresby, the antiquarian diarist. As we have noted earlier, he records visiting Turret House in 1712: 'Passing by the house where Mr Ashmole once lived, we visited the widow, who showed us the remains of Mr Tradescant's rarities, amongst which some valuable shells and Indian curiosities.'[28] By this date Ashmole's widow had been dead for eleven years, but her second husband, the stonemason John Reynolds, was in possession of the house and had taken as his new wife a Stepney widow called Mildred Prowde. It was presumably she to whom Thoresby refers.

Perhaps it was one of these shells that found its way into the Hunterian Collection in Glasgow: a *Strombus-listeri* T. Gray, still a very rare shell today. Its provenance can almost certainly be traced back to Tradescant, and it is considered to be his *Buccina striata*.[29]

Ashmole could not have expected to acquire the Tradescant family portraits, but perhaps we should be grateful that he did, as these were sent to Oxford with the original accessions. The collection, which is on view at the Ashmolean Museum, consists of the following paintings:

A portrait of John Tradescant I emerging from the clouds; possibly by Emanuel de Critz.

A portrait of John Tradescant I believed to have been painted posthumously and based on the above picture. It is attributed to Cornelius de Neve. The surrounding cartouche of flowers, fruit and vegetables may be from the hand of Alexander Marshal.

A portrait of an unknown lady (probably Hester Tradescant) painted in 1638 by an unknown British painter.

A double portrait of John Tradescant II with Hester, painted in 1656. It is attributed to Emanuel de Critz and was probably commissioned to commemorate publication of the *Musaeum Tradescantianum*.

A portrait of John Tradescant II with his neighbour Roger Friend and some of The Ark's more curious shells. These have been identified as coming from as far afield as China, the Moluccas, Zanzibar and the West Indies. This double portrait is now attributed to Thomas de Critz.

A portrait of Hester Tradescant with her two stepchildren; attributed to Emanuel de Critz.

A portrait of John Tradescant II leaning on a spade and dressed as a gardener in an open-necked shirt and fur-lined coat; possibly by Thomas de Critz.

A portrait of John Tradescant I on his deathbed in 1638; by an unknown painter.

Two separate portraits of John III and his sister Frances, both by the same unknown artist, painted about 1638.

A portrait of Hester Tradescant and her stepson John III painted in 1645 and now attributed to Thomas de Critz.

The following pictures, on view at the Ashmolean, are also believed to derive from the Tradescant collection:

A self-portrait of Cornelius de Neve II.

A portrait of a young man called Oliver de Critz and attributed to his half-brother Thomas but possibly a self-portrait of Thomas de Critz.

A portrait of Charles I after Van Dyck.

A portrait of Elizabeth Woodville, Queen to Edward IV, who died in 1492; by an unknown artist.[30]

There is another portrait of the younger Tradescant, now attributed to Thomas de Critz, in the National Portrait Gallery. At one time this portrait hung at Strawberry Hill in the collection of Horace Walpole, who associated the moss-covered skull with which Tradescant is portrayed with the remedy known as the 'Powder of Sympathy'. Unfortunately, he does not record on what this assumption was based. There was a magical treatment of that name, but Sir Kenelm Digby, who in 1662 was advertising 'Sympathetical powder . . . prepared by Promethean fire to cure all green wounds and the toothache',[31] makes no mention of this strange ingredient in his published account.[32] Dr Robert Hooke, a contemporary of Tradescant, does, however, refer to 'a soveraine remedy for ye falling sickness . . . made out of the mosse of a mans scull'.[33] If, as is considered possible, the symbolic objects in this painting relate to the death of John III in 1652, does this suggest that he was an epileptic? The gallery acquired the portrait from a dealer in 1897.

Chapter 17

The 'Principall Benefactors'

At the end of the *Musaeum Tradescantianum* is a list of the principal benefactors to the collection. There are 109 names, carefully arranged in order of precedence. Curiously, however, this order of precedence, so methodically worked out, is not correct for the year 1656, the date of the *Musaeum Tradescantianum*'s publication. To give just three examples, Lady Mary Villiers, the daughter of the Duke and Duchess of Buckingham, had by then been twice married. Her first wedding took place in 1635 when she was only twelve years old. By 1656 she was the Duchess of Richmond. Mr Nicholas, Secretary to the Navy, had been Sir Edward since 1641; and Sir Christopher Hatton, a courtier with antiquarian and gardening interests, had been elevated to the peerage some thirteen years earlier.

Some sort of an accessions book had obviously been kept for the collection and this list shows clearly how far back in time most of the items must have been presented, confirming that the bulk of the rarities were acquired in the time of the elder Tradescant. The fact that a number of benefactors had died some years before Tradescant opened his museum and even before he started to collect for the Duke of Buckingham indicates that he had made a hobby of collecting from an early age. All donations seem to have been made in the benefactors' lifetimes; such wills as have been checked reveal no mention of Tradescant's name.

Unfortunately in most cases there is no record of the actual gifts that were made, but a brief study of the lives of these patrons can tell us their interests, and in some cases their careers divulge the type of object that may have been contributed.

The lives of many of them are interwoven, not only with that of Tradescant, but with each other. Many fell within Buckingham's orbit and a surprising number were Catholic recusants. Above all, they were, almost without exception, Royalists.

It has already been shown how the King and Queen and the Buckingham family could have made their contribution. All Tradescant's other known employers are represented, too, and, while they would undoubtedly have allowed him to take seeds and cuttings from the plants that had prospered in his care, the list of benefactors does not include the names of those known to have sent plants (such as the Robins, the Morins or even Sir Peter Wyche), so that the conclusion must be drawn that only benefactors to the museum are included.

Robert Cecil was perhaps the person who first aroused Tradescant's collecting instincts. In 1607 Cecil had dispatched a young man on an East India Company ship to 'go for parrots, monkeys and marmosets'[1] and, as we have seen, Tradescant acquired an artificial bird and a great buffalo's horn for him in France. We know that his son William, the second Earl of Salisbury, donated '7 old maps of diverse countries' as Tradescant's name has been added in a later hand against this entry on an inventory of the contents of Hatfield House made in July 1612.[2] Unfortunately there are no maps as such listed in the collection, hut they are probably included among the 'several draughts' in section VII.

'Lady Wootton' was the widow of Tradescant's employer at Canterbury; her sole mark in history seems to have been wearing a gown to a royal wedding made from embroidered material that cost fifty pounds a yard.[3] She was Margaret, daughter of Philip, third Baron Wharton.

Obviously Sir Dudley Digges would have been in a good position to have presented some of the Russian objects, but he was also connected with the East India, Virginia, New England and North West Passage Companies. A 'store of unicorns' horns' was reputedly found on a journey for the last. Tradescant was heard telling Lord Carlisle about them, but he seems to have been sceptical about their origins: they were 'long and wreathed like that at Windsor, which I have heard to be nothing else but the snout of a fish, yet very precious against poison'.[4]

Tradescant's warrant makes it clear that his appointment at Oatlands was a contract to maintain the palace gardens, and it seems likely that he also found time to act as gardening adviser to a number of his benefactors. Unfortunately no records to prove this can be traced, but he would certainly have been quite free to do so after leaving Buckingham's employ, and possibly before then, as his previous terms of employment are unknown. It was common practice later in the century for a gardener of repute to tour the great estates. George London, for instance, spent three months of the year riding round on regular tours,[5] although it is not suggested that Tradescant did anything on the same scale. He is more likely to have supervised the laying out and planting of new gardens. The idea is not unreasonable. He was after all looking after his own garden in Lambeth, the royal garden at Oatlands and had accepted responsibility for the Oxford physic garden.

One possible employer is Lady Christian Leveson, the daughter of Sir Walter Mildmay and the second wife of Sir John Leveson of Halling, Kent.

After her husband's death in 1615 she continued to live at Halling, acting as guardian to their unmarried children. Certainly Tradescant trod 'the footeway' to her house, as Parkinson records that this 'worthy, diligent and painefull observer and preserver both of plants and all other natures varieties' found the common green beet growing there.[6] Parkinson also tells us that parsnips grew wild in the grounds.[7]

Another possible employer is Alathea Talbot, a rich heiress who, after her marriage to Thomas Howard, Earl of Arundel, came to be regarded as the 'chief lady of the Court and Kingdom'.[8] Her husband was considered the greatest patron of the arts, famed for transplanting 'Old Greece into England' and 'causing a whole army of old forraine Emperours, Captaines, and Senators all at once to land'.[9] His whole family became infected with his collecting enthusiasm, not least his son, Lord Maltravers, whose wife, Lady Elizabeth Stuart, daughter of the third Duke of Lennox, was also a benefactor. The Arundels owned houses at Highgate, London and Albury in Surrey, all with fine gardens.

Lord Arundel had first travelled to Italy with Inigo Jones in 1613, when he was shown the sights of Rome by another benefactor, George Gage. The Countess accompanied him and later went again to visit their sons who were studying there. On this occasion her husband was too busy at Court to accompany her, but he requested the French King that his wife should 'be used with all humanity' and be given 'leave to carry weapons and peeces, to diffende herselfe in these broken times'. When she finally left Venice on her journey home she had with her a large train and seventy bales of goods all sealed and exempted from customs by order of the Doge.[10]

Her husband, with apparently endless funds, had collectors buying for him all over Europe. These included two more benefactors, Sir Dudley Carleton, created Viscount Dorchester in 1628, at the Hague, and Sir Thomas Roe in Constantinople. Not content with their efforts, in 1624 Arundel also sent out as his personal agent his chaplain, the Rev. William Petty, a man whose knowledge, stamina and energy were unbounded.

Sir Thomas Roe, who was Ambassador to Turkey from 1621 to 1628, was asked by Arundel to smooth the way for Petty so that he could travel around the country buying up 'marbles'. Roe was himself endeavouring to collect antiquities not only for Arundel but also for the all-powerful Buckingham, whose favour he dared not lose. He had hoped that he could persuade Petty to divide such loot as he acquired — with ambassadorial help — between his two important patrons, but Petty would not have it and perpetually tried to deceive Roe by claiming that he had found nothing of interest.

Writing to Arundel in 1625, Roe said of Petty that he 'spareth no paynes nor arts to effect his service . . . I have done for Mr Petty whatsoever was in my power, by giving him forceable commands, and letters of recommendation . . . but your lordship knowing, that I have received the like from his grace the duke of Buckingham, and engaged my word to doe him service, he might judge it want of witt, or will, or creditt, if Mr Petty (who could doe nothing but by mee) should take all things before or from mee.'

Despite Petty's doublecrossing, Roe was unable to conceal his admiration for him: 'Ther was never man so fitted to an imployment, that encounters all accidents with so unwearied patience; eates with Greekes on their worst dayes; lyes with fishermen on plancks, at the best; is all things to all men, that he may obteyne his ends, which are your lordships service.'

Roe had to fall back on sending odd stones. One, 'taken out of the old pallace of Priam in Troy, cutt in horned shape, hut because I neither can tell of what it is, nor hath it any other bewty, but only the antiquity. . . I will not presume to send it you; yet I have delivered it to the same messenger, that your Lordship may see it, and throw it away.'[11]

Many of the objects sent back by Sir Thomas Roe, whose wife, the daughter of Sir Richard Gresham, was also a benefactor, were entrusted to the care of Anthony Wood, Captain of the *Rainbow*. Although it is possible that he was the 'Captain Wood' listed among the benefactors, John Wood, who, as has been related, was long connected with the Guinea Company, would seem to be the more likely candidate.

Sir Thomas Roe was also sending antiquities to William Laud, the Archbishop of Canterbury, who was building up a collection of coins and medals and was also interested in acquiring manuscripts. Laud, another benefactor, had become intimate with Buckingham as his confessor and was, of course, Tradescant's neighbour at Lambeth. In endeavouring to obtain manuscripts for the Archbishop, Roe was again frustrated by Petty. Writing to the Archbishop's chaplain, Roe complained that Petty 'by my meanes had admittance into the best library knowne of Greece, where are loades of old manuscripts; and hee used so fine arte, with the helpe of some of my servants, that hee conveyed away 22. I thought, I should have had my share, but hee was for himselfe: hee is a good chooser, saw all, or most, and tooke . . . I meant to have a review of that library; but hee gave it such a blow, under my trust, that since it hath beene locked up under two keys.'[12]

Prior to his appointment at Constantinople, Sir Thomas Roe had held, at the request and expense of the East India Company, the post of Ambassador to the Court of Jehangir, the Mogul Emperor of Hindustan. 'Honest Tom', as he was called, carried out his duties there with courage and perseverance, always insisting on the respect that he felt was due to him as the king's representative. His dignity and insistence won respect and raised British prestige. He always refused gifts for himself other than 'an horse or two, and sometimes a vest, or upper Garment made of slight Cloath of Gold, which the Mogul would first put upon his own back, and then give to the Ambassadour'.[13] The prince, the Emperor's son, similarly presented him with a 'cloke' of cloth of gold. 'I made reverence for it very unwillingly,' wrote Roe in his journal, but 'it is here reputed the highest favour to give a garment that has been worn by the Prince.'[14]

One of these unwanted gifts obviously found its way into the Tradescant collection. Sir Thomas's own interests lay in the collection of coins and oriental manuscripts, which in due course he presented to the Bodleian Library.

Viscount Dorchester was in turn Ambassador to Venice and the Hague. On Buckingham's behalf and with the assistance of the Catholic recusant George Gage, who seems to have acted as his agent, he arranged the exchange for marbles of Rubens's famous collection of pictures and tapestries and also sought out pictures for Arundel. Dorchester's wife went to Flushing in 1624 for a sale of Italian and Spanish goods taken from a prize, where she bought pictures on her husband's behalf, after he had received various commissions, including one from Buckingham. She also hoped to acquire beads of heliotrope, lapis lazuli, agate, crystals, hangings and tapestries.[15]

During his time in the Low Countries Dorchester met many talented artists, introducing their work to his patrons at home. He collected in a small way on his own account and was responsible for enriching the galleries of many others with greater means.

Dorchester died in 1632. In that same year Sir William Boswell was appointed Ambassador to the Hague, having previously been secretary to the Earl of Carlisle. Boswell sent over books and maps for the King and must have been a connoisseur of coins and medals because in the previous year he had been ordered, with two others, to put the King's coin collection 'into such order as they shall thinke fitt off' and was afterwards sworn a Gentleman of the Privy Chamber.[16]

George Gage was respected for his artistic knowledge and seems to have had some talent as a painter himself. In 1622 he was involved in secret negotiations over papal dispensation for the marriage then proposed between Prince Charles and the Spanish Infanta, to which end he spent eighteen months travelling between London, Rome and Spain. Various sums were paid to him at this time for his work 'in foreign parts for His Majesties special service'.[17]

James Hay, first Earl of Carlisle, was a Gentleman of the Bedchamber and a prominent courtier who travelled extensively on the Continent on diplomatic assignments and later became renowned for his extravagance and splendid hospitality. He was the inventor of the 'ante-supper' when tables laden with cold dishes were whisked away before any guest had had a chance to taste them, to be immediately replaced with an equally ostentatious array of hot dishes. After the proposed Spanish marriage had fallen through, he helped negotiate the marriage treaty between Charles I and Henrietta Maria. He rode into Paris on a horse shod with silver; when one shoe fell off to be fought over by the following crowd it was immediately replaced by another.

He was at one time Keeper of Nonsuch House and Park. He also had interests in the Caribbean, fitting out ships to trade with the Lesser Antilles.

Henry Cary, first Viscount Falkland, was made Comptroller of the Household under Buckingham, which position he sold in 1622, buying with the proceeds a six-mile-wide section of Newfoundland. His colony failed because of the inexperience of those sent out, but he enjoyed profits from it both in trade and fishing, the latter industry then employing an astonishing 250 ships and 10,000 men from England.

In 1637 Sir David Kirke was one of a group granted a charter for the whole of Newfoundland. Nine years earlier he, with his brother and a band of gallant followers, having previously won Novia Scotia for the Crown, captured the principal French territories in Canada, including Quebec. This feat has been described as 'the most brilliant naval exploit in colonial history'. The territories were returned to the French at the Peace of St Germaine in 1632. Kirke's Newfoundland charter gave him more or less a free hand in taxing colonists and he proceeded to extract the maximum until dismissed for unscrupulous behaviour in 1640.[18]

In February 1638 Kirke took out to Newfoundland John Scandouer, the King's deer-keeper, 'to take and bring over some dere for His Majesty', for which trip 'two tents of two roomes apeece' were drawn from the Master of the Tents.[19] Perhaps some antlers were passed on to Tradescant. Certainly Kirke and Falkland seem most likely to have contributed the very early Canadian material still remaining in the collection.

James Stanley, Lord Strange, heir to the sixth Earl of Derby, had travelled in France and Italy and possessed a fine library. He devoted himself to Manx interests and lived mostly at Castle Rushen.

The court fool, Lord Goring, having accompanied Charles and Buckingham on their abortive trip to Madrid, later participated in negotiating the marriage treaty of Charles I with the French princess. Afterwards he became in succession Vice-Chamberlain and Master of the Horse to Queen Henrietta Maria. Offices were heaped upon him and, like the Earl of Carlisle, he became renowned for his extravagance.

In 1633 he organized a syndicate to colonize the mouth of the Amazon. The venture collapsed after only one ship had been sent out, but he could perhaps have been the source of some of the South American items. His wife, also a benefactor, was the second daughter of Edward Nevill, sixth Lord Abergavenny. They lived at Danny in Sussex. Goring is another benefactor who had been further elevated before the *Musaeum Tradescantianum's* publication, having been made Earl of Norwich in 1644.

Baptist Hicks, first Viscount Campden, was the court silk merchant whose thriving business was carried on at the White Bear in Cheapside. He imported rich materials from abroad and also went in for money-lending. One of very few merchants to be honoured with a title, he had achieved his position through the influence of his brother, Sir Michael, who had worked for Robert Cecil.

'Lady Denbeigh', the wife of William Fielding, first Earl of Denbigh, was Buckingham's sister, Susan Villiers. Her husband, by this fortunate choice of a wife, became Master of the Great Wardrobe in 1622 and, despite his inexperience, was put in charge of the fleet in 1628. He seems to have had an adventurous disposition as he afterwards made a voyage to India out of curiosity.

'Lady Killegray' was Mary Woodhouse, a niece of Sir Francis Bacon and the wife of Sir Robert Killigrew, a courtier interested in the concoction of drugs and cordials who succeeded Dorchester as Ambassador to Holland. She seems to have had a connection with the Glovers' Company and was described as 'a cunning old woman, who had been herself too much, and was too long versed in amours'.[20]

Sir Henry Wotton, the half-brother of Edward, Lord Wotton, was Ambassador to Venice on and off for nearly twenty years. The first person to introduce Italian works of art to members of the English Court, he supervised the construction of the mosaic portrait of Robert Cecil for Hatfield House and later purchased pictures for Buckingham. He regarded himself as an expert on Venetian glassware and paid many visits to the Murano glassworks, often choosing pieces for his patrons back home. He is also known to have sent rose cuttings and melon seed to the King and fennel with 'a large direction' on how to dress it to Tradescant.[21]

Sir Kenelm Digby, despite having been brought up as a ward of archbishop Laud, remained a Catholic under the influence of his mother. While on a private visit to Spain, he had met Charles and Buckingham and became caught up in the ill-fated marriage negotiations. In the 1631 patent of the Guinea Company he is named as a member, and he acted as Deputy Governor for a year.

In 1628 Digby made a privateering expedition to the Mediterranean, successfully seizing foreign piratical merchantmen in the Turkish port of Alexandretta, then known as Scanderoon, transferring the spoils to his own ship and sailing off with them. It caused considerable local ill will, but in England he was regarded as a hero.

On the way home he called in at Melos, Delos and Mycenae to look for antiquities, successfully it seems, as it was reported that 'some of the Old-Greeke-Marble-bases, columnes, and altars were brought from the ruines of Apollo's temple at Delos, by that noble and absolutely compleat gentleman Sir Kenelme Digby Knight'.[22] Perhaps he passed on a few stones to Tradescant.

Digby also collected books and was fascinated by chemical experiments; although Evelyn described him as an 'arrant Mountebank',[23] he was invited to become a founder member of the Royal Society and, as the first to appreciate the importance of oxygen to the life of plants, read the members a paper on that subject.[24]

Sir Nathaniel Bacon probably donated 'a small Landskip' painted by himself. It is still in the Ashmolean collection and is probably the earliest landscape by an English artist in existence. The half-brother of Sir Francis Bacon, his recipe for a particular 'browne pinke' colour became famous. He is buried at Culford in Suffolk and the inscription on his monument describes him as 'well skilled in the history of plants, and in delineating them with his pencil'.[25]

Sir Henry Vane put himself into court by buying a Carver's place and in 1629 was appointed Comptroller of the King's Household. He held ambassadorial appointments in Sweden and the Low Countries, where he collected paintings and a book of Holbein's work for Arundel; he later visited Germany on diplomatic business.[26]

His son, another Henry, was married at the church of St Mary's, Lambeth, to Frances Wray and, although he was knighted in 1640 and had gone to New England in 1624, having a brief administration as Governor of Massachusetts, his father is more likely to have been the benefactor.

Sir Henry Palmer was Comptroller of the Navy and lived at Howletts, Bekesborne, Kent. Sir Robert Heath rose for a brief period to be Lord Chief Justice, being dismissed for political and religious reasons.

The corrupt and incompetent 'bottomless Bagge' was the man responsible for victualling and supplying the fleet. Buckingham's henchman Sir James Bagge was either fraudulent or careless but retained his position as Governor of Plymouth despite sending out ships supplied with rotten food and tackle and noxious drink. He was involved in an appalling case of corruption that was heard by the Star Chamber. It had been his responsibility to victual the fleet sent out on the ill-fated Isle of Rhé expedition, after which he even failed to pay the men who served on it, although he received large sums of money for which he was afterwards unable to account.[27]

Sir Peter Manwood, who probably donated the bestiary, had antiquarian interests, but his extravagant lifestyle involved him in financial difficulties and he was forced to leave the country in 1621. Suffering ill health, he returned to Hackinton, near Canterbury, in 1624 and died a year later.

Sir John Trevor had been made Keeper at Oatlands for life in 1603, but he died in 1630, the year of Tradescant's appointment. He was also a Councillor for Virginia and Surveyor of the Navy from 1609. In this last capacity he had close links with another benefactor, Phineas Pett, Master Shipwright to the Navy and Naval Commissioner.

Pett was renowned for the intricate models of the ships that he constructed, and, while the Ashmolean Museum has such a model, there is none listed in the *Musaeum Tradescantianum* (and such a prize exhibit surely would have been). Moreover this surviving example is now regarded as greatly inferior to Pett's workmanship and not of comparable date.

Pett had sailed on the *Unity* to Virginia in 1609, and Tradescant had sailed with him on the *Mercury*'s voyage to the Mediterranean in 1620. They must also have renewed acquaintance when, in command of the *Prince*, Pett brought Henrietta Maria over from Boulogne as a bride when Tradescant was acting as baggage-master to Buckingham.

Sir Clipsby Crew lived at Isleworth and Evelyn, after dining with him there, commented on his 'fine Indian hangings'.[28] Evidently he was a man with artistic tastes and an interest in gardens, as they had together seen some 'curious flowers' being cultivated near by.

Sir Alexander Gordon of Cluny was created a baronet in 1625 and six years later was sworn a Gentleman of the Privy Chamber despite being a Catholic recusant. Sir Butts Bacon was created a baronet in 1627 and was another half-brother of Francis Bacon. He was named 'Butts' after his mother, the heiress daughter of Sir William Butts who had been surgeon to Henry VIII. Sir Richard Wiseman of Thundersly in Essex was another baronet, created in 1628. 'Sir John Aemoote' was probably Sir John Achmouty, a Groom of the Bedchamber to James I, who had travelled in Italy and later to Paris with Lord Hay and who seems to have made his mark in history by his prowess at dancing, being esteemed one of 'the most principall and loftie' high dancers in Ben Jonson's *Irish Masque*.[29]

'Lady Graimcs' was probably the wife of Sir Richard Grimes, who, as the Duke of Buckingham's Master of the Horse, helped him and Charles on their secret mission to woo the Spanish Infanta in 1623. During that mission he returned at least once to bring eagerly awaited news to James I.

Of the five doctors, 'Owin' was probably the clergyman John Owen, son of 'the worthy and grave minister' of Burton Latimer, Northamptonshire, who, having succeeded his father as rector there, was later 'preferred beyond his expectation', being made a chaplain to the future King Charles and afterwards, in 1629, Bishop of St Asaph.[30]

Thomas Wharton, as we have seen, helped to prepare the museum catalogue. William Broad, although a prominent apothecary, never appears to have qualified as a doctor. A friend of Thomas Johnson, who revised Gerard's *Herbal*, he accompanied him on several botanizing expeditions around the country. He also wrote an introductory verse of commendation to Parkinson's *Paradisus*.

John Bugg(s) was also a member of these expeditions and seems to have been a man of strong character. He, too, was an apothecary and, when he was charged by the College of Physicians with practising physick, he refused to give an answer, 'behaving himself very insolently and saucily'. After he had the misfortune to lose several of his patients, he was sent to the Fleet Prison. Sir Robert Heath, then Lord Chief Justice, tried to obtain his release for the summer vacation, but the President of the College would not contemplate it,

Denton, too, got into trouble for private trading. When he returned home in the *Royal James* in 1621, all his cloves were sequestered and sold. When charged with the offence, he replied that 'he was not so very a fool as to serve so many years up and down from port to port and get nothing for himself'. The Court of the East India Company noted 'his insolency' and told him that, if all their factors were of his mind, there would be nothing for the Company. Buckingham interceded on his behalf and he appears to have remained with the Company until 1628.[38]

William Claiborne (Cleborne) went to Virginia as Surveyor in 1621 and seven years later received a licence to trade and explore the shores of the upper Chesapeake. Returning to England in 1629 he joined a firm of London merchants and two years later the King granted them a licence to trade with any part of the North American coast where a monopoly had not already been granted; in the following year he obtained a licence to trade with the Dutch plantations.

The younger brother of Lord de la Warr, Francis West first went to Virginia in 1609. He was sent upstream from Jamestown to overwinter at some falls with 120 men. The Governor, then John Smith, went up to inspect the settlement and, finding it too near the river and in danger of flooding, insisted on moving the encampment. But as soon as his back was turned West led the men back to their original site.

In the winter of the following year food was desperately short so he was sent to trade for grain at Potomac in one of the colony's three ships. After obtaining such supplies as he could, he sailed off to England with them, causing great distress to those remaining in the colony, who were left to endure such severe hunger and hardship that many of them died.

West should have been severely reprimanded, but, as by that time his brother was Governor, he was given another ship and sent back. He remained in the colony, being appointed Governor of New England in 1622.[39]

Captain Plumleigh, or 'Plumbey' as Tradescant called him, was also at the Isle of Rhé, where he was described as 'a younge sea Capt. half Papist halfe Protestante',[40] and in 1632 his flagship was the *Victory*. Captain Ireland was probably George Ireland, one of the 'seamen' sworn to give evidence for Phineas Pett at a commission of inquiry over the building of the *Prince Royal* in 1609.[41]

Thomas Trenchfield was an elder brother of Trinity House who lived at St Mary Cray. He died in 1646 at the age of sixty-seven and must have been a man of means as his will provided for the provision and endowment of four almshouses, whose inmates were to be nominated by Trinity House.[42]

Edward Nicholas began his career in the service of Edward, Lord Zouch, Lord Warden of the Cinque Ports, transferring to Buckingham when he succeeded to that post. Nicholas then became Secretary to the Admiralty Commissioners. A conscientious administrator, he was perpetually overworked, and his health suffered accordingly. He had a great interest in books and pictures, and he collected portraits of the celebrities of the day. An ardent Royalist, he was instructed by the King to sign the articles of surrender at Oxford in June 1646, being allowed six months' liberty to put his affairs in order before going into exile.[43] Mr Butterworth was probably his brother-in-law of that name.[44]

Mr John Slany, a merchant tailor of London, lived in Cornhill and was Governor of the Newfoundland Company between 1610 and 1628.

The merchant Mr James Bovey or Boovy is one of the few benefactors who probably made his donation to the younger Tradescant. Born in 1622, he travelled abroad extensively, learned five languages and became cashier to Sir Peter Vanlore, working out a table of all the exchanges of Europe. Exceedingly industrious, he retired through indisposition at the age of only thirty-two; he then studied law and became an expert on 'law merchant'. Aubrey described him as 'about 5 foot high, slender, strait, haire exceeding black & curling at the end, a dark hazell Eie of a middling size, but the most sprightly that I have ever beheld, browes and beard of the colour of his haire'.[45]

Thomas Howard was perhaps the third husband of Buckingham's daughter, Mary Villiers, a brother of Charles, first Earl of Carlisle, which title was only granted to him after the Hay peerage died out. Although they did not marry until 1664 he was presumably moving in the same circle.

The Offley brothers, Robert and Thomas, came from a Staffordshire family and were merchants connected with a variety of companies trading overseas. Of the two, Robert seems the most likely to have been a benefactor because he was probably the same Robert Offley who was a gentleman volunteer with Tradescant on the Mediterranean expedition of 1620.[46] The brothers helped to create the Eastland Company, which traded from Elbing with the lands around the Baltic. Robert was also connected with the East India, Virginia, Levant and North West Passage Companies. Thomas Offley was a member of the Muscovy Company and had connections with Bermuda.

Laurence Green, a prominent London merchant and a freeman of the Grocers' Company, was connected with the East India, Virginia, Levant, French, North West Passage, Muscovy and Spanish Companies. Another Laurence Green, probably his son, was appointed Consul at Smyrna in 1630 and petitioned the King six years later because, having done many services during those years, 'he has received no manner of allowance for his pains' whereupon he has 'made stay' of some of the merchants' goods. He 'prays letters of protection' as they now 'labour to arrest' him.[47]

'Mr Munke' must surely be Levinus Monk, who was secretary to Robert Cecil. In 1612 he was sent on diplomatic business to the Low Countries and afterwards accompanied the Princess Elizabeth to Heidelberg after her marriage to the Elector Palatine. By this time he held the appointment of a

Clerk to the Signet and was also receiving interest on money loaned to the Crown.[48] He died in 1623, reputedly worth £40,000, which, as Chamberlain commented, was 'very rich for a clarke of the signet'.[49]

Mr Sadler was perhaps either Thomas Sadler, with whom James I stayed on his visits to Salisbury, or his son Ralph, who married Anne, the daughter of the Lord Chief Justice, Sir Edward Coke. They had a lavish wedding with a magnificent feast.

At the age of fifteen Thomas Bushell entered Sir Francis Bacon's service and learned from him many secrets about the extraction of minerals. After Bacon's death, he lived for three years as a recluse on the tiny island of the Calf of Man. In 1636, after obtaining a grant of the royal mines of Cardiganshire and expending considerable sums in draining them, he carefully extracted both the silver and the lead, having first erected a mint on the site. It proved a sound investment.

Shortly before this, while work was being undertaken on his estate at Enstone, just north of Oxford, stone-cutters had exposed a rock of unusual shape. Bushell decided to build some curious and splendid waterworks around it and laid down pipes and cisterns for this purpose. There were fountains that played organ tunes and bird-songs while others produced artificial thunder and lightning. He added a banqueting house and a garden laid out with fruit trees and entertained the King and Queen there, who thought it all enormous fun.[50] To mark the occasion the Queen presented him with an Egyptian mummy which he put on display. Evelyn noted it on a later visit when he seemed rather shocked to find Bushell in 'a Grott where he lay in an hamac like an Indian'.[51]

'Mr Liggon' is probably the Richard Ligon who accompanied a Colonel Modyford to Barbados in 1647. He embarked on the *Achilles* 'having lost by a barbarous riot all that I had gotten from the painful travels of my youth and finding few friends not banished or dead'. It was obviously an unhappy time for Royalists.

En route they met a ship coming from 'Ginny' with a cargo of gold and elephants' teeth and the Captain, Blague by name, presented 'every gentleman of our company' with a present of rarities. Ligon spent three years in Barbados, returning home in 1650. He was familiar with The Ark, describing flies with 'great hornes, which we keep in boxes, and are shewed by John Tradescan'.[52]

George Thomason, Tradescant's 'Mr Tomasin', was a London bookseller who carried on his business at the Rose and Crown in St Paul's Churchyard. His fame lies in his gift to posterity of the historic collection of more than 33,000 publications printed during the civil war. Although a Royalist himself, Thomason's collection represented the views of both sides and was acquired and kept with great difficulty, being packed in trunks and stored with trusty friends around the country, often having to be moved to elude

5. Hester Tradescant with her stepson John III in 1645.
Attributed to Thomas de Critz

6, 7. The younger John Tradescant's children, John and Frances.
Artist unknown

8. The Tradescants' house in South Lambeth (left). The adjoining house belonged to Elias Ashmole. Watercolour by George Shepherd

9, 10. Two articles from the Tradescant collection: Powhatan's 'habit', now believed to be an ornament for a native temple, and an African drum of wood and elephant hide

11. Cherries by Alexander Marshal. From his florilegium, now in the Royal Library at Windsor

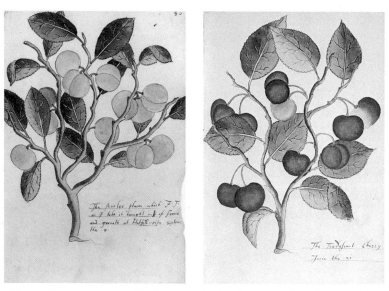

12, 13. Two pages from 'Tradescant's Orchard': the 'Amber plum' and the 'Tradescant Chery'

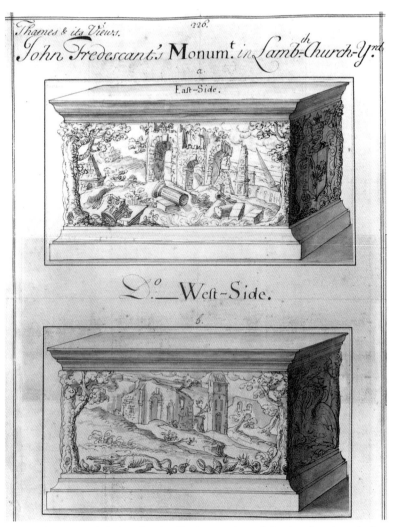

John Tredescant's Monum.t in Lamb-Church-Y.rd

a.

East-Side.

D.o — West-Side.

b.

14. The original design for the Tradescants' tomb in the churchyard of
St Mary-at-Lambeth. The east and west sides are reversed on the
actual tomb

advancing or retreating armies. Long after Thomason's death the collection was presented to the British Museum after it had been acquired by George III for less than it had cost originally.[53]

William Dell was secretary to Archbishop Laud and acted as his solicitor throughout his trial for treason, describing himself as 'the inconsolable servant' after Laud's execution. He should not be confused with the Puritan of the same name.[54]

It is possible that 'Mr Pergins' was the royal goldsmith Admondisham Perkins, to whom there were frequent payments for making gold and silver 'spangles' for the uniforms of the royal guard.[55] Moses Tryon was a rich London merchant and probably the benefactor of that name. 'Mr Woolfe' may have been the principal apothecary to both James I and Charles I, John Wolfgang Rumlero, who became known as John Wolf. The terms of his appointment show that he was responsible for the compounding and serving of all sweet waters, powders and other odoriferous things to the royal family.[56] There was also a John Wolfe who was treasurer of the Levant Company in Constantinople.

The most likely candidate for the role of 'Mr Browne' would seem to be the Norfolk doctor Thomas Browne, who was not knighted until 1671 when he was sixty-six. Browne was a Royalist renowned for his skill in physick, so if it is him it is surprising that he is not listed with the title of doctor. He was also a keen naturalist. When Evelyn visited him in the year of his knighthood he described his 'whole house & Garden being a Paradise & Cabinet of rarities, & that of the best collection, especially Medails, books, Plants, natural things'. He also had a collection of birds' eggs.[57] Such an accumulation must have taken many years to build up and could well have been started in the elder Tradescant's lifetime.

Several of the most skilful craftsmen of the day are named. 'Mr Butler' must surely be Richard Butler, the principal English glass artist of his time. He lived in the glaziers' quarter at Southwark and was responsible for the east window in the chapel at Hatfield. He also worked for Robert Cecil at Salisbury House in the Strand and in his shopping arcade, Britain's Burse, near by. Butler restored windows in Lambeth Palace chapel and seems also to have restored and dealt in antiques.

Rowland Bucket was twice master of the Painter Stainers' Company, whose arms were placed in a window of the company's hall after he had helped to 'beautify' it in 1630. He had painted the case of the Jacobean organ at Hatfield, having previously decorated an organ clock that Queen Elizabeth sent as a gift to the Sultan of Turkey. Bucket accompanied it all the way to Constantinople. He worked at both Salisbury House and Hatfield, where he painted canvases for the chapel, gilded picture frames and decorated chimney-pieces and furniture.

In fact he seems to have been a surprisingly versatile artist, painting at least one miniature, illuminating manuscripts and making gilt leather hangings for Althorp. In the 1630s he was living on the west side of St Martin's Lane in a substantial house let to him by the second Earl of Salisbury with courtiers and politicians as neighbours.[58]

The King's master mason, Nicholas Stone, is best remembered for his monumental statuary, but he also worked in most of the royal palaces, paving a room at Oatlands in 1636 and refixing a fountain after it was moved there from Greenwich in the following year. His notebook records various charges for making 'the head of Apollo, fairely carved in Portland stone, almost twice as bigge as the life'; for '6 Emperors heads, with their pedestals cast in plaister, molded from Antiques'; and for making 'statues in Portland stone of Apollo, Juno and Diana, 6 foote in hight with 3 pedestals'.[59] Surely at least one piece of Tradescant's statuary must have emanated from his hands?

'Mr Reeve' may have been John Reeve, who was sworn in as the royal 'ovall turner' in 1633 and who subsequently made 'picture boxes in Ivory' in the form of an oval and turned out round ivory balls by the dozen.[60] Or he may have been Richard Reeves, the eminent glass-grinder and optical instrument maker whose lenses and perspective glasses were regarded as the best in the world.[61] While the listed name corresponds more with the former and there are still 'divers sorts of Ivory-balls turned one within another' in the collection, there were also 'Severall sorts of Magnifying glasses: Triangular, Prismes, Cylinders' which might have been the work of the latter.

Francis Cline, usually spelt Clein, was born in Rostock in the Baltic Provinces, the son of a goldsmith. He worked in Denmark before coming to England to become chief designer for the Mortlake tapestry works, for which he drew many original designs. The tapestry works, founded in 1619, stood on the north side of Mortlake High Street and employed skilled workers from Flanders. Clein was also employed on drawing pictures for the King and book illustrations for George Sandys; he was reputed to have been the master of the portrait painter William Dobson.[62]

'Mr Phillips' is perhaps Fabian Philips, the antiquarian friend of Aubrey, who spent his time and money publishing books devoted to the Royalist cause.

There are a number of possible 'Mr Harisons', but the most likely contender is John Harrison, for many years the King's agent in Barbary, who spent his time travelling between the two countries endeavouring to effect the release of British slaves held there. He was responsible for the return of 260 British captives.[63]

Bartholomew Haggatt was a merchant connected with the East India and Levant Companies and was appointed Consul in Aleppo in 1614.

'Mr Snelling' is perhaps Erasmus Snelling, who built the large brick house with a belvedere at Greenwich later bought by Tradescant's friend Mark Cottle. It had an enclosed orchard covering four acres planted with five hundred cherry and other fruit trees. The garden also had arbours, a high walk and a mount. [64] Snelling later moved to South Lambeth.

There was a John Rowe who was a younger brother of Trinity House in 1629, a mariner and shipowner of London. 'Mr le Goulz' was Steven le Gouche, a 'merchant stranger' from Antwerp who lived in Candlewick Street, London, and supplied expensive jewellery – mainly diamonds – to the court.

'Gasper Calthoofe' was obviously Caspar Kalthoff, the inventive Dutchman employed by the second Marquess of Worcester, who from 1628 devoted his life to mechanical experimentation. Later Worcester established Kalthoff in a workshop at Vauxhall with William Lambert, a fellow benefactor, supervising castings. According to the parliamentary survey of 1645 the Vauxhall establishment consisted of a large melting house with seven furnaces, equipment for working various metals and two rooms containing models. Guns and diverse engines, including those for raising water and irrigation, were all produced under the patronage of the Marquess, who also strove to discover the elusive secret of perpetual motion. Kalthoff in fact patented several ideas for it.[65] The Marquess later compiled a *Century of Inventions* which included a description of a steam engine – an instrument of propulsion with 'an admirable and most forcible way to drive up water by fire'.

In 1640 Samuel Hartlib noted that Kalthoff had found an excellent invention for minting and an admirable way of 'boring into brasses and iron as if it were into wood'. Nine years later he added that 'Kalthof by a devise makes his Tooles or files worke of themselves' and in the following year had invented a new kind of door that 'can open conveniently on both sides, very neatly contrived'.

John Lanyon, as proofmaster to the Ordnance until 1641, must have known Alexander Norman and is no doubt the same Lanyon described by Hartlib in 1651 as having a wife and children, two of them of marriageable age, who lived in a country house in Essex, about twelve miles from London, with 'a curious garden'. Hartlib described him as being 'very metallical'. He discovered that good lamp wicks could be made from twisted paper dipped in oil, perfected a newly invented auger and built a boat motivated by wheels that could be turned by a dog. He also devised a coach with fourteen seats.

Hartlib also noted a Mr Owefield, 'an excellent smith' who lived in Gray's Inn, whose father was a 'great mineralist having beene much imploied in the tin and leaden mines of Wales'.[66] This latter is possibly the 'Mr Ofield' listed, who may perhaps have been connected with Bushell's Welsh mines, although there were several merchants with overseas connections with the same name.

John Benson was perhaps the Benson referred to by Hartlib, who made optical glass 'for multiplying of light' and later became engrossed in trying to produce 'artificial stones or jewels'.[67] One of the royal building contractors shared the same name.

There were several contemporary knights called John Smith; nor is the 'Mr Smith' identifiable, although it seems possible that he was the adventurous and colourful Captain John Smith. As we have seen, he left the elder Tradescant some books in his will.

Mr John Millen dwelt in Old Street where his nursery was reputed to grow 'the choicest fruits this kingdom yeelds'. Here could be had gooseberries, apples, cherries and pears as well as thirteen varieties of peaches ('all good ones'), six nectarines, five sorts of apricots and 'most of the best' plums.[68] A friend of both Parkinson and Tradescant, the Millen family were well off, describing themselves as 'gent'. John Millen died in 1635 and his two sons did not long outlive him.[69]

The traveller, author and antiquary Thomas Herbert only received his baronetcy at the Restoration. As a young man he had been given a place in the suite of Sir Dodmore Cotton when he was sent as Ambassador to the Persian Court, which gave Herbert the opportunity to travel widely in that country. On the journeys out and home again his ship dropped anchor at various places on the African and Indian coasts as well as at Madagascar and Mauritius.

Although Herbert had at first taken Parliament's side, he was won over to the King's cause when he was appointed to attend him during his confinement at Holdenby. Having been made a Groom of the Bedchamber, he served as Charles I's sole attendant during the last few months of his life and treasured the gifts the King bestowed on him at the scaffold.[70]

In 1680 Herbert wrote to Elias Ashmole saying that South Lambeth was 'a place I well know, having bin sundry times at Mr Tradescons (to whom I gave severall things I collected in my travaills) & was much delighted with his gardens', describing them as 'a place of much pleasure as well as privacy'.[71]

Chapter 18

The Tradescants' Plant Introductions

The number of plant introductions that can be reliably attributed to the Tradescants is difficult to assess. They undoubtedly brought back a few plants of their own gathering that were then new to Britain. Many more, which were first recorded as being grown in England at South Lambeth, came to them through friends and contacts abroad. Nevertheless, it is by no means easy to correlate the names used for such plants in botanical and horticultural literature before 1753 with the names used today or even to identify the plants concerned; indeed some identifications can be little more than guesses.

The botanical names in the early herbals have the simplicity of the vernacular names with which they were closely linked. Thus the *Buglossa sylvestris* and 'Wild Ochenzung' of Otto Brunfels in his *Herbarum Vivae Eicones* (1530) were exact equivalents, as were the *Digitalis purpurea* and 'Brauner Fingerhut', *Digitalis lutea* and 'Geeler Fingerhut' of Leonhard Fuchs's *De Historia Stirpium* (1542). Many of the names used, for example, by John Parkinson are such simple two-word names, although he also used such a name as *Keiri sive Leucoium luteum simplex vulgare* for the single yellow wallflower.

As the number of plants introduced into gardens and discovered in the wild continually increased during the sixteenth and seventeenth centuries, so the names used to distinguish them inevitably became longer and had frequently to be changed. Even such an old and well-known garden plant as the Dame's Violet (*Hesperis matronalis* L.) had received thirteen botanical names before 1753. In that year the Swedish naturalist Carl Linnaeus introduced consistent binomial nomenclature for species, in consequence of which that called *Hesperis matronalis* bears that name unchanged today. Linnaeus tried to maintain continuity by adopting the earlier names when appropriate (for instance, the species named *Digitalis purpurea* and *Digitalis lutea* by Fuchs have the same names today because Linnaeus adopted them), but in many cases he made a dramatic break with the older names, a large number of which became obsolete and are now forgotten.

196

In addition to the problems resulting from changes in names, there are often difficulties of identification because some species were inadequately described and illustrated in the earlier works. Thus it may not be easy and is sometimes impossible to ascertain with certainty the identity of a plant recorded as arriving on English soil some 300 years ago.

It must be pointed out that many of the introductions attributed to the Tradescants by Mea Allan[1] were plants that had arrived in England long before their time. Examples are the lilac (*Syringa vulgaris* L.), which was growing in Gerard's Holborn garden in 1596;[2] the Cornelian cherry (*Cornus mas* L.), which had been planted in the royal garden at Hampton Court by 1551;[3] and the white jasmine (*Jasminum officinale* L.), which was described by Turner in 1548 as already common in gardens about London.[4] The evening primrose (*Oenothera biennis* L.), sent from America to the botanic garden at Padua in 1619, was in England by 1621, according to John Goodyer.[5] The horse chestnut (*Aesculus hippocastanum* L.) is believed to have arrived by 1616.[6]

Dr P.J. Jarvis, in an article in the *Journal of the Society for the Bibliography of Natural History*, also includes a number of errors among his list of identifications and introductions.[7]

Another group of plants were all growing in English gardens by 1629 when Parkinson published his *Paradisus*. These include the strawberry tree (*Arbutus unedo* L.); the Virginian mulberry (*Morus rubra* L.); the Virginia creeper (*Parthenocissus quinquefolia* (L.) Planchon); the Pyracantha (*Pyracantha coccinea* M.J. Roemer); the shagbark hickory (*Carya ovata* K. Koch.); the black walnut (*Juglans nigra* L.) and the stagshorn sumach (*Rhus typhina* L.), although the latter was 'Onley kept as a rarity and ornament to a Garden or Orchard'. It seems likely that at least some of these may have come first into Tradescant's hands, either through Buckingham's plea 'to all merchants from all places' or through his own arrangements with friends abroad.

Tradescant's spiderwort (*Tradescantia virginiana* L.) was received in this way. 'This Spider-wort is of late knowledge, and for it the Christian world is indebted unto that painfull industrious searcher, and lover of all natures varieties, John Tradescant,' Parkinson recorded. He 'first received it of a friend, that brought it out of Virginia, thinking it to bee the Silke Grasse that groweth there, and hath imparted hereof, as of many other things, both to me and others'.[8]

This plant was originally classified as a 'Phalangium' because it was believed to be an antidote to the bite of the Phalangium spider. Curiously, it had reached Bavaria in the previous century, where it was painted along with a group of Mexican plants by the court artist Georg Hoefnagel, who died in 1600.[9] It is unlikely to have been the only American plant to reach mainland Europe in the sixteenth century.

Tradescant records receiving another spiderwort, with white flowers, in

1633 (the earlier introduction bearing blue), and by 1640 a third, with pink or reddish blooms, had turned up. This plant is of course the one commonly known as Moses in the bullrushes.

Our first scarlet runner beans also arrived in this way; Johnson relates that this bean with flowers 'of an elegant scarlet colour' was 'procured by Mr Tradescant',[10] and Parkinson informs us that it came from the West Indies.[11] Surprisingly this bean (*Phaseolus coccineus* L.) is omitted from Tradescant's 1634 garden list (unless he mistakenly catalogued it as 'Faba Americana', which seems unlikely).

Many of the Tradescants' introductions are described in these contemporary herbals. In 1629 Parkinson says of the 'Knobbed Mountaine Valerian' (*Valeriana globularifolia* DC): 'I had of the liberalitie of my loving friend John Tradescante, who in his travaile, and search of natures varieties, met with it, and imparted thereof unto me.'[12]

Of 'Trefoil Ladies smockes' (*Cardamine trifolia* L.) he records that it was 'sent me by my especiall good friend John Tradescante, who brought it among other dainty plants from beyond the Seas, and imparted thereof a roote to me'.[13] He also describes how John Tradescant was the 'first, as I thinke' to bring the Roman red lettuce 'into England'. In a letter to Parkinson, Tradescant had described how 'after one of them had been bound and whited, when the refuse was cut away, the rest weighed seventeene ounces'.[14]

Then there was an uncommon form of parsnip known as 'the Pine Parsnep' that 'as John Tradescante saith (who hath given me the relation of this, and many other of these garden plants to whom everyone is a debtor) the roote hereof is not altogether so pleasant as the other',[15] and the 'white diapred plum of Malta, scarce knowne to any in our Land but John Tradescante'.[16]

In 1633 Thomas Johnson's revised edition of Gerard's 1597 *Herbal* was published. He had paid a visit to South Lambeth in July of the previous year and noted that, among other plants growing there, were 'one or two yong' Asian plane trees (*Platanus orientalis* L.).[17] These had been received from the Guinea Company merchant Humphrey Slaney in 1629. The tree was already well known in England and Gerard, at some time before 1597, had received 'one of those rough buttons, being the fruite thereof',[18] from which, presumably, he grew the specimen in his Holborn garden listed in 1596.[19] Turner had noted 'two very young trees' in 1568,[20] and by 1582 Nonsuch Palace boasted a 'widespreading circular plane tree, its branches supported on posts, so that many people can sit beneath it'.[21]

Johnson also observed at Lambeth the horse chestnut,[22] which four years earlier Parkinson had recorded as being 'noursed up from the nuts sent us from Turky';[23] a 'Milke' or 'Shrub Trefoile' (*Cytisus sessilifolius* L);[24] a golden thistle with white spotted leaves (*Scolymus maculatus* L.);[25] seven varieties of garlic (*Allium* spp.);[26] a 'Spring large floured Gentian' (*Gentiana acaulis* L.) with flowers of an 'exquisite blew';[27] a variety of 'Silver Knapweed'

(*Centaurea alba* L.);[28] and a 'Snakeweed that was brought from Virginia' which was found to be 'agreeable in all points'[29] to the Cretan variety. This was the Virginian snake-root (*Aristolochia serpentaria* L.), the root of which was considered an antidote to the bite of adders and vipers.

Both 'Bean Trefoil' and 'Stinking Bean Trefoil' (*Laburnum anagyroides* Medicus and *Anagyris foetida* L.) were also to be seen at Lambeth.[30] While Gerard had been growing the former in 1596, he specifically states in his herbal of the following year that the latter was 'a stranger in England',[31] and so this is the first record of its cultivation in Britain. It is surprisingly omitted from Tradescant's 1634 list, but as it appears in 1656 perhaps it was still being 'noursed up' and was not on public view.

Goat's beard spiraea (*Aruncus dioicus* (Walter) Fernald.) was then known as 'Barba Capri' and Johnson had 'onley seene it growing with Mr Tradescant',[32] so it, too, can be considered an introduction. He also saw 'The impatient Lady-smocke' (*Cardamine impatiens* L.), 'first brought hither by that great Treasurer of Natures rarities, Mr John Tradescant';[33] and there were 'two shrubby starworts from Virginia',[34] although not yet in flower. One, a white-flowered species, is still called after Tradescant as *Aster tradescantii* L., and the other with 'small blewish floures' may perhaps be *Aster novi-belgii* L., the true Michaelmas daisy, although this plant is not generally considered to have arrived until 1710.

There was also the 'Geranium Indicum noctu odoratum or Sweet India Storksbill', which had but newly arrived and been 'brought into this kingdome, and to our knowledge, by the industry of Mr John Tradescant'.[35] This was *Pelargonium triste* (L.) Aiton, the sad geranium, which had arrived from René Morin in Paris in 1631. Evidently it had been brought to Europe by a Dutch ship stopping at the Cape of Good Hope. Cornut described and illustrated it as 'Geranium triste' in his book on Canadian and other little-known plants published in 1635.[36]

Like the many varieties of 'Beares eares' or auriculas that he noted growing at South Lambeth,[37] Johnson could not have seen Tradescant's Great Rose Daffodil in flower on this particular summer visit, but he regarded it as 'the largest and stateliest of all the rest',[38] and Parkinson called it 'this Prince of Daffodils'.[39] Although this double variety was still common at the end of the last century it is very rare today, if indeed it still exists. In 1874 an attempt was made to count the petals of one specimen of a similar variety, but after sixty-six had been removed the experiment was abandoned as too difficult. All parts of the flower become multiplicated and, in endeavouring to develop leaves as well as petals, the flower often shows as much green as yellow.[40] While the 'Great Rose Daffodil' was obviously an object of much admiration in the seventeenth century, many today would agree with L.A. Bowles who, in his *Handbook of Narcissus* (1934), described it as 'this heavy-headed over-loaded flower' and dismissed it as both 'clumsy and ugly'.

1 *Pseudonarcissus Hispanicus maximus aureus.* The great yellow Spanish bastard Daffodill. 2 *Pseudonarcissus Pyreneus variiformis* The Mountaine bastard Daffodill of diuers kindes. 3 *Pseudonarcissus Hispanicus maior albus* The greate white Spanish bastard Daffodill. 4 *Pseudonarcissus Hispanicus minor aluus* The little Spanish white bastard Daffodill. 6 *Pseudonarcissus tubo sexangulari.* The six cornered bastard Daffodill. 5 *Pseudonarcissus maximus aureus, siue Roseus Tradescanti,* John Tradescants great Rose Daffodill. 7 *Pseudonarcissus aureus Anglicus maximus,* Master Wilmers great double Daffodill 8 *Pseudonarcissus Hispanicus aureus flore pleno.* The double Spanish Daffodill, or Parkinsons double Daffodill. 9 *Pseudonarcissus Gallicus maior flore pleno,* The greater double French Daffodill. 10 *Pseudonarcissus Anglicus flore pleno,* The double English Daffodill, or Gerrards double Daffodill.

Tradescant's Great Rose Daffodil and other contemporary daffodils
(from John Parkinson's *Paradisus*)

Tradescant was also growing many choice tulips at this time, several of which were new. His collection included fifty flame-coloured varieties alone. Johnson, however, was able to admire 'in the Garden of my Kinde friend' the 'Ladies Slipper' (*Cypripedium calceolus* L.), a British native which then, as today, was 'reported to grow in Northern parts of the Kingdom',[41] and the 'Sea Lavander with the indented leafe' (*Limonium sinuatum* (L.) Miller)[42] from the Mediterranean region.

Tradescant's own copy of *Paradisus* lists his acquisitions between 1629 and 1633, and, of course, in the following year he printed his own garden list. These show that in 1629 he received three consignments of plants from Robin in Paris with some 'Renuncculus' (*Ranunculus asiaticus* L.) and anemones from one of the Morin brothers; in the following year a batch of plants arrived from Sir Peter Wyche, then British Ambassador in Constantinople.

In 1629 Humphrey Slaney sent him, in addition to the Oriental plane, a specimen of the smoke tree or Venetian sumach (*Cotinus coggygria* Scop.) which Tradescant records as 'Cogciggrya or shumahat'. He had received one from another source just beforehand which he called 'Cogciggrum Plinii'. These were a new introduction from southern Europe. Humphrey Slaney had headed the list of merchants that Buckingham had requested to send plants and other rarities, and these must still have been arriving even though the Duke was dead.

Other introductions in 1629 were Jupiter's beard (*Anthyilis barba-jovis* L.) and goat's thorn (*Astragalus massiliensis* (Miller) Lam.); in 1632 he received rough bindweed (*Smilax aspera* L.) and saw briar or sarsaparilla (*Smilax glauca* Walter), both also new, but as the last is not heard of again it was presumably lost.

Another 1632 introduction, tree purslane (*Atriplex halimus* L.), was described as 'Hulimus', becoming 'Halimus arborescens' two years later. It is a silver-grey bush from the Iberian peninsula. *Tiarella cordifolia* L., which he called 'Cortusa Americana', and 'Virga aurea Virgine', the Virginian golden rod (*Solidago canadensis* L.), were also introductions received in 1632.

Tradescant is considered responsible for the introduction of five types of rock-rose, the *Cistus crispus* L. and *C. populifolius* L., acquired in 1632, and the *C. clusii* Dunal, *C. psilosepalus* Sweet and *C. monspeliensis* L., all first listed in 1634 and, as already suggested, possibly picked up on his expedition to the Mediterranean. He was also growing several other varieties which were not new, although his 'Cistus Halimi folio' – the sun rose (*Halimium halimifolium* (L.) Willk.) – also first listed in 1634, was another introduction from the same area possibly gathered at the same time. His 'Cistus annuus Clus.' (*Helianthemum salicifolium* (L.) Miller) seems to have died out, as it disappears after 1634.

While Tradescant records the arrival of 'Sabina Bacsiffira' (*Juniperus sabina* L.) in 1633, a plant that had been growing in England since the fourteenth century,[43] the two other varieties of Sabina listed in 1656, 'Sabina vulgaris, sive stirilis, barren Savin' and 'Sabina stirilis cupressi facie', must still have been rare, as William Coles in 1657 also lists three Savines, which he calls the 'ordinary', the 'greater berried' and the 'gentle Savine with berries'. The first was regarded as quite common, but the other two were only to be found 'in some of our more curious Gardens, as in that of John Tradescants'.[44]

Various varieties of 'Clematis' are recorded, it then being the 'genericke name to all wooddy, winding plants'.[45] The 'Amaracock, sive Clematis Virginiana: the Virginian Clymer, or Passion flowre' of 1656 can be identified, with the 'Flos Passionis' of 1634, as *Passiflora incarnata* L., as described and illustrated by Johnson. It has been suggested that the 'Clematis Virginiana' listed in 1634 and repeated in 1656 with the English equivalent of 'Virginian Ladyes Bower' was an introduction of the rather insignificant white-flowering variety of that name. Although it is clearly a different plant from the passion flower, the suggestion is unlikely. Both plants are illustrated in the book of drawings by Alexander Marshal, now in the Royal Library at Windsor. From this the latter plant can be identified as *Gonolobus carolinensis* (Jacq.) Schultes.

Tradescant had bought 'two great medlar trees of naples' for the garden at Hatfield in 1611, and one of these, described as 'Mispilis Arona', arrived for his own garden in 1633; it was in fact the azarole (*Crataegus azarolus* L.), which was cultivated for its fruit in southern Europe. It, too, was probably being nursed up, as it is omitted in 1634 but reappears in 1656 and was still growing, although decaying, at the time of Ashmole's occupation.

In 1632 Tradescant recorded 'Oliva Cappadocia', the oleaster (*Eleagnus angustifolia* L.). In the following year he received another, recording it as 'Zisipha Capadocia'. Johnson reported that it was also being cultivated by Parkinson under that name in 1633,[46] but it must have been comparatively new to him as there is no mention of the plant in *Paradisus*. In 1634 Tradescant called it 'Olea sylvestris'. By 1656, however, the younger Tradescant was growing this plant under the name of 'Olea Bohemia', his 'Olea sylvestris' being *Olea europaea* L. var. *oleaster*.

Moon trefoil (*Medicago arborea* L.) was twice received by Tradescant, once in 1629 as 'Sittissos Amarantinum' and three years later as 'Cittissus maranthe', after which it thrived, appearing in both printed catalogues. It was growing in Gerard's garden in 1596,[47] and Parkinson described it as 'noursed up to furnish waste places in a garden'.[48] The plant has yellow flowers and flat pods that curl round like miniature rams' horns.

An introduction that seemingly failed to survive was the mastic tree, received as 'Lentiscus' (*Pistacia lentiscus* L.). It arrived in 1632, was recorded two years later but is not listed in 1656. Shrubby germander (*Teucrium fruticans* L.), which arrived in 1633 as 'Teucrum arboressence', is another delicate plant, an introduction from Portugal and the western Mediterranean, which seems to have met with the same fate as did the jujube tree (*Zizyphus jujuba* Miller). Parkinson described the last as 'so tender that it seldome abideth long in our Country'.[49]

In 1632 Tradescant received *Ornithogalum arabicum* L., a Mediterranean relative of the chincherinchee. Parkinson bemoaned the loss of some of these bulbs in 1629, claiming that he had been misled as to the careful treatment they required, but Tradescant, perhaps learning from his experience, had greater success as they appear in both later lists.

Poison ivy (*Toxicodendron radicans* (L.) D. Kuntze) was first received in 1632 as 'Frutex Canadencis Epimedium folio' and was another new plant, as was the 'Dronicum maior Americana' (*Rudbeckia laciniata* L.). His 'Bellis maior Americana Arboressence proliffra' received in 1633 can be identified as the North American biennual *Erigeron annuus* Pers.

Tradescant must have been delighted when 'Alowaye mucronata' appeared in 1633. This was probably an introduction of the American aloe (*Agave americana* L.). Although in the previous century Gerard had described the Oriental aloe as 'Aloe folio mucronato',[50] by this time the term was generally used for the American variety which, according to Parkinson, was brought from Mexico to Spain from whence it spread through Europe.

'Piemetum Realie' is a curious name to find listed in 1633. No contemporary herbal describes any plant with a similar name, and it is now suggested that Tradescant used this appellation for *Pimenta dioica* (L.) Merrill, the Jamaican pepper or allspice. As it is not heard of again it was presumably lost and perhaps reintroduced in 1793, the date generally accepted for its arrival.

'Aspick', which also arrived in 1633, is spike lavender (*Lavandula latifolia* Medicus). This was the French name for it at the time, and the oil that the variety yields is still called 'essence d'aspic' and is different from that of true lavender. It had been in England since at least 1597.

The first record of the following plants growing in England is in Tradescant's plant lists of 1629–33 and 1634.

1629–1633
Achillea clavennae L.
Aeonium arboreum (L.) Webb &
   Berth.
Amelanchier ovalis Medicus
Arundo donax L.
? *Asarum canadense* L.
? *Cyclamen libanoticum* Hildebr.
Erythronium americanum Ker-
   Gawl.
Eupatorium ageratoides L.

Sedum cepaea L.
? *Sisyrinchium bermudiana* L.
Spiraea hypericifolia L.
Zephyranthes atamasco Herb.

1634
Capparis breynia DC
? *Geranium maculatum* L.
? *Juglans cinerea* L.
Myagrum perfoliatum L.
Ononis speciosa Lag.

Pistacia terebinthus L.
Rosa Virginiana Miller
Rumex spinosus L.
Rumex vesicarius L.
Ruscus hypophyllum L.
Smilacina racemosa (L.) Desf.

Smilax aspera L. var. *maculata*
? Smilax herbacea L. or
    Menispermum canadense L.
? Thalictrum purpurascens L.
Vitis vinifera L. var.
    'Apiifolia'

He passed on a specimen of 'Laurus Alexandrina' (*Ruscus hypophyllum* L.) to Parkinson, who relates that he had it 'by the meanes of my good friend Master John Tradescant with whom it groweth'.[51]

'Auricula ursi maxima Tradescanti flo. obsolet.' first appears in 1634 and in 1656 is repeated in similar terms with the English equivalent 'Tradescant his greatest blush Beares ears'. As this plant is not given any epithet, such as 'American' or 'Indian', terms used almost synonymously at the time to describe arrivals from the New World, it is unlikely to be the *Dodecatheon meadia* L. suggested by Mea Allan.[52]

An improved variety of the 'Auricula Ursi flore obsoleto magno – The Spaniards blush Beares eare' mentioned by Parkinson in *Paradisus* seems much more probable. Describing it as 'larger than any of the other that I have seene', he explains that he gave it this name because the plant was 'of a duskie blush colour, resembling the blush of a Spaniard, whose tawney skinne cannot declare so pure a blush as the English can'.[53]

In 1640 Parkinson published his *Theatrum Botanicum*, which contains many more references to the Tradescants. The younger John had of course just returned from his first visit to Virginia, and Parkinson records that he brought back with him 'Virginian Winter Cherries' (*Physalis pubescens* L.);[54] the American plane tree (*Platanus occidentalis* L.);[55] a variety of 'Spicknard';[56] the Canadian columbine (*Aquilegia canadensis* L.),[57] an early variety with single red and yellow flowers which had reached Paris some years earlier as it is listed by Cornut and which may in fact have been the plant first received by the elder Tradescant in 1632; a 'Goodly Virginia grasse with a joynted spike';[58] the swamp cypress (*Taxodium distichum* (L.) Rich.);[59] a 'Strange maidenhaire' (*Adiantum pedatum* L.);[60] the Virginian bladder nut (*Staphylea trifolia* L.);[61] the 'great branched Burre reede of Virginia'[62] (? *Sparganium americanum* Nutt.); a 'Noble Liverwort' from Virginia with very dark leaves[63] (? *Hepatica americana* L.); 'The hollow leafed strange plant '– in fact the insectivorous and moisture-loving purple pitcher plant (*Sarracenia purpurea* L.) – which he lists as a 'Sea Marsh Buglosse';[64] and the 'sweete yellow climing Virginian Jasmine' (*Gelsemium sempervirens* (L.) Aiton) seen there by John Tradescant and from whom Parkinson had 'a plant risen of the seede'.[65]

'A wild mint of America'[66] was added hastily to the appendix at the back of *Theatrum* with no attribution for its arrival, and it seems possible that

Tradescant may have been responsible for this bergamot (*Monarda fistulosa* L.). Cornut, however, had included it as 'Origanum fistulosum Canadense', under which name it is also listed in 1656, suggesting that it may have come to England via Paris.

Although the elder Tradescant had died two years before the publication of *Theatrum*, it, too, includes many references to Parkinson's old friend. For instance, a 'yellow Starwort of Virginia' that had been brought back by George Gibbes, a Bath surgeon with a garden renowned for exotics, had 'flowred and seeded with none but Master Tradescant at South Lambeth'.[67]

His green fingers notwithstanding, Tradescant was not always successful. He had 'a sort' of plum tree 'that bore double flowers, but perished not long continuing with him',[68] while the 'Strawberry headed Trefoile of Portugall'[69] (? *Trifolium physodes* Bieb.), which Tradescant had received from Dr William Boel at Lisbon, perished with both him and Parkinson, and neither managed to procure replacements.

Dr Boel was a Dutchman who lived mainly in Lisbon but travelled widely. Parkinson described him as a 'very curious and cunning searcher of simples'.[70] He sent seeds and plants to various gardeners. Parkinson employed him in this capacity and was disgusted when Boel sent various rare seeds 'in love, as a lover of rare plants' to the amateur grower William Coys, whose garden at Stubbers in Essex was famed for producing the first yucca to flower in England.

'But to me of debt, for going into Spaine almost wholly on my charge hee brought mee little else for my mony, but while I beate the bush another catcheth and eateth the bird,' Parkinson complained.[71] Perhaps Tradescant, as a 'lover of rare plants', also got them from Boel 'in love'. Despite his grumbles, Parkinson recorded receiving many seeds, bulbs and other plants from Dr Boel.

The 'Double flowred Myrtle' was another of Tradescant's casualties. It was 'noursed up in the Gardens of the chiefe Lovers of rarities' and, while 'not over tender' yet was 'not so hardy . . . which Master Tradescant can sufficiently witnesse, who by a little neglect lost a good plant overtaken with the frost'.[72] This must have been the 'Mirtis flore pleno' (*Myrtus communis* L. var. *'Flore Pleno'*) received in 1633 and later described as 'Myrtus florida'.

Tradescant also kept at South Lambeth a 'very beautifull' kidneywort or pennywort with pale green leaves, also acquired from Boel;[73] and he was the first to receive the 'Strange Coltsfoot of America'[74] (? *Cacalia atriplicifolia* L.) 'from beyond sea', again passing on a plant to Parkinson. The 'supposed Wolfes bane of America'[75] (*Actaea alba* L.), which had come to Tradescant from Canada via Robin in Paris, was also 'imparted' to Parkinson after the roots had increased. Parkinson also described *Syringa x persica* L., the six-foot lilac-like shrub which was 'now to be seene' at South Lambeth.[76] It had reached Europe via the Venetian Ambassador to Constantinople before 1614,[77] and Tradescant had included it in his 1634 list.

Parkinson also described 'Tradescants Turkie purple Primrose'.[78] It had a yellow circle at the base and was evidently a form of *Primula vulgaris* subsp. *sibthorpii* which occurs in European Turkey and Asia Minor and would appear to be one of the parents of the coloured primroses of Western European gardens.

Parkinson's description of Tradescant's *Robinia pseudacacia* L., which by 1640 had already grown 'to be a very great tree, and of an exceeding height',[79] has led to the suggestion by Marjorie F. Warner that this tree first came to Europe through Tradescant. Its introduction has been accredited to Jean Robin, after whom it is named, but, in an article about the royal French botanists published in 1956, she claims that it was not documented in France until 1635, when Cornut listed it as 'Acacia Americana Robini' and stated that the tree had grown up in the Robins' Paris garden. The tree was probably transplanted to the Jardin Royal des Plantes Médicinales about five years after Robin's death in 1629; the first catalogue of that garden, issued in 1636, lists it as the 'Acatia Africana', under which title Cornut had also indexed it and as it may have been called in the Robins' garden.[80]

Although it has been stated by John Loudon and others that the *Robinia* reached Paris by 1601, there is no trace of it in Jean Robin's *Catalogus Stirpium* published in that year, which lists only the 'Acacia altera Matthioli' (*Calicotome spinosa* (L.) Link).

Tradescant first listed the *Robinia* in 1634, calling it 'Locusta Virginiana arbor', and as it is not recorded as having been received during the previous five years it seems likely that it came to him prior to 1629, possibly as a result of Buckingham's plea 'to all merchants' in 1625; he perhaps passed on seeds to his friend in Paris. Various American plants are believed to have reached Robin through Tradescant.

Today there still stands in the garden of Cobham Court at Bekesbourne, near Canterbury, a very fine old *Robinia*, held together with metal bands. This was once the Court House for the Lord Warden of the Cinque Ports, and the present owner likes to think that the tree was grown by the elder Tradescant when he was gardener to the Duke of Buckingham, who was Lord Warden between 1624 and 1628.

On his later trips to Virginia the younger John Tradescant came home with the tulip tree (*Liriodendron tulipifera* L.), which was said by John Evelyn to be growing 'very well with the Curious amongst us to a considerable Stature. I conceive it was first brought over by John Tradescant, under the Name of the Tulip-tree.' He added: 'I wish we had more of them; but they are difficult to elevate at first.'[81]

Philip Miller tells us that the Virginian maple (*Acer rubrum* L.) 'was rais'd from Seeds, which were brought from Virginia many Years since by Mr John

Tradescant, in his Garden at South Lambeth'.[82] Plukenet also commented on this tree: 'Arborem hanc magnitudine & proceritate eximiam, in Hort D. Joh. Tradescanti Lambethae ad Austrum'[83] ('This tree distinguished by its size and height in the garden of John Tradescant to the south of Lambeth').

Other plants probably brought back on these later journeys, as they are all first recorded as growing in England in the 1656 catalogue, include the hackberry (*Celtis occidentalis* L.), listed as 'Lotus arbor Virginiana, Virginian Nettle tree'; the colourful but scentless red and yellow trumpet honeysuckle (*Lonicera sempervirens* L.), described as 'Caprifoliū Virginianum arbor, Virginian Woodbine-tree'; the Virginian Yucca (*Yucca filamentosa* L.), described as 'Jucca Virginiana angustiore & breviore folio, The Virginian Jucca with shorter and narrower leaves', comparing it with the *Yucca gloriosa* L., an introduction from the previous century which was growing alongside it; and probably *Glycyrrhiza lepidota* Pursh., native to North America from Mexico to Canada, as the most likely equivalent for Tradescant's 'Glycyriza Brasiliensis'.

The 'Fox-Grape from Virginia' (*Vitis vulpina* L.), a variety first noted by Ralph Austen in his *A Treatise of Fruit Trees* (1653), probably arrived by Tradescant's hands, too; but his 'Vitis vinifera sylvestris Virginiana, Virginia wilde Vine' (*Vitis labrusca* L.) is more questionable, as it occurs in William Coys's 1616 list of Virginian plants and may already have been growing in his Essex garden.[84]

Tradescant named six vines in 1634 and referred to 'divers others', while fourteen are listed in 1656. Parkinson, however, relates that 'he hath twentie sorts growing with him, that hee never knew how or by what name to call them'.[85]

The 'Cabbage tree from Barbados' (*Roystonea oleracea* (Jacq.) Cook), the 'Prickly Costard apple from Barbados' (*Annona muricata* L.) and the 'Guavon from Barbados' (*Psidium guajava* L.) had also arrived at South Lambeth by 1656 and could have been procured by John junior had these plants reached Virginia by the time of his final visit or if he had contrived to visit the West Indies himself.

Also first recorded as growing in England in 1656 were various European plants. These included such varieties as the 'unsavory yellow Italian Jasmine' (*Jasminum humile* L.), a yellow-flowering evergreen often grown on a wall which apparently received this name because it originally arrived from Italy among orange trees, and *Echinospartum lusitanicum* (L.) Rothm. which is Tradescant's 'Genista Lusitanica'.

As there are no records of the plants received by the elder Tradescant between 1634 and his death four years later, it is possible that these new European plants arrived at South Lambeth during his lifetime; alternatively, some of the contacts that he built up may have continued for his son.

In his description of the service tree Parkinson in 1629 records, in addition to 'a wild kind', two varieties 'that are planted in orchards'. Although in fact this tree was already in Britain in Chaucer's time and had been planted for Henry VIII at Hampton Court,[86] Parkinson claimed that the rarer of these two varieties had been 'brought into this Land by John Tradescante'.[87] This was no doubt the 'Cormus' of 1634 – cormier being the French name for *Sorbus domestica* L. – which by 1656 was either already lost, as it was in the time of Ashmole's occupation, or was omitted by mistake.

This last possibility is a real one, as the catalogue contains many printing errors. For instance, 'Thlaspi Neronis Carotef: Lob: large tufted Mustard' does not correlate. The Latin should obviously read 'Thapsia', as listed in 1634, while the 'Thlaspi' to which the mustard refers has been omitted. A similar mistake has been made with 'Staechys Arabica', which is described as 'Arabian base Horehound' when in fact it must mean French lavender (*Lavandula stoechas* L.), although this duplicates 'Staechas, Cassidony or French Lavender'. It, too, was correctly listed in 1634 as 'Staechas Arabica'. Many other plants are also duplicated under different names.

The London plane, the ornament of so many city streets because of its ability to withstand pollution by shedding its bark scales, is considered by most authorities to be a hybrid of the Oriental and Occidental planes. But, while the Oriental plane thrives in England and produces good pollen, the Occidental plane is much less happy with the uncertain climate and seldom lives to an age to produce pollen. For this reason most botanists believe that the London plane must have bred in a warmer climate, possibly in Spain, and arrived here as a sapling.

The earliest known specimen of the London plane is at Oxford, having been preserved by the younger Bobart who became Keeper of the Physic Garden in 1680. He was the first to recognize that it was different from other varieties and dried a specimen for posterity. For this reason the Oxford Botanic Garden likes to claim that this useful tree first grew with them as Bobart was known to have been exchanging trees with the Montpelier region.

John Tradescant junior was of course growing both trees at South Lambeth from 1638 and may have continued to exchange plants with the Continent as his father had done before him. However, if the London plane did by some chance first grow with him it certainly went unrecognized in 1656.

On the strength of 'pine-pits' being discovered during redevelopment of the Oatlands Palace site, a find of which there is no record at Weybridge Museum, Mea Allan[88] has claimed that the younger Tradescant may have been growing pineapples during his time there as gardener.

If such pits were found, as is quite likely, they undoubtedly date from the occupation of the mid-eighteenth-century nurseryman Henry Scott, who used some of the old palace walls to form an enclosed garden. His trade card shows that he grew pineapples on the site from 1754.[89]

Growing pineapples in brick-lined pits containing fermenting tan bark did not become general until the 1720s, when this method was found to raise the soil to the necessary temperature. The first published account appeared in 1728, and three years later Philip Miller recorded in *The Gardener's Dictionary* that it was 'very lately' that the pineapple had produced fruit in European gardens, attributing the earliest success to the wealthy cloth merchant Pieter de la Court of Leiden, 'who after a great many trials with little or no success, did at length, hit upon a proper degree of heat and management'. He sent plants to Sir Matthew Decker, and a painting in the Fitzwilliam Museum at Cambridge records that in 1720 the result was a fruit deemed worthy of the royal table.

There is also the famous painting by Danckerts in the possession of the Marchioness of Cholmondeley, copies of which are at Ham House and elsewhere. This painting shows the gardener John Rose presenting the first pineapple grown in this country to Charles II and must have been painted between 1668, when the artist first arrived in England, and 1677, when Rose died. The house in the background, which has a classical façade, has been identified as Dorney Court, Berkshire, despite the fact that the latter is a splendid example of Tudor architecture, on the grounds that Rose is said to have worked there as gardener to Sir Philip Palmer. A tradition persists in the Palmer family that a carved stone pineapple was made to commemorate the occasion, which, it is claimed, took place soon after 1665.[90]

Dorney House, Weybridge, has also been suggested as the location for this picture, but this house, too, bears little resemblance to the one in Danckerts's painting, which is now believed to be a figment of the artist's imagination based on memories of his Dutch homeland.

By 1661 Rose was royal gardener at St James's Park, and no doubt the pineapple fit for the royal table was grown in the way described by Tilleman Bobart in a letter dated 14 October 1693, when on a visit to George London, Rose's former apprentice and successor to the royal appointment: 'Here is at this time a very fine Ananas near Ripe in the stove which is to be presented to ye Queen in few dayes.'[91]

No doubt Rose taught London this technique of growing the fruit. Danckerts's picture passed from the latter's grandson to the Rev. William Pennicott who in 1780 gave it to Horace Walpole for Strawberry Hill.

Certainly the pineapple is the type of novelty that would have appealed to the Tradescants' fascination with the strange and rare, and one can imagine them endeavouring to raise it if by some happy chance a suitable fruit had come into their hands; they exhibited a dried specimen in their museum. But even by the date of the younger Tradescant's death the fruit was barely known in England. On 9 August 1661 John Evelyn recorded: 'I first saw the famous Queene-pine brought from Barbados presented to his Majestic, but the first that were ever seene here in England were those sent to Cromwell, foure-yeares since.' Another seven years elapsed before he wrote: 'Standing by his Majestie at dinner in the Presence, There was of that rare fruite called the King-pine, (growing in Barbados & W. Indies), the first of them I had ever seen.[92]

A new arrival in 1632 was 'Caradache Americana' which Dr John Harvey suggests might be *Bromelia karatas* L., reputedly introduced in 1739. This plant is in fact the wild pineapple, a relation but not an edible fruit. It is disappointing to have to report that it does not seem to have survived, as there is no mention of it in either of the later plant lists.

It has also been suggested that Tradescant brought the first larch trees to Britain from Archangel in 1618. If he did introduce the larch at that time then it is more likely to have been the Siberian larch (*Larix sibirica* Ledeb.), but it is possible that he received the European larch (*Larix decidua* Miller) at a slightly later date and that the specimen Evelyn saw 'arriv'd to a flourishing, and ample Tree' near Chelmsford in 1664 was the result.[93]

In 1629 Parkinson described the European larch as 'rare, and noursed up but with a few', declaring that 'it groweth both slowly and becommeth not high' and that flowers and cones are borne 'not in our Land that I could heare', all of which indicate that it was a new arrival.[94] By 1640 it had become established, although, surprisingly, it does not appear in either of the Tradescants' garden lists. Two plants described in earlier editions as first growing with Tradescant, the *Rhododendrum hirsutum* L. and *Mimosa sensitiva* L., are now known to have been listed earlier, the former by Parkinson in 1629 as 'Ledum Alpinum . . . The Mountaine Sweet Holly Rose' and the latter by Bobart as growing in the Oxford Physic Garden in 1648. Although several suggestions regarding identifications on the Tradescants' plant lists have been put forward, the only definite change of identity is that for the 1634 'Carobe Americana' which is presumably the same as the '*Carob from Barbados*' on the 1656 list and which should now be regarded as *Hymenaea courbaril* L.

Another plant attributed by Mea Allan[95] to the younger Tradescant for its introduction is the humble plant (*Mimosa pudica* L.) listed in the 1656 catalogue. But Parkinson recorded that he had seen it growing 'in a pot' in the Chelsea garden of Sir John Danvers where 'diverse seeds being sowne therein about the middle of May, 1638. and 1639. some of them sprang up'.[96]

The first half of the seventeenth century was a period of intense horticultural activity, as indeed the previous half-century had been. Old World plants, for long cultivated with great skill in Persia, were gradually working their way westward via Vienna and Antwerp, and plants from America, even more exciting because they were entirely new, were also arriving. While some plants that can be attributed to the Tradescants, either for their introduction or for the first record of their cultivation in England, may have arrived at an earlier date and gone unregistered, their real achievement lay in cultivating them for all to admire in their botanic garden at South Lambeth and for making many new varieties as nurseryman's plants.

Appendix I

List of Plants Received by John Tradescant 1629–1633 (noted in his handwriting in the back of his copy of Parkinson's *Paradisus*)

In each of the three plant lists that follow, an asterisk (*) indicates a plant first grown in England by one or other of the Tradescants, and a dagger (†) indicates a plant introduced to England by one or other of the Tradescants (i.e. collected by their own hands). The symbols occur only at the first listing of the plant.

MODERN BOTANICAL NAME

Reseved since the Impression of this Booke

In primis	Sittissos Amarantinum	*Medicago arborea* L.
	*Barba Jovis	*Anthyllis barba-jovis* L.
	Poligolan	*Coronilla valentina* L.
	Digitalem lutem maior	*Digitalis grandiflora* Miller
	Frittillarie Aquitanica	*Fritillaria pyrenaica* L.
	Rosam Vittriensem	—
	*Cogciggrum Plinii	*Cotinus coggygria* Scop.

From Morine	The Great whyt Renuncculus single	
	on other sort of whyt Renuculus single	*Ranunculus asiaticus* L. cvs.
	Renuncculus Drape De Argent	
	Anemone Duble Greene with A littill leafe	—
	A thrice fayer Duble Anemone whyt Anemone	—
	On other sort of Dubble whyt Anemone	—

From Mr Robine	Tulipa perce maior	—
	Cardinallis planta 2	*Lobelia cardinalis* L.
	On Aaster	—

From Holland	On Vyola matronallis	*Hesperis matronalis* L.
	Plattanos Arbor	*Platanus orientalis* L.
	Cogciggrya or shumahat } from Mr Humfry Slaynie	*Cotinus coggygria* Scop.

From france Robyne	Iris Affracanis	*Iris filifolia* Boiss.
	Iris percyca	*Iris persica* L.
	6 Anemones tenuifollio Duble	*Anemone coronaria* L.
	4 latifollio Duble Anemones	*Anemone pavonina* Lam.

From Mounser Robyne	On German Rose of Mr Parkinson from Mounser Robine, which is called Rosa Austriaca flore phenissio	*Rosa foetida* Herrm. cv. '*Bicolor*'
	4 more Roses whearof Mr Tuggy Hathe two	—
	on strang vyene	—
	oñ Red Honnysoccle	—
	Two Irisses without Name	*Iris* spp.
	Arbutus slipes	*Arbutus unedo* L.
	*Tragacantha slipe	*Astragalus massiliensis* (Miller) Lam. (tragacantha)

Reseved in the yeare 1630 from forrin partes

	On Narciss	—
From Constanti- noble. Sr Peeter Wyche	On Ciclaman	
	4 Renuncculuses	
	Tullipe Caffa	} cvs.
	Tullipe perce	
	4 sortes of Anemones	

Reseved in the yeare 1631

L.W.	On tulupe Called the Coronell & on of Hir owne.	} cvs.

T.S.	On tulipe Brewer 3 collers sh welcom Hom Best Golyathe On Palmer more good tulipes unknowne	⎫
Mr Colfe	On Tulipe Beau withowt A Circle Blanck swisant Unick De Armenitier Mr Groves olyas Hollias Beu	⎬ cvs.
from W. Win	Blienburgh Admirall of 3 Collers olli van Dusport flamed Red & Whyt Crowne.	
Mr Renees	Two Holliasses	⎭

Reseved in the yeare 1631 from Mr Rene Morine

In primis	Renuncculus Asiaticus flore duplice luteo	—
	Narcissus Jacobei, Narcissus indicus, Narcissus flor rubro	*Sprekelia formosissima* (L.) Herb.
	Semper Eternum flore luteum	? *Helichrysum stoechas* (L.) DC.
	*Geranium noctu odorato	*Pelargonium triste* (L.) Aiton
from Bruxsells	6 Hiasinthes	⎫
	Narcissus medio luteus	
	Narcissus Narboniencis	⎬ cvs.
	Narcissus Mussart	⎭

In the yeare 1632.

Lotus Libica	? *Melilotus officinalis* (L.) Pall.
Phillerea	*Phillyrea angustifolia* L.
*Sarsaparilla	? *Smilax glauca* Walter
*Smilex Aspera	*Smilax aspera* L.
*Lentiscus	*Pistacia lentiscus* L.
Agnus Castus	*Vitex agnus-castus* L.
Cittissus maranthe	*Medicago arborea* L.
Absinthum arborescence	*Artemisia arborescens* L.
Cittisus panonicum Clusii	*Cytisus nigricans* L.
Pseudo Dictamnum	*Ballota acetabulosa* (L.) Benth.
Vyburnum	*Viburnum lantana* L.
Lauristinus folio Glabro	*Viburnum tinus* L.
*Cistus folis chrispus	*Cistus crispus* L.
*Cistus popelium folyo	*Cistus populifolius* L.
Cistus mas	*Cistus albidus* L.
*Cortusa Americana	*Tiarella cordifolia* L.
Thimum verum verum Hispanicum	*Thymus capitatus* (L.) Hoffm. & Link
Hisopium tenuifolio	*Hyssopus officinalis* L. var. *angustifolius*
Tragacantha	*Astragalus massiliensis* (Miller) Lam. (tragacantha)
*Amanker Lobellie	*Amelanchier ovalis* Med.
Frutex Coronaria flore pleno	*Philadelphus coronarius* L.
Mirtis florence	*Myrtus communis* L.
Sesely Ethiopicum	*Bupleurum fruticosum* L.
*Caradache Americana	? *Bromelia karatas* L.
Narcissus Tobago	? *Hymenocallis* sp.
Ornithogalum Arabicum	*Ornithogalum arabicum* L.
Iris percicus	*Iris persica* L.
*Absinthium umbelatum	*Achillea clavennae* L.
Absinthium folio Lavendula	*Artemisia caerulescens* L.
Auriggunum verum Hihipanicum	*Origanum vulgare* L. var. or *O. heracleoticum* L.
Tumariscus Itallica	*Myricaria germanica* Desv.

Lutea Creatica
Linaria odorata

Ieracium Indicum
Serpentaria
Arum mius   If 'mius' = 'minus' then
                   If 'mius' = 'majus' then
Iris Gloriossa
Coulchicum frittilaria
Fraxanello flore Rubro
Fraxsanela minor   }
*Herunde Hispanica
Chama Iredis 3 sorts
Iris Anglica variagata
Dentaria Herundelesie
Dentaria trefolia
Dentaria setfolia
Telethium maius & minus
Moluka
Sentaurum magnoni
Siclamen flore Albo

*Hulimus
Geranium 3 specius
Tithemali caracius
*Pistolochia
Hiasithus flore Albo
Chamalea tricockos
Tulipe Chistmaker
Tulipe se bloome
Tricoler Nomveell
Ratabet
The Lyon
Brandingburg
Oudenard
De Turbone
Tulipe swice
Tulipe Crowne
Tulipe Canadense
Otho Demeine

*Oliva Cappadocia

from the frencheman
The whyt Crown tulipe
Hiasinthus Brumalis
Narcissus totus Albus

Narcissus Constantinopolis

from Mr Ploves Brother
*Narcissus virginiana
Narcissus totus Albis

Narcissus De Diverse specie

Millefolium flore luteum
*Virga Aurea virgine

from Brussells 16 tulipes

Datisca cannabina L.
Linaria purpurea (L.) Miller or *Anarrhinum*
   bellidifolium (L.) Desf.
—
Plantago maritima L. var. *serpentina*
Colocasia antiquorum Schott.
Arisaema triphyllum (L.) Torrey
Iris florentina L. (form)
Fritillaria sp.

Dictamnus albus L.

Arundo donax L.
Iris pumila L.
Iris xiphioides Ehrh.
Plumbago europaea L.
Cardamine enneaphyllos (L.) Crantz.
Cardamine heptaphylla (Vill.) O.E. Schulz
Sedum telephium L. and ? *Sedum anacampseros* L.
Moluccella laevis L.
Centaurea centaurium L.
Cyclamen hederifolium Aiton or *C. purpurascens*
   Miller var.
Atriplex halimus L.
—
Euphorbia characias L.
Aristolochia pistolochia L.
Hyacinthus orientalis L.
Cneorum tricocum L.

cvs.

Eleagnus angustifolia L.

cv.
—
Narcissus tazetta L. subsp. *papyraceus* (Ker-Gawl.)
   Baker
Narcissus tazetta L.

Zephyranthes atamasco (L.) Herb.
Narcissus tazetta L. subsp. *papyraceus* (Ker-Gawl.)
   Baker
Narcissus spp.

Achillea tomentosa L.
Solidago canadensis L.

cvs.

In the yeare 1632
Fraxanella flore Albo
Fraxanella minor flore Albo   }   *Dictamnus albus* L.
*Dronicum maior Americana   *Rudbeckia laciniata* L.
*Eupatorem Nove Belgicum   *Eupatorium ageratoides* L.
Papaver Reas flore luteo, Radx papetum   *Meconopsis cambrica* (L.) Vig.
Pulegium servinom   *Mentha cervina* L.
*Frutex Canadencis Epimedium folio   *Toxicodendron radicans* (L.) D. Kuntze
*Aquilegi variagata Rubro et Albo   ? *Aquilegia canadensis* L.

In the yeare 1633
Abrotanum unguntaria   *Artemisia pontica* L.
Androsasa Mathiolie   *Androsace maxima* L.
Renunculus Lusetanycus odorata luteo   *Ramunculus bullatus* L. var.
Colis Jovis   *Salvia glutinosa* L.
*Bellis maior Americana Arboressence proliffra   *Erigeron annuus* (L.) Pers.
*Cepe Lobelii   *Sedum cepaea* L.
Aspick   *Lavandula latifolia* Medicus
Buglosa minor sempervirence   *Pentaglottis sempervirens* (L.) Tausch.
Fumaria Arboressence flore luteo semper vyrence
    variagata   ? *Fumaria capnoides* L.
*Asarum maius Americana   ? *Asarum canadense* L.
Absinthium Innodorum   *Artemisia crithmifolia* L.
Poligon Creticum verum luteo   *Cressa cretica* L.
*Phalangium virginianum flore Albo   *Tradescantia virginiana* L. var. *alba*
Scabiosa Alpina vera   *Cephalaria alpina* (L.) Roemer & Schultes
Galliosus panonica Clusii   *Lamium orvala* L.
*Teucrum arboressence   *Teucrium fruticans* L.
Aposinum Americana folis Asclepoyedes floribus
    purpureo   *Asclepias syriaca* L.
Viola luteo Americana arboressence   *Oenothera biennis* L.
Tordillium maius sive Sesseli Crettica   *Tordylium maximum* L.
Alkamilla pese leonis   *Alchemilla vulgaris* L.
Stelaria Argentina   ? *Centaurea solstitialis* L.
Fillapedulla Altra   ? *Pedicularis tuberosa* L.
Campanella Lactencis piramdalis   *Campanula pyramidalis* L.
Barba hersi Coronopi folio   ? *Crepis coronopifolia* L.
Cetterache   *Ceterach officinarum* DC.
Millifolium flore luteo   *Achillea tomentosa* L.
Cianus Constantinopilus   *Centaurea moschata* L.
Cottila marinum   *Tripleurospermum maritimum* (L.) Koch.
Absinthium tridentinum   *Artemisia austriaca* Jacq.
Hisopium mirtifolio   *Hyssopus officinalis* L. form.
Mar Rubium   *Marrubium vulgare* L.
Renunculus minor Bulbosa flore pleno   *Ranunculus bulbosus* L. var. *pleniflorus*
Saniccula Guttata Montana   *Saxifraga hirsuta* L.
Aster 4 species   *Aster* spp.
Abrottinum Altra   *Abrotanum arborescens* L.
Cardus Bulbosus monspellesis   *Cirsium tuberosum* (L.) All.
Balsamum sive Osimum oderatum   *Ocimum* sp.
*Ciclamen vernale flore Rubro odoratissima   ? *Cyclamen libanoticum* Hildebr.
Ciclamen Antiochum & withe them 2 others   *Cyclamen persicum* Miller
Narcissus Virginnianum   *Zephyranthes atamasco* (L.) Herb.
Narcissus indicus squamosus   *Haemanthus coccineus* L.
Ciclmen flore pleno, Albo et Rubro   *Cyclamen persicum* Miller
*Dence caninis flore Luteo   *Erythronium americanum* Ker-Gawl.
Frittilari flore luteo   ? *Fritillaria latifolia* Willd.

Frittilarie hispanica	*Fritillaria pyrenaica* L.
Hiasinthus Indicus tuberosa Radice	*Polianthes tuberosa* L.
Prumela flore flore purpureo	*Prunella grandiflora* (L.) Jacq.
*Gladiolus Canadencis	? *Sisyrinchium bermudiana* L.
*Alowaye mucronata	*Agave americana* L.
Mirtis flore pleno	*Myrtus communis* L. var. '*Flore Pleno*'
*Sedum arboressence	*Aeonium arboreum* (L.) Webb & Berth.
Casie Qorundum Clusii	*Osyris alba* L.
*Hipericon arboressence	*Spiraea hypericifolia* L.
Mispilis Arona	*Crataegus azarolus* L.
*Piemetum Realie	? *Pimenta dioica* (L.) Merrill
Alipum motesetie	*Globularia alypum* L.
*Annagiris feotida	*Anagyris foetida* L.
Jugibie Arabum	*Zizyphus jujuba* Miller
Zisipha Capadocia	*Eleagnus angustifolia* L.
Carobie	*Ceratonia siliqua* L.
Limonium minus Angustifolio	*Limonium binervosum* (G.E.Sm.) C.E. Salmon
Mariaranum sempervirence	*Origanum onites* L.
Sabina Bacsiffira	*Juniperus sabina* L.
Phlirea lattifolio	*Phillyrea latifolia* L.
Sicorum Grumosa Radice	*Cichorium intybus* L.
Capris vera	*Capparis spinosa* L.
Gnapphalium marinum et Cotonuri vulgi sive Bumbax humlis	*Otanthus maritimus* (L.) Hoffm. & Link (*Diotis candidissima* L.)
Martigon Canadencis	*Lilium canadense* L.
Saldanella Alpina	*Soldanella alpina* L.
Philex bacciffera	*Cystopteris bulbifera* Bernh.

Appendix II

Plantarum in Horto
John Tradescant's Plant List of 1634

PLANTARUM

IN HORTO

IOHANNEM TRADE-
SCANTI nascentium
Catalogus.

NOMINA
SOLVMMODO

Solis vulgata exhi-
bens.

Anno 1634.

Plantarum in Horto Iohannis Tradescanti, nascentium catalogus.

A

ABies.	*Abies alba* Miller and/or *Picea abies* (L.) Karsten
Abrotanum Mas.	*Artemisia abrotanum* L.
Abrotanum fœmina, *id est*, chamæcyperissus.	*Santolina chamaecyparissus* L.
Abrotanum Montanum	*Artemisia arborescens* L.
Absinthium arborescens.	? *Artemisia arborescens* L.
Absinthium folio Lavandulæ.	*Artemisia caerulescens* L.
Absinthium Marinum, *id* est, Seriphium.	*Artemisia maritima* L.
Absinthium Umbellatum, Clus.	*Achillea clavennae* L.
Absinthium Vulgare.	*Artemisia absinthium* L.
Acanthus sativus, *id est*, Branca ursina.	*Acanthus mollis* L.
Acanthus sylvestris.	*Acanthus spinosus* L.
Acetosa Hispanica maior.	? *Rumex lunaria* L.
Acetosa franca rotundi-folia, Lobellii.	*Rumex scutatus* L.
*Acetosa Indica.	*Rumex vesicarius* L.
Aconitum cæruleum, *id* est, Napellus.	*Aconitum napellus* L.
Aconitum lycoctonum, Luteum Hiemale.	*Aconitum lycoctonum* L. and *Eranthis hyemalis* (L.) Salisb.
Aconitum Ponticum luteum maius.	*Aconitum lycoctonum* L.
Aconitum Ponticum luteum minus.	*Aconitum vulparia* Reichb.
Acorus verus.	*Acorus calamus* L.
Agrimonia.	*Agrimonia eupatoria* L.
Agnus castus, *id* est, Vitex.	*Vitex agnus-castus* L.
Alaternus.	*Rhamnus alaternus* L.
Alopecuros vulgaris.	*Lagurus ovatus* L.
Alopecuros spica aspera.	*Cynosurus echinatus* L.
Alcea Veneta, *id* est, Alcea Vesicaria.	*Hibiscus trionum* L.
Alsine Repens Maxima.	*Cucubalus baccifer* L.
Allium Sativum.	*Allium sativum* L.
Allium maius (i) Scordoprassum.	*Allium scorodoprasum* L.
Althæa arborea Flo. alb. montis Olb.	*Lavatera olbia* L.
Althæa arborea Flo. purpureo.	? *Lavatera arborea* L.
Alyssum Clusii, i. Alyssum Plinii.	*Marrubium alysson* L.
Ameranthus spersa Pannicula.	*Amaranthus hypochondriacus* L.
Ameranthus holosericus.	*Celosia argentea* L. var. *cristata*
Amaranthus tricolor.	*Amaranthus gangeticus* L. var. *tricolor*
Ageratum.	*Achillea ageratum* L.
Anagallis tenuifolia Flo. Cæruleo.	*Anagallis linifolia* L. var. 'Monelli'
Ammi vulgatius.	*Ammi majus* L.
Amomum Plinii.	*Solanum pseudocapsicum* L.
Amygdalus.	*Prunus dulcis* (Miller) D.A. Webb
Alkakengi.	*Physalis alkakengi* L.
Anthora.	*Aconitum anthora* L.
Anemone latifolia Pavot. ma. Flo. plen.	*Anemone pavonina* Lam.
Anemone latif. Calchedonica Flo. plen.	—
Anemone latif. la Bruyne Flo. plen.	
Anemone latif. Rosea Flo. plen.	
Anemone latifolia albicans Flo. plen.	
Anemone latifolia Coccinea Flo. plen.	*Anemone pavonina* Lam.
Anemone latif. Potorine Flo. plen.	
Anemone latif. Superisse Flo. pleno.	
Anemone latif. Constantinopol. Flo. ple.	
Anemone latif. aliæ diversæ species.	—

Anemone tenuifol. rubro Flo. plen.
Anemone tenuifol. Albo Flo. pleno.
Anemone tenuifol. alba dilut. Flo: pleno.
Anemone tenuifol. mutabilis Flo. pleno.
Anemone tenuifol. viridis Flo. pleno.
Anemone tenuif, carnea vivacis Flo. pl.
Anemone tenuifol. scarlata Flo. plen.
Anemone tenuif. *Pink colour* Flo ple.
Anemone tenuif. pl. Coma-amaranthina.   *Anemone coronaria* L.
Anemone tenuif. Flo. pleno Roseo.
Anemone tenuifol. Flo. plen. variegata.
Anemone tenuif. Flo. plen. purpureo.
Anemone tenefol. flo. pleno purpureo dilutior.
Anemone tenuifol. flo. simplici Brancion.
Anemones flor. simp. diversæ species.   —
Angelica sativa.   *Angelica archangelica* L.
Antirrhinum maius flo. albo.   *Antirrhinum majus* L.
Antirrhinum minus flo. variegato.   *Misopates orontium* (L.) Raf.
Antirrhinum minus flo. albo.   *Asarina procumbens* (L.) Miller
Antirrhinum minus sylvestre.   ? *Chaenorhinum minus* (L.) Lange
Anthyllis leguminosa erecta flo. rubro.   *Anthyllis vulneraria* L. var.
Aquilegia rosea.
Aquilegia variegata albo & purpureo.
Aquilegia variegeta albo & rubro.   *Aquilegia vulgaris* L. vars.
Aquilegiæ magna diversitas.
Arbo Judæ.   *Cercis siliquastrum* L.
Arbor vitæ vel Thyia.   *Thuja occidentalis* L.
Arbutus, sive Unedo.   *Arbutus unedo* L.
Aristolochia rotunda radice.   *Aristolochia rotunda* L.
Aristolochia clematitis.   *Aristolochia clematitis* L.
Armeria holoserica.
Armeria flo. pleno.   *Dianthus barbatus* L.
Armeriæ flo: sim. magna diversitas.   —
Arum sylvestre.
Arum maculato folio.   *Arum maculatum* L.
Arum maius.   *Colocasia antiquorum* Schott.
Aracus Bæticus.   ? *Vicia lutea* L. form *hirta*
Aracus clematites.   ? *Vicia angustifolia* L. var. *bobartii*
Apocynum Americanum.   *Asclepias syriaca* L.
Apocynum alterum.   *Asclepias variegata* L.   } or vice versa.
Asarum vulgare.   *Asarum europaeum* L.
Arundo Hispanica, Donax.   *Arundo donax* L.
Asclepias flo. nigro.   *Vincetoxicum nigrum* (L.) Moench
Asclepias flo. albo.   *Vincetoxicum hirundinaria* Medicus
Asparagus sativus.   *Asparagus officinalis* L.
Astrantia nigra.   *Astrantia maior* L.
Astragalus Bæticus.   *Astragalus lusitanicus* Lam.
Astragalus Marinus.   *Astragalus boeticus* L.
Asphodelus minor, Clus.   *Asphodelus fistulosus* L.
Asperula flo. albo.   *Galium odoratum* (L.) Scop.
Asphodelus Lusitanicus.   *Asphodelus albus* Miller
*Aster cæruleus serotinus fruticans.   ? *Aster novi-belgii* L.
*Aster alter minor fruticans & præcocior.   ? *Aster paniculatus* Lam.
Atractylis.   *Carthamus lanatus* L.
Atriplex baccifera Maior.   *Chenopodium capitatum* (L.) Ascherson
Atriplex baccifera minor.   *Chenopodium virgatum* Thunb.
Atriplicis Varietates.   —
Avena nuda.   *Avena nuda* L.

Avellanæ Diversitates.

Corylus avellana L., *Corylus maxima* Miller and *Corylus colurna* L.

Auricula ursi flore albo.
Auricula Ursi flore luteo maximo.
Auricula Ursi folio Glabro.
Auricula ursi flore luteo Medio.
Auricula ursi albo & rubro variegata.
Auricula ursi Albo & Purpureo variegata.
Auricula ursi flo. Holoserico.
Auricula ursi flo. rubro.
Auricula ursi flo. Violacea.
Auricula ursi flo. fusco.
Auricula ursi Holoserica, Potrine.
Auricula ursi altera, Potrine.
*Auricula ursi maxima Tradescanti flo. obsolet.
Auriculæ ursi Diversæ species.

} *Primula auricula* L.

} *Primula* x *pubescens* Jacq.

B

BAlsamina fœmina.
Barba Jovis frutex.
Barba Hirci Tragi.
Ben Album.
Ben Rubrum.
Bellis maior.
Bellidis minoris magna diversitas.
*Beta spinosa Cretica Bauhiniu.
Beta sativa.
Betonica maior Danica.

Impatiens balsamina L.
Anthyllis barba-jovis L.
Tragopogon pratensis L.
Silene vulgaris (Moench) Garcke
Silene muscipula L.
Erigeron annuus (L.) Pers.
Bellis perennis L. vars.
Emex spinosus Necker
Beta vulgaris L.
? *Betonica hirsuta* L. (*Stachys danica* Schinz. & Thell.)

Bistorta maior.
Blattaria flore albo, & Violaceo.
Blattaria flore luteo.
Blattaria Maxima obsoleta.
Blattaria Maxima odorata flo. luteo.

Polygonum bistorta L.
Verbascum glabrum Miller and *V. phoeniceum* L.
Verbascum blattaria L.
—

Borago flore cærulea minima.
Borago flo. Albo.
Borago Sempervirens.
Botrys.
Brassica Marina latifolia.
Brassica Perfoliata.
Brassica foliis crispis.
Brassica Striata.
Brassica Hispanica.
Brassicæ Sabaudicæ, varietas.
Brunella flore albo.
Buglossa sativa.
Bolbo castanum maius.

Omphalodes verna Moench
Borago officinalis L. (form)
Pentaglottis sempervirens (L.) Tausch.
Chenopodium botrys L.
Crambe maritima L.
Conringia orientalis (L.) Dumort.

} *Brassica oleracea* L. var. *bullata*

Brassica vesicaria L.
Brassica oleracea L. var. *bullata* subvar. *sabauda*
Prunella vulgaris L. (form)
Anchusa officinalis L.
Bunium bulbocastanum L.

Buxus maior.
Buxus minor.
Buxus auratus.

} *Buxus sempervirens* L. (forms)

C

CAlamintha Montana praestantio.
Calceolus Mariae.
Calendula flo. pleno.
Calendula Prolifera.
Caltha Palustris flo. Pleno.

Calamintha grandiflora (L.) Moench
Cypripedium calceolus L.
} *Calendula officinalis* L. cvs.
Caltha palustris L. var. *plena*

Cassia Quorundam Clusii.
*Carobe Americana.
Canna Indica flo. Rubro.
Canna Indica flore luteo.
*†Cardamine impatiens.
Cardamine flore Pleno.
*†Cardamine trifolia.
Carduus globosus.
Carlina, i. chamaelæon albus.
Carduus chrysanthemus.
Carduus Benedictus.
Carduorum diversae species.
Caryophyllorum elegantium
   magna varietas.
Caryophyllus globosus latifol.
Caryophyllata montana.
Castanea equina.
Castanea vulgaris.
Centaurium maius fol. Helenii.
Centaurium maius Flo. luteo.
Centaurium alterum Clusii.
Cerasorum diversæ species.
Christophoriana.
Chamæ-irides variæ.
Chamæ-cerasus.
Chamæpitys secunda.
Chamelæa tricoccos.
Chelidonium maius.
Chelidonium mai. fol. quernis.
Chondrilla.
Chondrilla purpurea.
Chrysanthemum Creticum.
Chrysanthemu seget. bellidis fo.
Cichorium sativum.
Cinara sylvest. Bætica.
Cistus annuus Clus.
Cistus mas.
Cistus fœmina.
Cistus ledum.
Cistus Flo. albo.
Cistus Flo. albo alter.
Cistus foliis crispis.
Cistus ledum primum Clusii.
Cistus ledum latifol. secundum Clus.
*(?†)Cistus ledum quartum Clusii.
*(?†)Cistus ledum septimum Clusii.

*(?†)Cistus Halimi folio.
*(?†)Cistus quintus Clusii.
Clematis flore pleno.
Clematis flore cæruleo.
Clematis flore rubro.
*Clematis Virginiana.
Cochlearia Batavorum.
Coccigria.
Colchicum vernum.
Colchicum Flo. pleno.
Colchicum flo. albo.

Osyris alba L.
Hymenaea courbaril L.
Canna indica L.
Canna lutea Miller
Cardamine impatiens
Cardamine pratensis L. var. *flore pleno*
Cardamine trifolia L.
Echinops sphaerocephalus L.
Atractylis gummifera L.
Scolymus hispanicus L.
Cnicus benedictus L.
—

Dianthus caryophyllus L. cvs.

Armeria plantaginea Willd.
Geum rivale L.
Aesculus hippocastanum L.
Castanea sativa Miller
Centaurea rhapontica L.
Centaurea alpina L.
Centaurea centaurium L.
Prunus cerasus L. cvs.
Actaea spicata L.
Iris pumila L., etc.
Lonicera alpigena L.
Ajuga chamaepitys (L.) Schreb.
Cneorum tricoccum L.
Chelidonium majus L.
Chelidonium majus L. var. 'Laciniatum'
Lactuca perennis L.
Crupina vulgaris Cass.
Chrysanthemum coronarium L.
Chrysanthemum segetum L.
Cichorium intybus L.
Cynara humilis L.
Helianthemum salicifolium (L.) Miller
Cistus albidus L.
Ledum palustre L.
Cistus ladanifer L.
? *Cistus ladanifer* L. var. 'Albiflorus'
?*Cistus salvifolius* L.
Cistus crispus L.
Cistus laurifolius L.
Cistus populifolius L.
Cistus psilosepalus Sweet
? *Cistus clusii* Dunal or *Halimium umbellatum* (L. Spach.
Halimium halimifolium (L.) Willk.
Cistus monspeliensis L.

Clematis viticella L. vars.

? *Gonolobus carolinensis* (Jacq.) Schultes
Cochlearia officinalis L.
Cotinus coggygria Scop.
Bulbocodium vernum L.
Colchicum autumnale L. var. *flore pleno*
Colchicum autumnale L. var. *album*

Colchicum fritillariæ facie.
Colchicum Bizantinum.
Colchicum variegatum.
Colchicum vulgare.
Colchicum ex insula Chios.
Colchicum atro-purpureum.
Colutea vesicaria.
Colutea scorpoides.
Conyza maior vera.
Convolvulus minor folio Althææ.
Coriandrum.
Coronopus maior.
Cornus fructu rubro.
Cornus fructu albo.
Cornus sylvestris.
Corona imperialis.
Cormus.
Crocus Neapolitanus.
Crocus flore albo.
Crocus Mæsiacus luteus.
Crocus Mæsiacus flo. albo.
Crocus flo luteo.
Crocus Violaceus Maior.
Crocus Violaceus Minor.
Crocus flore cinereo.
Crocus Mæsiacus argentinus.
Crocus Mæsiacus luteo Duc.

Croci flore variegato Diversæ species.
Cortusa Matthioli.
Cortusa Americana.
Crupina.
Cruciata Gentiana.
Cucumer asininus.
Cyanus maior.
Cyani Hortensis varietates.
Cyclamen flore albo.

Cyclamen folio Hederæ.
Cyclamen folio Hederæ Italicum.
Cynoglossum minus.
Cynoglossum non descriptum.
Cyperus longus.
Cypressus.
Cytisus Maranthæ.
Cytisus primus Clusii.
Cytisus Secundus Clusii.

D

DElphinium flo. Pleno.
Dens caninus flo. albo.
Dens Caninus flore rubello.
Dentaria tryphylla.
Dentaria septifolia.
Dentillaria Rondeletii.
Digitalis flo. albo.
Digitalis variegata.
Digitalis Alba maior.

Colchicum lusitanum Brot.
Colchicum byzantinum Ker-Gawl.
Colchicum agrippinum Baker
Colchicum autumnale L.
Colchicum variegatum L.
Colchicum atropurpureum Stapf. apud Stearn
Colutea arborescens L.
Coronilla emerus L.
Inula conyza DC.
Convolvulus althaeoides L.
Coriandrum sativum L.
Plantago maritima L.
Cornus mas L.
Cornus mas L. var. 'Xanthocarpa'
Cornus sanguinea L.
Fritillaria imperialis L.
? *Sorbus domestica* L.
Crocus vernus All. (form)
Crocus vernus All. subsp. *albiflorus*
Crocus flavus Weston (form)
? *Crocus flavus* Weston var. '*Lacteus*'
? *Crocus flavus* Weston (form)
? *Crocus violaceus* Weston
Crocus vernus All.
? *Crocus cinericius* Weston
Crocus biflorus Miller
Crocus angustifolius Weston (*C. susianus* Ker-Gawl.)
Crocus versicolor Ker-Gawl., etc.
Cortusa matthioli L.
Tiarella cordifolia L.
Crupina vulgaris Cass.
Gentiana cruciata L.
Ecballium elaterium (L.) A. Rich.
Centaurea montana L.
Centaurea cyanus L. vars.
Cyclamen hederifolium Aiton or *C. purpurascens* Miller var.
Cyclamen repandum Sibth. & Sm.
Cyclamen hederifolium Aiton
Cynoglossum germanicum Jacq.
? *Cynoglossum cheirifolium* L.
Cyperus longus L.
Cupressus sempervirens L.
Medicago arborea L.
Chamaecytisus hirsutus (L.) Link
Cytisus sessilifolius L.

Delphinium consolida L. (form)
Erythronium dens-canis L. var. *album*
Erythronium dens-canis L.
Cardamine enneaphyllos (L.) Crantz.
Cardamine heptaphylla (Vill.) O.E. Schulz
Plumbago europaea L.
Digitalis purpurea L. var. *alba*
? *Digitalis grandiflora* Miller
—

Digitalis feruginea maior & minor.
Doronicum Americanum.
Draco Herba.
Dracuntium Maius, Serpentaria.
Draba flo. albo.

Digitalis ferruginea L. and *Digitalis parviflora* Jacq.
Rudbeckia laciniata L.
Artemisia dracunculus L.
Dracunculus vulgaris Schott.
Arabidopsis thaliana (L.) Heynh.

E

EChium.
Elleborus albus.
Elleborus albus flo. Atro-Rubente.
Elleborus Niger.
Elleboraster.
Endiviæ species.
Epemedium.
Eruca peregrina Clus.
Eruca Aragonica.
Eryngiun Marinum vulgare.
Eryngium Constantinopolitanum.
Eryngium planum.
Eryngium flo. luteo.
Eupatorium Novæ Belgiæ.
Equisetum Marinum.
Esula Maior.
Esula montana.
Esula minor.

Echium vulgare L.
Veratrum album L.
Veratrum nigrum L.
Helleborus niger L.
Helleborus foetidus L.
Cichorium endivia L.
Epimedium alpinum L.
Alyssum sinuatum L.
Diplotaxis tenuifolia (L.) DC.
Eryngium maritimum L.
Eryngium amethystinum L.
Eryngium planum L.
Eryngium campestre L.
Eupatorium ageratoides L.
Equisetum fluviatile L.
Euphorbia palustris L.
Euphorbia dulcis L.
Euphorbia esula L.

F

FAba Americana.
Fabarum Diversæ species.
Ferula.
Ferula Galbanifera.
Ficus.
Ficus Indica.
Flamula Jovis.
Flos Africanus.
Flos Africanus flo. Pleno.
Flos Constantinopolitanus flo Miniato.
Flos Constantinop. Flore rubro.
Flos Constantinop Flore pleno.
Flos passionis.
Flos solis maior.
Flos solis prolifera.
Fœniculum.
Fœniculum dulce.
Fraga spinosa sive hispida.
Fraga fructu albo.
Fraga maiora.
Fraga fructu viridi.
Fraga communis.
Fraxinella Flore albo minor.
Fraxinella purpur. mai.
Fraxinella Flo. rubro.
Fritillaria Flo. rubr.
Fritillaria Flo albo.
Fritillaria vulgaris maior & minor.
Fritillaria Aquitanica.
Frumenti Turcici variet. triplex.
Frutex Canadensis Epemedii folio.

? *Cassia alata* L.
Vicia faba L. vars.

} *Ferula communis* L.

Ficus carica L.
Opuntia vulgaris Miller
Clematis recta L.
Tagetes patula L.
Tagetes erecta L.

} *Lychnis chalcedonica* L. vars.

Passiflora incarnata L.
Helianthus annuus L.
Helianthus multiflorus L.
Foeniculum vulgare Miller
Foeniculum vulgare Miller var. 'Dulce '
Fragaria vesca L. var. *muricata*
Fragaria vesca L. var. *semperflorens*

} *Fragaria vesca* L. vars.

} *Dictamnus albus* L.

? *Fritillaria tubiformis* Gren. & Godr.

} *Fritillaria meleagris* L.

Fritillaria pyrenaica L.
Zea mays L.
Toxicodendron radicans (L.) D. Kuntze

Frutex coronaria Flo. pleno: Syringa Flo.   *Philadelphus coronarius* L.

G

GAlega Flo. carneo.   } *Galega officinalis* L.
Galega Flo. albo.

Genista hortensis.   *Cytisus scoparius* (L.) Link
Genista Hispanica.   *Spartium junceum* L.
Gentiana maior.   *Gentiana lutea* L.
Gentiana foliis Asclepiadis.   *Gentiana asclepiadea* L.
Gentianella alpina Helvetica.   *Gentiana acaulis* L.
Geranium indicum nocte odoratum.   *Pelargonium triste* (L.) Aiton
*Geranium Virginianum.   ? *Geranium maculatum* L.
Geranium tuberosa radice.   *Geranium tuberosum* L.
Geraneum non descriptum Dodonæi.   —
Geranium muscatum.   *Erodium moschatum* (L.) L'Hér.
Geranium oderatum longius radicatum.   *Geranium macrorrhizum* L.
Geranium Creticum.   *Erodium gruinum* (L.) L'Hér.
Gingidium.   *Ammi visnaga* Lam.
Gladiolus Byzantinus.   *Gladiolus byzantinus* Miller
Gladiolus Flo. albo.   *Gladiolus communis* L. or *Gladiolus italicus* Miller
Glaux æstiva supina Lusitanica.   *Glaux maritima* L.
Gnaphalium Flo. albo.   *Antennaria dioica* (L.) Gaertner
Gramen striatum.   *Phalaris arundinacea* L. var. 'Picta'
Graminis diversæ species.   —
Gratiola.   *Gratiola officinalis* L.
Grossularia maxima.
Grossularia maxima longa.
Grossularia cærulea.
Grossularia rubra maior rotunda.   } *Ribes uva-crispa* L. cvs.
Grossularia media species longa.
Grossularia rubra minor.
Grossularia spinosa.
Guaiacum Patavinum.   ? *Diospyros virginiana* L. and/or *D. lotus* L.

H

HAlimus arborescens.   *Atriplex halimus* L.
Hedysarum Clypeatum Lob.   *Hedysarum coronarium* L.
Hesperus Italica.   *Hesperis matronalis* L.
Hepatica Flo albo.
Hepatica Flo. cæruleo maior.
Hepatica Flo. cæruleo minor.
Hepatica Flo. albo.   } *Hepatica nobilis* Miller forms and cvs.
Hepatica Flo albo cum staminibus rubris.
Hepatica cærulea Flo. pleno.
Hepatica cærulea Flo pleno altera.
Herba Dória.   *Senecio doria* L.
Hieracium medio nigrum.   ? *Tolpis barbata* (L.) Gaertner
Hieracium lanuginosum Flo. luteo.   *Hieracium lanatum* Vill.
Hieracium dentis leonis facie.   *Leontodon hispidus* L.
Hippoglossum.   *Ruscus hypoglossum* L.
Hippomarathrum Lusitanicum.   *Seseli hippomarathrum* L.
Horminum Sylvestre Lusitan. flo. albo.   } *Salvia viridis* L. (forms)
Horminum Sylvestre Lusitan. flo. cæruleo.
Hypericum latifolium Lusitanicum.   ? *Hypericum caprifolium* Boiss. or *H. hircinum* L.
Hyacinthus Peruvianus flo. albo.   } *Scilla peruviana* L. (forms)
Hyacinthus Peruvianus, flo. Cæruleo.
Hyacinthus Comosus.   *Muscari comosum* Miller

Hyacinthus Paniculatus.
Hyacinthus Brumalis.
Hyacinthus Orientalis atro-Rubiens.
Hyacinthus Oriental. flo. albo.
Hyacinthus oriental. flo. Cæruleo.
Hyacinthus Pyrenæus flo. albo.
Hyacinthus Pyrenæus flo. Cæruleo.
Hyacinthus Botroides flo. albo.
Hyacinthus Botroides flo. cæruleo.
Hyacinthus flo. obsoleto, Clusii.
Hyoscyamus Albus.
Hyoscyamus Albus medio-pupereus.
Hyssopus sativa.
Hyssopus prolifera.
Hyssopus alba.
Hyssopus tenuifolia.
Hyssopus comosa.

I

JAcea maxima oderata.
Jacea æstiva elegans.
Jacea spinosa.
Jatea flo. luteo.
Jacobæa.
Jacobæa marina.
Jacobæa latifolia Bætica.
*Jasminum Persicum.
Jasminum Catalonicum flo. albo.
Jasminum flo. albo.
Jasminum flo. luteo.
Ilex.
Impatiens Herba Dodonæi, Persicaria siliquosa.
Irides Maiores variæ.
Iris Gloriosa.
Iris Susiana maior.
Iris Clusii flo. Pleno.
Iris Clusii flo. Albo.
Iris Clusii flo. Cæruleo.
Iris bulbosa Anglica maior flo. albo.
Iris Bulbosa Anglica Minor flo. albo.
Iris Bulbosa Anglica flo. Cæruleo.
Iris Persica.
Iris Bulbosa Africana.
Iris Bulbosa Anglica variegata.
Iris Bulbosa flo. luteo.
Iridis Bulbosæ aliæ Diversitates.
Irides humiles sive Chaerides variæ.
Juniperus minor.
Jucca.

K

KEyri maius simplex.
Keyri maius ferugineo flo. Pleno.
Keyri flo pleno Pyramidale.
Keyri. flo. Pleno vulgare.
Keyri flo. Peno aurato.
Keyri flo. albo simplex.

Muscari comosum Miller var. '*Monstrosum*'

Hyacinthus orientalis L. cvs.

Brimeura amethystina (L.) Chouard

Muscari botryoides (L.) Miller var. '*Album*'
Muscari botryoides (L.) Miller
Dipcadi serotinum (L.) Medicus
Hyoscyamus albus L.
Hyoscyamus niger L.

Hyssopus officinalis L. (forms)

Hyssopus officinalis var. '*Angustifolius*'
—

Centaurea moschata L. var. '*Imperialis*'
? *Centaurea cyanus* L.
? *Centaurea spinosa* L.
Centaurea collina L.
Senecio jacobaea L.
Senecio cineraria DC.
Senecio eriopus Willk.
Syringa x *persica* L.
Jasminum officinale L. var. '*Affine*'
Jasminum officinale L.
Jasminum humile L.
Quercus ilex L.
Impatiens noli-tangere L.
Iris germanica L. & other bearded Iris
? *Iris florentina* L. (form)
Iris susiana L.
? *Iris planifolia* (Miller) Fiori var.
Iris planifolia (Miller) Fiori var. '*Alba*'
Iris planifolia (Miller) Fiori

Iris xiphioides Ehrh. vars.

Iris persica L.
Iris filifolia Boiss.
Iris xiphioides Ehrh. cv.
Iris lusitanica Ker-Gawl.
—
Iris pumila L. vars. and *I. chamaeiris* Bertol. vars.
Juniperus communis L.
Yucca gloriosa L.

Cheiranthus cheiri L.

Matthiola incana (L.) R. Br. var. '*Annua*'

L

LAburnum maius.
Laburnum minus.
Lagopus flo. Rubro.
Lapathum Hortense.
Lathyrorum elegantium variæ species.
Lavendula
Lavendula multifido folio.
Laurus tinus folio glabro.
Laurus tinus.
Laurea cerasus.
Laurus Gallica.
*Laurus Alexandrina.
Leucojum Bulbosum maius.
Leucojum Bulbosum minus.
Leucojum arbo. flo. pleno rubro.
Leucojum arbo. flo. pleno albo.
Leucojum arbo, flo. pleno purpuræo.
Leucojum arbo. flo. pleno rubro variegato.
Leucojum arbo flo. pleno purpureo variegato.
Leucojum marinum.
Lilium album.
Lilium flore luteo.
Lilium convalium flo. albo.
Lilium convalium flo. rubro.
Lilium Constantinopolitanum.
Lili-asphodelus flore albo.
Lili-asphodelus flo. luteo.
Lilac Matthioli.
Limonium minus angustifolium.
Linaria oderata.

Lotus arbor.
Lotus Lybica.
Lotus coronata maxima Hispanica.
*Locusta Virginiana arbor.
Lupinus Indicus.
Lupinus candidus ex Candia.
Lupinus flore luteo.
Lupinus flo. Cæruleo minor.
Libanotis.
Lutea Cretica.
Lychnis sativa rubra flore pleno.
Lychnis coronaria pleno flo. albo.
Lychnis coronaria pleno flo. rubro.
Lychnis sylvestris Pyrenæus.
Lentiscus.

M

MAiorana.
Malva arborescens.
Malva maxima Hispan. striata.
Malva segetum Lusitanica.
Marum.
Mandragora mas.

Laburnum anagyroides Medicus
Laburnum alpinum (Miller) Bercht. & Presl.
Trifolium incarnatum L.
Rumex patientia L.

—

Lavandula angustifolia Miller
Lavandula multifida L.

} *Viburnum tinus* L. (forms)

Prunus laurocerasus L.
? *Laurus nobilis* L. (form)
Ruscus hypophyllum L.
Leucojum aestivum L.
Galanthus nivalis L. or *G. plicatus* Bieb.

} *Matthiola incana* (L.) R. Br. cvs.

Matthiola sinuata R. Br.
Lilium candidum L.
Lilium pyrenaicum Gouan
Convallaria majalis L.
Convallaria majalis L. var. '*Rosea*'
Lilium candidum L. var. '*Cernuum*'
Paradisea liliastrum (L.) Bertol.
Hemerocallis lilioasphodelus L.
Syringa vulgaris L.
Limonium binervosum (G.E. Sm.) C.E. Salmon
Linaria purpurea (L.) Miller or *Anarrhinum
   bellidifolium* (L.) Desf.
Celtis australis L.
? *Melilotus officinalis* (L.) Pallas.
Coronilla varia L.
Robinia pseudacacia L.
Lupinus perennis L.
? *Lupinus termis* Forsk.
Lupinus luteus L.
Lupinus varius L.
Laserpitium latifolium L.
Datisca cannabina L.
? *Lychnis chalcedonica* L. var. '*Rubra Plena*'

} *Lychnis coronaria* (L.) Desv.

Petrocoptis pyrenaica (J.P. Bergeret) A. Braun
Pistacia lentiscus L.

Majorana hortensis Moench
Hibiscus syriacus L.
Malva hispanica L.
? *Lavatera trimestris* L.
Thymus mastichina L.
Mandragora officinarum L.

Matricaria.
Matricaria flo. pleno. } *Chrysanthemum parthenium* (L.) Bernh. (forms)

Malum arantium. *Citrus aurantium* L.
Malum limonium. *Citrus limon* (L.) Burm. f.
Malum granatum. *Punica granatum* L.
Martagon Pompon. *Lilium pomponium* L.
Martagon Panonicum spadaceum. *Lilium carniolicum* Koch.
Martigon flo. albo punctato. *Lilium martagon* L. var. *'Albiflorum'*
Medica spinosa maior.
Medica transversis spinis.
Medica scoparia.
Medica elegans Catalonica.
Medica minor spinosa. } *Medicago intertexta* (L.) Miller, etc.
Medica doliata echinata.
Medica doliata ramosa.
Medica clypeata.
Meum. *Meum althamanticum* Jacq.
Melissa. *Melissa officinalis* L.
Melilotus Italica flo. lutea. *Melilotus italica* (L.) Lam.
Melilotus arborescens flo. albo. *Melilotus alba* Medicus
Mentha. *Mentha spicata* L.
Mentha crispa. *Mentha spicata* L. var. 'Crispa'
Mezereon album.
Mezereon rubrum. } *Daphne mezereum* L. (forms)
Milium album.
Milium nigrum. } *Panicum miliaceum* L.
Millefolium atrorubente flore. *Achillea millefolium* L. var. *rosea*
Morus. *Morus nigra* L.
Morus alba. *Morus alba* L.
Morus Virginiana. *Morus rubra* L.
Mollugo. *Galium mollugo* L.
Muscari flo. luteo. *Muscari macrocarpum* Sweet (forms)
Muscari flo. albo. *Muscari botryoides* (L.) Miller var. *album*
*Myagrum Monospermon. *Myagrum perfoliatum* L.
Myrrhys sativa. *Myrrhis odorata* (L.) Scop.
Myrtus latifolia. *Myrtus communis* L. (type)
Myrtus angustifolia. *Myrtus communis* L. var. *tarentina*
Myrtus florida. *Myrtus communis* L. var. *'Flore Pleno'*

N

NApellus. *Aconitum napellus* L.
Narcissus medio Croceus. *Narcissus tazetta* L.
Narcissus Anglic. flo. plen. Wilmot. *Narcissus pseudo-narcissus* L. f. *'Telamonius Plenus'*
*Narcissus Roseus maximus flo. pleno Tradescanti. *Narcissus plenissimus*
Narcissus Africanus Oderatus. *Narcissus* x *odorus* L.
Narcissus Africanus maior praecox. ? *Narcissus tazetta* L. (form)
Narcissus Indicus Jacobæus. *Sprekelia formosissima* (L.) Herb.
Narcissus Capa bonæ spei. *Crinum capense* Herb.
Narcissus tertius Matthioli. *Pancratium illyricum* L.
Narcissus montis Carmeli. *Narcissus tazetta* L. subsp. *lacticolor* Baker
Narcissus Virginianus. *Zephyranthes atamasco* Herb.
Narcissus medio fimbriatus. *Narcissus poeticus* L.
Narcissus Robinus maior. *Narcissus pseudo-narcissus* L. var.
Narcissus juncifolius luteo flo. ple. *Narcissus bulbocodium* L.
Narcissus humilis. *Narcissus minor* L.
Narcissus reflex flo. lut. *Narcissus triandrus* L. var. *concolor*
Narcissus reflex flo. alb. *Narcissus triandrus* L. var. *triandrus*

Narcissus oblong. calice flo. luteo.
Narcissus oblongo calice flo. albo.
Narcissus calice brevi.
Narcissus titesose.
Narcissus va Hecuus.
Narcissus omnium maximus.
Narcissus Montanus.
Narcissus Non-parell flo. alb.
Narcissus Non-parell.
Narcissus Constantinopolitan.
Narcissus totus albus.

Nasturtium Indicum.
Nigella flo. plen.
Nigella citrina.
Narcissus Matineus.
Nigello flo. simplici.
Nux juglans Virginiana.
*Nux juglans Canadensis.
Nux juglans Angliæ Novæ.
Nux juglans maior.
Nux juglans minor.

O

OEnanthe bulbosa marina venenosa.
Ononis non spinosa Pyrenaea.
*(?+) Ononis non spinos. oderata flo. luteo.
Ononis non spinos. aestiva minor flo. luteo.
Oleander flo. albo.
Oleander flo. rubro.
Origanum verum Hispanicum.
Ornithogalum Arabicum.
Ornithogalum Neopolitanum.
Ornithogalum maius flo. albo.
Orobus Venetus.
Olea sylvestris.

P

PÆonia mas.
Pæonia fœmina flo. simplici.
Pæonia fœmina flo. pleno.
Pæonia flo. pleno incarnato.
Pæonia flo. purpureo.
Paliurus.
Papas Americana flo. albo.
Papas Americana flo. purpureo.
Papaver rhæas flo. lut. radice perpetua.
Papaver rhæas flo. simplici.
Papaver rhæas flo. duplici.
Papaver nigrum capit. rotundis.
Papaver corniculatum flore luteo.
Pepo Americanus luteus.
Pepo Americanus viridis.
Periclymenum rectum 2, Clusii.
Periclymenum fructu cerasino.
Periclymenum hortense.

? *Narcissus triandrus* L. var. *concolor*
? *Narcissus triandrus* L. var. *loiseleurii*
—
—
Narcissus 'Van Heck'
Narcissus x *incomparabilis* Miller
Narcissus x *poculiformis* L.

Narcissus x *incomparabilis* Miller cvs.

Narcissus tazetta L.
Narcissus tazetta L. subsp. *papyraceus* (Ker-Gawl.) Baker
Tropaeolum minus L.
Nigella damascena L. var. 'Flore Pleno'
Nigella hispanica L.
Narcissus x *incomparabilis* Miller (form)
Nigella damascena L.
Carya ovata K. Koch.
Juglans cinerea L.
Juglans nigra L. } or vice versa.
Juglans regia L. var. *maxima*
Juglans regia L.

Oenanthe crocata L.
Ononis spinosa L. var.
Ononis speciosa Lag.
Ononis natrix L.

Nerium oleander L. (forms)

? *Origanum heracleoticum* L.
Ornithogalum arabicum L.
Ornithogalum nutans L.
Ornithogalum pyrenaicum L.
Lathyrus venetus (Miller) Wohlf.
Eleagnus angustifolia L. or *Olea europaea* L. var. *oleaster*

Paeonia mascula (L.) Miller

Paeonia officinalis L. cvs.

Paliurus spina-christi Miller

Solanum tuberosum L. (forms)

Meconopsis cambrica (L.) Vig.

Papaver rhoeas L. (forms)

Papaver somniferum L.
Glaucium flavum Crantz.

Cucurbita pepo L. (forms)

Lonicera nigra L.
? *Lonicera alpigena* L.
Lonicera caprifolium L.

Periclymenum Germanicum flo. rubro.

Lonicera periclymenum L. cv. 'Belgica' and/or 'Serotina'

Periploca.

Periploca graeca L.

Petroselinum hortense.
Petroselinum crispum.
Petroselinum Virginianum.

Petroselinum crispum (Miller) Nyman vars.

Phalangium Alobrogium Clusii.
Phalangium Virginianum Tradescanti.
Pistachia sativa.
Philyrea angustifolia.
Pimpinella sativa.
Pimpinella maior.
Pimpinella agrimonoides Colum.
Pistolochia Smilacis folio.
Pistolochia Virginiana.
Pisum Indicum.
Pisum perennes.
Pisum bacciferum.

—
Paradisea liliastrum Bertol.
Tradescantia virginiana L.
Pistachia vera L.
Phillyrea angustifolia L.
Poterium sanguisorba L.
Sanguisorba officinalis L.
Sanguisorba hybrida (L.) Nordborg
Aristolochia pistolochia L.
Aristolochia serpentaria L.
Cajanus indicus Spreng.
Vicia pisiformis L.
? Cardiospermum halicacabum L. or Abrus precatorius L.

Pisum quadratum.
Pisum maculatum.
Pinus.
Pinaster.
Plantago serrato folio.
Plantago rosea.
Platanus.
Polium montanum.
Polygala Valentina 1. Clusii.
Polygala Valentina 2. Clusii.
Poligonon marinum Lobelii.
Polygonatum Maius.
Polygonatum maius angustifolium.
Polygonatum minus.
*Polygonatum racemosum Virginianum.
Polygonatum alterum.
Pomum amoris medium.

Tetragonolobus purpureus Moench
? Dolichos lablab L.
Pinus pinea L.
Pinus pinaster Aiton
Plantago serraria L.
Plantago major L. var. 'Rosularis'
Platanus orientalis L.
Teucrium polium L.
Coronilla valentina L.
? Coronilla juncea L.
Polygomum raii Bab.
Polygonatum multiflorum (L.) All.
Polygonatum verticillatum (L.) All. var.
Polygonatum verticillatum (L.) All.
Smilacina racemosa (L.) Desf.
? Streptopus amplexifolius (L.) DC.
Lycopersicon esculentum Miller

Primula veris Flo. albo.
Primulæ veris albo flo. pleno.
Primula veris flo. pleno viride.

Primula vulgaris Hudson cvs.

Primula veris angustifolia flo. albo.
Primula veris angustifolia flo. rubro.
Primula veris flo. viride & albo. simpl.

Primula farinosa L. form alba
Primula farinosa L. (type)
Primula vulgaris Hudson cv.

Paralysis flo. viridante simplic.
Paralysis fatua.
Paralysis inodora geminata.
Paralysis flo. & calice crispo.

Primula veris L.

Psoudo dictamnum.
Ptarmica vulgaris.
Pulegium regale.
Pulegium carvinum.
Pyracantha.

Ballota acetabulosa (L.) Benth.
Achillea ptarmica L.
Mentha pulegium L.
Mentha cervina L.
Pyracantha coccinea M.J. Roemer

R

RAdix cava maior flo. purpureo.
Radix cava minor flo. albo.

Corydalis bulbosa (L.) DC. (forms)

Ranunculus Asiat. sang flo. Pl.
Renun. Asiat. tenuifol. pleno. flo. luteo.
Ranunculus Asiatic. flo. albo.
Ranunc. Asiaticus flo. rubro.
Ranunculus Asiati. flo. luteo.
Ranunc. Asiaticus folio papaveris.
Ranunc. Asiaticus *Drape de argentine.*
Ranunc. Ilyricus.
Ranunculus albus flore pleno.
Ranunc. aliæ diversitates.
Raphanus niger.
Reseda maior.
Rhodia radix.
Rapunculus.
Rhus myrtifolia.
Ribes fructu rubro.
Ribes fructu albo.
Ribes fructu nigro.
Ribesium dulce.
Rosa Austriaca Flore phœniceo.
Rosa provincialis.
Rosa provincialis Flore albo.
Rosa Vitriensis Flore pleno.
Rosa Incarnata.
Rosa Flore luteo pleno.
Rosa Flore luteo simplici.
Rosa muscata Flore pleno.
Rosa cinamomeæ.
Rosa cinamomeæ Flore albo.
Rosa Batavica.
Rosa provincialis Flore rubro.
Rosa alba variegatæ.
Rosa Flo. pleno elegans variegata.
Rosa Italica.
Rosa Francofurtiana.
Rosa Flore simplic. pomifera
*Rosa Virginiana.
*†Rosa Muscovitica.
Rosa Flore albo.
Rosa canina Flore pleno.
Rosa eglanteria.
Rosa eglanteria flo. pleno.
Rosa holoserica.
Rosa sempervirens.
Rosa Flore rubro.
Rosa Damascena.
Rosmarinus.
Rosemarinus auratus.
Rosemarinus Coronarius maximus.
Ruta canina.

S

SAbina.
Salvia variegata.
Salvia minor odoratissima.
Salvia hortensis rubra.
Salvia hortensis virides.

Ranunculus asiaticus L.

Ranunculus illyricus L.
Ranunculus aconitifolius L. var. '*Flore Pleno*'

Raphanus sativus L.
Reseda alba L.
Rhodiola rosea L.
Campanula rapunculus L.
Coriaria myrtifolia L.
Ribes rubrum L. (forms)
Ribes rubrum L. var. '*Fructu Albo*'
Ribes nigrum L.
Ribes rubrum L. var.
Rosa foetida J. Herrm. var. '*Bicolor*'
Rosa centifolia L.
Rosa centifolia L. var.

—

? *Rosa incarnata* Miller
Rosa hemisphaerica J. Herrm.
Rosa foetida J. Herrm.
Rosa moschata J. Herrm. var. '*Flore Pleno*'
Rosa majalis J. Herrm.

—

Rosa centifolia L.
Rosa centifolia L. var.

—

Rosa moschata J. Herrm.
Rosa francofurtana Muenchh.
Rosa villosa L.
Rosa virginiana Miller
? *Rosa acicularis* Lindl.
Rosa x alba L.

—

Rosa rubiginosa L.

Rosa gallica var. '*Holosericea*'
Rosa sempervirens L.
Rosa gallica L.
Rosa damascena Miller

Rosmarinus officinalis L. (forms)

Scrophularia canina L.

Juniperus sabina L.
Salvia officinalis L. var. *tricolor*
Salvia officinalis L. subsp. '*Minor*'
Salvia officinalis L. var. *purpurascens*
Salvia officinalis L. (form)

Salvia maior foliis crispis.	*Salvia officinalis* L. var. *crispa*
Sambucus aquatica.	*Viburnum opulus* L. or *Viburnum opulus* L. var. *sterile*
Sambucus foliis laciniatis.	*Sambucus nigra* L. var. 'Laciniata'
Sanicula Alpina guttata.	*Cortusa matthioli* L.
Saponaria Flore pleno.	*Saponaria officinalis* L. var. 'Plena'
Saxifraga aurea.	*Chrysosplenium oppositifolium* L.
Scabiosa Hispanica maior.	
Scabiosa Hispanica Clusii.	*Scabiosa stellata* L.
Scabiosa Indica.	
Scabiosa Indica Clusii.	*Scabiosa atropurpurea* L.
Scorpioides portulacæ folio.	*Coronilla scorpioides* (L.) Koch.
Scorpioides bupleurif. siliq. crasatorosa.	*Scorpiurus vermiculatus* L.
Scoipioides minor.	*Myosotis sylvatica* Hoffm. or *Myosotis discolor* Pers.
Scorpioides minor elegans.	*Myosotis arvensis* (L.) Hill
Scrophularia Pannonica Clu.	*Scrophularia vernalis* L.
Scrophularia Montis-Serrati.	*Scrophularia lucida* L.
Scorzonera.	*Scorzonera hispanica* L.
Securidaca minor.	*Astragalus hamosus* L.
Securidaca maior.	*Securigera securidaca* (L.) Degen. & Dörfler.
Securidaca perigrina Clusii.	*Biserrula pelecinus* L.
Sedum maius.	*Sempervivium tectorum* L.
Sedum elegans.	? *Saxifraga umbrosa* L.
*Sedum arborescens.	*Aeonium arboreum* (L.) Webb & Berth.
Serpentaria.	*Plantago maritima* L. var. *serpentina*
Seseli Æthiopicum frutex.	*Bupleurum fruticosum* L.
Sinapi Castiliæ novæ.	? *Sinapis hispanica* L.
Smilax aspera folio rotundo.	*Smilax aspera* L. (type)
*(?†)Smilax aspera fol. Maculata.	*Smilax aspera* L. var. *maculata*
*(?†)Smilax aspera levis.	? *Smilax herbacea* L. or *Menispermum canadense* L.
Solanum lethale.	*Atropa belladonna* L.
Spina solstitialis.	*Centaurea solstitialis* L.
Stæchas Arabica.	*Lavandula stoechas* L.
Stæchas Citrina.	*Helichrysum stoechas* (L.) DC.
Stachys Hispanica.	*Stachys ocymastrum* (L.) Briq.
Stachys spuria.	*Stachys germanica* L.
Stachylodendrum.	*Staphylea pinnata* L.
Stramonia flo. albo.	*Datura metel* L.
Stramonia flo. purpureo.	*Datura tatula* L.
Superbæ diversæ spec.	*Dianthus* spp.
Stœbe Salamantica.	*Centaurea salmantica* L.

T

TAmariscus Italica.	*Myricaria germanica* Desv.
Tamariscus minor.	*Tamarix anglica* Webb
Tamariscus vulgaris.	*Tamarix gallica* L.
Tanacetum.	*Tanacetum vulgare* L.
Tanacetum inodorum.	*Tanacetum corymbosum* L.
Tanacetum crispum.	*Tanacetum vulgare* L. subsp. *crispum*
Telephium maius.	*Sedum telephium* L.
Telephium minus.	? *Sedum anacampseros* L.
*(?†)Terebinthus vera.	*Pistacia terebinthus* L.
*Thalictrum Virginianum.	? *Thalictrum purpurascens* L. agg.
Thapsia Neronis Carotif. Lob.	*Elaeoselinum foetidum* (L.) Boiss.
Thlaspi umbellatum.	*Iberis amara* L.
Thymum verum Hispanicum.	*Coridothymus capitatus* (L.) Reichenb. f.
Tithymalus Charachia.	*Euphorbia characias* L.

Tithymalor diversæ species.   *Euphorbia* spp.

Trachelium album flo. pleno.   }
Trachelium cæruleum flo. ple.   *Campanula trachelium* L. vars.
*†Trifolium Barbaricum stellat. Tradesc.   *Trifolium stellatum* L.
Tulipar. eligant. maxima diversitas.   }
Tulipa. Num. 50 diversæ flamulæ.   *Tulipa gesneriana* L. cvs.
Triticum spica multiplici.   *Triticum* sp.

V

VAleriana Græca Dodon. flo. alb.   }
Valeriana Græca Flo. Cæruleo.   *Polemonium caeruleum* L.
Valeriana Dodonæi.   *Centranthus ruber* (L.) DC.
Verbascum salvi-folium.   *Phlomis fruticosa* L.
Verbascum Blattariæ folio.   ? *Verbascum blattaria* L.
Veronica mas.   *Veronica officinalis* L.
Veronica fœmina.   *Kickxia spuria* (L.) Dum.
Vinca pervinca maior.   *Vinca major* L.
Vinca pervinca minor.   *Vinca minor* L.
Viola Matronalis Flo. plen.   *Hesperis matronalis* L. cv.
Vergæ Aureæ quatuor spec.   *Solidago canadensis* L. and *S. virgaurea* L.
Vite sylvestris.   *Vitis vinifera* L. var. *sylvestris*
*Ulmeria perigrina Clusii.   *Aruncus dioicus* (Walter) Fernald.
Umbelicus Veneris.   *Umbilicus rupestris* (Salisb.) Dandy
Umbelicus Veneris Hispanicus.   ? *Omphalodes linifolia* (L.) Moench
Urtica Romana.   *Urtica pilulifera* L.

A Catalogue of Fruits

Apples.
DOctor Barchams Apple.
Pome de Rambure.
Master Williams.
Yellow Russeting.
Harry Apple.
Dutch Pearmaine.
Blacke Apple.
Barfolde Queninges.
Smelling Costard.
John apple.
Red master Williams.
Quince apple
Summer Permaine.
Winter Pearemaine.
Gillefloure Apple.
Ribon Apple
Pome Mater.
Russet Pippin.
Puffing Apple.
French Pippen.
Snouting.
Blandrille.
Torne Crab.
Great Russeting.
Summer Beiliboon.
Quince Crab.
Pome de Chastania.
Pome de Renet.

Pome de Carpandu.
Pome de Caluele.
Violet apple.
Darling apple.
Stoken apple.
Sack and Sugar.
Pidgions bill.
The Kings apple.
M. Molines apple.
Grey Costard.
Winter Belliboorue.
Little sweeting.
Yellow Spising.
Dari Gentles.
Livinges.
Mother Pipin.
Russet Peare apples.
Keelings.
Ginitings.
Black Pipin.

Peares
BInfield Peare.
Gergonell.
Sir Nathaniel Bacons great Peare.
Red Peare.
Rose water Peare.
Greenefield Peare.
Dego Peare.
Scarlet Peare.
French Popering.
Snow Peare.
Winter Boon Critian.
Summer Boon Critian.
Arundell Peare.
Pallas Peare.
Prince Peare.
Greene Peare.
Hedera de Besa.
Michaelmas Peare.
M. Motts Peare.
Paynted Peare.
Sliper Peare.
Greene Rowling.
Kings Peare.
Poyer Messer Ian.
Nutmeg Peare.
Bishops Peare.
Orenge Burgamott.
May Peare.
Swise Peare.
Summer Burgamot.
Hony Peare.
Mid-summer Peare.
Winter Burgamot.
Poyer de Poydre.
Portingale Peare.

Sugar Peare.
Double floure Peare.
Bloud Peare.
Poyer Fran Rial.
Winter Winsor.
Summer Winsor.
Poyer Irish Madam.
Poyer Dangobet.
Poyer de valet.
Poyer de Savoyse.

Plums
Moroco Plum.
Spanish Plum.
Blew peare plum.
Red peascod Plum.
White Plum.
Plum Dine.
Rath ripe Damaske violet.
Damaske Violet.
Verdoch Plum.
Friers Plum
Bowle Plum.
Nutmeg Plum.
White Rath ripe Plum.
Peake Plum.
Apricocke plum.
Orenge Plum.
Michaelmas damaske Plum.
Red Mirabolane.
White mirabolans.
The Monsiers Plum.
The Perdigon Plum.
The Kings Plum.
The Queenes Plum.
The white Perdigon.
The pruneola Plum.
The Diapre Plum of Malta.
The Diapre Plum.
The Imperiall Plum.
The Date Plum.
The Musle Plum.
The Damascene Plum.
The Irish Plum.
White Damaske violet plum.

Cheries
SWertes Cherie.
Seelinars Cherry.
The great Hart Cherry.
The great bearing Cherrie.
The Arch-Dukes Cherry.
The Spanish cherry.
The Luke Ward Cherry.
The Agriot Cherry.
The Chamelion Chery.
The dwarfe Hungarian chery.

Tradescants Chery.
The white Chery.
The cluster Chery.
The double floure Chery.
The May Chery.

Apricocks
†BArbarie Apricocks 2 sorts.
Small Holland Apricocke.
Masculine Apricocke.
Longe muske Apricock.
The ordinary Apricocke.

Nectorines
The Roman red Nectorine
Sir Edward Sillards ed Nectorine.
The little yellow Nectorine.
The white Nectorine.

Peaches
Tradescants double floured Peach.
The Queenes Peach.
The White Peach.
The Nutmeg Peach.
Peach de Troae.
Newington Peach.
Carnation Peach.
Spanish Peach.
De vine Peach.
Lions Peach.
Roman Peach.
Peach Pavi Jaune.

Vines
*The Parsly leaved Vine.   *Vitis vinifera* L. var. ' *Apiifolia*'
The Fronteneac Vine.
The great blew Grape.
The Potbaker Grape.
The reison Grape.
The currans Grape with divers others.

Appendix III

Musaeum Tradescantianum

Musæum Tradescantianum

OR

A COLLECTION

OF

RARITIES

PRESERVED

At *South-Lambeth* neer *London*

By

JOHN TRADESCANT

LONDON

Printed by *John Grismond*, and are to be sold by
Nathanael Brooke at the Angel in Cornhill,

M. DC. LVI.

C L.

ORNATISSIMISQUE VIRIS

PRÆSIDI & SOCIIS

Collegii Medicorum

Londinensium:

J. T.

Honoris ergo

D. Dq;

Anagr:

JOANNES TRADESCANTUS

Arte notus, annis cedas.
Natura, instans es: cedo.

Natura.—Senex.

DIALOGUS.

Nat. *Utrique* NOTUS ARTE *jam satis polo;*
   Utriusque deliciis satur;
   Favore maximi beatus Principis;
   Amore cultus omnium:
   Quid quæris ultra, terra quod donet, Senex.
   Famam quod ornet insuper?
  CEDAS, *molesti ne sient,* ANNIS *libens;*
   Linquasq linquentem domum.
Sen. NATURA, ES INSTANS: CEDO. *Nec verti potest*
   Stator supremi Numinis;
   Sed nec timeri debet, immensis beans
   Brevem dolorem gandiis.

To *John Tradescant* the younger, surviving.

Anagr:

JOHN TRADESCANT.

Cannot hide Arts.

Heire of thy Fathers goods, and his good parts,
  Which both preservest, & augment'st his store,
  Tracing th' ingenuous steps he trod before:
Proceed as thou begin'st, and win those hearts,
With gentle curt'sie, which admir'd his Arts.
  Whilst thou conceal'st thine own, & do'st deplore
  Thy want, compar'd with his, thou shew'st them more.
Modesty clouds not worth, but hate diverts,
  And shames base envy, ARTS he CANNOT HIDE
  That has them. Light through every chink is spy'd.

> *Nugas has ego, pessimus Poëta,*
> *Plantarum tamen, optimique amici*
> *Nusquam pessimus æstimater, egi.*
> GUALTERUS STONEHOUSUS
Theologus servus natus.

244

To the Ingenious
READER

For some *reasons* I apprehend my self engaged to give an *account* of *two* things, that refer to the ensuing *piece*: The one, for not *publishing* this *Catalogue* untill now: The other, of the *mode & manner* thereof, being partly *Latine* and partly *English*.

About three years agoe, (by the perswasion of some *friends*) I was resolved to take a *Catalogue* of those *Rarities* and *Curiosities* which my *Father* had scedulously *collected*, and my *selfe* with continued diligence have *augmented*, & hitherto *preserved* together: They then pressed me with that Argument, *That the enumeration of these Rarities, (being more for variety than any one place known in Europe could afford) would be an honour to our Nation, and a benefit to such ingenious persons as would become further enquirers into the various modes of Natures admirable workes, and the curious Imitators thereof:* I readily yeilded to the *thing* so urged, and with the assistance of two worthy *friends* (well acquainted with my design,) we then began it, and many *examinations* of the *materialls* themselves, & their *agreements* with severall Authors *compared*, a *Draught* was made, which they gave into my hands to examine over. Presently thereupon my *onely Sonne* dyed, one of *my Friends* fell very *sick* for about *a yeare*, and my *other Friend* by unhappy *Law-suits* much disturbed. Upon these accidents that *first Draught* lay neglected in *my hands* another year. Afterwards my said Friends call again upon me, and the designe of *Printing*, a-new *contrived*, onely the prefixed *Pictures* were not ready, and I found my kinde friend Mr *Hollar* then engaged for about tenne Moneths, for whose hand to finish the *Plates*, I was necessarily constrained to stay untill this time.

Now for the *materialls* themselves I reduce them unto two sorts; one *Naturall*, of which some are more familiarly known & named amongst us, as divers sorts of Birds, foure-footed Beasts and Fishes, to whom I have given usual *English* names. Others are lesse familiar, and as yet unfitted with apt *English* termes, as the shell-Creatures, Insects, Mineralls, Outlandish-Fruits, and the like, which are part of the *Materia Medica;* (Encroachers upon that faculty, may try how they can crack such shels.) The other sort is *Artificialls*, as Vtensills, Householdstuffe, Habits, Instruments of VVarre used by several Nations, rare curiosities of Art, &c. These are also expressed in *English*, (saving the Coynes, which would vary but little if Translated) for the ready satisfying whomsoever may desire a view thereof. The *Catalogue* of my *Garden* I have also added in the Conclusion (and given the names of the *Plants* both in *Latine* and *English*) that nothing may be wanting which at present comes within view, and might bee expected from

Your ready friend
JOHN TRADESCANT.

A view of the whole.

---

*These numbers refer to this book and not to the pages of the original *Musaeum Tradescantianum.*

Some kindes of Birds *their Egges, Beaks, Feathers, Clawes, and Spurres.*

1. *EGGES*

Cassawary, or Emeu, *vide Aldrov: p.* 542. *Harveum, G.A. p.* 61.
Crocodiles, Estridges,
Soland-goose, Squeedes (from *Scotland*).

Divers sorts of Egges from *Turkie:* one given for a Dragons egge.
Easter Egges of the Patriarchs of *Jerusalem.*

2. *BEAKS, or HEADS*

Cassawary, or Emeu, Griffin, Pellican, Shoveler, and thirty other severall forrain sorts, not found in any Author.
Aracari of *Brasil*, his beak four inches long, almost two thick, like a Turkes sword.
Ardeola *Brasil:* his beak three inches long, described, *Margrav:* 5. 13.

Guara of *Marahoon Brasil:* his beak like a *Poland* sword.
Jabira, *Brasil:* beak eleven inches long.
Macucagua, *Brasil: Margrav:* 5. 13.
Soco, Brasil: Margrav. 5. 5.
Tamatia, *Brasil: Margrav:* 5. 10.
Sixteen severall strange beaks of Birds from the East India's.

3. *FEATHERS*

Divers curious and beautifully coloured feathers of Birds from the West India's.
The breast of a Peacock from the West India's.
A white Plume.
Two feathers of the Phœnix tayle.

Tops of the white and black Herne, black and milke-white Herne.
Feathers of divers curious and strange forraign Birds.
Many several sorts of Hernes and Estridges feathers.

4. *CLAWES*

The claw of the bird Rock; who, as Authors report, is able to trusse an Elephant.
Eagles clawes.
Cock spurrs three inches long.

A legge and claw of the Cassaway or Emeu that dyed at S. *James's, Westminster.*
Twenty severall sorts of clawes of other strange birds, not found described by Authors.

5. *Whole BIRDS*

Kings-fisher from the *West India's.*
Divers Humming Birds, three sorts whereof are from *Virginia.*

A black bird with red shoulders and pinions, from *Virginia.*

Matuitui, the bigness of a Thrush, short neck and legges.

Bitterns two sorts, Batts— Red and blew Bird (from *Virginia*).

Penguin, which never flies for want of wings.

Puffin.

Pellican.

Shoveler.

Tropick bird.

Apous.

Fulica.

Dodar, from the Island *Mauritius*; it is not able to flie being so big.

White Partridge.

Spanish Partridge.

Wood-Pecker from the *West India's.*

Birds of Paradise, or Manucodiata; whereof divers sorts, some with, some without leggs.

Birds of Paradise from the Mount of *Moret*, described by *Hacluite.*

A small Grayish bird from the *East India's.*

A white Ousle, or white Black-bird.

The Gorara or Colymbus from *Muscovy*: And another taken upon the *Thames* and given by *Elias Ashmole*, Esq.

Many rare and beautifull Indian birds, not found described in Authors.

Barnacles, four sorts.

Solon Goose.

Squeede from the Basse in *Scotland.*

The Bustard as big as a Turky, usually taken by Greyhounds on *Newmarket-heath.*

Divers sorts of Birds-nests of various forms.

II

Fourfooted Beasts, with some Hides, Hornes, Hoofs.

Animalia quadrup.
1. *digit. vivipera.*
1. *fera.*

Lions head and teeth.

Lynxe's head.

Beares head, clawes, and skin.

Wolfes teeth.

Parde, Leopard's teeth.

Tygers head.

Gulo's legge.

2. semiferæ.

Hippopotamus.

Ai, Ignavus, Sloath, described by *Mar. p.* 221.

Fox, from *Virginia.*

Munkyes sceleton.

Brocks skin.

Beavers skin, teeth, testicles.

Otters skin, and head.

Musk Ratts, from *Virginia.*

Wilde Catt, from *Virginia.*

Cagui *Brasil:* described by *Margrav: pag,* 227.

Cat-a-mountaine.

Flying Squirrel.

Flinder mouse, from *West India.*

Rabbits, from *Ginny.*

Land Porcupine.

Foot of a *Ginny* Dogge.

Martin skin.

Civit-Catts-head and bones given by *T W.*

Dormouse.

Hares head, with rough horns three inches long.

Digitata. ovipara.

Tatus, *Echinus Brasiliensis*, described by *Aldrovand:* p. 480.

Armadilla, or Encubartado, two sorts: Tatu Apara, Tatu Tatupeba.

Alegator or Crocodile, from *Ægypt.*

Chamælion.

Gujana's or Lizards, seven sorts.

Lizards, from *Ireland.*

Snakes, seven or eight sorts.

Rattle Snakes.

Tajuguacu & Tamapara of *Tapanambis.*

Cloven and hairy-tongued Lizards, described by *Margr:* p. 237.

Lanhado.

Lacertus peregrinus Arabicus.

Ibyara, *Brasil: Margr: p.* 239.

Salamander.

Scincus.

Aspis.

Senembi, Iguana, *Margr: p.* 236.

Diverse Tortles or Tortouses.

A natural Dragon, above two inches long.

Quadrup. soliped.

Elephants head and tayle.

Onagrus head with horns.

Zebra's skin.

Monoceros horne.

Caput Equinum petrificatum.

Quadrup. bisulca.

Half of a Stags horn weighing 50 lb.

A Roe bucks horn, from *Cape de Verde*.
A Roe bucks head.
A Deeres horn, from *Greenland*.
A Bucks head with one horn double branched.
A Does head and horns, from Saint *James's* Parke
neer *London*.
The Rhinoceros—horn, jaw-bone, back-bone.
An *Indian* Goats horne.
Bisons head and horns.
Bonasus head and horns.

Antilops horn.
Elkes hoofes.
A Cowes tayle, from *Arabia*.
A Rams head with an upright cloven horn.
Boares tusks, round.
A Sowes head, from *Surat*.
Divers Horns answering to those, by Authors
attributed to the Ibex, Gazella, Hippelaphus,
Tragelaphus, Cervus palmatus, Camelopardalis,
&c.

III

Some Fishes and their parts.

Animalia aquatilia
1. *Sanguinea.*

A Bacatuaja Brasil: *Margr: p.* 161.
Acajamcu, Brasil: *Margr: p.* 163.
Araguagua, gladius Brasiliensis, *Marg: p.* 159.
The Boneeto.
Cunny fishes with horns.
The Dolphin.
A Dolphins head.
A Phocæna's head given by *T.W.*
A Dogge Fish.
A Grampus.
Guacucuja, Brasil: *Margr: p.* 143.
Guaja apara.
Hogge fish.
Sea Horses—head, teeth, pissle.
Iperuquiba, Brasil: *Margr: p.* 180.
King Crabbe.
Lump fishes.
Parrot fishes.
Poison fishes.
Paru, Brasil: *Marg:* 144.

Remora.
A Sharke.
Sword fishes, with several swords.
Swallow fish.
Shovell fish.
Sun fish.
Starre fish.
Sturgion.
Thunny fish.
Sea Wolfe.
Toad fish, and one with prickles.
The tayle of a Catt fish, Stinge ray.
The case of the spawn of the Stinge-ray.
A Whales skin, tayle, jawes, ribs, back-bone,
bladder, eare-bone, pupilla, as big as a pease.
Roches jaw-bone with flat teeth one inch and halfe
long.
Guamajaca guara. Bras: *Marg:* 159.
Guamajacu *ape*-Bras: *Marg:* 142.
Guazezua, Bras: *Margr:* 178. Spec. 2.
Unicornu marinum.
Caput *rosmari* cum dentibus cubitum longis.
Reri, Brasil: *Marg:* 188.

IV

Aquatilia exsanguinea Testacea.

Aporrhoides parvi, *Aristotelis.*
Ballani rubri, *Aldrov:*
Belliculi varii.
Buccinum parvum & striatum, *Rondel:*
Buccina parva varia.
Buccina striata, *Zoographi.*
Cancer Maia plurimis spinis horrens.
Cancer Maia. Guaja apara Brasil: *Marg:* 182.
Cancer macrochelis lutescens fluviatilis, *Matth:*
Chela cancri flavi *undulati.*
Chela astaci marini ex *Zoograph. Aldr.* p. 115.
Chamæ variæ.

Chama glycymeris, *Rond:*
Chama peloris, *Bellon:*
Chamulae variæ.
Conchæ veneris variæ.
Conchæ venereæ, *Aldr:* p. 557.
Conchylium, *Rond: Aldr:* p. 346.
Concha imbricata, *Rond:* minor, lævis.
Concha anatifera, Barnacles.
Concha margaritifera argentea cum lecto margari-
tarum.
Conchæ
candidæ, corallinæ (læves, asperæ), clathratæ,

depressæ, echinatæ, fasciatæ, longæ niveæ, miniatæ, Pictorum, Rhomboides, Rugatæ, spinosæ, squamosæ, anatifera.

Concha Persica major, minor.

Cochleæ
cælatæ, cylindroides variæ, depressæ, echinophoræ, *Rond:* muricatæ, perlatæ, rugosæ, umbilicatæ.

Dentalium quinque genera.

Echinometra, *Rond:*

Echinometra maxima pelagica spinis denudata.

Echinus spatagus.

Echini varii, spinis spoliati.

Echini minimi varii.

Entalia, vel Antalia.

Favago, *Arist: Aldrov:* p. 300.

Locusta maxima.

Lolligo major, *Aldrovan:* 67.

Mentula marina.

Mitulus cum striis.

Mituli fluvii *Thamesis.* myax *Dias:*

Murex
corocoides, lacteus, orthocentros purpurea, triangularis, & marmoreus.

Murices
marmorei varii, *spec.* 12, appendiculis asperis, coloribus variis.

Musculus margaritifer lævis.

Nautilus latinorum alter lævigatus & Ναυπλὸς.

Nautili primum, genus *Arist:*

Nautili testa rudi cortice & variegato.

Nautilus variis imaginibus extimo cortice nitidè insculptus ex Indiâ.

Nerites Bellonii.

Nerites varia genera.

Ovum marinum.

Ostreæ oblongæ Virginianæ.

Ostreæ arborum vamis annexæ.

Pagurus fœmina Venetorum.

Patellæ animalis Lepas, *Rond:*

Patella cypria striata.

Patellæ feræ, aures marinæ vel otia, *Aldr:* 551.

Pinna
aculeata, magna, parva.

Pinnæ byssus.

Penicillus marinus.

Pectines
eburnei, varii.

Pecten magnus depressus corallinus.

Pectunculi.

Pholas.

Polypus.

Purpuræ, *species* 7.

Purpura pentedactylis, *Aldr:* 286.

Rupes elegans artificialis testarum.

Solen
mas, fœmina unicolor glabra, onyx *Plin:*

Spondylus.

Stellæ marinæ
arborescentes, cartilagineæ, pectinatæ, rubræ, testaceæ.

Strombus magnus.

Tellinæ variæ, *Aldr:* 519.

Tridachnes, *Aldr:* 447.

Trochus
magnus, alter pyramidalis, *Aldrov:* p. 363.

Trochus Niloticus.

Tubuli marini vel siphunculi marini.

Turbines albi oblongi varii, & læves varii.

Turbines tuberosi parvi varii, *Aldrov:* p. 353.

Turben Angulosus.

Turben
magnus, auritus.

Turben
tuberosus, tuberculosus.

Turbines
angulosi, muricati, pentedactyli, tesserodactyli, ventricosi.

Turbinuli in spongiis degentes, *Aldro:* p. 363.

Umbilicus, *Rond:*

Urtica parva cinerea, *Rond:*

V

Insecta & Serpentes.

Alæ scarlettæ.

Aranea Virginiana.

Araneæ dens.

Buceros.

Bruchus viridis.

Bucroides.

Cicadæ variæ.

Cantharides.

Catena ex muscis Hispanicis.

Cerambyx.

Enena, Brasil: 2d. 3d. *Margr:* 247.

Erioceros hyacynthinus.

Erucæ nodosæ.

Guaruca eremembi Brasil: sisser, *Mar:* p. 255.

Grillo talpa tardi-gradus.

Grillus ex fusco nigricans.

Hyppocampus.

Hydrocantharus major Anglicus.

Jatatinga, curuculum, *Scalig: H.A. l.* 6. *Marg:* 255.

Labellæ
albæ, flavæ.

Locusta.

Locustæ Hispanicæ.
Locustæ perigrinæ.
Mololonthic, viridulus.
Muscatella armata Virginiana.
Nasicornis Virginianus.
Nasicornium species variæ pulcherrimæ.
Papiliones variæ.
Oestrus.
Phalæna cum pennâ ex capite.
Papilionum plurima genera.
Paipai Guaca, Brasil: *Marg: 255.*
Phalangium.
Phalangii Virginiani caput.
Pediculi cœti.
Platyceros.
Proscarobæus, cornu reflexo.
Quici miri. Insectum parallelogramma, *Aldrov:*
    254.
Quici, Brasil: cornutus, 20 internodiis, *Marg: 254.*
Scarabæi Virginiani cornua.
Scarabæus naso instar rostri navalis cornuto.

Scarabæus instar bufonis Virginianus.
Scarabæorum varia genera.
Scarabæi varii
    domestici.
    Jndici Orientales.
            Occidentales.
Scolopendra, Brasil: *Marg: 255. Muff: l. 2. c. 8.*
Scorpio terrestris.
Stellæ marinæ variæ.
Tipula.
Tambeiva Brasil: insectum, avellanæ. mole: *Marg:*
    255.
Ammodytes.
Amphisbæna.
Cæcilia.
Cenchris Bellonii.
Dipsas, Grevini.
Dryinus.
Seps.
Serpens marinus. *Aldrov:*
Anguis Æsculapii. Ova, sceleton.

VI

Fossilia.

1. Metallica.

Frustulum mineræ auri.
Chrysammonites
    Dendrites, Amonis cornu effigie.
Ramentum mineræ argenti.
Helcysma.
Argyroctenites varii
    majores, minores.
Conchites argentei obscuri coloris.
Æris
    minera, Pompholyx.
Lepis.
Diphryges.
Viride æris.
Santerna.
Pyrites ærosus globosus
    tessellatus, umbilicatus, pyriformis, carycoides.
Pyrites
    turbinatus, angulosus, conchytæ.
Cornu Ammonis
    helicoides, hoplites.
Cornu Ammonis striatum armaturâ æneâ lucente.
Belemnites hoplites.
Orichalcum.
Stanni minera.
Stannum Anglicum cum fluoribus variis.
Biacca Alexandrina.
Stelechites cum minerâ ferri.
Fluores varii cum minerâ ferri.

Cochleæ & conchæ sideroites ex agro Canta-
    brigiensi.
Chamites & turbinites siderites.
Siderocarites.
Sideromycetes.
Lapides ferruginei varii.
Stomoma, squama chalybis.
Ferrugo.
Plumbi vena variis mixta.
Glandes plumbariæ diversiformes.
Chamites molybdoites.
Stibium fossile.
Cerussa cinerea.
Lithargyrii species
    Chrysitis, Argyritis, molybditis.
Plumbum nigrum Virginianum.
Bismuthum.
Cadmia fossilis, lapis calamnaris.
Galena fossilis frugifera.

Metallica factitia.

Cadmiæ species quatuor
    placites, rhotites, onychites, ostracites.
Pompholyx.
Spodios.
Tutia Alexandrina.
    Botryites.
Alcyonia varia ponderosa instar spongiæ concreta.
Adarcion aluminis instar.

2. *Terræ.*

Porus Roseus 1. Alcionium primum.
Marga saxatilis.
Marga cum variis silicum differentiis.
Stenomarga, Agaricus mineralis, lac lunæ, ex
    dono *T.W.*
Terræ
    Cimolia, Chia, Lemnia, sigillata, Parætonii,
    Brunnus Anglicus.
Creta
    Syriaca, Selinusia.
Smectis Anglica.
Rubrica
    sinopica, fabrilis, Anglica laminata.
Ochra
    lutea, fossilis, Anglica, plumbaria factitia.
Rusma Turcarum.

3. *Succi concreti macri.*

Stalagmata varia ex aquis Eboracensibus concreta.
Lapis ex earundum aquarum stillicidio instar
    racemi uvarum concretus.
Coralium
    candidum, nigrum, rubrum.
Coralii frutices, alii instar
    Brassicæ, crassulæ, musci claviculati, &c.
Coraliorū differentiæ quatuordecim.
Stelechites coraloides varii.
Coralia hirsuta muscosa.
Coralium erythroleucon.
Coraliū rubrum cum antipathe.
Pseudocoraliū rubrū fungosum cum astris variis.
Pseudocoralium rubrum calamites.
Millepora Imperati. *Worm:* 235.
Sal fossilis Anglicus
    albus, ruber.
Stelechites salis.
Spumæ salis variæ.
Lapis salinus.
Sal gemma fossilis.
Sal è ramis arborum ex Indiâ.
Alumen nativum
    Cantabrigiense, Eboracense, Cantianum.
Aluminis rupei figuræ variæ.
Chalcanthi species
    Saxonicum, Bohemicum, Bagneum, Cyprium,
    Metallicum.
Lapis candidus Venetorum ex quo Borax fit.

4. *Succi concreti pingues.*

Auripigmentum.
Sandaracha.
Arsenicum.
Sulphur nativum.
Bitumen Dunelmense.
Carbo fossilis, ex quo varia artificialia.
Carbones ex Ætnâ.

Gagates.
Mummia.
Succinorum copia.

5. *Lapides selectiores.*

Lapides metallicos testulatos ex agro Richmon-
diensi effossos, dedit D⁹ *Man.*
Astragolites.
Buccinites.
Cochlites fasciatus
    convexus, concavus.
Ætitū differentiæ variæ cum callimis.
Gæodites.
Hæmatitum differentiæ variæ.
Cerauniorum varietas.
Chelonites.
Brontiæ, ombriæ, odontites.
Glossopetræ magnæ
    denticularæ, non denticulatæ.
Belemnites varii.
Osteocolli varii.
Umbilicus marinus Eboracensis.
Selenites, lapis specularis.
Encephalites magnus.
Lithophthalmites.
Muricites.
Chamæpectinites.
Buccinites.
Conchites.
Turbinites.
Rhombites.
Ophytes varii ex *Whitby* in agro Eboracensi.
Spongites.
Echinitum differentiæ decem.
Marmoris differentiæ variæ.
Marmor Eboracense maculosum.
Magnetes varii.
Lapis minii, vel cinnabaris fossilis.
Lapis
    nephriticus, hystericus, Hybernicus.
Lapides
    è Vesicâ hominis.
                  felleâ.
    è capite assellorum.
                  carpionum.
Coagulum Ætnæ.
Gypsum.
Pumex.
Talcum.
Smyris.
Ebenum fossile.
Crystallini fluores varii.
Lapilli transparentes Virginiani.

6. *Materiæ petrificatæ.*

Cucurbites.
Dactylites.

Pyrites & fructus varii.
Maxillæ cum dentibus.
Dentes varii petrificati.
Ilex petrificata, ex lacu Hybernico *Lough-neath*, ex dono D. *Wybard.*
Quercus cum ejusdem foliis.
Ulmus.
Sambucus cum ejus medullâ.
Fraxinus.
Muscus.
Guttulæ Knasburgenses.
Costa humana cum carne.
Ossa varia.
Caput simiæ.
Ungula equi.
Ovaria halecis.
Cancer totus.
patella cum pisce.
Cochleæ.
Siderites varii.
Ligna varia in ferrum versa.
Guttæ fontis vitrificatæ.

7. *Gemmæ.*

Adamantes Indici ex Decan.
Pseudoadamas Anglicus.
Carbunculi, pyropi, acriores.
Rubini, spinelli ex rupe veteri.
Rubicelli.
Granati
    Orientales ex Cambaia, occidentales, Bohemici.

Hyacinthi coccei & crocei ex oriente.
Amethistus violaceus orientalis.
Saphirus
    albus, cæruleus.
Opalorum differentiæ quædam ex Indiâ.
Smaragdi
    Scythici, Britannici.
Prasii.
Berilli crystallini.
Sardii, corneoli varii.
Onychites.
Achates Indici.
Jaspides virides & purpurei.
Heliotropii varii.
Chrysolithi, topasii Arabici.
Crystalli varii Anglici.
Calcedonius, onyx candida.
Malachites, species Jaspidis.
Oculus cati vel Beli.
Turcosa, Turcois.
Astroites, stellaris lapis.
Asteria vera ex agro Staffordiensi.
Alectorius.
Chelidonius.
Garatronius, crapaudina.
Lapis manati vel tuberonum.
Margaritæ
    Indicæ, Anglicæ, Scoticæ, Virginianæ.
Lapis
    Armenius, Lazuli, limacis.
Lapis Bezoar
    orientalis, occidentalis.

VII

Fructus Exotici.

Acajuiba, acajuti & itimabova, *Marg:* 99.
Ambare, juglandis mole.
Ahovay Thereti, nolæ Cannibalium.
Anacock, phaseoli genus.
Ananas, malo citrio minor.
Anacardia varia.
Avellanæ Indicæ, juglandis mole.
Apeiba, Brasil: *Marg:* 124.
Avellanæ purgatrices, Ben magnum.
Aratica
    Ape, Aponhe, *Margr:* 93, Pana.
Avacari, myrto similis.
Almendras de Peru. *Worm:* 18.
Aurantium nigrum.
Balanus myrepsica.
Banana, musa Alpini.
Bangue semen cannabino minus.
Betele.
Billingbing.
Boramez, agni Scythici pellis portiuncula.

Brindones, intùs rubentes instar sanguinis.
Buna, grana acida continet.
Bon, fructus.
Cachos.
Carambola, siliquæ quadrangulares & pentagonæ.
Capsicum.
Cardamoma
    majora, minora.
Cajus instar ovi anserini.
Cazavi ex herba yuccâ.
Cacâo, potus ejus Chocolate dicitur.
Cevadella, hordeolum.
Cocculæ orientales instar racemi corymborum.
Cajete vel Cochine. Brasil. *Marg:* 123.
Caraguata, Brasil: *Piso.*
Cereiba, Brasil: *Marg:* 128.
Nucum Cocorum varia genera.
Coco nux ex Maldiviâ. *Auger:* Clutius speciatim
    nominat. pag. 8.
Cocci varia genera.

Copaiba Brasil: *Margr:* 130.
Castanea, cornu caprini specie.
Castaneæ equinæ testa.
Cucurbitæ variæ.
Cucurbita, calabassæ.
Coni
 cedri, Abietis, terebinthi.
Cubebæ.
Curcas candidus, avellanæ mole.
Dactylus ebrius.
Daturæ semina.
Durionis fructus echinatus.
Duriaon cum Buanâ, *Clus:* 65.
Fabæ rubræ, Brasil.
Fabæ purgatrices.
Faufel, Areca.
Fructus
 ridiculato cono, Piceæ, Suberis,
 Ilicis triplicis bacciferæ.
                    coccigeræ.
                    glandiferæ. vel
                    galliferæ—
                         Pummukoner.
                         Maummenark.
Cedri & Laricis, platani Virginianæ, gummi-
arboris Virginianæ, squamosi Indici varii,
dysentericus, varii, animalium diversorum
speciem ferentes.
Guanabanus.
Guaganas semina.
Guiraparibu, Brasil: *Marg:* 119.
Guitiiba. *Marg:* 114.
Ibacurapari.
Jangomus, sorbo similis.
Jambolones, olivæ similis.
Jaca ex Goâ instar cucurbitæ, ex trunco prodit.
Juglans nigra Virginiana.
Icicaribu, Brasil. *Marg:* 98.
Janipaba, Bras: *Marg:* 92.
Ibati, Brasil. *Marg:* 20.
Jamacuru, Brasil. *Piso* 100.
Jetica, *Marg:* p. 16.
Jaborandi, *Pis:* 97.
Lancium racemi.
Lobus niger membranosus.
Lobus ex *Windondaw* Virginiâ.
Lobus echinoides ex Brasiliâ.
Lobus echinoides. *Bonduch.* mates Indorum.
Malacactos.
Mangostans, Jambos, mole aurantii.
Mangas, ovo anserino major.
Mehen bethene cum capillis.
Mehen bethene sine capillis.
Mungo nigrum.
Moringa fructus pedalis.
Mandubiguacu, nux purgatrix.
Mucuna, Bras: *Marg:* 19.
Meyney vel nequamel.

Mecaxuchitl, piperis oblongi instar miscetur
cocco.
Myrobalani
 citrinæ, emblicæ, Indicæ, & chepulæ.
Nux
 Moschata cum mace, Indica, Pistachia, vomica.
Nimbo instar olivæ subluter.
Palmeto sylvestris fructus.
Phaseoli varii.
Phaseolus arborescens.
Phaseolus Indicus.
Pochicria Virginiana.

Radices.

Radices
 Caopeba, Brasil: Chinæ, Contrayarvæ, Dari-
 agen, Jalapiæ, Labrundinæ, Matalistæ, Mecho-
 acan, Sarsaparill, Tagion Guineæ.

Miscelanea.

Folia Thee.
Fungus
 sambucinus, rosæ.
Boletus cervi.
Pila stagnalis.
Orabanche.
Coni
 cupressi, pini.

Ligna.

Agallochum.
Aspalathum gummosum.
Caoba, *i.e.* saccharinum.
Cocogola.
Colubrinum.
Cinnamomi lignum.
Bdellium.
Corylinum tortilatam.
Cupressinum.
Fætidum.
Guajacum.
Hebenum.
Levissimum è Siam:
Nephriticum.
Rhodium.
Santalinum.
Strumosa ligna varia.

Semina.

Ammeos.
Amomi.
Bombacis.
Cardamomi utriúsque.
Baccæ
 hederæ, juniperi, lauri, paridis, myrti.
Carthami.
Cataputiæ utriúsque.
Colocynthidos.
Citrulli.

T.S.	On tulipe Brewer 3 collers sh welcom	⎫
	Hom Best Golyathe	
	On Palmer more good tulipes unknowne	
Mr Colfe	On Tulipe Beau withowt A Circle	
	Blanck swisant	
	Unick De Armenitier	⎬ cvs.
	Mr Groves olyas	
	Hollias Beu	
from W. Win	Blienburgh Admirall of 3 Collers olli van	
	Dusport flamed Red & Whyt Crowne.	
Mr Renees	Two Holliasses	⎭

Reseved in the yeare 1631 from Mr Rene Morine

In primis	Renuncculus Asiaticus flore duplice luteo	—
	Narcissus Jacobei, Narcissus indicus,	*Sprekelia formosissima* (L.) Herb.
	Narcissus flor rubro	
	Semper Eternum flore luteum	? *Helichrysum stoechas* (L.) DC.
	*Geranium noctu odorato	*Pelargonium triste* (L.) Aiton
from Bruxsells	6 Hiasinthes	⎫
	Narcissus medio luteus	
	Narcissus Narboniencis	⎬ cvs.
	Narcissus Mussart	⎭

In the yeare 1632.

Lotus Libica	? *Melilotus officinalis* (L.) Pall.
Phillerea	*Phillyrea angustifolia* L.
*Sarsaparilla	? *Smilax glauca* Walter
*Smilex Aspera	*Smilax aspera* L.
*Lentiscus	*Pistacia lentiscus* L.
Agnus Castus	*Vitex agnus-castus* L.
Cittissus maranthe	*Medicago arborea* L.
Absinthum arborescence	*Artemisia arborescens* L.
Cittisus panonicum Clusii	*Cytisus nigricans* L.
Pseudo Dictamnum	*Ballota acetabulosa* (L.) Benth.
Vyburnum	*Viburnum lantana* L.
Lauristinus folio Glabro	*Viburnum tinus* L.
*Cistus folis chrispus	*Cistus crispus* L.
*Cistus popelium folyo	*Cistus populifolius* L.
Cistus mas	*Cistus albidus* L.
*Cortusa Americana	*Tiarella cordifolia* L.
Thimum verum verum Hispanicum	*Thymus capitatus* (L.) Hoffm. & Link
Hisopium tenuifolio	*Hyssopus officinalis* L. var. *angustifolius*
Tragacantha	*Astragalus massiliensis* (Miller) Lam. (tragacantha)
*Amanker Lobellie	*Amelanchier ovalis* Med.
Frutex Coronaria flore pleno	*Philadelphus coronarius* L.
Mirtis florence	*Myrtus communis* L.
Sesely Ethiopicum	*Bupleurum fruticosum* L.
*Caradache Americana	? *Bromelia karatas* L.
Narcissus Tobago	? *Hymenocallis* sp.
Ornithogalum Arabicum	*Ornithogalum arabicum* L.
Iris percicus	*Iris persica* L.
*Absinthium umbelatum	*Achillea clavennae* L.
Absinthium folio Lavendula	*Artemisia caerulescens* L.
Auriggunum verum Hihipanicum	*Origanum vulgare* L. var. or *O. heracleoticum* L.
Tumariscus Itallica	*Myricaria germanica* Desv.

Alchanet.
Madder.
Brasil.
Redwood.
Cochinell.
Campeigiana.
Campeichia.

Brasiletto:
Orchall.
Arnotto.
Flores Carthami.
Minium.
Cinnabrium.

4. *For Blewes.*

Lapis Lazuli.
Ultramarin.
Virditer.
Woade.

Nele.
Indico, divers sorts.
Logwood.

5. *For White.*

Cerussa.

Album.

VIII

Mechanick artificiall Works in Carvings, Turnings, Sowings and Paintings.

Severall Heads cut on Agates.
Divers Figures cut on Shells.
Variety of Figures cut in crystalls.
Divers sorts of Doublets.
Divers sorts of Ambers, with
   Flyes, Spiders (naturall.)
A Bird sitting on a pearch naturall.
Comelian-cup. Amber-cup, and
   Amber-bottle turned. A Crystall bottle.
Severall things rarely cut in Corall.
Divers sorts of Corall, one with Mosse in it.
Divers things cut on Plum-stones.
Heliotropian spoone.
Many cups of Agates.
Cornelian thum-cases of the Turks.
Several curious paintings in little forms, very
   antient.
Splene-stones, divers sorts.
The Indian lip-stone which they wear in the lip.
A little Box with the 12 Apostles in it.
A silver Box with 6 divisions.
Turkish Alkaron in a silver box.
The Roman measure called *Ligula.*
Divers sorts of Purses of Outlandish work in gold
   and silver.

Jupiter, Jo and *Mercury* wrought in Tent-stitch.
Divers sorts of Straw-worke wrought with a
   needle.
Cloath spun of the downe of yellow feathers.
Chirurgeons Instruments framed upon the points
   of needles.
Halfe a Hasle-nut with 70 pieces of houshold-
   stuffe in it.
A Cherry-stone holding 10 dozen of Tortois-
   shell combs, made by *Edward Gibbons.*
A nest of 52 wooden-cups turned within each
   other as thin as paper.
A Hollow cut in wood, that will fit a round,
   square and ovall figure.
The story of the Prodigall son carved in wood:
   Antient.
Persius and *Andromeda* carved in an Ivory table.
Figures and stories neatly carved upon Plum-
   stones, Apricock-stones, Cherry-stones, Peach-
   stones, &c.
A Cherry-stone, upon one side S. *Geo:* and the
   Dragon, perfectly cut: and on the other side 88
   Emperours faces.
The martyrdome of the Bishop of *Amphipolis*
   carved in Alabaster.

Several Landskips, Beasts, Cities, Rocks, naturally wrought in stones.

Landskips, Stories, Trees, Figures (cut in Paper by some of the Emperours).

Divers rare and antient pieces carved in Ivory.

Two figures carved in stone by *Hans Holben.*

A large piece of Fortification cut in wood.

A Deske of one entire piece of wood rarely carved.

A modall of the Tower of *Strasburg* carved in wood.

A rare piece of hollow-carved worke in fashion of a Book.

A Cherry-stone with a dozen of wooden-spoons in it.

A dozen of silver Spoons in a little box.

Flea chains of silver and gold with 300 links a piece and yet but an inch long.

A dozen of little Sheers.

Little chains of silver, gold, and straws, small as haire.

Divers curiosities of turned work in Amber, Ivory.

A little wheele and spindle turned in Amber.

A cup turned in a pepper-corne and garnished with Ivory.

A set of Chesse-men in a peppercorn turned in Ivory.

Divers sorts of Ivory-balls turned one within another, some 6, some 12 folds; very excellent work.

Rolls of the Barkes of Trees wherein are graved the China, Arabian, and Eastern Languages.

Plates engraved in
    Gold, Silver, Copper.

Divers medalls cast off in several metalls.

A Copper-plate enameled with the story of the Salutation.

Divers rich enamell'd plates of
    Gold, Silver, Copper, Brasse.

An ancient annointing Box of guilt-brasse.

Effigies of divers Personages of honor, note and quality.

Severall figures, heads, and effigies cast of in plaister of *Paris.*

Several sorts of imbost Wax-works curious.

Phaëton with his Chariot and Horses, excellent wax-works.

Divers figures moulded and painted.

A glasse-hatt-band spun in fine threds.

A glasse-basket full of several fruits.

Back-work wrought upon glasse.

Variety of glasse in many curious forms.

Backside work acht upon crystall.

Two severall modells of the Sepulcher at *Jerusalem;* one in wood: the other in plaister.

Mosaick work of divers sorts.

Severall draughts and pieces of painting of sundry excellent Masters.

A small Landskip drawn by Sir *Nath: Bacon.*

The figure of a Man singing, and a Woman playing on the Lute, in 4° paper; The shadow of the worke being *David's* Psalmes in Dutch.

Prince of *Orange's* picture shadowed with writing in afore-recited manner.

Old *Parre's* picture.

A Booke of Mr. TRADESCANT'S choicest Flowers and Plants, exquisitely limned in vellum, by Mr. *Alex: Marshall.*

A book of all the Stories in the glasse-windowes of *Sancta Sophia,* lim'd in vellum by a Jew.

Divers sorts of pictures wrought in feathers.

A little Box made of straw and silke.

Indian books made of *Phillyrea.*

Indian paper made of
    Grasses, Straw, Rinds of trees.

With large margents full of figures and divers colours.

Babylonian combs.

Severall Indian combs, one of reeds.

IX

Variety of Rarities.

Indian morris-bells of shells and fruits.

Indian musicall Instruments.

Indian Idol made of Feathers, in shape of a Dog.

Indian fiddle.

Spanish Timbrell.

Instrument which the Indians sound at Sun-rising.

Portugall musicall Instrument like a hoop, with divers brasse plates.

A choice piece of perspective in a black Ivory case.

A Canow & Picture of an Indian with his Bow and Dart, taken 10 leagues at Sea. *An°.*—76.

A bundle of Tobacco, *Amazonian.*

Birds-nests from *China.*

Indian Conjurors rattle, wherewith he calls up Spirits.

Indian *Pa*God.

The Idol *Osiris. Anubis,* the Sheep, the Beetle, the Dog, which the Egyptians worshipped. Mr. *Sandys.*

A Gamaha with *Jesus, Joseph* and *Mary,* in Italian capitall letters.

A Gamaha with a Fish in it.

A Gamaha of a Deaths-head.

A Circumcision-Knife of stone, and the instrument to take up the *præputium* of silver.

Jewes Philacteries with the Commandements, writ in Hebrew.

A piece of Stone of Saint *John Baptists* Tombe.

A piece of the Stone of *Sarrigo*-Castle where *Hellen* of *Greece* was born.

A piece of the Stone of the Oracle of *Apollo*.

A piece of the Stone of *Diana's* Tomb.

An Orange gathered from a Tree that grew over *Zebulon's* Tombe.

Severall sorts of Magnifying glasses: Triangular, Prismes, Cylinders.

Antient Iron-Money in crosse-plates, like Anchors, preserved in *Pontefract*-Castle, *Yorkeshire*.

Several Assayes of Money.

A Brazen-ball to warme the Nunnes hands.

A piece of one of the Logges of *Bagmere* in *Cheshire*, neer *Breereton*.

A Trunion of Capt: *Drake's* Ship.

Divers sorts of Indian Jakes.

Several sorts of Cymballs.

Cassava Bread 2 sorts.

The Padre Guardians staffe of *Jerusalem*, made of a branch of one of the 70 Palme-Trees of Elam, which he gave to Sir *Tho: Roe*.

A glasse-horne for annointing Kings.

2 Roman Urnes.

A Roman sacrificing-earthen-Cup, with the word *CAMPANION* printed in the bottome.

Tarriers of Wood made like our Tyring-Irons.

Tarriers of Wood like Rolles to set Table-dishes on.

Indian Tresles to hang a payr of Skales on, of black varnisht wood.

The plyable Mazer wood, being warmed in water will work to any form.

Blood that rained in the *Isle of Wight*, attested by Sir *Jo: Oglander*.

A Hand of Jet usually given to Children, in *Turky*, to preserve them from Witchcraft.

X

Warlike Instruments.

Poleaxe with a Pistoll.

Poleaxe and Pistoll with a Mill and Crosse-bow in it for either Arrow or Bullet.

German Poleaxes.

Count *Mansfield's* Poleaxe, called *Pussacon*.

Indian square-pointed Dagger, broad and flat.

Japan Sword and Dagger.

Moores Daggers, 2 sorts.

Severall sorts of Daggers.

Javelin
    Japan, Turkish.

Indian Lance.

Molocco Sword.

Targets from the *East India* of—
    Reeds, Leather, Skins, and Crocodill-skin.

Bowes 12, Arrowes 20, Quivers 12, Darts 60 (From *India, China, Canada, Virginia, Ginny, Turkey, Persia*).

Drums two sorts; 1. from *Ginny* of a whole piece of wood; 2^d. from *India* of copper.

Targets several sorts, *viz:*
    Knights Templers, Britaine, *Isidore* the Monk, Roman, Japan, Græcian, *Roguza.*

Indian drumming Target.

Ginny Drum made of one piece.

China Armour.

Knife wherewith *Hudson* was killed in the *North-West* passage, or *Hudson's* Bay.

Knives from Ginny, 3 sorts.

Knives from *Muscovy*.

A *Damascus* knife perfum'd in the casting.

Roman Darts headed with copper, taken neer *Pontefract, Yorkesh.*

Moddels for a Cannon, with the appurtenances.

Tamahack, 6 sorts.

Poisoned Creeses, or Daggers—
    2 waved, 2 plain.

Iron Manacle taken in the Spanish-Fleet.—88.

Sithe, Symiter, Steletto (from *Turkey*).

Souldiers Coat of Armour.

Skaling ladders 6 sorts of wood and ropes, and iron pullies; 2 with joints of wood closed in a staffe.

A Sempitan or Trunck wherewith they execute men to death with poysoned Arrowes.

XI
Garments, Vestures, Habits, Ornaments.

An Arabian vest.
A Russian vest.
A Portugall habit.
A Turkish vest.
A Brackmans vest of Leaves of Aloes
A Virginian habit of Beares-skin.
A Babylonian vest.
A Greinland-habit.
A Match-coat from—
    Virginia of Feathers.
    Canada.   Deer-skin.
Match-coat from *Greenland* of the Intrails of Fishes.
Pohatan, King of *Virginia's* habit all embroidered with shells, or Roanoke.
A Match-coat of *Virginia* made of Racoune-skins.
Crownes
    Indian, Amazonian.
Swabes suit.
Henry the 8
    his Stirrups, Haukes-hoods, Gloves.
Barbary Spurres pointed sharp like a Bodkin.
K. great Porter's Boots.
Little *Ieffreyes* Boots.
Little *Ieffreyes* Masking-suit.
Boots from
    Lapland, Greenland, Muscovy, Babylonian, Russian, Persian.
Shooes to walk on Snow without sinking.
Spurres from *Turkey.*
Moores Cap.
Chappenes, 20 sorts.
Tartarian Whips.
Scourges of Sinewes.
Disciplines of wire, quilted cotton.
A Fryers Discipline with silver rowels.
A lacrymaticall Urne for Teares, of glasse.
Girdles of the length of the Sepulchre.
Nunnes penitentiall Girdles of Haire.
Cordilier Girdles of
    silke, pearle, straw, cotton, curious worke.
Jewes girdle and purse.
Girdle, Indian.
Borâchios for wine.
Hat-bands of Porcupine quills beaten flat and dyde.
A payre of Scotch gloves wrapt up like a ball.
A linnen Shirt woven without either seam or stitch, 2 yards long.
A vestall Nunnes head-dresse, of tiffany curiously crisped.
Duke of *Muscovy's* vest wrought with gold upon the breast and armes.

Case of Indian bands and caps made of the rinds of trees.
Shirts and smocks, Indian.
Turkish shash.
Brabant Womans cap and cuffs.
Polander Priests cap.
Handkerchiffs of severall sorts of excellent needle-work.
Edward the Confessors knit-gloves.
Anne of Bullens Night-vayle embroidered with silver.
Anne of Bullens silke knit-gloves.
Henry 8, hawking-glove, hawks-hood, dogs-coller.
Severall sorts of girdles from *Ierusalem* weaved in gold, silver, and silk.
A Caule of haire, excellent work.
Russia stockens without heels.
Hat of very fine straw or bent.
A hat-band made of the sting-ray.
Bands and cuffs of straw.
Indian monteroes.
Shooes from *Peru, Canada, Mogull, China, Japan, Cormandell, Barbery, Turky, Venice, Rhode, Malta, Greneland, Poland, Portugall, Spaine, Russia* shod with Iron, *East India.*
Sandals of wood, from *China.*
Sandals made of twigs.
Severall sorts of Sandals.
Choppenes for Ladyes from *Malta, Venice.*
Womans breeches from the *Abissenes.*
Divers night-caps made of grasse, from the *West Indies.*
Turkish belt wrought with gold.
Rich vest from the *great Mogull.*
Napkins made of the rinds of trees.
Variety of Indian Crownes made of divers sorts of feathers.
Severall attires and ornaments made of most beautifull feathers.
A Hat-band of glasse spun into fine threads.
Variety of Chains, made of the teeth of Serpents and wilde beasts, which the Indians weare.
Bracelets from *Guiny.*
Bracelets of Indian fruits.
Severall steel-chains of curious work, from *Spaine.*
Black Indian girdles made of Wampam peek, the best sort.
A Bracelet made of thighes of Indian flyes.
Purses of the barks and rindes of trees.
A Purse made of a Toad-skin, a handfull long.
Virginian purses imbroidered with Roanoake.
A Coat lyned with *Agnus Scythicus.*
West Indian thred.

XII

Utensils.

A Roman Lamp.

A Lethern Tobacco-pipe.

A *Ginny* Lanthorn.

Indian Ladle.

Dishes of gourd shells, Indian.

Ginny drinking-cups made of birch.

Indian pillow.

Chaffing-dish, gridiron, spits, and to roast egges and apples; all to be done with one fire, and all in a modell of iron.

Desk for a book. Rack to hang a cloak on. (Of carved Whalebone).

Indian cradle.

An Indian hollow low stoole.

An Indian little round table.

China ware, purple and green.

Mazer dishes.

Indian long pepper-boxes.

Cup of Rhinoceros, Unicorn, & Albado's hornes.

Divers dishes of mother of pearle.

A branched Candlestick turned in Ivory.

An Indian dish made of excellent red earth, with a Nest of Snakes in the bottome.

A casting bottle of marbled-glasse.

Variety of *China* dishes.

A Table-cloath of grasse very curiously waved.

Divers transparent Ivory-cups.

Severall cups of Amber turned.

Cup made of Albado horn.

Skades to slide with.

Hamaccoes, five several sorts.

A *Portugall*-Whisk of haire to beat away flyes from horses and camels.

Tobacco-pipes, 30 sorts from *Brasil, Virginia, China, India, Amazonia.*

Visnago, a Spanish tooth-picker.

Turkish tooth-brush.

Gurgolets to poure water into their mouthes without touching it.

Baskets to carry those Gurgolets, Indian.

Plates made of Rushes, *Ginny.*

Turks budget.

A Turkish Inkhorn.

An Italian lock, *Custos pudicitiae.*

An *Umbrella.*

Ventilo's of *Palmeto* leafe, Turkish feathers, Straw, Leather, Sedge.

Indian baskets 20 sorts.

German locks 6 sorts.

Fannes of skins and rushes.

Tartarian saddle with stirrups of wood with a hollow wherein he keeps his meat alwayes warm.

Divers sorts of Indian weights and skales.

Beads strung upon stiffe wyers, and set in four-square frames wherewith the Indians cast account.

A Turks travelling bucket of leather.

An Indian leather-case wrought in gold.

Letter-cases made of the rindes of trees and grasses.

A copper Letter-case an inch long, taken in the *Isle of Ree* with a Letter in it, which was swallowed by a Woman, and found.

A choice polished steel for a looking-glasse in an Ivory frame, cut in curious figures.

Divers sorts of Looking-glasses of severall formes.

A steel-glasse that showes a long face on one side, and a broad on the other.

XIII

Nomismata.

Aurea.

Græca.

Lysimachus.

Britannica.

Cunobelinus, *vid: Cambd: Brit: Tab:* 1. N.3.

Alius, ibid: N. 8.

Sex, incerta.

Latina.

Scipio Africanus.

Cicero.

Augustus.

Nero.

Fl: Jul: Constantius.

Fl: Valentinianus.

Fl: Gratianus.

Valentinianus Jun:

Fl: Honorius.

Arcadius.

Justinus.

Constans & Constantinus.

Justinianus II.

Constantinus VIII & Romanus.

Moderna.
Sextus V. Pont: Max:
Clemens VIII. Pont: Max:
Urbanus VIII. Pont: Max:
Ferdinandus & Eliz: Hisp.
Philippus II. Rex Hisp.
Carolus Rex Francorum.
Jacobus V. Rex Scotorum.
Casimirus Rex Polon:
Stephanus Rex Polon:
Conradus II. Ro: Rex Dux & Gub: Reip: Gen:
Emanuel Filib: Dux Sabaud:

Gulielmus Dux Mantuæ.
Ferdinandus Dux Mant:
Ranut Far: Placent: Dux IV.
Moneta Aurea.
Provinc: fœder: Belg:
Westfrisiæ.
Civitas Metensis.
Civitas Campen.
Venetian Ducat, half Ducat.
Spanish Pistoll, half-Pistoll.
French Pistoll, half Pistoll.

Nomismata Hebraica.
Argentum.

Siclus
Hemisiclus.
Characteribus Samaritanis signati.

Siclus
Hemisiclus.
Characteribus Chaldaicis signati.

Nomismata Graca.
Argentum.

Stater-
Alexandri, Athenarum, Ephesiorum, Macedonum.
Tridrachma
Rhodiornm, Siculorum.
Didrachma
Tarentinorum, Syracusanorum.

Drachma
Alexandri, Gælensinum, Armeniorum, Siriphiorum, Rhegiorum. Massiliensium.
Triobolus
Actiorum, Apolloniatum, Dyrrachinorum, Rhodinorum.

Ærea.

Demetrii.
Lysimachi.
Athenarum.

Panormi.
Syracusarum.
Rhodi.

Nomismata Romana, secunda Familia.
Argentea.

M': AEMILIus LEPidus.
M. Æmilius LEPIDVS.
M. ANTonius IMP.
{ ANTonius.
{ AVGustus IIIVIR R. P. C. LEG. IIII.
ANT. AVG. IIIVIR. R. P. C. LEG. VI.
ANT. AVG. IIIVIR. R. P. C. LEG. XIIII.
ANT. AVG. IIIVIR. R. P. C. LEG. XX.
M': AQVILlius M. F. M N.
M: Aurelius SCAVRus.
Augustus CÆSAR. IMP. VII.
Castor & Pollux equitantes.
L. Calphurnius PISO FRVGI.
C. CASSIus.
L. Cassius LONGINus IIIV.

Q. CASSIVS Longinus.
Q. Cæcilius Mettellus PIus.
L CAESIVS.
TI. CLAVDius TI.F. AP.N.
P. CLODIVS. M. F.
T. CLOVLIus.
C. COIL (Cœlius) CALDus.
M'. CORDIVS RVFVS IIIVIR.
CN. Cornelius LENTulus.
L. Cornelius SCIPio ASIAticus.
CN. DOMITius Ahenobarbus.
C. EGNATIVS. CN. F. CN. N.
C. FABIus CF.
N. FABIVS C.F. Pictor.
L. FLAMINius CILO.

C. FVNDANius Fundulus.
C. HOSSIDIus C. F. GETA. IIIVIR.
Julius CAESAR. *Eliphas*
Julius CAESAR. *Anchises*
L. Junius BRVTVS.
{ L.MANLIVS PROQ.
{ L. Cornelius SVLLA.
L. Marcius PHILIPPVS.
L.MEMMius GAL.
Q.Minutius THERmus M.F.
M. Papirius CARBOnus.
M. PLAETORIus CESTianus.
{ Q. POMPEIus Q. F. RVFVS.
{ L. Cornelius SVLLA.
C. Porcius CATO. Manii filius.

L. RVBRIus Dossenus.
L. SCRIBONius LIBO.
TI.SEMPRONIVS GRACCVS IIIVIR.
C. SERVILIus M.F.
C. SERVILIus C. F.
Q. Servilius CAEPIOnus.
C. SVLPICIus C. F.
L. THORIVS BALBVS.
Q. TITIus.
L. TITVRIus SABINus.
P. Titurius SABINus.
C. VALerius FLACCus.
L. VALERIus FLACCus.
C. VIBIVS. C. F. PANSA.

Nomismata Imperatorum.
Argentea.

C. Julius Cæar.
Marcus Antonius.
Augustus.
Tiberius.
Nero Claud: Drusus Germ:
Caius.
Claudius.
Nero.
Ser: Galba.
M. Otho.
A. Vitellius.
Vespasianus.
Titus.
Domitianus.
Nerva.
Trajanus.
Hadrianus.
Sabina Hadriani.
Antoninus Pius.
Faustina Pii:
M. Aur: Antoninus.
Faustina Marci.
Lucilla Veri.
L. Æl: Aurel: Commodus.
Crispina Commodi.
P. Helvius Pertinax.
L. Sept: Severus.
M. Aurel: Antoninus Caracalla.
Caracallæ Caput barbatum.
P. Septim: Geta.
M. Aur: Antoninus Elagabalus.

Elagabali Caput barbatum.
Julia Mæsa.
Julia Mamæa.
M. Aurel: Sever: Alexander.
Maximinus.
M. Clod: Pupienus Maximus.
M. Ant: Gordianus.
M. Jul: Philippus.
M. Otacilla Severa Philippi.
M. Jul: Philippus. Jun:
Q. Trajanus Decius.
C. Herennius Etruscus Mes: Dec:
C. Vibius Trebonianus Gallus.
C. Vibius Volusianus.
P. Licinius Valerianus.
P. Licinius Gallienus.
Corn: Solonina Gallieni.
P. Licinius Valerianus.
M. Cassius Latienus Postumus.
Fl: Julius Constantius.
Fl: Julius Constans.
Magnentius.
Fl: Claud: Julianus.
Juliani Caput barbatum.
Valentinianus.
Fl: Gratianus.
Fl: Magnus Maximus.
Honorius.
Valens.
Theodosius.
Arcadius.

Ærea.

	Magnitudo.		Magnitudo
C. Julius Cæsar.	1 &2.	P. Lic: Corn: Saloninus Valerianus.	2.
M. Agrippa, Lucii F.	2.	M. Cass: Lat: Posthumus.	3.
Augustus.	1. 2.	M. Aur: Victorinus.	3.
Tiberius.	1. 2.	P. Pives: Tetricus.	3.
Germanicus.	2.	C. Pives: Tetricus.	3.
Agrippina.	1.	M. Aurel: Claudius.	2.
Caius.	1.	L. Domitius Aurelian⁹.	2.
Claudius.	1. 2.	M. Claud: Tacitus.	2.
Nero.	1. 2.	M. Annius Florianus.	2.
Galba.	2.	M. Aurel: Probus.	2.
Otho.	1.	Probi caput barbatum.	
Vitellius.	1.	C. Valer: Dioclesianus.	2, & 3.
Vespasianus.	1. 2.	Carausius.	2.
Titus.	1. 2.	Allectus.	2.
Domitianus.	1. 2.	M. Aur: Valer: Maximianus.	2. 3.
Nerva.	1. 2.	Fl: Valer: Constantius.	2. 3.
Trajanus.	1. 2.	Fl: Jul: Helena.	3.
Hadrianus.	1. 2.	C. Gal: Val: Maximianus.	3.
Antoninus Pius.	1. 2.	C. Gal: Val. Maximinus.	3.
Faustina.	2.	Fl: Valer: Constantius.	2. 3.
M. Aurel: Antoninus.	1. 2.	Fl: Max: Fausta.	3.
Faustina Marci.	1.	Fl: Jul: Crispus.	3.
L. Aurel: Verus.	1.	M. Aur: Val: Maxentius.	3.
Lucilla Lucii Veri.	1.	C. Val: Licinianus Licinius.	2.3.
L Æl: Aur: Commodus.	1. 2.	Licinius Junior.	3.
Commodi Caput Barbatū.	1.	Fl: Claud: Constantinus Jun:	3.
L. Sept: Severus.	1.	Fl: Julius Constans.	2. 3.
M. Aur: Ant: Caracalla.	1. 2.	Fl: Julius Constantius.	2. 3.
Julia Mæsa.	1.	Magnentius.	2. 3.
Julia Mamæa.	1.	Decentius.	2.
M. Aur: Sever: Alexander.	1. 2.	Fl: Valentinianus.	3.
Maximinus.	1.	Fl: Gratianus.	3.
M. Ant: Gordianus.	1. 2.	Valentinianus II.	3.
M. Jul: Philippus.	1. 2.	Honorius	3.
M. Octacilla Sev: Philippa	1. 2.	Valens.	3.
M. Jul: Philippus Jun:	1. 2.	Theodosius.	2.
Q. Trajanus Decius.	1.	Tiberius Mauritius.	1.
Barbia Orbiana Decii.	2.	Justinianus II.	1.
Vibius Trebonianus Gallus.	2.	Leontius.	
P. Licinius Gallienus.	2.	Michael. *vide Strada, fol.* 319.	2.
		Constantius XI. *ib. fol.* 322.	2.

Argentea quædam inserenda.

L. Aurelius Verus.	Julia Scemias.
M. Opel: Macrinus.	Heren: Etruscilla Volusiani.

XIV

Medalls.
Gold.

Pope Sixtus *V.*
Pope Clement *VIII.*
Pope Uurban *VIII.*

Elizabeth *the Daughter of* Andrew *King of* Poland.
Upon the Coronation of King CHARLES in
   Scotland.

Silver.

Moses.
David & Bathsheba, Lot & his 2 daughters.
Priam.
Hellen.
Pallas.
Alexander.
Mithridates.
Camillus Dictator.
Lucretia.
Artimesia.
Dido.
Julius Cæsar.
Herod *and* Josias *King of* Juda.
Pope Clement *VIII.*
Pope Urban *VIII.*
Maximilianus Magnanimus, Mary *daughter and*
   heire of Charles *Duke of* Burgundy.
Rodolphus *II.* Emperour *of* Germ:
Matthias *and* Maximilian (*Archdukes of* Austria).
Ferdinand *II upon his Coronation.*
The Effigies of eleven of the Austrian *family.*
All the Armes *of the* Empire *upon a* Peacocks tayle.
JAMES *King of* England, &c.
Queen ANNE.
King JAMES, *Queen* ANNE, *Prince* HENRY.
King CHARLES.
King CHARLES *and Queen* MARY.
Upon King CHARLES his Coronation at West-
   minster.

Upon the Isle of Ree *Voyage.*
Upon His Coronation *in* Scotland.
Upon Prince CHARLES *his Birth.*
Upon JAMES *Duke of* Yorke *his Birth.*
Prince CHARLES.
Philip *the II. K. of* Spaine, 1557.
Philip *the II. and* Anne *his Wife.*
Lewis *XIII. King of* France.
Queen Mother.
John *II. King of* Sweden.
Gustavus Adolphus *King of* Sw:
Gustavus Adolphus, *and* Maria *and* Elianora.
Upon Gustavus *his* death.
Christina *Queen of* Sweden.
Christian *IV. King of* Denmarke.
Maximilian *King of* Bohemia *and* Hungaria, 1563.
Ignatius Loyala.
Cardinall Richlieu.
Frederick Henry *Prince of* Orange, 1625.
Maurice *Pr: of* Orange, 1632.
John Frederick *Duke of* Saxony.
Ernestus *Count* Mansfield.
Albertus Durer. 1514.
Lawren: Staberus *Orator*, 1536.
John a Leyden.
Pomponius Bellieuræus, 1598.
Upon the Comet, 1618. 19. *Nov.*
A Lady *suckling her* Father *in Prison.*

Copper and Lead.

Æneas.
Alcibiades.
Conon.
Mithridates.
Solon.
Themistocles.
Timotheus.
Hanniball.
Scipio.

Brutus.
Camillus Dict:
C. Marius.
Charles *the great.*
Charles *the V.* 1521.
Pope Julius *II.*
Pope Sixtus *V.*
Philip *II. King of* Spaine, 1588.
Philip *the IV.*

Henry *IV King of* France.
Henry *IV. and* Maria Augusta.
Maria Aug: Gall: *and* Navar: Regin:
Lewis *XI. King of* France.
Lewis *XIII.*
Leopold *Archduke of* Austria.
Mar: Magdalena *Archdutchesse of* Austria.
Maria Austria.
Gabriel *King of* Hungaria.
Elizabeth *Queen of* Hungaria.
Cardinall Granvelanus.
Charles *Duke of* Burgundy, 1467.
Frederick *Count* Pallatine.
Marcus Antonius Memmo, *Duke of* Venice.
Frederick Gonzaga *Duke of* Mantua.
Lotharing: Archiep: Treveriensis.
Antonius Perrenot Archiep:
    Mechlin:
Franciscus Medicis.

Ni: Brulartus a Sillery Franc: & Navar: Canc:
Antonius B. de Burgundia.
Albertus Durer:
Lodovicus Ariost: Poet:
Michael Angelus.
Andreas Doria.
George Fetzel.
Joan Baptista Houwart.
Joan Riette.
Stephanus de Witt.
Antonius van Rossendael, 1632.
In memory of the Jubile *at* Francof. 1617.
Strasburg, 1628.
In memory of 1588.
Upon the Synod *of* Dort.

Divers old Saxon *Coynes.*
Severall old English, *or* Esterling *pieces of Money.*

Severall sorts of Moderne Moneyes from most Countreys in Europe, As also from

India.
Bengalla.
Pegu.
Lira.

Turkey
    Aspers, Shehees.
200 *severall sorts of* Dollers.

Moneyes from beleagured Cities, &c. viz:

Breda, 1625.
Bruxells.
Bergen up Zoon.
Pomfract.

Newarke
    1645, 1646.
and divers other places.

CATALOGUS

Plantarum in Horto Johannis Tredescanti, *nascentium.*

MODERN BOTANICAL NAME**

	MODERN BOTANICAL NAME**
ABelmosch AEgyptiorum s: alcea. *The* yellow Marsh Mallow.	*Hibiscus abelmoschus* L.
Abies { Mas Foemi- na. } *The* { Male Female } *Firre tree.*	*Abies alba* Miller
	Picea abies (L.) Karst.
Abrotanum — Mas. *Southern wood*	*Artemisia abrotanum* L.
Foemina. Chamæ Cyparissus *Lavender Cotton.*	*Santolina chamaecyparissus* L.
Unguentare.	*Artemisia pontica* L.
Silvestre. *Common Southern wood.*	*Artemisia campestris* L.
Inodorum. *Unsavory Southern wood.*	? *Artemisia inodora* Willd.
Arborescens. *Tree Southern wood.*	*Artemisia arborescens* L.
Marinum. *Romane Wormwood.*	*Artemisia pontica* L.
Romanum tennifolum. *Roman Wormwood with fine leaves.*	*Artemisia pontica* L.
Marinum, *sc.* Serephium. *Sea-Wormwood.*	*Artemisia maritima* L.
Marinū folio Lavendulæ. *Sea-wormewood with Lavender-leaves.*	*Artemisia caerulescens* L.
Absinthium — Vulgare. *Common Wormwood.*	*Artemisia absinthium* L.
Umbellatum Clusii. *Clusius his white Wormwood.*	*Achillea clavennae* L.
Tridentinum Lobeli, *his Austrian wormwood.*	*Artemisia austriaca* Jacq.
Acacia. *The binding Bean-tree.*	*Acacia arabica* Willd.
Acacia Indica.	*Accacia farnesiana* (L.) Willd.
Acanthus — Sylvestris. *The wilde Beares breech.*	*Acanthus spinosus* L.
Sativus, *scil.* Branca Ursina. *The manured Beares breech.*	*Acanthus mollis* L.
Aculeatus. *Prickly Beares breech.*	*Acanthus spinosus* L. var. spinosissimus
Acer — Majus Latifolium, sive Pseudoplatanus. *The great Maple or Cycamore tree.*	*Acer pseudoplatanus* L.
Minus vulgare. *The cōmon Maple tree.*	*Acer campestre* L.
* † Virginianum Tradescanti. *Tradescant's Virginian Maple*	*Acer rubrum* L.
* † Virginianum alterum, *his other Virginian Maple.*	? *Platanus occidentalis* L. or *Acer* sp.
Acetosa — Hispanica major, *great Spanish Sorrell.*	? *Rumex lunaria* L.
Franca rotundifol: lobel: *round-leafed Sorrell.*	*Rumex scutatus* L.

**Most of these identifications were independently proposed by Dr J.H. Harvey, working largely from the illustrations in Gerard's *Herbal* amended by Johnson in 1633 and in Parkinson's *Paradisus*. Some names have been brought into line with recent taxonomic changes by Dr W.T. Stearn.

	Indica, seu vescicaria; *Indian or American Sorrell.*	*Rumex vesicarius* L.
Acetosa	Vulgare, *common Sorrell.*	*Rumex acetosa* L.
	Minima, sive Oxalis minima; *Sheeps Sorrell.*	*Rumex acetosella* L.
Acinos Anglica, *our English wild Basil.*		*Acinos arvensis* (Lam.) Dandy
	Hyemale, Winter Wolfesbane.	*Eranthis hyemalis* Salisb.
	Salutiferum, sive Anthora, *wholsome Helmet flowre.*	*Aconitum anthora* L.
	Luteum ponticum majus, *the greater yellow Wolfesbane.*	*Aconitum lycoctonum* L.
	Luteum ponticum minus, *the lesser yellow Wolfesbane.*	*Aconitum vulparia* Reichb.
Aconitum	Cæruleum, *sc.* Napellus, *blew Helmet flowre.*	*Aconitum napellus* L.
	Bacciferū, sive Christophoriana; *herb Christopher.*	*Actaea spicata* L.
	Americanum racemosum fructu albo; *Indian branched Wolfesbane with white fruit.*	*Actaea alba* Miller
	Flore Delphinii, *Wolfesbane with Larkesheele-flowers.*	*Delphinium elatum* L.
	verus, sive calamus aromaticus officinarum; *sweet smelling flagge.*	*Acorus calamus* L.
Acorus	palustris; *yellow water-flagge, or Flore de Luce.*	*Iris pseudacorus* L.

Ageratum flore luteo; *yellow Maudline.*	*Achillea ageratum* L.
Agnus castus virtex; *the Chast tree.*	*Vitex agnus-castus* L.
Agrimonia, *Agrimony.*	*Agrimonia eupatoria* L.
Alaternus; *ever-green Privet.*	*Rhamnus alaternus* L.

Alcea	Veneta; *Venice Mallow.*	*Hibiscus trionum* L.
	vulgaris; *Vervine Mallow.*	*Malva moschata* L.

Alchimilla, pes Leonis; *Ladies Mantle.*	*Alchemilla vulgaris* L.
Alkekengi, *Winter-cherries.*	*Physalis alkekengi* L.
Alliaria, *Sauce alone, Jack by the hedge.*	*Alliaria petiolata* (Bieb.) Cavara & Grande
Allioporrum, sive Scorodoprasson; *or great Turkey Garlick.*	*Allium scorodoprasum* L.

	Sativum, *Garlick.*	*Allium sativum* L.
	Latifolium, ursinum, Ramsous.	*Allium ursinum* L.
Allium	Silvestre tenuifolium, *Crow-Garlick.*	*Allium vineale* L.
	majus Scorodoprasson; *great Turkey Garlick.*	*Allium scorodoprasum* L.

Aloe Hispanica, *Aloes of Spaine.*	*Aloe vera* (L.) Burm. f.

	maxima Anglica, *greatest English Fox-taile grasse.*	*Alopecurus pratensis* L.
Alopecuros	minima, *least Fox-taile-grasse.*	? *Koeleria cristata* (L.) Pers.
	spica aspera.	*Cynosurus echinatus* L.
	baccifera, *berry-bearing Chickweed.*	*Cucubalus baccifer* L.
	baccifera repens, Clusii. Cacubalum Plinii. *great spreading Chickweed.*	? *Cucubalus baccifer* L.
	maxima, *greatest Chickweed.*	*Myosoton aquaticum* (L.) Moench
	major, *great Chickweed.*	? *Stellaria neglecta* Weihe.
Alsine	hederacea, *Ivy Chickweed.*	*Veronica hederifolia* L.
	foliis veronicæ, *speedwell Chickweed.*	*Veronica arvensis* L.
	aquatica major, *great Water-Chickweed.*	*Myosoton aquaticum* (L.) Moench
	hirsuta Myosotis. Ad: *Mouseare Chickweed.*	*Cerastium holosteoides* Fries.
	vulgaris, *common Marsh Mallowes.*	*Althaea officinalis* L.
Althæa	arborea flore Purpureo, *purple tree Mallow.*	? *Lavatera arborea* L.

Althæa	arborea flore albo, fundo Purpureo, montis Olbiæ.	*Lavatera olbia* L.
	montis Olbi, Morini.	*Lavatera olbia* L. (form ?)
Alyssum	Dioscoridis, *Madwort of Dioscorides.*	*Fibigia (Farsetia) clypeata* (L.) Medicus
	Clusii, Galeni; *Galens Madwort according to Clusius.*	*Marrubium alysson* L.

Amaranthus purpureus major paniculis sparsis; *great Floramour or purple flowre gentle.* — *Amaranthus hypochondriacus* L.

Amaracock, sive Clematis Virginiana; *the Virginian Clymer, or Passion flowre.* — *Passiflora incarnata* L.

Amaranthus	major purpureus; *great purple Flowre gentle.*	*Amaranthus caudatus* L.
	purpureus minor elegans; *neat lesser purple Flowre gentle.*	*Celosia argentea* L.
	tricolor; *spotted or variable Flowre gentle.*	*Amaranthus gangeticus* L. var. *tricolor*
	purpureus major paniculis sparsis, *great Flowre Armour, or purple Flowre-gentle.*	*Amaranthus hypochondriacus* L.
	viridis Novæ Angliæ; *green Flowre gentle from New-*England.	*Amaranthus hybridus* L.
	holosericus; *crimson velvet-Flowre gentle.*	*Celosia argentea* L. var. *cristata*
	cristatus.	*Celosia cristata* L. (type)

Amelanchier Lobeli; *French hony sweet wort.* — *Amelanchier ovalis* Medicus

Ammi vulgare, Dod: *Bishops weed.* — *Ammi majus* L.

Amomum Plinii, Pseudocapsicum Dodonai; *Winter Cherry-tree.* — *Solanum pseudocapsicum* L.

Amygdalus; *the Almond-tree.* — *Prunus dulcis* (Miller) D.A. Webb

Anagallis	tenuifolia flore cæruleo. Monelli, *Narrow-leafed Pimpernell with blew flowres.*	*Anagallis monellii* L.
	flore cæruleo mai: Monelli	? *Anagallis monellii* L.
	mas flore Phœniceo; *male red Pimpernell.*	*Anagallis arvensis* L.
	fœmina flore cæruleo; *female blew Pimpernell.*	*Anagallis foemina* Miller
	flore Luteo; *yellow flowre Pimpernell.*	*Lysimachia nemorum* L.
	aquatica vulgaris, sive Becabunga; *Water Pimpernell, or Brooklyme.*	*Veronica beccabunga* L.
	aquatica, sive Becabunga major; *the greater Brooklyme.*	*Veronica anagallis-aquatica* L.

Anagyris foetida; *stinking beane Treefoile.* — *Anagyris foetida* L.

Androsaemon	sive Climenum Italorū; *Tutsan or Park-leaves.*	*Hypericum androsaemum* L.
	magnum; *Tutsan, or great St. Johns wort.*	*Hypericum hirsutum* L.

Anemone	latifolia pavot. ma: flore pleno; *great double Orange tawny Anemone, with broad leaves.*	*Anemone pavonina* Lam.
	latif: Chalcedonica flo: pleno; *double Orange tawney Anemone of* Constantinople, *or Spanish Marigold.*	*Anemone fulgens* (DC) Rchb.
	Anemones { *violet, peach, Encarnadine, white, amaranth.* }	
	latif: Rosea flore pleno; *double Rose-coloured Anemone with broad leaves.*	*Anemone pavonina* Lam.
	latif: albicans flo: pleno; *double pale blush Anemone with broad leaves.*	
	latif: coccinea flo: pleno; *double scarlet Anemone with broad leaves.*	
	latif: potorine flo: pleno.	

Pyrites & fructus varii.
Maxillæ cum dentibus.
Dentes varii petrificati.
Ilex petrificata, ex lacu Hybernico *Lough-neath*, ex
   dono D. *Wybard.*
Quercus cum ejusdem foliis.
Ulmus.
Sambucus cum ejus medullâ.
Fraxinus.
Muscus.
Guttulæ Knasburgenses.
Costa humana cum carne.
Ossa varia.
Caput simiæ.
Ungula equi.
Ovaria halecis.
Cancer totus.
patella cum pisce.
Cochleæ.
Siderites varii.
Ligna varia in ferrum versa.
Guttæ fontis vitrificatæ.

7. *Gemmæ.*

Adamantes Indici ex Decan.
Pseudoadamas Anglicus.
Carbunculi, pyropi, acriores.
Rubini, spinelli ex rupe veteri.
Rubicelli.
Granati
   Orientales ex Cambaia, occidentales, Bohemici.

Hyacinthi coccei & crocei ex oriente.
Amethistus violaceus orientalis.
Saphirus
   albus, cæruleus.
Opalorum differentiæ quædam ex Indiâ.
Smaragdi
   Scythici, Britannici.
Prasii.
Berilli crystallini.
Sardii, corneoli varii.
Onychites.
Achates Indici.
Jaspides virides & purpurei.
Heliotropii varii.
Chrysolithi, topasii Arabici.
Crystalli varii Anglici.
Calcedonius, onyx candida.
Malachites, species Jaspidis.
Oculus cati vel Beli.
Turcosa, Turcois.
Astroites, stellaris lapis.
Asteria vera ex agro Staffordiensi.
Alectorius.
Chelidonius.
Garatronius, crapaudina.
Lapis manati vel tuberonum.
Margaritæ
   Indicæ, Anglicæ, Scoticæ, Virginianæ.
Lapis
   Armenius, Lazuli, limacis.
Lapis Bezoar
   orientalis, occidentalis.

VII

Fructus Exotici.

Acajuiba, acajuti & itimabova, *Marg:* 99.
Ambare, juglandis mole.
Ahovay Thereti, nolæ Cannibalium.
Anacock, phaseoli genus.
Ananas, malo citrio minor.
Anacardia varia.
Avellanæ Indicæ, juglandis mole.
Apeiba, Brasil: *Marg:* 124.
Avellanæ purgatrices, Ben magnum.
Aratica
   Ape, Aponhe, *Margr:* 93, Pana.
Avacari, myrto similis.
Almendras de Peru. *Worm:* 18.
Aurantium nigrum.
Balanus myrepsica.
Banana, musa Alpini.
Bangue semen cannabino minus.
Betele.
Billingbing.
Boramez, agni Scythici pellis portiuncula.

Brindones, intùs rubentes instar sanguinis.
Buna, grana acida continet.
Bon, fructus.
Cachos.
Carambola, siliquæ quadrangulares & pentagonæ.
Capsicum.
Cardamoma
   majora, minora.
Cajus instar ovi anserini.
Cazavi ex herba yuccâ.
Cacâo, potus ejus Chocolate dicitur.
Cevadella, hordeolum.
Cocculæ orientales instar racemi corymborum.
Cajete vel Cochine. Brasil. *Marg:* 123.
Caraguata, Brasil: *Piso.*
Cereiba, Brasil: *Marg:* 128.
Nucum Cocorum varia genera.
Coco nux ex Maldiviâ. *Auger:* Clutius speciatim
   nominat. pag. 8.
Cocci varia genera.

Antirrhinū	medium flore incarnato, *middle incarnadine Snapdragon.*	*Antirrhinum majus* L. (form)
	minus flore variegato, *small party-coloured Snapdragon.*	*Misopates orontium* (L.) Raf.
	minus flore albo, *small white Snapdragon.*	? *Asarina procumbens* Miller
Apacha, *yellow wilde Vetch.*		*Lathyrus aphaca* L.
Apios, *vide* Lathyrus.		
Apium	hortense, *garden-Parsley.*	*Petroselinum crispum* (Miller) Nyman
	ampl: & angustifolio, *large narrow-leafed Parsley.*	*Petroselinum crispum* vars.
	crispum, *curled Parsley.*	
	Virginianum, *Virginia Parsley.*	—
	silvestre, sive thisselinum, *wilde Parsley.*	*Peucedanum palustre* (L.) Moench.
	selinum Venetorum, *Venetian Parsley.*	*Athamanta macedonica* Sprengel
	perfoliatū seu Smirnium Creticum, *thorow-leafed Parsley of* Candy.	*Smyrnium rotundifolium* Miller
Apium sive Paludapium, *Smallage*		*Apium graveolens* L.
Apocynum	Americanum, *American Dogs bane.*	*Asclepias variegata* L. (or vice
	alterum.	*Asclepias syriaca* L. versa)
Aquilegia	†Virginiana, *Virginian Columbine.*	*Aquilegia canadensis* L.
	variegata albo & purpureo, *striped Columbine white and purple.*	
	variegata albo & rubro, *party-coloured Columbine white and red.*	?*Aquilegia vulgaris* L. vars.
	rosea variegata variabilis, *Rose Columbine.*	
	roseo flore multiplici variorum colorum, *double Rose Columbine in severall colours.*	
	vulg. diversorum colorum, *ordinary single Columbines of divers colours.*	*Aquilegia vulgaris* L.
Arabis sive Draba, *Arabian Mustard.*		*Lepidium draba* L.
Aracus	Bæticus, *the Spanish chichling Peas.*	? *Vicia lutea* L. form *hirta*
	clematites, *the running wilde chichling Peas.*	? *Vicia angustifolia* L. var. *bobartii*
Arbor	vitæ vel Thuyæ, *Tree of life.*	*Thuja occidentalis* L.
	Judæ flore rubro, *Judas tree with red flowres.*	*Cercis siliquastrum* L.
Herba	*†sensitiva elegantissima, *the sensitive plant.*	*Mimosa sensitiva* L.
	sensitiva humilis, *from* Barbados, *the low sensitive shrub.*	*Mimosa pudica* L.
Arbutus, sive Virido, *the Strawberry-tree.*		*Arbutus unedo* L.
Argemone	capitulo rotundiore, *round-headed Bastard with Poppie.*	*Papaver hybridum* L.
	capitulo longiore, *long-headed Bastard with Poppie.*	*Papaver argemone* L.
Argentina sive Potentilla, *Silver weed, Wilde Tansey.*		*Potentilla anserina* L.
Aristolochia	clematitis, *the running-rooted Birthwort.*	*Aristolochia clematitis* L.
	rotunda radice, *round rooted Birthwort.*	*Aristolochia rotunda* L.
	longa, *long rooted Birthwort.*	*Aristolochia longa* L.
Armeria	holoserica, *crimson Sweet-Williams.*	*Dianthus barbatus* L.
	flore pleno, *double flowred Sweet-Williams.*	*Dianthus barbatus* L. 'Flore Pleno'
	flo: simpl: magna diversitas, *great variety of Sweet-Williams with single flowres.*	*Dianthus barbatus* L. (forms)
	sylvestris, *Deptford Pinke.*	*Dianthus armeria* L.
Artemisia vulgaris, *common Mugwort.*		*Artemisia vulgaris* L.
Arum	vulgare, *Wake Robin, Cuckowpintle.*	*Arum maculatum* L. (form)
	maculis nigris, *blacke spotted Wake Robin, Priests-pintle.*	*Arum maculatum* L. (form)

Arum	{ majus.	*Colocasia antiquorum* Schott.
	foliis laciniatis, seu Dracuntiū,	*Dracunculus vulgaris* Schott.
	striatum album elegans, *Morini.*	*Arum italicum* Miller
Arisarum		*Arisarum vulgare* Targ.-Tozz.
Arundo	{ Hispanica, seu Δουας, *Spanish Reed, or*	*Arundo donax* L.
	Cane.	
	Indica foliis striatis, *Morin:*	*Arundo donax* L. 'Variegata'
Asarum vulgare, *common Asarabacca.*		*Asarum europaeum* L.
Ascyrum vulgare, *ordinary St. Peters Wort.*		*Hypericum maculatum* Crantz.
Asclepias	{ flore albo, *white flowred Swallowort.*	*Vincetoxicum hirundinaria* Medicus
	flore nigro, *Swallowort with black flowres.*	*Vincetoxicum nigrum* Moench
Asparagus sativus, *Garden Asparagus.*		*Asparagus officinalis* L.
Asperula	{ flore albo, *white Woodroof.*	*Galium odoratum* (L.) Scop.
	flore cæruleo, *blew Woodroof.*	*Asperula arvensis* L.
Asphodelus	{ minor, Clusii *his small Asphodill.*	*Asphodelus fistulosus* L.
	Lusetanicus, *Portugall Asphodill.*	*Asphodelus albus* Miller
	Indicus nondum descriptus, *Morini.*	? *Crinum americanum* L.
Asplenium, *Ceterach, Spleen wort.*		*Ceterach officinarum* DC.
Asplenii & Polytrici, species quinque, *Morini.*		(ferns)
Aster	{ Italorum, *Italian Starwort:*	*Aster amellus* L.
	Virginianus fructicosus, Ger: emasc:	*Aster tradescanti* L.
	fructicosus, Ger: ema: precocior.	*Aster paniculatus* Lam.
	cæruleus serotinus fructicans.	? *Aster novi-belgii* L.
Astragulus	{ Bæticus, Clusii *his Spanish milke Vetch.*	*Astragalus lusitanicus* Lam.
	Marinus, *Sea Spanish milke Vetch.*	*Astragalus boeticus* L.
Atractylis, *Distaffe Thistle.*		*Carthamus lanatus* L.
Atriplex	{ baccifera { major, *greater Arrache.*	*Chenopodium capitatum* Aschers.
	{ minor, *lesser Arrache.*	*Chenopodium virgatum* Thunb.
	sativa alba, *manured White Arrache.*	} *Atriplex hortensis* L. vars.
	sativa rubra, *manured red Arrache.*	
	olida, *stinking Arrache, Notchweed or*	*Chenopodium vulvaria* L.
	Vulvaria.	
Atriplicis varietates, *severall sorts of Arrache.*		—
Avellanæ diversitates, *variety of Filbeards and Nuts.*		*Corylus* spp. and vars.
Avena nuda, *naked Oates.*		*Avena nuda* L.
Auricula ursi	{ flore albo, *white coloured Beares eares.*	
	flore luteo maximo, *greatest yellow Beares*	
	eares.	} *Primula auricula* L.
	folio glabro, *smooth leafed Beares eares.*	
	flore luteo medio, *middle yellow Bears eares.*	
	albo & rubro variegata, *striped white and red*	—
	Bears eares.	
	albo & purpureo variegata, *party-coloured*	—
	and purple Bears eares.	
	flore holoserico, *crimson-velvet Beares ears.*	—
	flore rubro, *red Bears ears.*	? *Primula integrifolia* L.
	flore violaceo, *violet-coloured Beares eares.*	? *Primula halleri* Honck.
	flore fusco, *Hare-coloured Beares eares.*	—
	Holoserica, Potrine, *silken Beares eares.*	—
	altera Potrine.	—
	maxima Tradescanti flore obsoleto,	—
	Tradescant his greatest blush Beares ears.	
	diversæ species, *several sorts of Beares ears.*	—
Azadorach, *the Bead tree.*		*Melia azedarach* L.

B.

BAccharis Monspeliensium, *French-Bacchar.* Gerards *Plowmans*   *Inula conyza* DC.
    Spicknard.

Balaustium, *sc*: Malus Punica, *Pomegranat tree.*   *Punica granatum* L. cv. 'Flore Pleno'

Ballote, *sc*: Marrubium nigrum fætidum, *stinking black Horehound.*   *Ballota nigra* L.

Balsamina cacumerina. *Balsam Apple, Apple of Ierusalem.*   *Momordica balsamina* L.

Balsamum Alpinum, Ges: Camer: *Sweet Mountaine Rose.*   *Rhododendron hirsutum* L.

Barba Jovis, frutex, *the silver bush.*   *Anthyllis barba-jovis* L.

Barba Hirci, *sc*: Tragapogon, *Goates-Beard.*   *Tragopogon pratensis* L.

Bardana
- major, *the greater Burdock.* — *Arctium lappa* L.
- minor vel Arctium, *the lesser Burdock.* — *Xanthium strumarium* L.

Battatos, Potatoes.   *Ipomoea batatas* (L.) Lam.

Behen
- album, *white spatling Poppy.* — *Silene vulgaris* (Moench) Garcke
- rubrum, *red spatling Poppy.* — *Silene dioica* (L.) Clairv.

major campestris, *Great field-Dasie.*   *Leucanthemum vulgare* Lam.

major Americana umbellata, *Great tufted American Dasie.*   *Erigeron annuus* (L.) Pers.

Bellis
- hortensis flore rubro variegata, *red garden striped Dasie.*
- hortensis flore albo pleno, *white garden Dasie with a double flowre.*
- hortensis flore albo prolifera, *white garden childing Dasie.*
- hortensis flore varia prolifera, *changeable Dasie.*
- flore rubro fistuloso.
- flore car: *blush coloured Dasies:*

   Bellis perennis L.

Bellidis minoris magna diversitas, *great variety of lesser Dasies.*

Belvidere Italis, *sc*: Linaria magna Scoporia, *Broom Toadflax.*   *Kochia scoparia* Schrader

Berberis fructu rub: *red Berberies.*   *Berberis vulgaris* L.

Beta
- rubra sativa, *garden red Beets.*
- viridis vulgatior, *common green Beet.*
- rubra Romana, vel rubra rapæ radice, *red Roman Beets.*

   Beta vulgaris L. (forms)

- alba major platiculis, *greater white flat stalked Beet.* — *Beta vulgaris* L. var. 'Maritima'
- spinosa Cretica, *prickly Beets of* Candy. — *Emex spinosus* Necker

major Daniæ, *broad-leafed Betony of* Denmarke.   ? *Betonica hirsuta* L. (*Stachys danica* Schinz. & Thell.)

Betonica
- vulgaris sive minor flo: purpureo, *common wood Betony.* — *Betonica officinalis* L.
- pureo, *common wood Betony.* — —
- aquatica, *water Betony.* — *Scrophularia auriculata* L.

Betula, *the Birch tree.*   *Betula pendula* Roth. and B. pubescens Ehrh.

Betulus, *the Hornbean tree.*   *Carpinus betulus* L.

Bifolium sive Ophris, *Bisole or Twablade.*   *Listera ovata* (L.) R.Br.

Bistorta, *Snakeweed.*   *Polygonum bistorta* L.

Blataria
- flore luteo, *yellow flowred Moth Mullein.* — *Verbascum blattaria* L.
- flore albo, *Moth Mullein with white flowres.* — *Verbascum glabrum* Miller
- ma: exautica flo: absoleto, *Moth Mullein &c.*
- flore purpureo, *purple Moth Mullein.* — *Verbascum phoeniceum* L.
- flore cæruleo minima, *the least blew flowred Moth Mullein.* — ? *Salvia aethiopis* L.
- major flo: luteo, *great Moth Mullein.* — ? *Verbascum boerhavii* Willd.
- maxima oderata flo: luteo, *great sweet yellow Moth Mullein.* — —

Blitum
- album sylvestre minus, *small wilde white Blite.* — *Amaranthus blitum* L.
- rubrum sylv: minus, *small wild red Blite.* — *Amaranthus lividus* L.
- Polyspermon, *wilde Blite with much seed.* — *Chenopodium polyspermum* L.
- majus albo, *great white Blite.* — *Chenopodium foliosum* Aschers.

Bolbonach sive Viola lunaris, *the white Sattin flowre.*		*Lunaria annua* L.
Bonus Henricus, *common or English Mercury.*		*Chenopodium bonus-henricus* L.
	flore cæruleo & flore albo, *blew and white Borage.*	*Borago officinalis* L. & var.
	foliis variegatis, *Borage with various leaves.*	*Borago officinalis* L. var.
	semper vivens, *ever-living Borage.*	*Pentaglottis sempervirens* (L.) Tausch.
Borago		
	minima semper vivens, seu symphitum minus, *the least ever-living Borage.*	} *Omphalodes verna* Moench
	flore cæruleo minima, *smallest Borage.*	
Botrys Mexicano, *the Mexican Oake of Jerusalem.*		*Chenopodium ambrosioides* L.
	sylvestris, *wilde Coleworts.*	*Brassica oleracea* L.
	marina latifolia, *broad-leafed sea Colewort.*	*Crambe maritima* L.
	perfoliata, *thorow-leafed Cole wort.*	*Conringia orientalis* (L.) Dumort.
Brassica	foliis crispis, *Colewort with curled leaves.*	} *Brassica oleracea* L. var. *bullata* (forms)
	striata, *ridged or furrowed Colewort.*	
	Hispanica, *Spanish Colewort.*	*Brassica vesicaria* L.
	Sabaudica, varietas, *Savoy Cabages.*	*Brassica oleracea* L. var. *bullata* subvar. 'Sabauda'
Bryonia	alba, *white Briony.*	*Bryonia dioica* Jacq.
	nigra, *black Briony.*	*Tamus communis* L.
	sativum, *garden Buglosse.*	*Anchusa officinalis* L.
Buglosū	luteum, Ger: *lang de Beef.*	*Picris echioides* L.
	sylvestre, *wilde Buglosse.*	*Lycopsis arvensis* L.
	vulg: flo: cæruleo, *ordinary blew flowred Bugle.*	*Ajuga reptans* L.
Bugula	flore albo, *Bugle with a White flowre.*	*Ajuga genevensis* L.
	flore carneo, *Bugle with blush-coloured flowres.*	*Ajuga genevensis* L. (form)
	majus, *great earth Chestnut*	*Bunium bulbocastanum* L.
Bulbocastanum	minus vulgare, *lesser earth Chestnut.*	*Conopodium majus* (Gouan) Loret
Buphthalmium verum Delacamp: vel Chrysanthemū Valentinum Clusii, *true Oxeye, or Clusius his Spanish Corne Marigold.*		*Anacyclus valentinus* L.
	major vulgaris, *common Shepherds purse.*	*Capsella bursa-pastoris* (L.) Medicus
Bursa pastoris	minor, *small Shepherds purse.*	*Capsella rubella* Reuter
	major, *great Box.*	*Buxus sempervirens* L.
	minor, *small Box.*	*B. sempervirens* L. var. 'Suffruticosa'
Buxus	auratus, *gilded Box.*	} *Buxus sempervirens* L. (forms)
	auratus alter foliis minoribus, *another sort of gilded Box with small leaves.*	

C.

(? †) Cabbage tree from Barbados.		*Roystonea oleracea* (Jacq.) Cook
Cacalia. *Colts foot.*		? *Adenostyles alliariae* (Gouan) Kerner or *Adenostyles alpina* (L.) Bluff & Fingerh.
Cachrys vera, *sc*: libanotis Ferulæ folio, *Fennel leafed herb Frankinsence.*		*Cachrys libanotis* L.
	montana præstantior, *great mountaine Calamint.*	*Calamintha grandiflora* (L.) Moench
Calamintha	montana pulegii odore, *field Calamint.*	*Calamintha nepeta* (L.) Savi.
	aquatica, *water Calamint.*	*Mentha arvensis* L.
Calamagrostis, *Sheergras.*		*Calamagrostis epigejos* (L.) Roth.
Calceolus Mariae, *Ladyes slipper.*		*Cypripedium calceolus* L.

Calendula
- max: flore pleno, *greatest double Marigolds.* — Calendula officinalis L. var. 'Flore Pleno'
- maxim: prolifera, *greatest fruitfull Marigold.* — Calendula officinalis L. var. 'Prolifera'
- maxim: flo: luteo, *greatest yellow Marigold.* — Calendula officinalis L.

Caltha palustris, flore pleno, *double Marsh Marigold.* — Caltha palustris L. var. plena

Camelina, *Treacle Wormeseed.* — Erysimum cheiranthoides L.

Campanula
- lactescens Persici folia flo: cæruleo, *blew peach-leafed flowre.* — Campanula persicifolia L.
- lactescens Pers: flore albo *white peached leafed Belflowre.* — Campanula persicifolia L. var. alba
- minor rotundifolio, *small Belflowre.* — Campanula rotundifolia L.
- lact: minor sive rapuncules. — Campanula rapunculus L.

Canabis
- sativa, *sown Hemp.* — Cannabis sativa L.
- spuria elegans, *the fine bastard Hemp.* — Galeopsis speciosa Miller
- aquat: *Water Hemp.* — Bidens tripartita L.

Canna
- Indica flore rubro, *red flowred Indian Cane.* — Canna indica L.
- Indica flore luteo, *yellow Indian Cane.* — Canna lutea Miller

Capillus veneris, *common Maidenhaire.* — Adiantum capillus-veneris L.

Capparis. — Capparis spinosa L.

Caprifoliū
- Germanicum flore rubro serotinum, *the German red indented Honisuckle.* — Lonicera periclymenum L. var. 'Serotina'
- Italicum perfoliatum præcox, *double Italian early ripe Honisuckle.* — Lonicera caprifolium L.
- vulgare, *ordinary Woodbine.* — Lonicera periclymenum L.
- *†Virginianum arbor, *Virginian Woodbine-tree.* — Lonicera sempervirens L.
- surrectum fructu rubro, *red upright Honisuckle.* — ? Lonicera xylosteum L.

Capsicum Indicum, *Ginny paper.* — Capsicum annuum L.
Capsicum rotundum surrectum, *Morini.* — Capsicum frutescens L.
Capsicum alterum, *Morini.* — C. frutescens L. (form)

Cardamine
- flore pleno, *double Ladyes-smock.* — Cardamine pratensis L. var. 'Flore Pleno'
- trifolia, *three-leafed Lady-smock.* — Cardamine trifolia L.
- minus sive Sium minus impatiens, *impatient Ladyes smock.* — Cardamine impatiens L.
- vulgare, *common Ladyes-smock.* — Cardamine pratensis L.

Cardiaca, *Motherwort.* — Leonurus cardiaca L.

Carduorum diversae species, *divers other sorts of Thistles.* — (including *Scolymus maculatus* L.)

Cardu'
- lacteus S. Mariae, *Lady Thistle.* — Silybum marianum (L.) Gaertner
- Globosus, spherocephalus, ma: perrennis, *Globe Thistle.* — Echinops sphaerocephalus L.
- Stellatus, *Starre Thistle.* — Centaurea calcitrapa L.
- Benedictus, *blessed Thistle.* — Cnicus benedictus L.
- Moschatus, *Moske Thistle.* — Carduus nutans L.
- Solstitialis, *Saint Barnabies Thistle.* — Centaurea solstitialis L.
- Lanceatus, *speare Thistle.* — Cirsium vulgare (Savi) Ten.
- vulgaris, *way Thistle.* — Cirsium arvense (L.) Scop.

Carlina major, seu Chamælion album, *greater Carline Thistle.* — Atractylis gummifera L.
Carob *from Barbados.* — Hymenaea courbaril L.
Carum flore albo, *white-flowred Carawayes.* — Carum carvi L.

Caryophillata
- montana, Clusii, *his red mountain Avens.* — Geum rivale L.
- vulgaris, *common Avens, herb Bennet.* — Geum urbanum L.

Caryophillorum
- hortensium flore pleno vario in colore differ: *double Carnations or Gilliflowers of various colours.* — Dianthus caryophyllus L. (forms and cvs.)

Caryophillorum { flore simplici vario in colore different: *single Carnations or Gilliflowers of severall colours.* elegantium magna varietas, *severall sorts of great dainty Gilliflowers or Carnations.*	*Dianthus caryophyllus* L. (forms and cvs.)
Caryophillus { marinus mi: *small Thrift, or Sea Gilliflower.* globosus latifolius, *Globe Gilliflower with broad leaves.*	*Armeria maritima* (Miller) Willd. *Armeria plantaginea* Willd.
Castanea { equina, *horse Chesnut-tree.* vulgaris, *Chesnut-tree.*	*Aesculus hippocastanum* L. *Castanea sativa* Miller
Catanance, *crimson grasse Fetch.*	*Lathyrus nissolia* L.
Caucalis { major, *great rough wilde Parsley.* peucedani, fol: *Hogs Parsley.*	*Daucus muricatus* L. *Selinum pyrenaeum* Gouan
Cauda Equina, *Horse-taile.*	*Equisetum* spp.
Cauda Muris, *Mouse-taile.*	*Myosurus minimus* L.
Celastrus, Alaternus, *ever-green Privet.*	*Rhamnus alaternus* L. var. 'Glaber'
Centaurium { luteum perfoliatum, *yellow Centory.* vulgare, *common Centory.* minus vulgare, *little common Centory.* majus fol: Helenii, *course great Centory.* majus flore luteo, *great yellow Centory.* alterum Clusii, *Clusius his Centory.*	*Blackstonia perfoliata* (L.) Hudson *Centaurium erythraea* Rafn. *Centaurium pulchellum* (Sw.) Druce *Centaurea rhaponticum* L. *Centaurea alpina* L. *Centaurea centaurium* L.
Cœpea Lobelii, *Lobel's Orpine.*	*Sedum cepaea* L.
Cœrasus { flore pleno, *double flowred Cherry.* Ramosus seu Padus Theoph: *the clustred Cherry.*	*Prunus cerasus* L. cv. 'Rhexii' *Prunus fruticosa* Pall.
Cærasorium diversæ species, *diverse kindes of Cherries.*	*Prunus cerasus* L. vars.
Cerefolium, *common Chervill.*	*Anthriscus cerefolium* (L.) Hoffm.
Cerinthe { flore luteo, *yellow Honeywort.* flore rubro, *white Honeywort.* flore variegato, *striped Honeywort.*	*Cerinthe aspera* Roth. ? *Cerinthe major* L. (form) ? *Cerinthe major* L.
Ceterach, Asplenium, *Spleen-wort.*	*Ceterach officinarum* DC.
Chamæcistus flo: luteo, *Dwarfe-Cistus, or little Sunflower.*	*Helianthemum nummularium* (L.) Miller
Chamæcerasus, *Dwarfe-Cherry.*	*Lonicera alpigena* L.
Chamædrys { sylvestris, sc: Tencrium, *wilde Germander.* laciniata, *Germander with fine cut leaves.*	*Veronica chamaedrys* L. *Teucrium botrys* L.
Chamæirides variæ, *severall Dwarfe Flowerdeluces.*	*Iris pumila* L; *I. chamaeiris* Bertol.
Chamæiris Constantinopolitana. *Mor.*	*Iris pumila* L. var.
Chamelæa tricoccos, *Widow waile.*	*Cneorum tricoccum* L.
Chamæmelum { flore pleno, *double flowred Camomill.* flore simplici, *single flowred Camomill.*	*Chamaemelum nobile* (L.) All. var. 'Flore Pleno' *Chamaemelum nobile* (L.) All.
Chamænerium, *Rosebay Willow.*	*Chamaenerium angustifolium* (L.) Scop.
Chamæpytis, *Groundpine.*	*Ajuga chamaepitys* (L.) Schreb.
Cheledonium { majus laciniatum, *great fine cut Celandine.* mas vulgare, *common male Calendine.* minus, *Pilewort.* majus fol: quernis, *great oake-leafed Celandine.*	*Chelidonium majus* L. var. 'Laciniatum' *Chelidonium majus* L. *Ranunculus ficaria* L. *Chelidonium majus* L. var. 'Laciniatum'
Condrilla { Gum Succory. purpurea, *Purple Gum Succory.*	*Lactuca perennis* L. *Crupina vulgaris* Cass.
Christophoriana, *herb Christopher.*	*Actaea spicata* L.

Christopho- riana fructu	{ albo / rubro } Morini.	*Actaea alba* (L.) Miller *Actaea rubra* Willd.
Chrysanthemum	Creticum, *Candy corn Marygold.* segetum, bellidis fol: *Dasie-leafed corne Marygold.*	*Chrysanthemum coronarium* L. *Chrysanthemum segetum* L.
Cichoreum	flore albo, *white Succory.* sativum, *garden Succory.* sylv: flo: cæruleo, *wilde blew Succory.*	*Cichorium intybus* L. var. *album* *Cichorium intybus* L. cv. *Cichorium intybus* L.
Cicuta vulgaris, *common Hemlock.*		*Conium maculatum* L.
Cinara sylvestris Bætica, *Spanish wilde Artichock.*		*Cynara humilis* L.
Circæa	lutetiana major, *the greater Inchanters Nightshade.* lutetiana minor, *small Inchanters Nightshade.*	*Circaea lutetiana* L. *Circaea alpina* L.
Cirsium Anglicanum, *single-headed Thistle.*		*Cirsium dissectum* (L.) Hill
Cistus	mas prima Clusii, *male Cistus or Holyrose.* fœmina Rosmarini folio, *Rosemary-leafed Cistus.* ledon flore albo, *white-gum Cistus or sweet Holyrose.* flore albo alter, *another white Cistus.* foliis Crispis, *Cistus with crisped leaves.* ledon primum Clusii, *sweet bearing Cistus.* ledon latif: secundum Clusii, *sweet Cistus with black poplar leaves.* ledon quartum Clusii, *sweet gumme Cistus with hoary-leaves.* ledon septimum Clusii, *sweet Cistus with hoary rough or Rosemary leaves.* Halami folio, *Sea-Purslan leafed Cistus.* quintus Clusii, *Cistus with the smaller Olive leaves.*	*Cistus albidus* L. *Ledum palustre* L. *Cistus ladanifer* L. var. '*Albiflorus*' ? *Cistus salvifolius* L. *Cistus crispus* L. *Cistus laurifolius* L. *Cistus populifolius* L. *Cistus psilosepalus* Sweet ? *Cistus clusii* Dunal or *Halimium umbellatum* (L.) Spach. *Halimium halimifolium* (L.) Willk. *Cistus monspeliensis* L.
Clematis	peregrina flo: pleno atropurpureo, *double purple Ladyes Bower.* peregrina flore purpureo, *purple Ladyes Bower.* Daphnoides ma: flo: violaceo, *great violet-colour Periwincle.* Daphn: minor flore albo simplici, *little white Periwincle.* Daphn: minor flore violaceo simpl: *little single violet coloured Periwincle.* Daph: minor flore purpureo pleno, *little purple double Periwincle.* Panonica cæruleo, secunda Clusii, *the greater Hungarian Climer, with blew flower.* Virginiana, *Virginian Ladyes Bower.*	*Clematis viticella* L. var. '*Flore Pleno*' *Clematis viticella* L. *Vinca major* L. *Vinca minor* L. var. *alba* *Vinca minor* L. (type) *Vinca minor* L. var. '*Multiplex*' *Clematis integrifolia* L. ? *Gonolobus carolinensis* (Jacq.) Schultes
Clematis sylvestris, i. Viorna, *Travellers Joy.*		*Clematis vitalba* L.
Clinopodium vulg: *wilde Basil.*		*Acinos arvensis* (Lam.) Dandy
Cochlearia	Batavorum, *or Sea Scurvigrasse.* vulgaris, longo & sinuato folio, *common Scurvigrasse.* montana Anglica, *English mountain Scurvigrasse.* Borealis folio ampliss:	*Cochlearia officinalis* L. *Cochlearia anglica* L. *Cochlearia officinalis* L. subsp. *alpina* (Bab.) Hook. ? *Cochlearia danica* L.

	autumnale flo: simplice albo, *white Saffron of Autumne with single flower.* — Colchicum autumnale L. cv. 'Album'
	autumnale flore simplice purpureo, *purple Saffron of Autumne with single flower.* — Colchicum autumnale L. (type)
	Purpureum flore pleno amplo Autum: *large double purple Saffron of Autumne.* — Colchicum autumnale L. cv. 'Flore Pleno'
	Autumnale flore pleno variegato amplo, *large double party-coloured Saffron of Autumne.* — Colchicum autumnale L. ? var. 'Striatum'
Colchicum	Autumnale flore atropurpureo, *darke purple meadow Saffron of Autumne.* — Colchicum atropurpureum Stapf. apud Stearn
	Vernum, *meadow Saffron of the Spring.* — Bulbocodium vernum L.
	fritillariæ facie, *chequered meadow Saffron.* — Colchicum lusitanum Brot.
	Bizantinum, *meadow Saffron of Constantinople.* — Colchicum byzantinum Ker-Gawl.
	variegatum, *party-coloured meadow Saffron.* — Colchicum agrippinum Baker
	vulgare, *common meadow Saffron.* — Colchicum autumnale L. (type)
	ex Insula Chios, *Saffron of Chio or Sio.* — Colchicum variegatum L.

Colus Jovis, *Jupiters Distaffe.* — Salvia glutinosa L.

Colutea	vesicaria, *great bastard Senna.* — Colutea arborescens L.
	Scorpoides, *Scorpion podded bastard Senna.* — Coronilla emerus L.
Coniza	major, *sc:* Baccharis Monsp: *great Flebane.* — Inula conyza DC.
	media, *middle Flebane.* — Pulicaria dysenterica (L.) Bernh.
	minima, *dwarfe Flebane.* — Pulicaria vulgaris Gaertner
Consolida	major flore albo, *great white Comfrey.* — Symphytum officinale L.
	major flore purpureo, *great purple Comfrey.* — Symphytum officinale L. (form)
	major flo: luteo, *great Comfrey with yellow flowers.* — Symphytum tuberosum L.
Convolvulus	Azureus folio hederatio. — Ipomoea hederacea (L.) Jacq.
	Coronatus elegans, *Morini.* — ? Convolvulus cneorum L.
	major purpureus, *great purple Bindweed.* — Ipomoea purpurea Roth.
	minor elegans, *little dainty Bindweed.* — Convolvulus tricolor L.
	Virginianus, cordato folio flore obsoleto *Tradescanti.* — ? Ipomoea lacunosa L.
	minor folio Althææ, *little Mallow-leafed Bindweed.* — Convolvulus althaeoides L.

Coriandrum, *Coriander.* — Coriandrum sativum L.

Cornus	mas fructu rubro, *male red Cornell tree, or Cornelian Cherry tree.* — Cornus mas L.
	fœmina fructu albo, *white female Cornell tree.* — Cornus mas L. var. 'Xanthocarpa'
	sylvestris, *wilde Cornell tree.* — Cornus sanguinea L.

Corona Imperialis, *Crown Imperiall.* — Fritillaria imperialis L.
Corona Imperialis flore luteo, *Morini.* — Fritillaria imperialis L. var. 'Maxima lutea'

Coronopus	major. — Plantago maritima L.
	minor, *Buckshorne Plantane.* — Plantago coronopus L.
	Ruellii, *Swines Cresses.* — Coronopus squamatus (Forsk.) Aschers.

Cortusa	Matheoli, *Beares eare Sanicle.* — Cortusa matthioli L.
	Americana, *Sanicle of America.* — Tiarella cordifolia L.
Corylus	major, *great Woodnut or Hasel nut.* — Corylus maxima Miller
	minus, *lesser Hasel nut.* — Corylus avellana L. (form)
	fructu rubro sativa, *red Filbeard.* ⎫ ? Corylus maxima Miller vars.
	fructu oblongo sativa, *long Filbeard.* ⎭
	sylvestris, *the Hasle nut-tree.* — Corylus avellana L.

Costus hortensis sive Balsamita, *Costmary.* — Chrysanthemum balsamita L.

Cotula
{ non fœtida flore pleno, *double Mayweed without scent.* — *Matricaria recutita* L. var. 'Flore Pleno'
fœtida & non fœt: flo: simpli: *single flowred Mayweed with a strong and no scent.* — *Anthemis cotula* L. and *Matricaria recutita* L. }

Cotyledon, *Navelhwort or Pennywort.* — *Umbilicus rupestris* (Salisb.) Dandy

Cratæogenon Euphrosine, Ger: *Eyebright CowWheat.* — *Odontites verna* (Bell) Dum.

Crocus
{
Neopolitanus, *Saffron of Naples.* — *Crocus vernus* All. (form)
flore albo, *white flowred Saffron.* — *Crocus vernus* All. subsp. *albiflorus*
Mæsiacus luteus, *Yellow Saffron of Mesia.* — *Crocus aureus* Sibth. & Sm.
Mæsiacus flore albo, *white Saffron of Mesia.* — ? *Crocus aureus* var. 'Lacteus'
flore luteo, *yellow Saffron.* — ? *Crocus aureus* Sibth. & Sm. (form)
Violaceus major, *great violet-coloured Saffron.* — ? *Crocus violaceus* Weston
Violaceus minor, *small violet-coloured Saffron.* — *Crocus vernus* All.
flore cinereo, *ash-coloured Saffron.* — ? *Crocus cinericius* Weston
Mæsiacus argentinus, *silver coloured Saffron of Mesia.* — *Crocus biflorus* Miller
Mæsiacus luteo Duc: *yellow-Saffron of Mesia, or Duke Crocus.* — *Crocus susianus* Ker-Gawl.
}

Croci flore variegato diversæ species, *divers kindes of sky-coloured Saffrons.* — *Crocus versicolor* Ker-Gawl., etc.

Cruciata
{ Crosswort. — *Cruciata laevipes* Opiz.
Gentiana. — *Gentiana cruciata* L. }

Crupina Belgarum, *beard creper*, Park: 786. — *Crupina vulgaris* Cass.

Cucumis sylv: *sc*: Assininus, *wilde Cucumer.* — *Ecballium elaterium* A. Rich.

Cupressus
{
mas, *male Cypresse.* — *Cupressus sempervirens* L.
fœmina, *female Cypresse.* — *C. sempervirens* var. 'Horizontalis'
*†Virginiana Tradescāti, *Tradescant's Virginian Cypresse.* — *Taxodium distichum* (L.) Rich.
}

Cuscuta, *Dodder.* — *Cuscuta europaea* L., etc.

Cyanus
{
major latifolius, *great broad-leafed Blew-bottle.* — *Centaurea montana* L.
Orientalis odoratissimus, *sc*: Floridus Turcicus, *the Sultans Flower.* — *Centaurea moschata* L.
}

Cyani hortensis variæ in colore differentiæ, *severall sorts of garden-corne flowers of different colours.* — *Centaurea cyanus* L. vars.

Cyanus Constantinopolitanus flore albo, *Morini.* — *Centaurea moschata* L. var. 'Alba'

Cyclamen
{
Autumnale flo: albo, *white flower Autumn Sowbread.* — *Cyclamen hederifolium* Aiton or *C. purpurascens* Miller var.
Aut: flo: purpureo, *purple Autumne Sowbread.* — *Cyclamen europaeum* L.
Radice Anemones, *Anemone rooted Sowbread.* — —
folio Hederæ, *Ivy-leafed Sowbread.* — *Cyclamen repandum* Sibth. & Sm.
folio Hederæ Italicum, *Ivy-leafed Italian Sowbread.* — *Cyclamen hederifolium* Aiton
}

Cymbalaria, *bastard Navelwort.* — *Cymbalaria muralis* Gaertner, Meyer & Scherb.

Cynocrambe, *Dogge Mercury.* — *Mercurialis perennis* L.

Cynoglossum
{
flore albo, *white flowred Hounds-tongue.* — *Cynoglossum officinale* L. ? var. 'Bicolor'
flore viride, criticum forte. — *C. Creticum* Miller or *C. cheirifolium* L.
minus, *small Houndstongue.* — *Cynoglossum germanicum* Jacq.
non descriptum, *Houndstongue not hitherto described.* — *C. cheirifolium* L. or *C. creticum* Miller
vulgare, *great Houndstongue.* — *Cynoglossum officinale* L.
}

Cytisus

Maranthæ, *the supposed tree Cytissus or Horned tree Trefoyle.*   *Medicago arborea* L.

primus Clusii, *the German hoary tree Trefoyle.*   *Chamaecytisus hirsutus* (L.) Link

secundus Clusii, *long-leafed Austrian Cytisus.*   *Cytisus sessilifolius* L. (and *Chamaecytisus austriacus* (L.) Link)

Marantæ sive Cyti scorpioides, *Morini.*   ? *Coronilla scorpioides* (L.) Koch.

D.

Daucus vulgaris, *wilde Carrot, or Birds-nest.*   *Daucus carota* L.

Delphinium

sc. Consolida regalis, flo: pleno cæruleo, *wilde Larkspur with double blew flowers.*

flore pleno albo, *Larkspur with double white flowers.*

flo: pleno carneo, *Larkspur with double blush-coloured flowers.*   *Delphinium consolida* L. vars.

flore pleno albo cærulescente, *double Larkspurre with white and blewish flowers.*

flore simpl: diversorum colorum, *single Larkespur of divers colours.*

Dens leonis

flore rubro, *Dandelion with red flowers.*   *Erythronium dens-canis* L.

flore albo, *white Dandelion.*   *Erythronium dens-canis* L. var. *album*

vulgaris, *common Dandelion.*   *Taraxacum officinale* Weber.

Dentaria

major, *great-toothed violet Toothwort, or Lungwort.*   *Cardamine bulbifera* (L.) Crantz.

triphillon, *Trefoile Corallwort.*   *Cardamine enneaphyllos* (L.) Crantz.

pentaphillon, *Cinquefoile Corallwort.*   *Cardamine pentaphyllos* (L.) Crantz.

Dentillaria Rondeletii, Plumbago Plinii, *Pliny's Leadwort.*   *Plumbago europaea* L.

Digitalis

major flo: albo, *great white Foxglove.*   *Digitalis purpurea* L. var. *alba*

major flo: purpureo, *great purple Foxglove.*   *Digitalis purpurea* L. (type)

angustifolio subluteo, *yellowish small-leafed Foxglove.*   *Digitalis lutea* L.

variegata, *striped Foxglove.*   ? *Digitalis grandiflora* Miller

ferruginea major & minor, *great and small dun-coloured Foxglove.*   *Digitalis ferruginea* L. and *Digitalis parviflora* Jacq.

Virginiana angustissimo folio Tradescanti, *Narrowest leafed Virginian Foxglove.*   *Chelone glabra* L.

Hispanica ferruginea minor angustifolia, *Morini.*   *Digitalis obscura* L.

Dipsacus

major, *great wilde Teasell, or Venus Bason.*   *Dipsacus fullonum* L. subsp. *sativus*

minor, sim: Virga Pastoris, *small wilde Teasell.*   *Dipsacus pilosus* L.

vulgaris, *c̄omon wilde Teasell.*   *Dipsacus fullonum* L.

Doronicum

Romanum, *great Doronicum or mountain Marygold.*   *Doronicum plantagineum* L.

Americanum, *Leopards bane of America.*   *Rudbeckia laciniata* L.

Romanum rotundifoli: *great Doronicum with round leaves.*   *Doronicum pardalianches* L.

Draba

major flore luteo, Solidago Saracenica, *great yellow Cresse.*   *Sisymbrium strictissimum* L.

repens flo: albo, *creeping white Cresse.*   *Arabidopsis thaliana* (L.) Heynh.

Draco herba, *Taragon*. — Artemisia dracunculus L.

Dracontium majus, Serpentaria, *great Dragons*. — Dracunculus vulgaris Schott.

Dulca-amara
{
  i. Solanum lignosum flo: cæruleo,
  woody Nightshade.
  flo: albo, *white flowery Nightshade*.
} — Solanum dulcamara L. (forms)

E.

Ebulus, *Danewort*, *Dwarfe Elder*. — Sambucus ebulus L.

Echium vulgare, *Vipers Bugloss*. — Echium vulgare L.

Elatine
{
  Dioscorid: sive Veronica fœmina Fuschii,
  female Fluellin or Speedwell.
  Math: altera Dod:
}
— Kickxia spuria (L.) Dum.
— Kickxia elatine (L.) Dum.

Endiviæ species variæ, *divers kindes of Endive*. — Cichorium endivia L. (cvs.)

Enula Campana, Helenum, *Elecampane*. — Inula helenium L.

Epimedium, *Barrenwort*. — Epimedium alpinum L.

Epimedium fructicans Virginiana, sive hedera trifolia candensis cornut: — Rhus radicans L.

Epimelis, *Dwarfe Medlar*. — Amelanchier ovalis Medicus

Equisetum
{
  Marinum, *Sea Horsetaile*.
  majus palustre, *great marsh Horsetaile*.
  prætense majus, *great meadow Horsetaile*.
  peregrina Clusii, *Clusius his strange Rocket*.
}
— Equisetum fluviatile L.
— Equisetum telmateia Ehrh.
— ? Equisetum arvense L.
— Alyssum sinuatum L.

Eruca
{
  Aragonica, *great garden Rocket*.
  sativa, *garden Rocket*.
}
— Diplotaxis tenuifolia (L.) DC.
— Eruca sativa Miller

Eryngium
{
  Constantinopolitanum, *Sea-Holly from Constantinople*.
  planum, *smooth sea-Holly*.
  flore luteo, *Sea-Holly with yellow flower*.
  marinum vulgare, *our ordinary Sea-Holly*.
}
— Eryngium amethystinum L.
— Eryngium planum L.
— Eryngium campestre L.
— Eryngium maritimum L.

Esula
{
  major Germanica, *water Spurge*.
  montana, *mountain Spurge*.
  minor, *small Spurge*.
  hortensis, *garden Spurge*.
}
— Euphorbia palustris L.
— ? Euphorbia dulcis L.
— Euphorbia esula L.
— Euphorbia lathyris L.

Evonimus Theophrasti, *Prickwood, Spindletree*. — Euonymus europaeus L.

Eupatorium
{
  Noviæ belgia.
  canabinum mas, *Water hemp or hemp Agrimony*.
  Novæ Angliæ, *hemplike Agrimony of New England*.
}
— Eupatorium ageratoides L.
— Bidens cernua L.
— Eupatorium maculatum L.

Euphrasia, *Eyebright*. — Euphrasia nitidula Reuter

F.

Faba
{
  sativa major albicans, *great garden whitish Beans*.
  sativa major rubicunda, *great garden red Beans*.
  minor alba, *lesser white Beane*.
  minor nigra, *greater black Beane*.
  Græca, sive pisum nigrum Camerarii, *the old Greekish Beane*.
  Americanae, *American beanes*.
}
— Vicia faba L. (forms)
— Vicia faba L. var. 'Minor'
— Vicia narbonensis L.
— ? Cassia alata L.

Fago-triticum, id fagopyron, Dod: *sc*: frumentum Saracenicum, *Buckwheat*. — Fagopyrum esculentum Moench

Fagus, *the Beech tree*. — Fagus sylvatica L.

Ferrum equinum
{
  majus, *the greater Horshoe Vetch*.
  minus siliquis in summitate.
}
— Hippocrepis unisiliquosa L.
— Hippocrepis comosa L.

Ferula
{
  Fennell =
  Galbanifera, *gum-bearing Fennell*.
}
— Ferula communis L.

Festuca, *wilde Oates.*	*Bromus sterilis* L.
Ficus Indicus minor, Opuntia, *lesser Indian Figge.*	*Opuntia vulgaris* Miller
Ficus Indica echinata elegans, *Morini.*	*Melocactus communis* Link & Otto
Ficus diversæ species, *severall kindes of Figges.*	*Ficus carica* L. (cvs.)
Filipendula { vulgaris, *Dropwort.*	*Filipendula vulgaris* Moench
aquatica, *vide* Oenanthe.	*Oenanthe fistulosa* L.
florida, Osmunda regalis, *Water-Ferne, or Sun-Royall.*	*Osmunda regalis* L.
Filix { mas ramosa pinulis latis densis minutim incisis, *common male Ferne.*	*Dryopteris filix-mas* (L.) Schott.
ramosa major, sive fœmina, *female Ferne, or Brakes.*	*Pteridium aquilinum* (L.) Kuhn
Flamula Jovis subrecta, *upright Virgine Bower.*	*Clematis recta* L.
Flamulæ variæ	*Ranunculus lingua* L., *Ranunculus flammula* L., etc.
Adonis, *Flower of Love, Rose-a-Ruby.*	*Adonis annua* L.
Affricanus major, *great French Marigold.*	*Tagetes erecta* L.
Affricanus minor, *lesser French Marigold.*	*Tagetes patula* L.
Constantinopolitanus flore Miniato, *Nonsuch or Flower of Constantinople.*	
Constantinop: flore rubro, *Nonsuch with red flower.*	} *Lychnis chalcedonica* L. (forms)
Flos { Constantinop: flore pleno, *double Nonsuch.*	*Lychnis chalcedonica* L. var. 'Rubra Plena'
Passionis, vel Maracōc: *Passion-flower.*	*Passiflora incarnata* L.
Solis major, *greater Sun-flower.*	*Helianthus annuus* L.
Solis prolifera, *childing Sunne-flower.*	*Helianthus multiflorus* L.
Solis, semine nigro & variegato, *Sun-flower with black and party-coloured Seeds.*	*Helianthus* spp.
	Foeniculum vulgare Miller
Fenicula { Fennell.	*F. vulgare* Miller var. 'Dulce'
dulce, *sweet Fennell.*	
Foenugrecum.	*Trigonella foenum-graecum* L.
fructu rubro major, *great red Strawberry.*	*Fragaria vesca* L.
fructu rubro minor, *little white Strawberry.*	? hybrids and/or forms
Fragaria { spinosa sive hispida, *prickly Strawberry.*	*Fragaria vesca* L. var. 'Muricata'
na: Novæ Angliæ nondum descript: *New England Strawberry.*	*Fragaria virginiana* Duch.
vulgaris, *ordinary Strawberry.*	*Fragaria vesca* L.
flo: albo minor, *lesser White bastard Dittaine.*	*Dictamnus albus* L.
Fraxinella { flore purpureo major, *great purple Dittaine.*	*Dictamnus albus* var. 'Purpureus'
flore rubro, *bastard Dittaine with a red flower.*	*Dictamnus albus* (form)
flore rubro, *red checkered Daffodill.*	? *Fritillaria tubiformis* Gren. & Godr.
flore albo, *the White Fritillaria.*	*Fritillaria meleagris* L. (form)
flore luteo, *yellow Fritillaria.*	*Fritillaria latifolia* Willd. var. 'Lutea'
Fritillaria { vulgaris major & minor, *common checker Daffodill the greater and the lesser.*	*Fritillaria meleagris* L. (forms)
Aquitanica flore gemino.	*Fritillaria pyrenaica* L.
Frumenti Turcici variet: triplex.	*Zea mays* L.
Frutex { Canadensis Epimedii folio.	*Toxicodendron radicans* (L.) D. Kuntze
Coronaria flo: pleno, Syringæ flore.	*Philadelphus coronarius* L.
Fumaria vulgaris, *Fumitory.*	*Fumaria officinalis* L.

G.

Galega	flo: albo, *white flowered Goats-rue.*	*Galega officinalis* L. var. '*Alba*'
	flore cæruleo, *blew-flowred Goats-rue.*	*Galega officinalis* L.
	maj: flore cæruleo, *great blew-flowred Goats-rue.*	*Galega officinalis* L. (form)
	flore car: *blush-coloured Goats-rue.*	*Galega officinalis* L. var. '*Carnea*'
Galeopsis, *Hedge-nettle.*		*Stachys sylvatica* L.
Gallium	flore luteo, *Ladyes bedstraw. Cheese-rening.*	*Galium verum* L.
	flore albo, *white-flowred Ladyes bedstraw.*	*Galium palustre* L.
Genista	Hispanica, *Spanish Broome.*	*Spartium junceum* L.
	*Lusitanica, *Portugall Broome.*	*Echinospartum lusitanicum* (L.) Rothm.
	spinosa, *Furze, Whins, Gorsse.*	*Ulex europaeus* L.
Genistella, *needle Furze, or petty Whin.*		*Genista anglica* L.
Gentiana	major, *great Gentian.*	*Gentiana lutea* L.
	foliis Asclepiadis, *Swallowwort Gentian.*	*Gentiana asclepiadea* L.
	Cruciata, *Crosse-wort Gentian.*	*Gentiana cruciata* L.
Gentianella	Verna, *Felwort of the Spring.*	*Gentiana nivalis* L. or *Gentianella anglica* Pugsl.
	Fugax autumnalis, *bastard or dwarf Felwort.*	*Gentianella amarella* (L.) Börner
	Alpina Helvetica.	*Gentiana acaulis* L.
Geranium	Batracoides flore cæruleo, *blew-flowered Crowfoot Cranesbill.*	*Geranium pratense* L.
	Batracoides flo: albo, *white-flowred Cranesbill.*	*Geranium pratense* L. var. '*Album*'
	Batracoides flore variegato, *strip-coloured Crowfoot Cranesbill.*	*G. pratense* L. var. '*Striatum*'
	Romanum variegatum, *variable stript Cranesbill.*	*Geranium striatum* L.
	Fuscum, *spotted Cranesbill.*	*Geranium phaeum* L.
	Virginianum, *Virginian Cranesbill.*	? *Geranium maculatum* L.
	longius Radicatum, *long-rooted Cranesbill.*	*Geranium macrorrhizum* L.
	Haematodes, *sc*: sanguinale, *red or bloody Cranesbill.*	*Geranium sanguineum* L.
	Moschatum, *musked Cranesbill.*	*Erodium moschatum* (L.) L'Hér.
	Creticum, *Candy Cranesbill.*	*Erodium gruinum* (L.) L'Hér.
	Indicum nocte odoratum, *sweet Indian Cranesbill.*	*Pelargonium triste* (L.) Aiton
	tuberosa radice, *tuberous or bulbed Cranesbill.*	*Geranium tuberosum* L.
	non descriptum Dodonæi.	—
	Arvense inodorum, *cerne Cranesbill.*	*Erodium cicutarium* (L.) L'Hér.
Gingidium, *Chervill.*		*Ammi visnaga* Lam.
Gladiolus	Bizantinus major flo: purpureo, *great purple flowred Gladiole from Constantinople.*	*Gladiolus byzantinus* Miller
	minor flo: albo, *small white-flowered Gladiole.*	*Gladiolus italicus* Miller (forms)
	minor flo: purpureo, *small purple Gladiole.*	
	Indicus Suertii, *Morin.*	? *Sisyrinchium bermudiana* L.
Glastum, *sc*: Isatis, *Woade.*		*Isatis tinctoria* L.
Glaux	vulgaris leguminosa, *wilde Liquorice, or Liquorice Hatchet-Vetch.*	*Astragalus glycyphyllos* L.
	æstiva supina Lusitanica.	? *Glaux maritima* L.
Glycyrrhiza, *Liquorice.*		*Glycyrrhiza glabra* L.

*†Glycyriza Brasiliensis.	? *Glycyrrhiza lepidota* Pursh.
	Americanum, *Livelong, or Life-everlasting*. — *Anaphalis margaritacea* Benth. & Hook. f.
	Anglicu longiore fol: *common Cudweed with long leaves*. — *Gnaphalium sylvaticum* L.
Gnaphaliū	Indic: *Indian Cudweed*. — ? *Helichrysum orientale* (L.) Gaertner
	flore albo, *White-flowered Cudweed*. — *Antennaria dioica* (L.) Gaertner
	minus repens, *small Cudweed*. — *Filago minima* (Smith) Pers.
	vulgare, *Cudweed, or Cottonweed*. — *Gnaphalium uliginosum* L.
	arundinaceum ma: sive Calamogrostis, *Sheer-grasse, wilde Reed*. — *Calamagrostis epigejos* (L.) Roth.
	striatum, *striped Grasse*. — *Phalaris arundinacea* L. var. ' Picta'
	plumosum, *Vetched Grasse*. — *Stipa pennata* Hudson
	parnassi, *Grasse of Parnassus, or white Liverwort*. — *Parnassia palustris* L.
Gramen	Alopecurinum majus, *great Foxtaile grasse*. — ? *Alopecurus mvosuroides* Hudson
	Alopecurinum minus, *small bastard Foxtaile*. — ? *Alopecurus aequalis* Sobol.
	Tremulum, lupuli glumis. — *Briza maxima* L.
	Junceum sive busoniū, *Toad-grasse*. — *Juncus bufonius* L.
	Cyperoides, *Cyprus grasse*. — *Carex otrubae* Podp.
	Leucanthemum, *Stitchwort*. — *Stellaria holostea* L.
Graminis aliæ diversæ species, *divers other sorts of Grasse*. — —	
Gratiola, *Grasse Poley*.	*Gratiola officinalis* L.
	maxima, *greatest Gooseberry*.
	maxima longa, *greatest long Gooseberry*.
	cærulea, *blew Gooseberry*.
	rubra major rotunda, *greater red round Goosberry*.
Grossularia	media species longa, *middle long sort of Goosberryes*. — *Ribes uva-crispa* L. cvs.
	rubra minor, *small red Gooseberry*.
	spinosa, *prickly Gooseberry*.
	vulgaris, *the cōmon Gooseberry*.
Guaiacum Patavinum, *Indian Date-Plum tree*.	? *Diospyros virginiana* L. and/or D. *lotus* L.
*(?†)Guavon *from Barbados*.	*Psidium guajava* L.

H.

Halicacabus sive Alkakenge, *Winter-Cherryes*.	*Physalis alkekengi* L.
Halimus arborescens, primus Clusii.	*Atriplex halimus* L.
	arborea, *climing or berried Ivy*.
	helix, *barren or creeping Ivy*. — *Hedera helix* L.
Hedera	Virginiana, sc: vitis, *Virginian Ivy, or Vine*. — *Parthenocissus quinquefolia* (L.) Planchon
	terrestris, *ground Ivy or Alehoofe*. — *Glechoma hederacea* L.
Hedysarum	Clipiatum, *French Hunisuckle*. — *Hedysarum coronarium* L.
	Peregrina, *strange hatchet-Vetch*. — *Biserrula pelecinus* L.
Helleborine, *wilde white Hellebore*.	*Epipactis latifolia* (L.) All. or Cephalanthera damasonium (Miller) Druce
	albus flore herbaceo. — *Veratrum album* L.
	albus flo: atrorubente, *white Hellebore with a dark red flower*. — *Veratrum nigrum* L.
Helleborus	niger verus serotinus, *true black Hellebore*. — ? *Helleborus orientalis* Lam.
	niger verus præcotior, *early true Hellebore*. — *Helleborus niger* L.
	niger flore viridi Bauhin: *black Hellebore of Bauhinus with green flowers*. — *Helleborus viridis* L.

Helleborus	niger foetidus Bauhi: *Bauhinus his blacke stinking Hellebore*.	*Helleborus foetidus* L.
	niger ferulaceus, *Fennell-leafed bastard black Hellebore*.	*Adonis vernalis* L.

Helleboraster, *bastard Hellebore*. — *Helleborus foetidus* L.

Hepatica	flore albo, *Hepatica or Liverwort with white flower*.	*Hepatica nobilis* Miller var. 'Alba'
	flore cæruleo major, *greater blew Hepatica*.	*Hepatica nobilis* Miller var. 'Caerulea'
	flore cæruleo minor, *lesser blew Hepatica*.	
	flore rubro, *red Hepatica*.	*Hepatica nobilis* Miller var. 'Rubra'
	flore albo puncticulato, *white speckled Hepatica*.	*Hepatica nobilis* Miller var. 'Marmorata'
	flore violaceo multiplici, *double violet-coloured Hepatica*.	
	flore cæruleo multiplici, *double blew Hepatica*.	*Hepatica nobilis* Miller vars. 'Flore Pleno'
	flore albo cum staminibus rubris.	
	cæruleo flore pleno altera, *another double blew Hepatica*.	

Herba	Doria, *Dorius his Woundwort*.	*Senecio doria* L.
	Paris, Solanum quadrifolium bacciferum Bauhi: *herb Paris, one berry*.	*Paris quadrifolia* L.
	Mimosa viva, *sc*: sensisica, *sensible Plant or Herb of Life*.	*Mimosa sensitiva* L.
	Mimosa altera sive humilis, *humble Plant*.	*Mimosa pudica* L.

Hermodactylus, *Hermodactyls*. — ? *Hermodactylus tuberosus* Miller
Herniaria, *rupture-wort*. — *Herniaria glabra* L.
Hesperis Italica, *Dames Violets of Italy*. — *Hesperis matronalis* L.

Hieracium	medio nigrū, *smaller black Hawkweed*.	? *Tolpis barbata* (L.) Gaertner
	lanuginosum flore luteo.	? *Hieracium lanatum* Waldst.
	asperum, *rough Hawkweed, or yellow succory*.	*Picris hieracioides* L.
	majus, *Hawkweed*.	*Crepis tectorum* L.

Hippoglossum, *Horsetongue*. — *Ruscus hypoglossum* L.
Hippolapathum, *Monks Rubarbe*. — *Rumex patientia* L.
Hippomarathrum Lusitanicum, *great Portugall Fennell*. — *Seseli hippomarathrum* L.
Hipposelinum, olus atrum, *Allisanders*. — *Smyrnium olusatrum* L.

Holostium	medium, *middle Toad-grass*.	*Juncus bufonius* L. vars.
	minus, *lesser Toad grass*.	

Hordeum	spurium spontanum, *Wall-Barley, or wilde Rye*.	*Hordeum murinum* L.
	nudum, *bastard Wheat*.	*Hordeum distichon* L. var. 'Nudum'
	Hermophrodicum.	*Hordeum* sp.

Horminum	sativum, *garden-Clary*.	*Salvia sclarea* L.
	sylvestre, sive oculus Christi, *wilde Clary*.	*Salvia horminoides* Pourr.
	glutinosum luteum, sive colus Jovis, *yellow wilde Clary, or Jupiters Distaffe*.	*Salvia glutinosa* L.
	Creticum, forte aut horminum exoticum Robini, *Candy Clary*.	? *Salvia triloba* L.
	sylvestre Lusitan: flore albo *Wilde Portugall Clary with white flowers*.	*Salvia viridis* L. (forms)
	sylvestre Lusitan: flore cæruleo, *wilde Portugall Clary with blew flowers*.	

Hyacinthus	Anglicus flore albo, & flo: purpureo, *the White and purple Harebell or English lacynth*.	
	Anglicus flo: cæruleo, *blew English lacynth*.	Endymion non-scriptus (L.) Garcke (forms)
	Anglicus flore cæruleo Dilutiore.	
	Angl: flore purpurascente.	
	Angl: colore Amethystino, *the Amethist coloured English lacynth*.	
	Autumnalis major Indicus tuberosa radici, *great Autumne Indian knobbed lacynth*.	Polianthes tuberosa L.
	Botroides flore albo, *white Muske grape flower*.	Muscari botryoides (L.) Miller var. 'Album'
	Botroides flo: cæruleo, *blew Muske grape flower*.	Muscari botryoides (L.) Miller
	Botroides flore violaceo, *violet coloured Muske grape flower*.	? Muscari atlanticum Boiss. & Reuter
	Brumalis, *Winter lacynth*.	Hyacinthus orientalis L. (form)
	comosus calamistratus purpureus.	Muscari comosum (L.) Miller
	comosus calamistratus violaceus.	(forms)
	comosus vulgaris, *common-haired lacynth*.	Muscari comosum (L.) Miller
	Orientalis flore albo Brumalis, *white Winter Orientall lacynth*.	
	Orient: flore cæruleo multiplici polyanthos.	
	Orient: atro-rubens.	Hyacinthus orientalis L. (cvs.)
	Orient: caule foliosa, *bushy stalked Orientall lacynth*.	
	Orient: flore cæruleo, *blew Orientall lacynth*.	
	Peruvianus flore albo stellaris, *white starry lacynth of Peru*.	Scilla peruviana L. var. 'Alba'
	Peruv: flore cæruleo stellaris, *blew starry lacynth of Peru*.	Scilla peruviana L.
	stellatus minor flore albo, *small white starry lacynth*.	Scilla bifolia L. var. 'Alba'
	stellatus flore cæruleo, Someri-dicta, *blew starry lacynth, or Somers starry lacynth*.	Scilla italica L.
	stellatus flore purp: *purple starry lacynth*.	Scilla bifolia L.
	Autumnalis minor Anglicus, *small Autumne English lacynth*.	Scilla autumnalis L.
	Paniculatus, *Panicke lacynth*.	Muscari comosum Mill. var. 'Monstrosum'
	Pyrenæus flore albo, *white Pyrenean lacynth*.	Brimeura amethystina (L.) Chouard (forms)
	Pyrenæus flore cæruleo, *blew Pyrenean lacynth*.	
	flore obsoleto Clusii, *Clusius's whale lacynth*.	Dipcadi serotinum (L.) Medicus
	Indicus Bulbosus & tuberosus, *Morini*.	Polianthes tuberosa L.
Hyropiper, *Arsmart*.		Polygonum hydropiper L.
Hyoscyamus	albus rotundifolius, *white roundleafed Henbane*.	Hyoscyamus albus L.
	niger, *black Henbane*.	Hyoscyamus niger L.
	luteus, *Candy Henbane*, vide Park: fol. 364.	Hyoscyamus aureus L.
	Peruvianus, *sc*: Tabacum verum fœminæ.	Nicotiana tabacum L.
	albus medio purpureus.	? Hyoscyamus niger L.

	arborescens, *Tree S. Johns wort.*	*Spiraea hypericifolia* L.
	non perfoliatum Ascyrum dictum, *S. Peters wort.*	*Hypericum maculatum* Crantz.
	non perfoliatum Ascyrum villosum supinum dictum, *creeping S. Peters wort.*	*Hypericum elodes* L.

Hypericum
- arborescens, *Tree S. Johns wort.* — *Spiraea hypericifolia* L.
- non perfoliatum Ascyrum dictum, *S. Peters wort.* — *Hypericum maculatum* Crantz.
- non perfoliatum Ascyrum villosum supinum dictum, *creeping S. Peters wort.* — *Hypericum elodes* L.
- Bacciferum, *scil*: Androsæmum, *Tutsan or Parkeleaves.* — *Hypericum androsaemum* L.
- Hypericoides dicta sive Androsæmum magnum, *great S. Johns wort.* — *Hypericum hirsutum* L.
- Pulchrum Tragi, *upright S. Johns wort.* — *Hypericum pulchrum* L.
- vulgaris, *common S. Johns wort.* — *Hypericum perforatum* L.
- repens, *creeping St. Johns wort.* — *Hypericum humifusum* L.
- tomentosum, *wooly S. Johns wort.* — *Hypericum tomentosum* L.

Hypochæris, *Swines Succory.* — *Hyoseris radiata* L.

Hyssopus
- sativa, *garden Hyssope.* — *Hyssopus officinalis* L.
- prolifera, *childing Hyssope.* — *Hyssopus officinalis* L. (form)
- alba, *white Hyssope.* — *H. officinalis* L. var. 'Albus'
- tenuifolia, *thin-leafed Hyssope.* — *H. officinalis* L. var. 'Angustifolius'
- comosa. — *H. officinalis* L. (form)

I.

Jacea
- maxima odorata, *greatest sweet-scented Knapweed.* — *Centaurea moschata* L. var. 'Imperialis'
- major lutea capite spinoso, *greater yellow Knapweed with a prickly head.* — *Centaurea collina* L.
- nigra, *Knapweed Mate fellon.* — *Centaurea nigra* L.
- æstiva elegans, *dainty Summer Knapweed.* — ? *Centaurea cyanus* L.
- vulgaris, vel nigra, *cōmon Knapweed.* — *Centaurea nigra* L.

Jacobæa
- marina vulgo cinerario, *Sea Ragwort.* — *Senecio cineraria* DC.
- vulgaris, *common Ragwort.* — *Senecio jacobaea* L.
- minor muralis, *small Rugwort, or Seggrum.* — ? *Senecio erucifolius* L.
- latifolia Bætica, *broad-leafed Spanish Rugwort.* — *Senecio eriopus* Willk.

Jasminum
- Hispanicum flo: albo vulg: *common white Spanish Jasmine.* — *Jasminum officinale* L. var. 'Affine'
- Americanum amplo flore Phœniceo. — *Campsis radicans* (L.) Seem.
- Indicum flore luteo odorato, *Morini.* — *Jasminum odoratissimum* L.
- *Italicum luteum inodorum, *unsavory yellow Italian Jasmine.* — *Jasminum humile* L.
- Persicum flo: violaceo, *violet-coloured Persian Jasmine.* — *Syringa* x *persica* L.

Iberis major, *sc*: lepidium, *great Sciatica Cresses.* — *Lepidium iberis* L.

Ilex, *the Holme Oake.* — *Quercus ilex* L.

Impatiens herba Dodonei, *sc*: Persicaria siliquosa, *wilde Mercury, called Quick in hand.* — *Impatiens noli-tangere* L.

Imperatoria, *common Masterwort.* — *Peucedanum ostruthium* (L.) Koch.

Irio, sive Erysimum, *Banke-Cresses.* — *Sisymbrium officinale* (L.) Scop.

Illecebra minor acris, v. vermicularis, *Stone-croppe.* — *Sedum acre* L.

Irides majores variæ, *severall sorts of great Fower de luces.* — *Iris germanica* L., etc. (*I. pallida, I. sambucina*)

Iris
- gloriosa, *the goodly Flower de luce.* — ? *Iris florentina* L. form
- Susiana major, *the Susian Flower de luce.* — *Iris susiana* L.
- Clusii flore pleno, *large Flower de luce of Clusius.* — ? *Iris planifolia* (Miller) Fiori var.
- Clusii flore albo, *Clusius his white Flower de luce.* — *Iris planifolia* (Miller) Fiori var. 'Alba'

	Clusii flo: cæruleo, *Clusius his blew Flower de luce.*	*Iris planifolia* (Miller) Fiori
	bulbosa Anglica major flore albo, *great white Bulbous English Flower de luce.*	*Iris xiphioides* Ehrh. vars.
	bulbosa Anglica flore cæruleo, *blew Bulbous English Flower de luce.*	
	Persica, *Persian Flower de luce.*	*Iris persica* L.
Iris	bulbosa Africana, *Bulbous African Flower de luce.*	*Iris filifolia* Boiss.
	bulbosa Anglica variegata, *Bulbous English variable Flower de luce.*	*Iris xiphioides* Ehrh. var.
	bulbosa flore lutea, *Bulbous yellow Flower de luce.*	*Iris lusitanica* Ker-Gawl.
	palustris lutea, *water Flower de luce.*	*Iris pseudacorus* L.
	marmoria Romano, *Roman Flower de luce.*	? *Iris* sp.

Iridis bulbosæ aliæ diversitates, *several sorts of Bulbous Flower de luces.* —

Irides humiles sive Chamæirides variæ, *divers kindes of dwarfe Flower de luces.* *Iris pumila* L. vars. and *Iris chamaeiris* Bertol. vars.

Juniperus	Bacciferus, *berry-bearing Juniper.*	*Juniperus communis* L. (form)
	minor, *common Juniper-tree.*	*Juniperus communis* L.

Jucca Indica orientalis planta, *East-Indian Jucca.* *Yucca gloriosa* L.
*†Jucca Virginiana angustiore & breviore folio, *The Virginian Jucca with shorter and narrower leaves.* *Yucca filamentosa* L.

K.

	flore luteo pleno, *double yellow Walflower.*	*Cheiranthus cheiri* L.
	flore luteo virescente majus, *the greater greenish yellow Walflower.*	
	majus ferrugineo flo: ple: *great Duncoloured double Walflower.*	*Cheiranthus cheiri* L. cvs.
	flore luteo simplex vulg: *common single Walflower.*	
Keiri	flore albo simplex, *white Walflower.*	*Matthiola incana* (L.) R. Br. var. 'Annua'
	flore pleno pyramidale, *the spired double Walflower.*	
	flore pleno vulgare, *common double Walflower.*	*Cheiranthus cheiri* L. cvs.
	flore pleno auratū, *double gilded Walflower.*	

L.

Laburnum	majus, *greater Beane Trefoile.*	*Laburnum anagyroides* Medicus
	minus, *lesser Beane Trefoile.*	*Laburnum alpinum* Bercht. & Presl.
	Aug: sativa, *common garden Lettice.*	*Lactuca sativa* L.
	agnina latifolia, *broad Cornesallet, or Lambs Lettice.*	*Valerianella locusta* (L.) Betcke
Lactuca	sylvestris, Endiviæ foliis, *Endive leafed wilde Lettice.*	*Lactuca serriola* L.
	major foliis pennatis, *long-headed Haresfoot.*	*Trifolium rubens* L.
Lagapus	flore rubro, *red flowred Haresfoot.*	*Trifolium incarnatum* L.
	vulgaris, *common Haresfoot.*	*Trifolium arvense* L.
	sylvestre flore albo, *Archangel, dead Nettle.*	*Lamium album* L.
Lamium	sylv: flo: rubro, *red Archangel.*	*Lamium purpureum* L.
	flo: luteo, *yellow Archangel.*	*Lamiastrum galeobdolon* (L.) Ehrend. & Polat.

Lamium	{ Pannonicum flo: rubro, *Hungary red* / *Archangel.*	*Lamium orvala* L.
Lampsana, *Dock Cresse.*		*Lapsana communis* L.
Lapathū	{ sanguineum, *bloodwort.*	*Rumex sanguineus* L.
	hortense, *Monks Rubarb.*	*Rumex patientia* L.
	acutum, *common Dock.*	*Rumex conglomeratus* Murr.
Lappa	{ major, *vide* Bardana.	*Arctium lappa* L.
	minor, sive Arctium.	*Xanthium strumarium* L.
Lathyrus	{ major latif: radice perpetua, *great broad-leafed Chichling, or Pease everlasting.*	*Lathyrus latifolius* L.
	major angustifolius, *grasse-leafed Chichling.*	*Lathyrus sativus* L.
	arvensis repens, tuberosus: Apios Fuschii,	*Lathyrus tuberosus* L.
	Tragi, Terræ glandes, *Pease Earth nutts.*	
	angustifolius semine maculoso, *sc*:	? *Lathyrus clymenum* L.
	Ægyptians common narrow-leafed wilde Chichling, or Ægyptian Chichling.	
	sylv: mi: Catananes D.	*Lathyrus nissolia* L.
	Æstivus flore luteo Lusitanico. *Roelii.*	? *Lathyrus annuus* L.
Lavendula	{ Major, sive vulgaris, *garden Lavender.*	
	angustifolia, *small spike Lavender.*	} *Lavandula angustifolia* Miller
	flore cæruleo, *blew-flowered Lavender.*	
	latifolia, *broad leafed Lavender.*	*Lavandula latifolia* (L.) Vill.
	multifida, *jagged Lavender.*	*Lavandula multifida* L.
Laureola, *Spurge Laurell.*		*Daphne laureola* L.
Laurocerasus, *Cherry Bay.*		*Prunus laurocerasus* L.
Laurus	{ vulgar: *common Bay-tree.*	*Laurus nobilis* L.
	tinus, *wilde Bay.*	*Viburnum tinus* L.
	tinus Lusitanicus, folio glabro, *smooth wilde Bay of Portugall.*	*Viburnum tinus* L. var. *lucidum* Aiton
	Alexandrina vera, *true Laurell of Alexandria.*	*Ruscus hypophyllum* L.
	Gallica, *French Bayes.*	? *Laurus nobilis* L. (form)
Lens palustris, *wild Lentill, Ducks meat.*		*Lemna minor* L.
Lepidium piperitis, *Pepperwort or Dittander.*		*Lepidium latifolium* L.
Leucojum	{ bulbosum triphyllon, *Bulbous-violet of three leaves.*	*Galanthus nivalis* L.
	bulbosū Hexaphyllon, *Bulbous-violet of six leaves.*	*Leucojum vernum* L.
	bulb: Hexaph: ma: polyanthemum.	*Leucojum aestivum* L.
	bulbosum majus, *greater bulbous-violet.*	*Leucojum aestivum* L. var.
	bulbosum minus, *lesser Bulbous violet*	*Galanthus nivalis* L. or *G. plicatus* Bieb.
Leucojum	{ arbor: flore pleno rubro, *double red stocke Gilliflower.*	
	arbo: flo: pleno albo, *double white stock Gilliflower.*	
	arbo: flo: pleno purpureo, *double purple stock Gilliflower.*	} *Matthiola incana* (L.) R. Br.
	arbo: flo: pleno rubro variegato, *double striped red stock Gilliflower.*	
	arbo: flo: pleno purpureo, *double striped purple stock Gilliflower.*	
	marinum, *Sea stock Gilliflower.*	*Matthiola sinuata* R. Br.
Levisticum, *i*, ligusticum, *Lovage.*		*Levisticum officinale* Koch.
Libanotis, Theophrast: *the true herbe Frankinsence of Theophrastus.*		*Laserpitium latifolium* L.
Lichen, *Liverwort.*		*Marchantia polymorpha* L.
Ligustrum, vulgare, *Privet.*		*Ligustrum vulgare* L.

Liliasphodelus	flore luteo, *yellow day Lilly.*	*Hemerocallis lilioasphodelus* L.
	flore pheniceo, *the old red day Lilly.*	*Hemerocallis fulva* (L.) L.
	flore albo, *white red Lilly.*	*Paradisea liliastrum* Bertol.
Lilium	album, *white Lilly.*	*Lilium candidum* L.
	album latifolium, *white Lilly with a broad leaf.*	? *Lilium candidum* L. (form)
	album polyanthemum Affricanum flor: multip: *the white many flower Affrican Lilly.*	*Ornithogalum latifolium* L.
	Convallium flore albo, *white Lilly Convall, May Lilly with white flowers.*	*Convallaria majalis* L.
	Convallium flo: rubello, *scarlet Lilly of the Valley.*	*Convallaria majalis* L. var. 'Rosea'
	flore luteo, *yellow Lilly.*	*Lilium pyrenaicum* Gouan
	Constantinopolitanum, *Lilly of Constantinople.*	*Lilium candidum* L. var. 'Cernuum'
	cruentum Bulbiferum, *the red Bulbous Lilly.*	*Lilium bulbiferum* L.
	rubrum, *red Lilly, fiery red bulbed Lilly.*	*Lilium bulbiferum* L. var.
	candidum flore plenissimo, *Morini.*	*Lilium candidum* L. cv.

Lilio Narcissus Indicus, *Morini.* — ? *Amaryllis belladonna* L.
Lilac – Matthioli, Syringa, *Pipe-tree.* — *Syringa vulgaris* L.
Limonium minus angustifolium, *small narrow-leafed Lavender.* — *Limonium binervosum* (G.E.Sm.) C.E. Salmon

*†Seamarch Buglosse, Park: 1234. — *Sarracenia purpurea* L.

Linaria	oderata, *sweet Flaxweed.*	*Linaria purpurea* (L.) Miller or *Anarrhinum bellidifolium* (L.) Desf.
	vulgaris, *common Toadflax.*	*Linaria vulgaris* Miller

Lingua cervina, *Hearts-tongue.* — *Phyllitis scolopendrium* (L.) Newm.

Linum	sylvestre catharticum, *Mill-mountaine.*	*Linum catharticum* L.
	vulgare sativum, *garden-flax*	*Linum usitatissimum* L.

Lithospermū, Milliū folis, *great Grumbell.* — *Lithospermum purpureo-caeruleum* L.

Locusta Virginiana arbor, *Virginian Locus tree.* — *Robinia pseudacacia* L.

Lolium	album, *white Darnell.*	*Lolium temulentum* L.
	rubrum, *red Darnell.*	*Lolium perenne* L.
Lotus	arbor, *Nettle tree.*	*Celtis australis* L.
	*†arbor Virginiana, *Virginian Nettle tree.*	*Celtis occidentalis* L.
	Libica, *lesser pile Trefoile.*	? *Melilotus officinalis* (L.) Pallas.
	coronata maxima Hispanica.	*Coronilla varia* L.
	Tetragonolobus, Pisum quadratum, *square codded Pease.*	*Tetragonolobus purpureus* Moench

Lonchitis vulgaris, *rough Spleenwort.* — *Blechnum spicant* (L.) Roth.
Lunaria minor, *small Moonwort.* — *Botrychium lunaria* (L.) Swartz.

Lupinus	albus sativus, *white garden Lupine.*	*Lupinus albus* L.
	cæruleus latifolius, medius angustifol: luteus, *yellow Lupine.*	*Lupinus hirsutus* L. and *Lupinus luteus* L.
	Indicus, *Indian Lupine.*	*Lupinus perennis* L.
	candidus ex Candio, *white Lupine from Candy.*	? *Lupinus termis* Forsk.
	flo: cæruleo minor, *lesser blew Lupine.*	*Lupinus varius* L.
Lupulus	cultivus, *garden Hops.*	*Humulus lupulus* L. (form)
	sylvestris, *wilde Hops.*	*Humulus lupulus* L.

Lutea Cretica, *Would or Diers weed of Candy.* — *Datisca cannabina* L.
Lutum, herba luteola, *Diers weed.* — *Reseda luteola* L.

Lychnis	sylvestris flore albo multiplici, *double wilde Campion with a white flower.*	*Silene alba* (Miller) E.H.L. Krause var. 'Multiplex'

Lychnis	sylvestris flore rubro multipl: *double wilde Campion with a red flower.*	*Silene dioica* (L.) Clairv. var. *'Multiplex'*
	Chalcedonica flo: miniato ple: *double flower of Bristoll or Nonsuch.*	*Lychnis chalcedonica* L. var. *'Rubra Plena'*
	Chalcedonica flo: miniato simplici: *single Nonsuch or flower of Bristoll or Constantinople.*	*Lychnis chalcedonica* L.
	Chalc: flo: albo, *white Campion of Constantinople.*	*Lychnis chalcedonica* L. var. *'Alba'*
	Coronaria flore albo, *white rose Campion.*	*Lychnis coronaria* (L.) Desr. (form)
	Coronaria flore rubro, *red rose Campion.*	*Lychnis coronaria* (L.) Desr.
	Coronaria flore variegat: *variable rose Campion.*	*Lychnis coronaria* (L.) Desr. (form)
	sylvestris flo: albo & flo: rubello, *white and scarlet wilde Campion.*	*Silene alba* (Miller) Krause and *Silene dioica* (L.) Clairv.
	Marina Anglica, *Sea rose Campion.*	*Silene maritima* With.
	sylvestris Pyrenæa, *the wilde Pyrenean Campion.*	*Petrocoptis pyrenaica* (J.P. Bergeret) A. Braun

Lysimachia	lutea, *yellow Willow Weed.*	*Lysimachia vulgaris* L.
	galariculata cærulea, *blewheaded Willow Weed.*	*Scutellaria galericulata* L.
	spicata cærulea, *blew-spiked Willow weed.*	*Veronica austriaca* L.
	siliquosa folio salicis, *codded Loosestrife, with Willow leaves.*	*Epilobium dodonaei* Vill.
	Virginiana lutea, *yellow Willow herbe of Virginia.*	*Oenothera biennis* L.
	purpurea spicata, *purple spikeheaded Loosestrife.*	*Lythrum salicaria* L.
	siliquosa sylvestris hirsuta, *hairy wilde codded Loosestrife.*	*Epilobium hirsutum* L.
	siliquosa glabra, *smooth-codde Willow-weed.*	*Epilobium montanum* L.

M.

Majorana	annua nobilis, *the best yearly Marjoram.*	*Majorana hortensis* Moench
	nobilis perpetua, *the best everlasting Marjoram.*	*Majorana hortensis* Moench var. *'Tenuifolium'*
	nobilis perpetua foliis variegatis, *the perpetuall best changeable Marjoram.*	*Majorana hortensis* Moench var. *'Variegatum'*
	vulgaris foliis luteis, *the common yellow Marjoram.*	*Origanum onites* L. var. *'Aureum'*
	Anglica semper virens, *the ever-green English Marjoram.*	*Origanum onites* L.

Mali domesticæ species variæ, *very many sorts of choice Apple trees.*	*Malus domestica* Borkh. cvs.

Malva	Indica arborescens, *Indian tree Holliock.*	*Hibiscus syriacus* L.
	major vulgaris, *great ordinary Mallow.*	*Malva sylvestris* L.
	pumila, *the small Mallow.*	*Malva neglecta* Wallr.
	flore luteo ex Tartaria, *Tartarian yellow Mallow.*	*Abutilon avicennae* Gaertner
	Crispa, *French Mallows.*	*Malva crispa* L.
	hortensis diversorum colorum. *garden Mallowes of divers colours.*	*Alcea rosea* L.
	maxima Hispanica striata, *great Spanish striped Mallow.*	*Malva hispanica* L.
	segetum Lusitanica, *the Portugall corn Mallow.*	? *Lavatera trimestris* L.

Malum	aurantium major, *great Orange-tree.*	*Citrus aurantium* L.
	limonium, *Lemon-tree.*	*Citrus limon* (L.) Burm. f.
	granatum, *Pomegranat-tree.*	*Punica granatum* (L.)
	insanum fructu purpureo.	*Solanum melongena* L.
Mandragoras, *Mandrake.*		*Mandragora officinarum* L.
Marrubium	album vulgare, *common Horehound.*	*Marrubium vulgare* L.
	nigrum, Ballote, *stinking black Horehound.*	*Ballota nigra* L.
Marum, *herb Mastick.*		*Thymus mastichina* L.
Martagon	Pannonicum spadaceum, *bright red Martagon of Hungary.*	*Lilium carniolicum* Koch.
	Pompenū, *Martagon Pompony, or early red Martagon.*	*Lilium pomponium* L.
	flore albo punctato, *the white Martagon.*	*Lilium martagon* L. var. 'Albiflorum'
Matricaria	flore pleno, *double Fetherfew.*	*Chrysanthemum parthenium* (L.) Bernh. var. 'Flore Pleno'
	bullato flore, *naked Fetherfew.*	*C. parthenium* (L.) Bernh. (form)
	flore simplici vulgaris, *common Fetherfew.*	*C. parthenium* (L.) Bernh.
Medica	spinosa major, *greater thorny Medica or Claver.*	*Medicago intertexta* (L.) Miller
	transversis spinis, *the prickly Medick.*	
	scoparia, *the brush Medick.*	
	eligans Catalonica, *Dainty Catalonian Claver.*	*Medicago intertexta* (L.) Miller (forms)
	minor spinosa, *lesser thorny Claver.*	
	doliata echinata, *the tublike-hedghog Medick.*	
	doliata ramosa, *the tub-branched Medick.*	
	clypeata, *the helmet Medick.*	? *Medicago scutellata* (L.) Miller
Melampyrum album, *white Cow-wheat.*		*Melampyrum cristatum* L.
Melilotus	Italica flore luteo, *Italian Melilote with yellow flower.*	*Melilotus italica* (L.) Lam.
	Hispanica flore albo, *Spanish Mellilote with White flower.*	? *Melilotus alba* Medicus (forms)
	arborescens flore albo, *tree Mellilote with white flower.*	
	vulgaris, *common Mellilote.*	*Melilotus altissima* Thuill.
Melissa	Turcica flore albo, *Turkie-Balme with white flower.*	*Dracocephalum moldavica* Lam. or *Cedronella triphylla* Moench
	vulgaris, *common garden Balm.*	*Melissa officinalis* L.
Mentha	citrata sive Ocimi odore, *the Basil smelling Mint.*	*Mentha citrata* Ehrh.
	crispa, *crisped or curled Mint.*	*Mentha spicata* L. var. 'Crispa'
	hortensis, *garden Mint.*	*Mentha spicata* L.
Mentastrum	niveū Anglicū, *the white English wilde Mint.*	*Mentha longifolia* (L.) Hudson var. 'Mollissima'
	vulgare, *common wilde Mint.*	*Mentha longifolia* (L.) Hudson
Mercurialis	mas, *French male Mercury.*	*Mercurialis annua* L.
	fœmina, *French female Mercury.*	
	Anglica, bonus Henricus, *English Mercury.*	*Chenopodium bonus-henricus* L.
Mespilus	fructu magno, *great Medler.*	*Mespilus germanica* L. (forms or cvs.)
	fructu medio, *middle sort of Medler.*	
	vulg: seu minor, *ordinary small sort of Medler.*	
	aronia Neopolitana, *Medler of Naples.*	*Crataegus azarolus* L.
Meum athamanticum, *Mew or Spignell.*		*Meum athamanticum* Jacq.

Mezeræon	album	Daphne mezereum L. var. 'Alba'
	rubrum	Daphne mezereum L.
	semine nigro, *black Millet.*	Panicum miliaceum L. (form)
Milium	semine flavo, *Millet with yellow seed.*	Setaria italica (L.) Beauv. (form)
	album, *common white Millet.*	Panicum miliaceum L. (form)
	majus album, *great white flowered Yarrow.*	? Achillea nobilis L.
	ma: purpureum, *great purple Yarrow.*	Achillea millefolium L. var. 'Rosea'
	minus luteum, *small yellow Yarrow.*	Achillea tomentosa L.
Millefoliū	atro rubente flore, *ruddy black Yarrow.*	? Achillea millefolium L. (form)
	vulgare, *Yarrow, or Milfoile.*	Achillea millefolium L.
	sive Maratriphyllum, fore & semine Baccunculi aquat: *water-Fennel, Crowfoot Milfoile.*	Ranunculus trichophyllus Chaix
Millegrana, *Allseed.*		Radiola linoides Roth.
Mirabilia Peruviana	flore albo & purp: *Marvell of Peru with white and purple flowers.*	Mirabilis jalapa L.
	flore luteo & rubro, *Marvell of Peru with yellow and red flowers.*	
Mirabilia *from Barbados.*		? Mirabilis dichotoma L.
Moly	Moly *or wilde Garlick.*	Allium subhirsutum L.
	Virginianum Bauhini, *Bauhins Virginian Moly.*	Tradescantia virginiana L.
Mollugo, *Madder.*		? Galium mollugo L.
Morsus Diaboli, *Devils bit.*		Succisa pratensis Moench
Morsus Ranæ, *Frogge bit.*		Hydrocharis morsus-ranae L.
Morus	nigra, *black Mulbury.*	Morus nigra L.
	alba, *white Mulbury.*	Morus alba L.
	Virginiana, *Virginian Mulbury*	Morus rubra L.
	terrestris vulgaris, *common Mosse.*	Hypnum velutinum L.
	terrestris scoparius, *Beesome Mosse.*	? Bryum scoparium L.
Muscus	Pixidatus, *Cuppe or Challice Mosse.*	Cladonia pyxidata (L.) Hoffm.
	clavatus, *club Mosse.*	Lycopodium clavatum L.
	arboreus, *tree Mosse.*	? Usnea plicata (L.) Wigg.
	filicinus, *Fern like Mosse.*	Hypnum parietinum L.
	Coralloides, *Coraline Mosse.*	? Cladonia rangiferina (L.) Wigg.
Muscari	flore luteo.	Muscari macrocarpum Sweet
	flore albo.	Muscari botryoides (L) Miller
Myagrum monospermon, *one grain'd gold of pleasure.*		Myagrum perfoliatum L.
Myosotis	scorpoides palustr: *Water-Scorpion grasse.*	Myosotis scorpioides L.
	scorpo: arvensis, *Mouseare Scorpion grasse.*	Myosotis arvensis (L.) Hill
Myrrhis sativus, *sweet Ferne.*		Myrrhis odorata (L.) Scop.
Myrtus	latifolia, *great leafed Myrtle.*	Myrtus communis L. (type)
	angustifolia, *small Myrtle.*	Myrtus communis L. var. tarentina
	florida.	Myrtus communis L. cv. 'Flore Pleno'

N.

Napellus, *Monkes hood.*		Aconitum napellus L.
Narcissus	medio Croceus, *meane yellow Daffodill.*	Narcissus tazetta L.
	Anglic: flo: pleno Wilmot: *Wilmots double Daffodill.*	Narcissus pseudo-narcissus L. f. Telamonius Plenus
	roseus maximus flore pleno Tradescanti, *Tradescant's great rose Daffodill.*	Narcissus plenissimus
	Africanus odoratus, *sweet Daffodill of Africa.*	Narcissus x odorus L.
	Africanus major præcox, *great early African Daffodill.*	? Narcissus tazetta L. (form)
	Indicus Jacobæus, *Indian Daffodill.*	Sprekelia formosissima Herb.

Narcissus	Capa bonæ spei, *Daffodill from the Cape of good Hope.*	Crinum capense Herb.
	tertius Matthioli, *great white sea Daffodill.*	Pancratium illyricum L.
	Montis Carmeli, *Daffodill from Mount Carmel.*	? Narcissus tazetta L. subsp. lacticolor Baker
	Virginianus, *Virginian Daffodill.*	Zephyranthes atamasco Herb.
	medio fimbriatus, *mean ringed Daffodill.*	Narcissus poeticus L.
	Robinus major.	Narcissus pseudo-narcissus L. var.
	Indicus bifolius flore rubro, squamosa radice, *Morini.*	Haemanthus coccineus L.
	juncifolius luteo flore pleno, *great yellow rush Daffodill.*	Narcissus bulbocodium L. var.
	humilis, *dwarfe Daffodill.*	Narcissus minor L.
	reflex flo: lut: *yellow Daffodill whose flowers turn upwards.*	Narcissus triandrus L. var. concolor
	relex flo: albo, *white turning Daffodill.*	Narcissus triandrus L. var. triandrus
	oblong: calice flo: luteo, *yellow Daffodill with a long cup.*	? Narcissus triandrus L. var. concolor
	oblong: calice flore albo, *white Daffodill with a long cup.*	? Narcissus triandrus L. var. loiseleurii
	calice brevi, *short cupp'd Daffodill.*	—
	titesose.	
	va Hecuus.	Narcissus 'Van Heck'
	omnium maximus, *great Nonsuch Daffodill.*	Narcissus x incomparabilis Miller
	montanus, *mountaine Daffodill.*	Narcissus x poculiformis L.
	Non-pareil flore albo, *white peerlesse Daffodill.*	Narcissus x incomparabilis Miller cvs.
	Non-pareil, *Nonpareill or peerlesse Daffodill.*	
	Constantinopolitanus, *Daffadill from Constantinople.*	? Narcissus tazetta L.
	totus albus, *milk-white Daffodill.*	Narcissus tazetta L. subsp. papyraceus (Ker-Gawl.) Baker
	Matinesse, *the Lady Mattenesse's Daffodill.*	N. x incomparabilis Miller (form)
Lilio Narcissus Indicus, *Morini.*		? Amaryllis belladonna L.
Narsturtium	Indicum, *Indian Cresse.*	Tropaeolum minus L.
	hortense crispum, *curled garden Cresse.*	Lepidium sativum L. (forms)
	hort: angustifolium & latifolium, *great and small leafed Cresse.*	
	Hyemale, sc: Barbaræa, *Bank-Cresse.*	Barbarea vulgaris R. Br.
Nepeta, Mentha Cattaria, *Neppe.*		Nepeta cataria L.
Nicotiana, *English Tobacco.*		Nicotiana rustica L.
Nidus avis, sive Satyrion abortivum, *Birds nest.*		Neottia nidus-avis (L.) Rich.
Nigella	flo: pleno, *double Nigella.*	Nigella damascena L. var. 'Flore Pleno'
	citrina, *yellowish seeded Nigella.*	Nigella hispanica L.
	flo: simplici, *single Nigella.*	Nigella damascena L.
	Romana, *Fennell flower, or Roman Nigella.*	Nigella sativa L.
Nummularia	major, *great Moneywort.*	Lysimachia nummularia L.
	minor, *flore purpurascente.*	Anagallis tenella (L.) L.
	juglans Virginiana, *Wallnut of Virginia.*	Carya ovata K. Koch.
	vesicaria, *Bladder-nut.*	Staphylea pinnata L.
	castanea Equina, *Horse-Chestnut.*	Aesculus hippocastanum L.
Nux	Juglans Canadensis, *Walnut of Canada.*	Juglans cinerea L. or J. nigra L.
	Juglans Angliæ novæ, *Walnut of New England.*	Juglans nigra L. or J cinerea L.
	Juglans major, *great Walnut.*	Juglans regia L. var. maxima
	Juglans minor, *small Walnut.*	Juglans regia L.

O.

Ocimum	vulgare, *common Basil.*	*Ocimum basilicum* L.
	sylv: sive Clinopodium vulg: *wilde Basil.*	*Clinopodium vulgare* L.
Oculus Christi, *wilde Clary.*		*Salvia horminoides* Pourr.
Oenanthe	bulbosa marina venenosa, *the poysonous sea Dropwort.*	*Oenanthe crocata* L.
	aquatica, *water Dropwort.*	*Oenanthe fistulosa* L.
Olea	sativa, *manured Olive.*	*Olea europaea* L.
	sylvestris, *Wilde Olive.*	*Olea europaea* L. var. *oleaster*
	Bohemia, *Bohemian Olive.*	*Elaeagnus angustifolia* L.
Oleander	flore albo, *Rose-bay with white flowers.*	*Nerium oleander* L. (form)
	flore rubro, *Rose-bay with red flowers.*	*Nerium oleander* L.
Olus album, *Dod.*		*Valerianella locusta* (L.) Betcke
Onobrichis	caput Gallinaceum, *Cockshead.*	*Onobrychis viciifolia* Scop.
	flore purpureo, *purple Cockshead.*	*Astragalus onobrychis* L.
Ononis	non spinosa Pyrenæa, *the smooth Pyrenean harrow.*	*Ononis spinosa* L. var.
	non spinosa oderata flore luteo, *sweet smooth Rest-harrow with yellow flowers.*	*Ononis speciosa* Lag.
	non spinosa æstiva minor flore luteo, *small smooth Summer Rest-harrow with yellow flowers.*	*Ononis natrix* L.
	spinosa, *prickly Rest harrow.*	*Ononis spinosa* L.
Ophyoglosson, *Adders tongue.*		*Ophioglossum vulgatum* L.
Ophris, sive Bifolium, *Tway blade.*		*Listera ovata* (L.) R. Br.
Orchis	melissias, *Bee Orchis, or Satyrion.*	*Ophrys apifera* Hudson
	albo calcare oblongo, sive Testiculus Vulpinus, *Gnat Satyrion.*	*Platanthera bifolia* (L.) Rich.
	flore albo odorato, *Lady Traces.*	*Herminium monorchis* (L.) R. Br.
	flo: luteo odorato, *Lady Traces with yellow flower.*	*Spiranthes aestivalis* (Porr.) L.C.M. Rich.
	palmata montana maculata, *whitehanded Orchis.*	*Dactylorhiza maculata* (L.) Sóo. (white form)
	palmata palustris latifolia, *Marish Satyrion.*	*Dactylorhiza incarnata* (L.) Sóo
	palmata palustris maculata, *spotted Marish Satyrion.*	? *Dactylorhiza traunsteineri* (Sauter) Sóo.
Origanum	Anglicanum, *wilde Marjoram.*	*Origanum vulgare* L.
	fistulosum Canadense.	*Monarda fistulosa* L.
	verum Hispanicū, *true Spanish Marjoram.*	*Origanum heracleoticum* L.
Ornithogalum	Neapolitanum maj: *great Sarreflower of Naples.*	*Ornithogalum nutans* L.
	Arabicum, *Starre-flower of Arabia.*	*Ornithogalum arabicum* L.
	majus flo: albo, *great white Starre-flower.*	*Ornithogalum pyrenaicum* L.
	purpureum, *purple Starre-flower.*	*Endymion hispanicus* (Miller) Chouard
	spicatum, *spiked Starre of Bethlehem.*	? *Ornithogalum narbonense* L.
Ornithopodium	majus, *great Birds foot.*	*Ornithopus perpusillus* L. var.
	minus, *small Birds foot.*	*Ornithopus perpusillus* L. (type).
Orobus	Venetus, *blew upright everlasting Pease.*	*Lathyrus venetus* (Miller) Wohlf.
	Pannonicus Clusii, *Hungarian.*	*Lathyrus vernus* Bernh.
Osmunda regalis, Filix florida, *water-Ferne, or Osmund Royall.*		*Osmunda regalis* L.
Oxyacantha	Dioscoridis, spina alba major.	? *Crataegus monogyna* Jacq.
	Gal: spina acuta *Dod:* vulg: *Berberis.*	*Berberis vulgaris* L.
	berberis absque nucleis.	*Berberis vulgaris* var. 'Asperma'
Oxys trifolia	flore albo, *wood-Sorrell with white flower.*	*Oxalis acetosella* L.
	flore luteo carniculato, *yellow flowered Wood-Sorrell.*	*Oxalis corniculata* L.

P.

Paliurus, *Christs Thorne*

Palma Christi
{ mas, *male hand Orchys*
foemina, *female hand Orchys.*

Pœonia
{ mas flore simplici, *single male Piony.*
fœmina flore simplici, *single female Piony.*
fœmina flore pleno, *double female Piony.*
flore pleno incarnato.
flore purpureo, *purple Piony.*

Panax coloni, *Clownes Alheale.*

Pappas
{ solanum tuberosum Esculentū Bauhin: *Virginian Potatoes.*
Americanum flore albo, *white flowred American Potatoes.*
Amer: flo: purp: *Potatoes from America with purple flower.*

Papaver
{ spumeum, sive Behen alb: *spatling Poppy.*
rhæas flore luteo radice perpetua.
rhæas flore simplici, *single Poppy.*
rhæas flore duplici, *double Poppy.*
nigrum capit: rotundis.
corniculatum flore luteo, *horn Poppy.*
rhæas, *red Poppy, Corn rose.*

Paralysis
{ flore viridante simplic: *single green Cowslip.*
fatua, *foolish Cowslip, or Jack-an-Apes on Horsback.*
inodora geminata, *double Oxlips, or Hose in Hose.*
flo: & calice crispo, *curled Cowslips or Gaskins.*

Parietaria, *Pellitory of the Wall.*

Paronychia
{ folio alsine vulgaris, *Chickweed, whitlow Chickweed.*
Rutae folio altera Ger: sedum, *Rue whitlow grasse.*

Pastinaca
{ latif: sativa, *garden Parsnip.*
latifol: sylvestris, *great wilde Parsnip.*
aquatica, *sc:* Sium Dioscoridis, *water Parsnip.*

Pathenium, *Feverfew.*

Pecten veneris, *Shepherds Needle, or Venus Combe.*

Pedicularis
{ rubra, *red Ratle, or Lousewort.*
pratensis lutea, *yellow Ratle Coxcombe.*

Pentaphyllon
{ elatium & heptaphyllum luteū erectum.
repens vulg: flore luteo, *yellow creeping Cinquefoyle, or Five-leafed grasse.*
minus, *small Cinquefoyle.*
rubrū palustre, *marsh Cinquefoyle.*

Pepo
{ Americanus luteus, *yellow Ponpian from America.*
Americanus viridis, *green American Pompian.*

Perchpier Anglorum, *Parsley breakestone.*

Perfoliata vulgaris, *common Thorow-wax.*

Paliurus spina-christi Miller
Dactylorhiza incarnata (L.) Sóo.
Dactylorhiza fuchsii (Druce) Sóo.
Paeonia mascula (L.) Miller
Paeonia officinalis L.

} *Paeonia officinalis* L. vars.

Stachys palustris L.
Helianthus tuberosus L.

} *Solanum tuberosum* L. (forms)

Silene vulgaris (Moench) Garcke
Meconopsis cambrica (L.) Vig.
Papaver rhoeas L.
Papaver rhoeas L. var.
Papaver somniferum L.
Glaucium flavum Crantz.
Papaver rhoeas L.

} *Primula veris* L. (forms)

Parietaria diffusa Mert. & Koch.
Erophila verna (L.) Chevall.

Saxifraga tridactylites L.

} *Pastinaca sativa* L. (forms)

Sium latifolium L.

Chrysanthemum parthenium (L.) Bernh.
Scandix pecten-veneris L.
Pedicularis sylvatica L.
Rhinanthus minor L.
Potentilla erecta (L.) Räusch.
Potentilla reptans L.

Potentilla tabernaemontani Aschers.
Potentilla palustris (L.) Scop.

} *Cucurbita pepo* L. (forms).

Aphanes arvensis L.
Bupleurum rotundifolium L.

Periclymenum	rectum 2. Clusii, *upright Woodbine.*	*Lonicera nigra* L.
	fructu ceracino.	? *Lonicera alpigena* L.
	hortense, *garden Woodbine.*	*Lonicera caprifolium* L.
	Germ: flo: rubro, *red Woodbine.*	*Lonicera periclymenum* L. cv. 'Belgica' or 'Serotina'
	sylvestris, *wilde Woodbine.*	*Lonicera periclymenum* L.
Periploca, *Dogs bane.*		*Periploca graeca* L.
Persicaria	siliquosa, *codded Arsmart.*	*Impatiens noli-tangere* L.
	maculosa, flore albo & rubro, *spotted Arsmart with white and red flower.*	*Polygonum persicaria* L.
	urens, flore albo & rubro, *white and red quick Arsmart.*	*Polygonum hydropiper* L.
	Virginiana, *Virginian Arsmart.*	*Polygonum virginianum* L.
Petasitis, *Butter-burre.*		*Petasites hybridus* (L.) Gaertner., Mey. & Scherb.

Petroselinum, *vide* Apium.
Peucedanum, *Hogs-fewell, or Sulphur-wort.*   *Peucedanum officinale* L.

Phalangium	Alobrogum Clusii, *Savoy Spiderwort.*	*Paradisea liliastrum* Bertol.
	Virginianū Tradescanti, *Tradescants Virginian Spiderwort.*	*Tradescantia virginiana* L.
Phalaris	sativa, *Canary seed.*	*Phalaris canariensis* L.
	pratensis minor, *Quaking grass or Cowquake.*	*Briza media* L.
Phaseolus	Indicus flo: miniato, semine nigro.	*Phaseolus coccineus* L.
	Indicus flore miniato, semine variegato.	
Phaseolorum variæ species.		*Phaseolus vulgaris* L. etc.
Philyrea angustifolia, *narow-leafed mock Privet.*		*Phillyrea angustifolia* L.
Phyllitis	vulg: lingua Cervina, *Harts-tongue.*	*Phyllitis scolopendrium* (L.) Newm.
	multifida, finger *Harts-tongue.*	*Phyllitis scolopendrium* (L.) Newm. var. *multifida*
Pilosella	major Dod: *great Mouseare.*	*Hieracium holosericeum* Backh.
	repens, *creeping Mouseare.*	*Hieracium pilosella* L.
Pimpinella	sive sanguisorba maj. *great Burnet.*	*Sanguisorba officinalis* L.
	sanguisorba min: *small or little Burnet.*	*Pimpinella saxifraga* L.
	saxifraga, *Burnet saxifrage.*	*Pimpinella major* (L.) Hudson
	sativa, *garden Burnet.*	*Poterium sanguisorba* L.
	agrimonoides Colum.	*Sanguisorba hybrida* (L.) Nordborg
	sylv: vulg: *common Burnet.*	*Sanguisorba officinalis* L.
Pinus, *Pine-tree.*		*Pinus pinea* L.
Pinaster, *dwarfe Pine tree.*		*Pinus pinaster* Aiton
Pirola, *Winter green.*		*Pyrola rotundifolia* L.
Pistolochia	smilacis folio.	*Aristolochia pistolochia* L.
	Virginiana, *Virginian Snakeweed.*	*Aristolochia serpentaria* L.
Pisum	perenne, *Pease everlasting.*	*Vicia pisiformis* L.
	bacciferum.	? *Cardiospermum halicacabum* L.
	maculatum, *spotted Pease.*	? *Dolichos lablab* L.
	majus, *rouncivall Pease.*	*Pisum sativum* L. (forms)
	minus, *field Pease.*	
	quadratum, lotus quad: *square Pease.*	*Tetragonolobus purpureus* Moench
	vulgare, *garden Pease.*	*Pisum sativum* L.
Plantago	major rosea, *great rose Plantane.*	*Plantago major* L. var. 'Rosularis'
	rosea spicata, sive quinque nervia rosea, *spiked rose Ribwort.*	*Plantago lanceolata* L. var.
	serato folio, *Plantane with dented leaves.*	*Plantago serraria* L.
	aquatica major, *great water Plantane.*	*Alisma plantago-aquatica* L.
	aquatica minor, *small water Plantane.*	*Damasonium alisma* Miller
	vulgaris, *common Plantane.*	*Plantago major* L.

Platanus, *Plane tree.* — Platanus orientalis L.

Polium montanum, *Poley mountaine.* — Teucrium polium L.

Polygala
- Valentina, 1. Clusii, *ever-green Sene of Valentia.* — Coronilla valentina L.
- Valentina, 2. Clusii. — ? Coronilla juncea L.
- flore cæruleo, *blew Milkwort.* ⎫
- flore albo, *white Milkwort.* ⎬ Polygala vulgaris L. (forms)
- flore rubro, *red Milkwort.* ⎭

Polygonatum
- majus, sigillum Solomonis, *broad leafed Solomons seal.* — Polygonatum odoratum (Miller) Druce
- angustifoliū, *narrow-leafed Solomons seal.* — Polygonatum verticillatum (L.) All. var.
- minus, *small Solomons seal.* — Polygonatum verticillatum (L.) All.
- racemosum Virginianum, *cluster like Solomon's seale of Virginia.* — Smilacina racemosa (L.) Desf.
- alterum. — ? Streptopus amplexifolius (L.) DC.
- vulgare, *Solomons seal.* — Polygonatum multiflorum (L.) All.

Polygonum
- marinum Lobelii, *Lobel's sea-Knotgrasse.* — Polygonum raii Bab.
- mas vulgare, *common Knotgrasse.* — Polygonum aviculare L. agg.
- selinoides, Perpierre Anglorū, *Parsley Pert.* — Scleranthus annuus L.

Pomum aureum, fructu luteo, *Morini.* ⎫
(?†) Prickly Costard, apple from Barbados. ⎬ Annona muricata L.
Poma amoris, *Apples of Love.* ⎫
Pomum amoris medium, *middle-sized Apples of Love.* ⎬ Lycopersicon esculentum Miller cvs.
Pomum amoris fructu, Phoeniceo rubro, *Morini.* ⎭

Populus
- *†alba Virginiana Tradescanti, Tradescant's white Virginina Poplar.* — ? Liriodendron tulipifera L.
- alba, *white Poplar tree.* — Populus alba L.
- nigra, *black Poplar tree.* — Populus nigra L.
- tremula, sive Lybica, *the Aspen tree.* — Populus tremula L.

Porrum vulgare, *common Leeks.* — Allium porrum L.

Portulaca
- marina, *sea Purslan.* — Halimione portulacoides (L.) Aellen
- sativa, *garden Purslan.* — Portulaca oleracea L. var. sativa
- aquat: sive Alsine rotundifol: *water Purslan.* — Lythrum portula (L.) D.A. Webb

Potamogeiton
- angustifol: *small Pondweed.* — Polygonum amphibium L.
- latif: *great Pondweed.* — Potamogeton natans L.

Potentilla, sive Argentina, *wilde Tansey.* — Potentilla anserina L.

Primula
- veris, flore albo, *white Primrose.* ⎫
- veris, albo, flore pleno, *double white Primrose.* ⎬ Primula vulgaris Hudson cvs.
- veris, flore pleno viride, *double green Primrose.* ⎭
- veris, angustifolia flore albo, *narrow leafed white Primrose.* — Primula farinosa L. (form) *alba*
- veris, angustifolia flore rubro, *narrow-leafed red Primrose.* — Primula farinosa L. (type)
- veris, flo: viridi & albo simpl: *single green and white Primrose.* — Primula vulgaris Hudson cv.
- veris major, *field Cowslips.* — Primula veris L.
- veris minor, *field Primrose.* — Primula vulgaris Hudson
- *veris vulg: flore purpureo, purple Primrose.* — Primula vulgaris Hudson subsp. sibthorpii (Hoffmanns) W.W.Sm. & Forrest

Prunus
- sylvestris, *Bullace tree.* — Prunus domestica L. subsp. *institia*
- sylvestris fructu minore serotino, *the Slowe tree, or blacke Thorne.* — Prunus spinosa L.

Prunus	Myrobolanus, *purging Indian Plumme.*	? *Diospyros lotus* L. and/or D. *Virginiana* L. or *Chrysobalanus icaco* L.
Prunella	{ flore albo, *White Selfeheale.* vulgaris, *Selfeheale.*	*Prunella grandiflora* L. var. '*Alba*' *Prunella vulgaris* L.

Pseudo-Dictamnus, *bastard Dittany.* — *Ballota acetabulosa* (L.) Benth.

Pseudo Narcissus vulgaris, *our common English wilde bastard Daffodill.* — *Narcissus pseudo-narcissus* L.

Pseudo Rhabarbarum, Rhabarbarum Monachorum, *Monks Rhubarbe.* — *Rumex patientia* L.

Psyllium, Coniza, *Fleawort.* — *Plantago indica* L.

Ptarmica	flore pleno, *double flowered Sneezwort.*	*Achillea ptarmica* L. var. '*Flore Pleno*'
	vulgaris, *Sneezwort, bastard Pellitory.*	*Achillea ptarmica* L.
	flore duplici, *Morini.*	*Achillea ptarmica* L. cv.
Pulegium	Regale, *great Penyroyall, Pudding grasse.*	*Mentha pulegium* L. var. '*Erecta*'
	minus vulgare, *small Penyroyall.*	*Mentha pulegium* L.
	Cervinum, *Harts Penyroyall.*	*Mentha cervina* L.
Pulmonaria	flore albo, *white-flowered Lungwort.*	*Pulmonaria officinalis* L. var. '*Alba*'
	flore purpureo maj: Germanicum.	? *Pulmonaria longifolia* (Bast.) Bor.
	flore purpureo vulg: *common purple flowred Lungwort.*	? *Pulmonaria officinalis* L.
	Galloru Hieralitis, *the lesser French or golden Lungwort.*	*Hieracium exotericum* Jord.
	maculosa, *spotted Lungwort.*	*Pulmonaria officinalis* L. (form)
Pulsatilla	{ flore violaceo, *purple Pasque flower.* vulgaris, *single Pasque flower.*	*Pulsatilla vulgaris* Miller (form) *Pulsatilla vulgaris* Miller
Pyrocantha	{ vulg: *ever-green Thorne.* Virginiana ma: non hyemalis virescit.	*Pyracantha coccinea* M.J. Roemer ? *Crataegus persistens* Sarg.

Q.

Quercus vulgaris, *common Oake.* — *Quercus robur* L.

Quinque nerva	{ vulg: *common Ribwort.* Rosea, *rose Ribwort.*	*Plantago lanceolata* L. *Plantago lanceolata* L. (form)

Qamoclet Indorum. — *Quamoclit pennata* Boj.

R.

Radix	cava major flore purpureo, *great purple Hollow root.*	*Corydalis bulbosa* (L.) DC.
	cava minor flore albo, *small white Hollow root.*	*Corydalis bulbosa* (L.) DC. var. '*Albiflora*'
	cava vulgaris, *common Hollow root.*	? *Corydalis solida* (L.) Sw.
Ranunculus	albus flore pleno, *double white Crowfoot.*	*Ranunculus aconitifolius* L. var. '*Flore Pleno*'
	arvensis echinatus flore luteo, *yellow rough-headed Crowfoot of Fallow field.*	*Ranunculus arvensis* L.
	aquatilis, *water Crowfoot.*	*Ranunculus aquatilis* L.
	Asiaticus sangu: flore pleno, *double Asian Crowfoot with a blood-red flower.*	
	Asiat: tenuifol: pleno flo: luteo, *thin-leafed Asian Crowfoot with double yellow flower.*	*Ranunculus asiaticus* L. cvs.
	Asiat: flore albo, *white Asian Crowfoot.*	
	Lusitanicus odoratus flore duplici, *Morini.*	*Ranunculus bullatus* L. var.
	Asiaticus flore rubro, *red Asian Crowfoot.*	
	Asiat: flore luteo, *yellow Asian Crowfoot.*	
	Asat: folio papaveris, *Asian Crowfoot with a Poppy-leaf.*	*Ranunculus asiaticus* L. cvs.
	Asiat: Drape de argentine.	

	Illyricus, *Crowfoot of Sclavonia.*	
	Illyricus major, *greater Crowfoot of Sclavonia.*	} *Ranunculus illyricus* L.
	radice grumosa, folio rutæ, flo: pleno.	*Callianthemum rutaefolium* C.A. Mey. var.
	aquaticus hederaceus luteus, *Ivy leafed water-Crowfoot.*	*Ranunculus hederaceus* L.
Ranunculus	hortensis flore luteo pleno, *double yellow garden-Crowfoot.*	*Ranunculus acris* L. var. 'Flore Pleno'
	vulg: repens flore pleno, *common creeping Crowfoot with double flower.*	*Ranunculus repens* L. var. 'Flore Pleno'
	pratensis, *meddow-Crowfoot.*	*Ranunculus acris* L.
	Virginianus, *Virginian Crowfoot.*	*Sanguinaria canadensis* L.
	albus multiflorus, *double white Crowfoot.*	*? Ranunculus aconitifolius* L. var.
	Globosus, *Globe Crowfoot.*	*Trollius europaeus* L.
	aquaticus, *water-Radish.*	*Rorippa amphibia* (L.) Besser.
Raphanus	rusticanus, *Horse-Radish.*	*Armoracia rusticana* Gaertner
	niger per annū, *black Radish.*	*Raphanus sativus* L. var.
	sativus, *garden-Radish.*	*Raphanus sativus* L.
Rapistrum arvorum, *Charlock.*		*Sinapis arvensis* L.
	radice rotunda, *round Turnips.*	
Rapum	radice oblonga, *long Turnips.*	} *Brassica rapa* L. (forms)
	radice lutea, *yellow Turnips.*	?
Rapuntium, *Rampions.*		*Phyteuma spicatum* L.
Rha capitatum folio enulæ, *Morini.*		*Centaurea rhapontica* L.
	major, *great base wilde Rochet.*	*Reseda alba* L.
Reseda	ma: Italica flore albo, *Italian Rocket with white flower.*	*Reseda alba* L. (form)
	minor, flore albo lutescente.	*Reseda lutea* L.
Rhabarbarum verum, *true Rubarbe.*		*Rheum rhaponticum* L.
Rhamnus	min: Dioscoridis, *small Buckthorne.*	*? Rhamnus pumilus* Turra.
	Catharticus, *Buckthorne.*	*Rhamnus catharticus* L.
Rhus Plinii myrtifolia Monspeliensium, *Virginian: Jasmini foliis.*		*Coriaria myrtifolia* L. and *Rhus typhina* L.
Ribesium dulce, *sweet wilde Currans.*		*Ribes rubrum* L. var.
	fructu rubro, *red Currans.*	*Ribes rubrum* L.
Ribes	fructu albo, *white Currans.*	*Ribes rubrum* L. var. 'Fructu Albo'
	fructu nigro, *black Currans.*	*Ribes nigrum* L.
	fructu spinoso, *prickly Currans.*	*? Ribes uva-crispa* L.
Ricinus Austrica flore Phœniceo, *Palma Christi of Austria, or great Spurge with Vermilion-flower.*		*? Jatropha gossypifolia* L.
Rorella, *sc:* Ros solis, *Sun-dew, or Rosa solis.*		*Drosera rotundifolia* L.
	Provincialis, *Province Rose.*	
	Provincialis flore albo, *white Province Rose.*	} *Rosa centifolia* L. cvs.
	Provincialis flore rubro, *red Province Rose.*	
	vitriensis flore pleno.	—
	Incarnata, *carnation Rose.*	*? Rosa incarnata* Miller
Rosa	flo: pleno luteo, *double yellow Rose.*	*Rosa hemisphaerica* J. Herrm.
	flore luteo simplici, *single yellow Rose.*	*Rosa foetida* J. Herrm.
	muscata flore pleno, *double Muske Rose.*	*Rosa moschata* J. Herrm. var. 'Flore Pleno'
	Italica, sive muscata flo: simp: *single Muske Rose.*	*Rosa moschata* J. Herrm.
	Cynamonia flore pleno, *Cinamon Rose.*	*Rosa majalis* J. Herrm. var.
	Cinamonia flore albo, *white Cinamon Rose.*	—
	Francofurtiana, *Frankford Rose.*	*Rosa francofurtana* Muenchh.

	Batavica.	*Rosa centifolia* L.
	alba variegata, *white variable Rose.*	—
	flo: pleno elegans variegata, *dainty double variable Rose.*	—
	flore simplici pomifera, *single apple Rose.*	*Rosa villosa* L.
	Virginiana, *Virginian Rose.*	*Rosa virginiana* Miller
	Moscovita, *Moscovie Rose.*	? *Rosa acicularis* Lindl.
	canina flore pleno, *double Dogrose.*	—
	canina flore simplici, *single Dogrose.*	*Rosa canina* L.
	Eglanteria flore pleno, *double Eglantine or sweet-Bryerbush.*	*Rosa rubiginosa* L. var. '*Duplex*'
Rosa	Eglanteria flore simplici, *single Egglantine Rose.*	*Rosa rubiginosa* L.
	holoserica, *velvet Rose.*	*Rosa gallica* L. var. '*Holosericea*'
	semper virens, *ever-green Rosebush.*	*Rosa sempervirens* L.
	flore rubro, *red Rose.*	*Rosa gallica* L.
	flore albo, *white Rose.*	*Rosa* x *alba* L.
	Damascena, *Damaske Rose.*	*Rosa damascena* Miller
	mensalis, *monthly Rose.*	*Rosa* x *bifera* Hurst
	Warneri, *Warner's Rose.*	—
	sylv: pimpinellæ folio, *Burnet Rose.*	*Rosa pimpinellifolia* L.
	Austriaca flore Phœniceo, *Vermilian Rose of Austria.*	*Rosa foetida* J. Herrm. var. '*Bicolor*'
	Hieorchuntina.	*Anastatica hierochuntica* L.
Rosmarinus	Coronarius latifolius, *great Rosemary.* Coronarius angustifolius, *narrow leafed Rosemary.* foliis aureis, *gilded Rosemary.* foliis argenteis, *silverd Rosemary.* Coronarius maximus.	*Rosmarinus officinalis* L. vars.
Rubia	Major tinctorum, *great garden-Madder.*	*Rubia tinctorum* L.
	minor, *small Madder.*	? *Galium pumilum* Murr.
	sylvestris.	*Rubia peregrina* L.
	Idæus fructu albo & rubro, *white and red Raspberries.*	*Rubus idaeus* L. vars.
Rubus	Idæus non spinosus, gratissimo odore flo: purpureo.	*Rubus odoratus* L.
	sylvestris, *the Bramble-bush, or Blackberry-bush.*	*Rubus fruticosus* L. agg.
Ruscus, Bruscus, Oximersine, *Butchers Broome.*		*Ruscus aculeatus* L.
Ruta	hortensis, *garden-Rue.*	*Ruta graveolens* L.
	muraria, sive salvia vitæ, *Wall-Rue.*	*Asplenium ruta-muraria* L.
	pratensis, sive Thalictrum, *meddow-Rue.*	*Thalictrum flavum* L.

S.

Sabina	baccifera, *Berry bearing Savin.*	*Juniperus sabina* L.
	vulgaris, sive stirilis, *barren Savin.*	*Juniperus sabina* L. ? var. '*Mas*'
	stirilis cupressi facie.	*Juniperus sabina* L. var. '*Erecta*'
Sagitaria	major, *broad Arrowhead.*	*Sagittaria sagittifolia* L.
	minor, *small Arrowhead.*	*Sagittaria sagittifolia* L. var. *parvifolia*
Saginæ spergula, *Spurry.*		*Spergula arvensis* L.
	humilis angustifolia, *the Osier.*	*Salix purpurea* L.
Salix	caprea rotundif: *round-leafed Sallow, or great Goats-Willow.* caprea latifolia, *broad or rather long-leafed Willow, small Goats Willow.*	*Salix caprea* L. (forms)
	vulgaris arborescens longis, angustis foliis, *common Willow.*	*Salix alba* L.

	variegata, *painted Sage.*	*Salvia officinalis* L. var. *tricolor*
	hortensis rubra, *red garden-Sage.*	*Salvia officinalis* L. var. *purpurascens*
Salvia	hortensis viridis, *green garden-Sage.*	*Salvia officinalis* L.
	major foliis crispis, *great crisped Sage.*	*Salvia officinalis* L. var. *crispa*
	minor odoratissima.	*Salvia officinalis* L. subsp. 'Minor'
	agrestis, *Wood Sage.*	*Teucrium scorodonia* L.
	aquatica, *water-Elder.*	*Viburnum opulus* L.
	vulgaris, *common Elder.*	*Sambucus nigra* L.
Sambucus	aquatica simplex, *single marsh-Elder.*	*Viburnum opulus* L.
	Rosea, *sc:* aquatica multiplex Ro: *the Gelder Rose.*	*Viburnum opulus* L. var. *sterile*
	laciniatis foliis, *jagged Elder.*	*Sambucus nigra* L. var. 'Laciniata'
	vera vulgaris, *Sanicle.*	*Sanicula europaea* L.
Sanicula	alpina guttata, sive Auricula ursi, *spotted Sanicle of the Alpes.*	*Cortusa matthioli* L.
	Hispanica guttata, *Spanish spotted Sanicle.*	*Saxifraga hirsuta* L.
	flore pleno, *double Soapwort.*	*Saponaria officinalis* L. var. 'Plena'
	flore simplice, *single-flowered Soapwort.*	*Saponaria officinalis* L.
	Alpina flo: pleno, *double Soapwort of the Alpes.*	*Saponaria ocymoides* L. var.
Saponaria	concava *sc:* exautica folio caulem obtigentem R. *hallow-Felwort or Soapwort.*	*Saponaria officinalis* L. (form)
Satureia	semper virens, *Winter-Savory.*	*Satureia montana* L.
	annua, *Summer Savory.*	*Satureia hortensis* L.

Satyrion, *vide* Orchy's.

	alba, *white Saxifrage.*	*Saxifraga granulata* L.
	aurea, *golden Saxifrage.*	*Chrysoplenium oppositifolium* L.
	Anglicana alsine folio, *English Saxifrage with Chickweed leaves*	*Sagina procumbens* L.
Saxifraga	Angl: umbellata *sc:* facie seseli, *common Saxifrage.*	*Silaum silaus* (L.) Schinz. & Thell.
	pimpinella major, *great burnet Saxifrage.*	*Pimpinella major* (L.) Hudson
	pimpinella minor, *small burnet Saxifrage.*	*Pimpinella saxifraga* L.
	Hispanica major, *great Spanish Scabious.*	
	Hispanica Clusii, *Clusius his Spanish Scabious.*	*Scabiosa stellata* L. ? vars.
Scabiosa	Indica, *Indian Scabious.*	*Scabiosa atropurpurea* L.
	Indica Clusii, *Clusius his Indian Scabious.*	*Scabiosa atropurpurea* L.
	major, *common Scabious.*	*Knautia arvensis* (L.) Coult.
	minor, *small Scabious.*	*Scabiosa columbaria* L.
	minor, sive Ovilla, *Sheeps Scabious.*	*Jasione montana* L.

Scammonium, *Scamony.* — *Convolvulus scammonia* L.
Scandix, Pecten Veneris. — *Scandix pecten-veneris* L.
Scolopendria, Ceterah, *Spleenwort.* — *Ceterach officinarum* DC.
Scordium, *water Germander.* — *Teucrium scordium* L.

	portulacæ folio, *Scorpions grasse with Purslan leaves.*	*Coronilla scorpioides* (L.) Koch.
	bupleurifol: siliq: crassa torosa, *smooth-codded thick Caterpillers.*	*Scorpiurus vermiculatus* L.
Scorpioides	min: *small Scorpions grass.*	? *Myosotis sylvatica* Hoffm. or M. discolor Pers.
	minor elegans, *dainty small Scorpions grasse.*	*Myosotis arvensis* (L.) Hill
	sive Viperaria.	*Scorzonera hispanica* L.
	angustifolio, *narrow-leafed Vipers prasse.*	*Scorzonera graminifolia* L.
Scorzonera	Constantina tuberosa radice flore carneo, *Morini.*	? *Scorzonera purpurea* L. subsp. *rosea*

Scrophularia	montis Serrati, *Tradescant his strange Figwort.*	*Scrophularia lucida* L.
	vulgaris, *Brown wort.*	*Scrophularia nodosa* L.
	Pannonica Clusii, *Clusius his Hungarian Figwort.*	*Scrophularia vernalis* L.
Secale, *Rye.*		*Secale cereale* L.
Securidaca	minor, *small hatchet Vetch.*	*Astragalus hamosus* L.
	major, *great hatchet Vetch.*	*Securigera securidaca* (L.) Degen & Dörfler
Sedum	perigrina Clusii, *strange hatchet Vetch.*	*Biserrula pelecinus* L.
	majus, *great Housleek.*	*Sempervivum tectorum* L.
	arborescens, *tree-Housleek.*	*Aeonium arboreum* (L.) Webb & Berth.
	elegans, *dainty Housleek.*	? *Saxifraga umbrosa* L.
	majus hæmatoides, *Prickmaddam.*	*Sedum reflexum* L.

Sempervivi variæ species non vulgares, *Morini.*
Senecio, Erigerum, *Groundsell.*

		Senecio vulgaris L.
Serpillum	vulgare, *common wilde Time.*	*Thymus serpyllum* L. agg.
	citratum, *Lemmon Time.*	*Thymus* x *citriodorus* Schreb.

Serpentaria, *grasse Plantane.*

		Plantago maritima L. var. *serpentina*
Serratula, *Sawwort.*		*Serratula tinctoria* L.
Seseli	Æthiopicum frutex, *shrub Harwort of Æthiopia.*	*Bupleurum fruticosum* L.
	Massiliense, *Hartwort of Marselles.*	*Seseli tortuosum* L.
	Creticum *sc:* caucalis vera, *Hartwort of Candy.*	*Tordylium maximum* L.
Sideritis	humilis lato obtuso folio, *petty Alheale.*	*Stachys arvensis* (L.) L.
	prima herba Judaica, *Jewes Ironwort.*	? *Sideritis romana* L.
	Anglica strumosa radice, *sc:* Panax Coloni, *Clowns Woundwort, or Clownes Alheale.*	*Stachys palustris* L.
Sinapi	sativum, *garden Mustard.*	*Brassica nigra* L.
	sylvestre, *wilde Mustard.*	? *Erucastrum gallicum* (Willd.) O.E. Schultz.
	Castiliæ novæ.	? *Sinapis hispanica* L.
	semine albo, *White Mustard.*	*Sinapis alba* L.
Sisarum, *Skirrets.*		*Sium sisarum* L.

Sison, Petrosolinum Macedonicum, *bastard stone-Parsley.* — *Sison amomum* L.

Smilax	aspera folio rotundo, *prickly Birdweed with a round leafe.*	*Smilax aspera* L. (type)
	aspera folio maculato, *spotted prickly Birdweed.*	? *Smilax aspera* L. var. *maculata*
	aspera levis.	? *Smilax herbacea* L. or *Menispermum canadense* L.

Smyrnium Creticum, *Candy Alexander.* — *Smyrnium rotundifolium* Miller

Solanum	lethale, *deadly Nightshade.*	*Atropa belladonna* L.
	hortense, *garden Nightshade.*	*Solanum nigrum* L.
	lignosū, *sc:* Dulcamara, *bittersweet, or Woody Nightshade.*	*Solanum dulcamara* L.
	arborescens Virgin: *Virginian tree Nightshade.*	? *Solanum virginianum* L. or *Phytolacca americana* L.
Soldinella	Alpina, *mountain Birdweed.*	*Soldanella alpina* Willd.
	vulgaris.	*Calystegia soldanella* (L.) R. Br.

Solidago Saracenica, *Saracens confound.* — *Senecio fluviatilis* Wallr.

Sonchus	asper vulgi, *prickly Thistle.*	*Sonchus asper* (L.) Hill
	lævis laciniatus vulgaris, *common Sowthistle.*	*Sonchus oleraceus* L. (forms)
	lævis latifol: *broad-leafed Sowthistle.*	

Sophia Chirurgorum, *Flix weed.*
Descurania sophia (L.) Webb
ex Prantl.

Sorbus
- torminalis, *common Service-tree.*
- sylvestr: Alpina, ornus, *Quickentree, Roane-tree, Wilde Service-tree.*

Sorbus torminalis (L.) Crantz.
Sorbus aucuparia L.

Sparganum *†
- ramosum Angl: *branched English Burweed.*
- ram: Virgin: *branched Virginian Burweed.*

Sparganium erectum L.
Sparganium americanum Nutt.

Spartum Anglicanū, *great English Matweed or Helme.*
Ammophila arenaria (L.) Link

Speculum Veneris, *Venus Lookingglasse.*
Legousia speculum-veneris (L.)
Chaix

Spinachia, *Spinage.*
Spinacia oleracea L.

Spina Solstitialis, Carduus Solstitialis.
Centaurea solstitialis L.

Spodylium, *Cow-Parsnip.*
Heracleum sphondylium L.

Stæchys
- Arabica, *Arabian base Horehound.*
- Cririna.
- Hispanica, *Spanish base Horehound.*
- spuria.

Lavandula stoechas L.
Helichrysum stoechas (L.) DC.
Stachys ocymastrum (L.) Briq.
Stachys germanica L.

*†Staphylodendron Virginianum, *Virginian Bladernut.*
Staphylea trifolia L.

Stæbe Salamantica Clusii, *Clusius's Spanish silver Knapweed.*
Centaurea salmantica L.

Stæchas, *Cassidony or French Lavender.*
Lavandula stoechas L.

Stellata aquatica, *Water-Starwort.*
Stellaria alsine Grimm

Stramonia
- flore albo, *white Thorne Apple.*
- flore purpur: *purple Thorn-Apple.*

Datura metel L.
Datura tatula L.

Syringa
- Italica flore albo simplici & mult: *single and double Pipe-tree.*
- Arabium flore cæruleo, *blew Pipe-tree of Arabia.*

Philadelphus coronarius L. and
P. coronarius L. var.
'Dianthiflorus'
Syringa vulgaris L.

T.

Tabacum, *Tobacco.*
Nicotiana tabacum L.

Tamariscus
- Italica, *Italian Tamarisk.*
- vulgaris, *ordinary Tamarisk.*

Myricaria germanica (L.) Desv.
Tamarix gallica L.

Tanacetum
- crispum Anglicū, *English crisped Tansey.*
- vulgare, *common Tansey.*
- variegatū, *party coloured Tansey.*
- inodorum, *unsavory Tansey.*

Tanacetum vulgare L. subsp.
crispum
Tanacetum vulgare L.
Tanacetum vulgare L. var.
Chrysanthemum corymbosum L.

Tapsia latifolia.
Thapsia villosa L.

Tapsus barbatus, *sc*: Verbascum, *Mullein, Hagtaper.*
Verbascum thapsus L.

Taxus, *Yew-tree.*
Taxus baccata L.

Telephium
- vulgare, *common Orphin, Livelong.*
- majus, *great Orpin.*
- minus, *small Orpin.*

Sedum telephium L.
Sedum telephium L. var.
? Sedum anacampseros L.

Terebinthus vera, *the Turpentine tree.*
Pistacia terebinthus L.

Tenerium arborescens.
Teucrium fruticans L.

Thalictrum
- *sc*: Thaleitrum Aug: *bastard Rhubarb, Meadow Rue.*
- Virginianum.

Thalictrum flavum L.

? Thalictrum purpurascens L. agg.

Thlaspi
- Neronis Carotef: Lob: *large tufted Mustard.*
- umbellatum, *tufted Mustard.*

Elaeoselinum foetidum (L.) Boiss.
(and Iberis umbellata L.)
? Iberis amara L.

Thymum
- durius, *common Tyme.*
- moschatum, *muske Tyme.*

Thymus vulgaris L.
Coridothymus capitatus (L.)
Reichenb. fil.

Tilia
- mas, *male Line tree.*
- fœmina, *female Line tree.*

Tilia x vulgaris Hayne

Tithymalus	Charachias, *wood Spurge.*	*Euphorbia characias* L.
	helioscopus, *sun Spurge.*	*Euphorbia helioscopia* L.

Tithymalorum diversæ species, *divers other sorts of Spurges.* — *Euphorbia* spp.

Tormentilla, *Tormentill.* — *Potentilla erecta* (L.) Räusch.

Trachelium

Americanum flore rubro, seu planta Cardinalis, *the rich crimson Cardinall flower.* — *Lobelia cardinalis* L.

majus flo: albo multiplici, *great double White Canterbury Bells.*

majus flore albo simplici, *great single white Canterbury Bells.*

ma: flore violaceo simplici, *great single violet-coloured Canterbury Bells.* — *Campanula trachelium* L. vars.

ma: flore violaceo multipl: *great double violet-coloured Canterbury Bells.* — *Campanula trachelium* L. var. 'Flore Pleno'

Gygantinū, *Gyants Throatwort.* — *Campanula latifolia* L.

minus, *small Throatwort.* — *Campanula glomerata* L.

cæruleum flo: pleno, *double blew Canterbury Bells.* — *Campanula trachelium* L. var. 'Flore Pleno'

Tragacantha, *Goates Thorne.* — *Astragalus massiliensis* (Miller) Lam. (tragacantha)

Tragapogon

flore luteo, *yellow Goats beard.* — *Tragopogon pratensis* L.

flore purpureo, *purple Goats beard.* — *Tragopogon porrifolius* L.

flo: cæruleo, *blew Goats beard.* — ? *Tragopogon porrifolius* L. var.

Tragopyron, *Buck Wheat.* — *Fagopyrum esculentum* Moench

Trichomanes, *vide* Capillus Veneris. — *Adiantum capillus-veneris* L.

Trifolium

fragiferum, *strawberry Trefoile.* — *Trifolium fragiferum* L.

pratense flo: rubro, *purple.* — *Trifolium pratense* L.

odoratum, *sweet Trefoile.* — *Trigonella caerulea* (L.) Ser.

flore albo, *white flowred Trefoile.* — *Trifolium repens* L.

cardatum, *heart Trefoyle.* — *Medicago arabica* (L.) Hudson

Lagapogon, *Hæresfoot.* — *Trifolium arvense* L.

aquaticum, *marsh-Trefoyle, or Bucks beans.* — *Menyanthes trifoliata* L.

lupulinum, *hop-Trefoyle.* — *Medicago lupulina* L.

acetosum, *sc:* lujula, *Wood-Sorrell.* — *Oxalis corniculata* L.

stellatum glabrum, *smooth starry-leafed Trefoyle.* — *Trifolium squamosum* L.

Tripolium, *Sea Starwort.* — *Aster tripolium* L.

Triticum

sive siligo spica mutica, *white Wheat.* — *Triticum aestivum* L.

aristis circumvallatum, *red Wheat.* — ? *Triticum turgidum* L.

spica multiplici. — *Triticum* sp.

Tubera Indica folia gladioli facie, *Morin.* — ? *Xyris indica* L.

Tuliparum eligant: maxima diversitas, *great variety of gallant Tulips,*

Admirall of England.
Admirall de Man.
Anvers.
Agat Robin.
Beswicke.
Carpenter.
Cipio.
Donquer Voilque.
Generall Duke.
Generall Holland.
Generall Branchion.
Generall Conde.
Iris Daley.
Luis Portugall.

— *Tulipa gesneriana* L. cvs.

Morillion d'Alger.
Matre Harlas.
Moulswicke.
Nonsuites.
Palto de Layden.
Pas Cittadell.
Paragon vas Vileson.
Paragon Liskins. } *Tulipa gesneriana* L. cvs.
Pas bell Leon.
Pas Odenard.
Pintres.
Satine.
Superiomen.
Tricolor crownes.
Viceroy.
Zebulom.

Turritis major, *Towers Mustard*.		*Turritis glabra* L.
Tussilago, *Coltsfoot*.		*Tussilago farfara* L.
Typha palustris, *Catts-taile, Reedmasse*.		*Typha latifolia* L.
Valeriana	vera, seu Phu majus, *great water Valerian*.	*Valeriana phu* L.
	vera, *sc*: Phu minus, *small water Valerian*.	*Valeriana officinalis* L.
	Græca, flore cæruleo, *blew Greek Valerian*.	*Polemonium caeruleum* L.
	Græca, flore albo, *white Greek Valerian*.	*Polemonium caeruleum* L. (form)
	hortensis, *garden-Valerian*.	*Valeriana officinalis* L. (form)
	annua Indica, *annual Indian Valerian*.	*Fedia cornucopiae* DC.
	Dodonæi.	*Centranthus ruber* (L.) DC.
	sylvestris minor, *small wilde Valerian*.	*Valeriana dioica* L.
	salvifoliū, *sage-leafed Mullein*.	? *Phlomis fruticosa* L.
	blattariæ folio.	? *Verbascum blattaria* L.
Verbascum	album vulgare, Tapsus barbatus communis, *common Mullein*.	*Verbascum thapsus* L.
	nigrum, *black Mullein*.	*Verbascum nigrum* L.
Verbena communis, *common Vervaine*.		*Verbena officinalis* L.
Veronica	mas repens, *creeping male Speedwell*.	*Veronica officinalis* L.
	fœm: Elatine, *female Fluellin*.	*Kickxia spuria* (L.) Dum.
	recta spicata, *upright Speedwell*.	*Veronica spicata* L.
Viburnum, *Wayfaring tree, Cotton tree*.		*Viburnum lantana* L.
Vicia vulgaris, *common Vetch or Fitch*.		*Vicia sativa* L.
Vinca pervinca	major, *great Periwinckle*.	*Vinca major* L.
	minor, *small Periwincle*.	*Vinca minor* L.

Viola — Matronalis flo: albo simpl: *single white Dames Violet*.
Matron: flore albo pleno, *double white Dames Violet*. } *Hesperis matronalis* L. cvs.
Matron: flore purpureo simplici, *single purple Dames Violet*.

Tricolor, *sc*: Deapensia repens flo: luteo ampliss: *great yellow Pansies or Hearts Ease*. } *Viola tricolor* L. (forms)
Tricolor assurgens Versicolor.

Pentigonia *sc*: speculum Veneris. — *Legousia hybrida* (L.) Delarb.

Martia flore pleno, cæruleo, *double blew Violet*.
Martia flore cæruleo simpl: *single blew Violet*. } *Viola odorata* L.
Mar: flo: pleno cineritio.
Mar: flo: simpl: rubro, *red single Violet*

inodora, *sc*: canina, *field Violet*. — *Viola riviniana* Reichenb.

Viola	{ flore luteo, *yellow Violet*.	*Viola lutea* Hudson
	aquat: *sc*: Millefol: aquat:	*Hottonia palustris* L.
Viorna vulgi, *Travellers Joy*.		*Clematis vitalba* L.
	{ Canadensis.	*Solidago canadensis* L.
Virga aurea	{ serratis foliis, *golden Rod with dented leaves*.	*Solidago virgaurea* L. (form)
	vulgaris, *ordinary golden Rod*.	*Solidago virgaurea* L.
Virga pastoris, *vide* Dipsacus minor.		*Dipsacus pilosus* L.
Vitedera Virginiana, *vide* Hedera Virginiana.		*Parthenocissus quinquefolia* (L.) Planchon

Ulmaria
{ Perigrina Clusii, *Clusius his strange Meadesweet*. — *Aruncus dioicus* (Walter) Fernald.
{ *sc*: Regina prati, *common Meadesweet*. — *Filipendula ulmaria* (L.) Maxim.

Umbilicus Veneris
{ verus, *Navellwort, Kidneywort*. — *Umbilicus rupestris* (Salisb.) Dandy
{ Hispanicus, *Spanish Navellwort*. — ? *Omphalodes linifolia* (L.) Moench

Vitis
vinifera
{ fructu albo. — *Vitis vinifera* L.
{ foliis laciniatis, *Parsley-Vine*. — *Vitis vinifera* L. var. 'Apiifolia'
{ ? †sylvestris Virginiana, *Virginia wilde Vine*. — *Vitis labrusca* L.

variegata, *party-coloured Grape*. — —
†vulpina Virginiana, *Fox-Grape from Virginia*. — *Vitis vulpina* L.
alba, *white Grape*.
cærulea, *blue Grape*.
Rhenensis, *Rhenish Grape*.

Amber Grape.
Burlett white and red.
Currant Grape.   } *Vitis vinifera* L. cvs.
Muskadell Grape.
Frontignack or Musk-grape, white and red.
Black Grape of Orleans.

Urtica
{ urens major, *great wilde Nettle*. — *Urtica dioica* L.
{ urens minor, *small wilde Nettle*. — *Urtica urens* L.
{ Iners, lamium, *dead Nettle*. — *Lamium album* L.
{ Romana, *Roman Nettle*. — *Urtica pilulifera* L.
{ ma: Americana, *great American Nettle*. — *Urtica canadensis* L.

X.

Xyris sive spotula fœtida, *stinking Gladdon*.	*Iris foetidissima* L.
Xanthium, *vide* Bardana minor.	*Xanthium strumarium* L.

Principall Benefactors
to the precedent
Collection

{King *Charles.*
{Queen *Mary.*
{*George* Duke of *Buckingham.*
{Lady *Katharine* Dutchess of
    Buck:
William Laud Archbishop of *Cant:*
Robert Earle of *Salisbury.*
William Earle of *Salisbury.*
    Earle of *Carlisle.*
Lord Viscount *Dorchester.*
Lord Viscount *Faulkland.*
Lord *Strange.*
Lord *Goring.*
Lord *Cambden.*
Countesse of *Arundell.*
Lady *Matrevers.*
Lady *Denbeigh.*
Lady *Wootton.*
Lady *Mary Villers.*
Lady *Goring.*
Lady *Killegray.*
Lady *Christian Leviston.*
Sir *Thomas Roe.*
Sir *Christopher Hatton.*
Sir *Henry VVooton.*
Sir *Kenelme Digby.*
Sir *Nathanael Bacon.*
Sir *Butts Bacon.*
Sir *Dudly Diggs.*
Sir *Henry Vane.*
Sir *Henry Palmer.*
Sir *Robert Heath.*
Sir *Peter Manwood.*
Sir *John Trever.*
Sir *William Boswell.*
Sir *Clipsby Crew.*
Sir *Alexander Gourdon.*
Sir *James Bagg.*
Sir *David Kirke.*
Sir *Richard Wiseman.*
Sir *John Smith.*
Sir *John Wieldes.*
Sir *Henry Meldree.*
Sir *John Aemoote.*
Lady *Roe.*
Lady *Graimes.*
Doctor *Owin.*
Doctor *John Hill.*
Doctor *Thomas Wharton.*
Doctor *William Broad.*
Doctor *Bugg.*
William Murray Esq.
William Curteene Esq.
Elias Ashmole Esq.
Captain *Weddell.*
Captain *Plumbey.*

Captain *Ireland.*
Captain *Cleborne.*
Captain *Prim.*
Captain *Wood.*
Captain *West.*
Captain *Swanley.*
Captain *Adam Denton.*
Captain *Trenchfield.*
Captain *David Atchinson.*
Mr. *Nicolas,* Secretary to the Navy.
Mr. *John Slany* Merchant.
Mr. *Charleton* Merchant.
Mr. *James Boovy* Merchant.
Mr. *John Millen.*
Mr. *Thomas Howard.*
Mr. *White of Burntwood.*
Mr. *Ofield.*
Mr. *Ofley.*
Mr. *Greene.*
Mr. *Munke.*
Mr. *Sadler.*
Mr. *Bushell.*
Mr. *Liggon.*
Mr. *George Tomasin.*
Mr. *Dells.*
Mr. *Gage.*
Mr. *Pergins.*
Mr. *Robert Martyn.*
Mr. *Trion.*
Mr. *Woolfe.*
Mr. *Browne.*
Mr. *Martin Masters.*
Mr. *Butler.*
Mr. *Phillips.*
Mr. *Harison.*
Mr. *Pette.*
Mr. *Short.*
Mr. *Bound.*
Mr. *Stone.*
Mr. *Bartholomew Hagatt.*
Mr. *Reeve.*
Mr. *Francis Cline.*
Mr. *Thomas Herbert.*
Mr. *Rowland Bucket.*
Mr. *Snelling.*
Mr. *Rowe.*
Mr. *Smith.*
Mr. *Butterworth.*
Mr. *le Goulz.*
Mr. *William Martyn.*
Mr. *Lanyon.*
Mr. *Gasper Calthoofe.*
Mr. *William Lambert.*
Mr. *John Benson.*

FINIS

References

The following abbreviations are used in the references:
BM: British Museum
CSP: Calendar of State Papers
CSPC: Calendar of State Papers Colonial
CSPD: Calendar of State Papers Domestic
DNB: Dictionary of National Biography
HMC: Historical Manuscripts Commission
HH: Hatfield House
PCC: Prerogative Court of Canterbury
PRO: Public Record Office

Introduction

1. Ashmole MS 1494.
2. *Diary of the Journey of the Duke of Stettin–Pomerania in 1602*, Transactions of the Royal Historical Society, New Series, No. 6 (1892).
3. *Philosophical Transactions*, No. 137 (January and February 1677/78).
4. BM, Royal MS 18A LXXI: *The Cabanet Royal*.
5. John Evelyn, *Diary*, 15 September 1657.
6. Samuel Pepys, *Diary*, 31 August 1661.
7. HMC 25, *Le Fleming MSS* (1890).
8. Henry Farley, *From St Paules Church Her Bill for the Parliament* (1621), p. 19.
9. *The Travels of Peter Mundy*, Hakluyt Society, Vol. III, Part I (1919).
10. Francis Bacon, 'Of Gardens' (1625).
11. Sir Henry Wotton, *The Elements of Architecture* (1624).
12. Thomas Hyll, *The Gardener's Labyrinth* (1577).
13. Gervase Markham, *Markham's Farwell to Husbandry* (1620).
14. Ralph Austen, *A Treatise of Fruit-Trees* (1665).
15. Sandra Raphael, 'John Evelyn's *Elysium Britannicum*', *The Garden* (November 1977).

Chapter 1

1. Anthony A. Wood, *Athenae Oxonienses*, Vol. IV, 3rd edn (1820).
2. HMC 9, Cecil MSS, Vol. XVIII (1940).
3. A. Suckling, *History and Antiquities of Suffolk* (1846).
4. Norwich, 165 Godsalve. (I am grateful to Peter Northeast for this reference.)
5. Suffolk Record Office, 1C/AA1/9/249.
6. Ibid., 1C/AA1/45/108.
7. BM, Add. MS 19,081.
8. Norwich, 219 Corant.
9. BM, Add. MS 19081.
10. Suffolk Record Office, 1C/AA1/27/278.

11. BM, Add. MS 19081.
12. Suffolk Record Office, 1C/AA1/32/123.
13. Mea Allan, *The Tradescants* (1964), p. 58.
14. Guildhall, MS 9535/1, *Register of Ordinations 1559–77*.
15. Guildhall, MS 5602/2.
16. Guildhall, MS 5633.
17. Guildhall, MS 5602/2.
18. *The Letters of John Chamberlain*, ed. N.E. McClure (1939).
19. John Gerard, *Herbal* (1597), p. 624; ibid., ed. Thomas Johnson (1633), pp. 764 and 766.
20. BM, Add. MS 72338.

Chapter 2

1. HH Accounts 160/1.
2. HMC 9, Cecil MSS, Vol. XIX (1965).
3. BM, Lansdowne MS 107, f. 51.
4. W.B. Rye, *England as Seen by Foreigners* (1865).
5. BM, Add. MS 27278, f. 24.
6. PRO, SP 14/52, f. 17.
7. PRO, SP 14/58.
8. HH Accounts 160/1.
9. Ibid.
10. HH Gen. 3/20.
11. HH Bills 72/12.
12. BM Add. MS 72339.
13. HH Accounts 160/1.
14. Ibid.
15. PRO, SP 14/61.
16. John Evelyn, *Diary*, 11 March 1642.
17. Thomas Fuller, *The Worthies of England*, ed. J. Freeman (1952).
18. HH Accounts 160/1.
19. PRO, SP 14/57.
20. HH Cecil Papers 142/122.
21. HH Accounts 160/1.
22. HH Gen. 11/25.
23. Sir William Brereton Bt, *Travels in Holland, United Provinces, England, Scotland and Ireland 1634–1635*, Chetham Society, Vol. I (1844).
24. John Ray, *Observations Made in a Journey Through Part of the Low Countries, Germany, Italy and France* (1673).
25. HH Bills 58/2.
26. John Parkinson, *Paradisi in Sole Paradisus Terrestris* (1629), p. 571.
27. HH Bills 58/3.
28. Ibid.
29. Gerard, *Herbal*, ed. Johnson, op. cit., p. 1593.
30. Parkinson, *Paradisus*, op. cit., p. 93.
31. HH Bills 58/3.
32. *The Letters of John Chamberlain*, op. cit.

33. HH Gen. 11/25.
34. HH Bills 67b.
35. HH Bills 58/2.
36 Edward A. Bunyard, 'John Tradescant, Senior', *Journal of Pomology*, Vol. I (1919–20).
37. George Brookshaw, *The Horticultural Repository* (1823).
38. Parkinson, *Paradisus*, op. cit., p. 574.
39. Ibid., p. 179.
40. Ibid., p. 574.
41. Ibid., p. 528.
42. Ibid., p. 520.
43. HH Bills 58/2.
44. HMC 75, Downshire MSS, Vol. III (1938).
45. HH Box G/13.
46. Gerard, *Herbal*, op. cit., p. 389.
47. M.F. Warner, 'Jean and Vespasien Robin', *National Horticultural Magazine*, Vol. 35 (1956).
48. HH Gen. 11/25.
49. HH Bills 58/31.
50. HH Gen. 11/25; HH Bills 58/31.
51. Parkinson, *Paradisus*, op. cit. p. 582.
52. Philip Miller, *The Gardener's Dictionary* (1743).
53. PRO, SP 14/63.
54. HH Bills 58/31.
55. HH Gen. 11/25.
56. Ibid.
57. HH Box G/13.
58. John Evelyn, *Sylva* (1664), p. 43.
59. Samuel Hartlib, *Universal Husbandry Improved* (1650).
60. HH Bills 70.
61. PRO, SP 14/57; Paula Henderson, 'A Shared Passion: The Cecils and Their Gardens', *Patronage, Culture and Power: The Early Cecils 1558–1612*, ed. Pauline Croft (2002)
62. HH FP 2nd supplement 1/176.
63. HH Bills 59.
64. Ibid.
65. Parkinson, *Paradisus*, op. cit., p. 445.
66. Gough drawings, 3a Bodleian Library.
67. HH Bills 69.
68. Ibid.
69. HH Bills 65/3.
70. HH Bills 79.
71. HH Accounts 128/1.
72. HH Bills 77.
73. HH Bills 82.
74. HH Accounts 160/1.
75. HH Boxes G/13 and G/14.
76. HH Accounts 14/14.
77. HH Accounts 13/18.
78. PRO, SP 14/67, f. 62.

79. HH Gen. 3/20.
80. PRO, SP 14/67, f. 63.
81. Ibid., f. 62.
82. PRO, SP 14/48.
83. HH Box U/71.
84. HH Accounts 160/1.
85. S. Sorbiere, *A Voyage to England* (1709).
86. HH Manor Papers.
87 HH Bills 71.
88. HH Manor Papers.

Chapter 3
1. Parkinson, *Paradisus*, op. cit., p. 152.
2. HH Gen. 7/13.
3. PRO, SP 14/36.
4. *A Relation of a Short Survey of the Western Counties Made by a Lieutenant of the Military Company in Norwich 1635*, ed. L.G. Wickham Legg, Camden Miscellany, Vol. XVI (1936).
5. PRO, SP 14/113.
6. Ashmole MS 824.
7. Parkinson, *Paradisus*, op. cit., p. 378.
8. John Parkinson, *Theatrum Botanicum* (1656), pp. 343–4.
9. Parkinson, *Paradisus*, op. cit., p. 141.
10. PRO, CO 1/2.
11. C.E. Hatch, *The First Seventeen Years: Virginia 1607–1624*, Jamestown 350th Anniversary Historic Booklets, No. 6 (1957).
12. D.L. Edwards, *A History of the King's School·Canterbury* (1957).

Chapter 4
1. Ashmole MS 824, ff. 175–86.
2. J. von Hamel, *England and Russia* (1854).
3. Parkinson, *Paradisus*, p. 346.
4. Parkinson, *Theatrum*, p. 1017.
5. G.S. Boulger, The First Russian Botanist', *Journal of Botany*, Vol. 82 (1895).
6. Parkinson, *Theatrum*, p. 705.
7 W.F. Ryan, *John Tradescant's Russian Abacus*, Oxford Slavonic Papers, New Series, Vol. V (1972).

Chapter 5
1. Parkinson, *Paradisus*, op. cit., p. 579.
2. J.S. Corbett, *England in the Mediterranean 1603–1713* (1904).
3. Ashmole MS 824, f. 149; PRO, SP 14/122, no. 106.
4. Gerard, *Herbal*, ed. Johnson, op. cit., p. 1208.
5. Parkinson, *Paradisus*, op. cit., p. 190.
6. Ibid., p. 430.

7. Parkinson, *Theatrum*, op. cit., p. 1511.
8. Parkinson, *Paradisus*, op. cit., p. 512.
9. *HMC 8th Report*, Appendix (Part II) (1881), p. 41.

Chapter 6

1. PRO, SP 14/133.
2. Evelyn, *Diary*, 10 July 1656.
3 Evelyn, *Sylva*, op. cit., p. 115.
4. Quoted in Hugh Ross Williamson, *George Villiers, First Duke of Buckingham* (1940), p. 121.
5. PRO, C 66/2359.
6. BM, Add. MS 12,528.
7. Ibid.
8. HMC 60, *Mar and Kellie MSS 1234–1708* and *1356–1743* (1930 and 1904).
9. Evelyn, *Diary*, 14 August 1654.
10. Thomas Fuller, *The Worthies of England*, op. cit.
11. P. Finch, *History of Burley-on-the-Hill, Rutland* (1901).
12. PRO, SP 14/176.
13. BM, Harl. MS 1576, f. 642.
14. *CSP Venetian* 1623–25.
15. *Mémoires et Négociations Secrètes de M. de Rusdorff*, Vol. I (1789), p. 579.
16. BM, Add. MS 12,528.
17. Ibid.
18. Margaret Toynbee, 'The Wedding Journey of King Charles I', *Archeologia Cantiana* (1955).
19. G. Goodman, *The Court of James I*, Vol. II (1839).
20. PRO, SP 16/4, ff. 155 and 156.
21. F.P. and M.M. Verney, *Memoirs of the Verney Family During the Seventeenth Century* (1904).
22. J.W. Blake, 'The Farm of the Guinea Trade', *Essays in British and Irish History* (1949).
23. PRO, SP 16/166 and SP 16/530.
24. PRO, E 351/3264.
25. PRO, LS 13/169.
26. BM, Add. MS 12,528.
27. BM, Add. MS 26,051.
28. T. Birch, *The Court and Times of Charles I*, Vol. I (1848).
29. *Miscellaneous State Papers 1501–1726*, Vol. II, ed. 2nd Earl of Hardwicke (1778).
30. BM, Add. MS 6,703.
31. PRO, SP 16/81.
32. BM, Add. MS 6,703; Ashmole MS 824.
33. PRO, SP 16/82.
34. Gerard, *Herbal*, ed. Johnson, op. cit., p. 1099.
35. Parkinson, *Theatrum*, op. cit., p. 624.
36. Gerard, *Herbal*, ed. Johnson, op. cit., p. 998.
37. PCC 31 Sadler.
38. Pierre Borel, *Les Antiquitez* (1649).

Chapter 7

1. I am grateful to David Sturdy for information about the Tradescants' Lambeth house and garden.
2. Minet Library, Lambeth, P2/35.
3. PRO, E 179/186/436, 448, 454, 465.
4. 'Vauxhall and South Lambeth: An 18th-century Lease', *Surrey Archaeological Collections*, Vol. 28 (1915).
5. Rev. James Granger, *Supplement to Biographical History of England* (1774).
6. *Surrey Hearth Tax* 1664, C.A.F. Meekings (ed.), Surrey Record Society, Vol. XVII, Nos. XLI and XLII (1940).
7. Ashmole MS 860.
8. Thomas Powell, *Humane Industry* (1661).
9. John Cleveland, 'Upon Sir Thomas Martin', in *Poems* (1651).
10. Robert Herrick, 'Epigram upon Madam Ursly', in *Hesperides* (1648).
11. John Oldham, 'Satires upon the Jesuits', in *The Works of Mr John Oldham* (1684).
12. Charles Hoole, *A New Discovery of the Old Art of Teaching Schoole* (1660).
13. Gerard, *Herbal*, ed. Johnson, op. cit., p. 1545.
14. Francis Willughby, *Ornithologia* (1676); John Ray, *Ornithology* (1678).
15. Richard Leigh, *The Transproser Rehears'd* (1673).
16. Parkinson, *Paradisus*, op. cit., p. 575.
17. Gerard, *Herbal*, ed. Johnson, op. cit., p. 489.
18. Northampton Record Office, Finch-Hatton MS 2423.
19. Cumbria Record Office, *Le Fleming MSS*, WD/Ry (492), (243), (260).
20. BM, Add. MS 22,466.
21. Pierre Borel, *Les Antiquitez*, op. cit.
22. Ed. M. Exwood and H.L. Lehman, *The Journal of William Schellinks' Travels in England 1661–1663*, Camden Society, Fifth Series, I (1993).
23. Sir Andrew Balfour, *Letters Written to a Freind . . .* (1700), pp. 24 and 65.
24. HMC 9, Cecil MSS, Vol. XXII (1971).
25. K.H. Schaible, 'Geschichte der Deutschen in England', *Englische Studien*, Vol. X (1887).
26. S. Hartlib, *Ephemerides*, MS in University of Sheffield Library.

Chapter 8

1. PRO, E 404/153, Part 2, 29.
2. PRO, E 403/2749–2756.
3. PRO, SO 3/10.
4. PRO, E 351/3269.
5. East Sussex Record Office, Glynde MSS 239, 240, 249, 253; PRO, A01 /2485/344 and A01 2487/356.
6. Hartlib, *Ephemerides*, op. cit.
7. M.A. Everett Green (ed.), *Letters of Queen Henrietta Maria* (1857).
8. PRO, LR 2/297, f. 109.
9. PRO, E 351/3253.
10. PRO, E 351/3253, 3255 and 3259.
11. PRO, E 351/3265.
12. PRO, E 403/2606.

13. PRO, E 351/3268.
14. PRO, E 404/154, 99.
15. N. Lib. Wales, Wynnstay MS 181.
16. PRO, E 351/3269.
17. Gerard, *Herbal*, ed. Johnson, op. cit., p. 1515.
18. India Office Records B/16.
19. PRO, LC 5/134, ff. 79 and 91.
20. *The Inventories and Valuations of the King's Goods 1649–1651*, ed. Oliver Millar, Walpole Society Publications, Vol. XLIII (1972).
21. Magdalen College, MS 367, f. 76.
22. Bodleian Library, MS Twyne 6/287.
23. R. Vyse and S. Tomlinson, *Matriculation Register 1615–1647*. I am grateful to David Sturdy for this reference.
24. Arthur MacGregor, *Tradescant's Rarities* (1983), p. 9.

Chapter 9

1. Guildhall, MS 10232.
2. PRO, WO 54/11, 12, 13; E 101 674/11.
3. Parish Register of St Mary's, Lambeth.
4. *Lambeth Churchwardens' Accounts 1504–1645 and Vestry Book 1610*, Vol II, Surrey Record Society, Vol. XX (1950).
5. Guildhall, MS 3390/1 and 2.
6. *Lambeth Churchwardens' Accounts*, op. cit.
7. Parkinson, *Paradisus*, op. cit., pp. 346, 378 and 389.
8. William Coles, *The Art of Simpling* (1656).
9. S. Denne, *Historical Particulars of Lambeth* (1795).
10. Parkinson, *Theatrum*, op. cit., p. 1050.
11. PRO, CO 1/1.
12. J.A.F. Bekkers, *Correspondence of John Morris with Johannes de Laet 1634–1649* (1970).
13. PCC Lee 63.
14. Parkinson, *Paradisus*, op. cit., p. 610.
15. Essex Record Office, D/DHt T 34/29.
16. PRO, E 403/2757.
17. Minet Library, Lambeth, P 2/35.
18. Evelyn, *Diary*, 10 June 1658.
19. I am grateful to Mr R.O. Dennys, MVO, OBE, FSA, Somerset Herald of Arms, for supplying this information.
20. J. Nichols, *The History and Antiquities of the Parish of Lambeth in the County of Surrey* (1786).
21. *Visitation of Suffolk 1664–1668*, Harleian Society, Vol. LXI (1910).
22. *Allegations for Marriage Licences*, Harleian Society, Vol. XXVI (1887).
23. *Lambeth Churchwardens' Accounts*, op. cit.

Chapter 10

1. PRO, SP 38/18.
2. PRO, E 351/3272.

3. David Brown, *Catalogue of the Drawings of the Ashmolean Museum*, Vol. 4 (1982).
4. Sir Thomas Herbert, *Memoirs of the Last Two Years* (1839).
5. Felix Herbet, *Le Château de Fontainebleau* (1937).
6. Bodleian Library, Ballard MS 2.
7. Parkinson, *Theatrum*, op. cit., p. 1565.
8. PRO, SP 28/194
9. N.M. Nugent, *Cavaliers and Pioneers* (1934).
10. *Calendar of Virginia State Papers 1652–1781*, ed. W. P. Palmer, Vol I (1875).
11. Peter Force, *Tracts Relating to North America*, Vol. III (1844).
12. Martha W. Hiden (ed.), 'Accompts of the Tristram and Jane', *The Virginia Magazine of History and Biography*, Vol. LXII (1954).
13. William Strachey, *The History of Travaile into Virginia* (1849).
14. Captain John Smith, *General History of Virginia* (1624).
15. Force, *Tracts Relating to North America*, op. cit.
16. *The Garden Book of Sir Thomas Hanmer Bart* (1933).
17. Quoted in Alicia Amherst, *A History of Gardening in England* (1910).
18. Webster R. Crowley Jr, 'Early America in Plant Names', Part I, *The Morton Arboretum Quarterly*, Vol. 12, No. 2 (1976).
19. *Allegations for Marriage Licences*, op. cit.
20. PRO, WO 54/10–18; A01/1841/54 and 55; A01/1842/56 and 57; AO1/1843/59–62; A01/1844/63, 64 and 65a.
21. T.C. Dale, *The Inhabitants of London in 1638* (1931).
22. PRO, WO 51/1.
23. PRO, SP 16/539, Part I, f. 71.
24. PRO, WO 54/18.
25. Guildhall, MSS 5602/3; 5614/1–4; 5603/3.
26. Guildhall, MSS 5603/4; 5602/3; 5602/4.

Chapter 11
1. *The Inventories and Valuations of the King's Goods 1649–1651*, op. cit.
2. H.D. Schepelern, *Breve fra og til Ole Worm III*, Copenhagen (1968).
3. Hartlib, *Universal Husbandry Improved*, op. cit.
4. Hartlib, *Ephemerides*, op. cit.
5. *The Winthrop Papers*, Vol. V, 1645–1649, Allyn Bailey Forbes (ed.) (1947).
6. J,A.F. Bekkers, *Correspondence of John Morris . . .*, op. cit.
7. BM, Add. MS 32,093, f. 367.
8. Schepelern, *Breve fra og til Ole Worm III*, op. cit.
9. Ashmole MSS 860 and 1136, f. 27.
10. Nugent, *Cavaliers and Pioneers*, op. cit.

Chapter 12
1. Ashmole MS 1136, f. 22.
2. Ashmole MS 430, f. 70; in code, quoted in C.H. Josten, *Elias Ashmole* (1966).
3. Ashmole MS 1136, f. 20.
4. Ashmole MS 374, f. 144; quoted in Josten, *Elias Ashmole*, op. cit.
5. Ashmole MS 1136, f. 27.

6. Ibid.
7. C.H. L'Estrange Ewen (ed.), *Witch Hunting and Witch Trials* (1929).
8. Ashmole MSS 1136, ff. 27 and 28 and 394, f. 57.
9. Ashmole MS 1136, f. 28.
10. Evelyn, *Diary*, 9 August 1661.
11. R.T. Gunther, 'The Garden of the Rev. Walter Stonehouse at Darfield Rectory, in Yorkshire, 1640', *The Gardener's Chronicle*, 15 May 1920.
12. Ashmole MS 826, ff. 33 and 34.
13. G.K. Fortescue and R.F. Sharp, *The Thomason Tracts* (1908).
14. Bodleian Library, 8° V 90 Art. (MS note in).
15. *The Dramatic Records of Sir Henry Herbert*, ed. J.Q. Adams, Cornell Studies in English, No. 3 (1917).
16. PRO, SP 29/38.
17. W.B. Gurdon, 'The Gurdon Papers', *The East Anglian*, New Series, Vol. IV (1892).
18. Thomas Flatman, *Poems and Songs* (1674).
19. PRO, SP 29/38.
20. *Surrey Quarter Sessions Records, The Order Book for 1659–1661*, Surrey Record Society, Vol. XIII, No. XXXV (1934); *Surrey Quarter Sessions Records, Order Book and Sessions Rolls 1661–1663*, Surrey Record Society, Vol. XIV, No. XXXVI (1935).

Chapter 13

1. Hartlib, *Ephemerides*, op. cit.
2. S. Pepys, *Diary*, 24 October 1660.
3. Evelyn, *Diary*, 23 July 1678.
4. See C.H. Josten, *Elias Ashmole*, Vol. I (1966), pp. 4–5.
5. Ashmole MS 1136, f. 34.
6. PRO, C 7/454/1.
7. Ibid.
8. Ashmole MS 860, p. 513.
9. PCC Laud 72.
10. Minet Library, Lambeth, P2/35.
11. Ashmole MS 1136, f. 37.
12. PRO, C 7/454/1.
13. Ashmole MS 1136, f. 39.
14. PRO, C 37/70, 71 and 72.
15. PRO, C 33/221/744.
16. Minet Library, Lambeth, P3/A.
17. *Private Correspondence and Miscellaneous Papers of Samuel Pepys, 1679–1703*, ed. J.R. Tanner (1926).

Chapter 14

1. Ashmole MS 1136, f. 41.
2. *Surrey Quarter Sessions Records: Order Book and Sessions Rolls 1666–1668*, Surrey County Council (Records and Ancient Monuments Committee), Vol. IX (1951).
3. *The Autobiography of Henry Newcome*, ed. Richard Parkinson (1852).

4. BM, Sloane MS 3988.
5. Ashmole MS 1136, f. 44.
6. John Harvey, *Early Nurserymen* (1974).
7. J. Gibson, 'A Short Account of Several Gardens Near London', *Archaeologia*, Vol. XII (1796).
8. BM, Add. MS 29,572, f. 295.
9. Ashmole MS 243, f. 189, quoted in Josten, *Elias Ashmole*, op. cit.
10. Ashmole MS 1136, f. 51.
11. PRO, C 7/541/2.
12. Ashmole MS 1136, f. 51.
13. Bodleian Library, MS Rawl. D 912/668.
14. Ashmole MS 1136, f. 58.
15. PCC Reeve 54.
16. Mary Edmond, *Limners and Picturemakers*, Walpole Society Publications, Vol. XLVII (1978–80).

Chapter 15

1. Ashmole MS 1136, f. 58.
2. Ibid.
3. PRO, C 10/209/69.
4. Ashmole MS 1136, f. 59.
5. Count Lorenzo Magalotti, *Relazioni d'Inghilterra 1668 e 1688*, Accademia Toscana di Scienze e Lettere 'La Columbaria', Studi No. 23 (1972).
6. Count Lorenzo Magalotti, *Travels of Cosmo the Third Grand Duke of Tuscany Through England During the Reign of King Charles the Second* (1669) (1821).
7. PRO, C 7/541/2.
8. Izaak Walton, *The Compleat Angler*, 5th edn (1792).
9. Guildhall, MS 1758.
10. Evelyn, *Diary*, 23 July, 1678.
11. Quoted in Michael Hunter, *Science and Society in Restoration England* (1981).
12. Bodleian Library, 4° Rawl. 156 (MS letter in).
13. *The Life and Times of Anthony Wood*, ed. A. Clark (1891).
14. HMC 25, *Le Fleming MSS* (1890).
15. Mrs J.C. Cole, 'William Byrd, Stonecutter and Mason', *Oxoniensia*, Vol. XIV (1949).
16. Ashmole MS 1136, f. 75.
17. R.T. Gunther, *Early Science in Oxford*, Vol. XII (1939).
18. Ashmolean Museum, MS 1/1.
19. Ibid., 1/2 and 1/3.
20. R.F. Ovenell, 'The Tradescant Dodo', *Archives of Natural History* (1992), Vol. 19, No. 2, pp. 145–52.
21. *The Academy*, No. 446 (20 November 1880).
22. K.C. Davies and J. Hull, *The Zoological Collections of the Oxford University Museum* (1976).
23. *Ashmolean Museum Reports* 1914–33.
24. Ralph Thoresby, *Diary* (1830), 1 June 1712.
25. BM, Add. MSS 29,572 and 29,573.

26. *Elias Ashmole, His House and Lands at South Lambeth*, Surrey Archaeological Collections, Vol II (1864).
27. Anthony Powell, *John Aubrey and His Friends* (1948); John Aubrey, *The Natural History and Antiquities of the County of Surrey* (1719).
28. *Stukely Papers, Vol. III*, Surtees Society, Vol. 80 (1885).
29. W. Watson, 'Some Account of the Remains of John Tradescant's Garden at Lambeth', *Philosophical Transactions*, Vol. XLVI (1749).
30. *The London Magazine or Gentleman's Monthly Intelligence*, Vol. XX (1751).
31. *Philosophical Transactions*, Vol. LXIII (1773).
32. Philip Miller, *The Gardener's Dictionary* (1743).
33. BM, Add. MS 29,572.
34. Parkinson, *Paradisus*, op. cit., p. 152.

Chapter 16

1. John Evelyn, *Numismata* (1697).
2. PRO, C 7/541/2.
3. *Englische Studien*, Vol. X (1887), op. cit.
4. Ashmole MS 1131, f. 96.
5. *The Travels of Peter Mundy*, op. cit.
6. Ashmole MS 1131, f. 95.
7. Evelyn, *Diary*, 17 September 1657.
8. Willughby, *Ornithologia*, op. cit.
9. *Encyclopedia Britannica*, 11th edn (1910).
10. Ibid.
11. *Notes and Queries*, 1st series, Vol. V (1852), p. 386.
12. *DNB*.
13. Ashmole MS 1461.
14. Evelyn, *Diary*, 1 August 1682.
15. Sir William Sanderson, *Graphice* (1658).
16. BM Print Room, MS Freind.
17. Thomas Birch, *History of the Royal Society*, Vol. II (1756).
18. Hartlib, *Ephemerides*, op. cit.
19. Philip L. Barbour, *The Three Worlds of Captain John Smith* (1948).
20. Ashmole MS 735.
21. Ashmole MS 1758.
22. Ashmole MS 34.
23. Ashmole MS 1752.
24. *Quarterly Review*, Vol. 102, No. 204 (October 1857).
25. Ashmole MS 1465.
26. Bodleian Library, Antiq. C.E. 1629/1.
27. PCC 97 Fane.
28. Thoresby, *Diary*, op. cit., 1 June 1712.
29. I am grateful to Dr Helen Brock and Mr David Houston for this information.
30. The Ashmolean Museum, *Complete Illustrated Catalogue of Paintings 2004*, ed. C. Casley, C. Harrison and J. Whiteley.
31. Daniel Lysons, 'Collectanea' (1660–1825), a scrapbook of newspaper cuttings in the British Library.

32. Sir Kenelm Digby, *A Late Discourse . . . Touching the Cure of Wounds by the Powder of Sympathy . . .* (1658).
33. Guildhall, MS 1758.

Chapter 17

1. *CSPC East Indies, China and Japan 1513–1616* (1862), p. 146.
2. HH MSS Box B8.
3. Birch, *The Court and Times of Charles I*, op. cit.
4. Ibid.
5. Harvey, *Early Nurserymen*, op. cit.
6. Parkinson, *Paradisus*, op. cit., p. 489.
7. Parkinson, *Theatrum*, op. cit., p. 944.
8. M.F.S. Hervey, *Correspondence and Collections of Thomas Howard, Earl of Arundel* (1921).
9. Henry Peacham, *The Compleat Gentleman* (1634).
10. Hervey, *Correspondence and Collections . . .* , op. cit.
11. Sir Thomas Roe, *Negotiations* (1740).
12. Ibid.
13. Edward Terry, *A Voyage to East-India* (1655).
14. Sir Thomas Roe, *Journal* (1732).
15. W. Noel Sainsbury (ed.), *Papers Relating to Rubens* (1859).
16. BM, Add. MS 6395; PRO, LC 5/132, ff. 225 and 302.
17. PRO, E 403/2742, 2743, 2751–3.
18. D.W. Prowse, *A History of Newfoundland* (1896).
19. PRO, LC 5/134, ff. 232 and 236.
20. *DNB*.
21. David Mathew, *The Jacobean Age* (1938); Parkinson, *Paradisus*, op. cit., p. 494.
22. Peacham, *The Compleat Gentleman*, op. cit.
23. Evelyn, *Diary*, 7 November 1651.
24. John F. Fulton, 'Sir Kenelm Digby FRS', in Sir Harold Hartley (ed.), *The Royal Society* (1960).
25. *DNB*.
26. Ibid.; Hervey, *Correspondence and Collections . . .* , op. cit.
27. S.R. Gardiner, *History of England* (1965).
28. Evelyn, *Diary*, 28 February 1648.
29. *The Letters of John Chamberlain*, op. cit.
30. David Lloyd, *Memoirs of the Lives* (1668).
31. Cecil Wall, *A History of the Worshipful Society of Apothecaries of London*, Vol. I, arr. H.C. Cameron, ed. E. Ashworth Underwood (1963); Charles Goodall, *The Royal College of Physicians in London* (1684).
32. PRO, LC 5/132.
33. *DNB*; Edward Edwards, *Lives of the Founders of the British Museum* (1969).
34. *CSPC East Indies, China and Japan 1622–1624* (1878); *CSPC East Indies and Persia 1630–1634* (1892).
35. BM, Add. MS 6,703; Birch, *The Court and Times of Charles I*, op. cit.
36. *DNB*.
37. G.G. Harris, *The Trinity House of Deptford* (1969).

38. *CSPC East India, China and Japan 1513–1616* (1862); ibid., *1617–1621* (1870).
39. Barbour, *The Three Worlds of Captain John Smith*, op. cit.
40. BM, Add. MS 26,051.
41. P. Pett, *Autobiography*, ed. W.G. Perrin (1918).
42. Harris, *The Trinity House of Deptford*, op. cit.
43. Donald Nicholas, *Mr Secretary Nicholas* (1955).
44. *CSPD 1633–1634* (1863); ibid., *1636–1637* (1867).
45. John Aubrey, *The Oxford Cabinet* (1797).
46. Ashmole MS 824, f. 168.
47. *CSPD 1636–1637* (1867).
48. PRO, E 403/2733.
49. *The Letters of John Chamberlain*, op. cit.
50. J.W. Gough, *The Superlative Prodigall* (1932).
51. Evelyn, *Diary*, 20 October 1664.
52. Richard Ligon, *A True and Exact History of the Island of Barbados* (1657).
53. Edward Miller, *That Noble Cabinet* (1973); *Bibliographica*, Vol. III (1897).
54. H.R. Trevor-Roper, 'William Dell', *English Historical Review*, Vol. LXII (1947).
55. PRO, E 403/2743, 2744.
56. PRO, LS 13/280; LC 5/132 and 134.
57. Evelyn, *Diary*, 18 October 1671.
58. Edward Croft Murray, *Decorative Painting in England 1537–1837*, Vol. I (1962).
59. W. L. Spiers, *The Notebook and Account Book of Nicholas Stone*, Walpole Society Publications, Vol. VII (1918–19).
60. PRO, LC 5/132 and 134.
61. E.G.R. Taylor, *The Mathematical Practitioner of Tudor and Stuart England* (1954).
62. Croft Murray, *Decorative Painting in England 1537–1637*, op. cit.
63. *DNB*; PRO, E 403/2745 and 2746.
64. *Hasted's History of Kent*, ed. H.H. Drake (1886).
65. Henry Dircks, *The Life, Times and Scientific Labours of the Second Marquis of Worcester* (1863); G. Doorman, *Patents for Inventions* (1942).
66. Hartlib, Ephemerides, op. cit.
67. Ibid.
68. Gerard, *Herbal*, ed. Johnson, op. cit.
69. Harvey, *Early Nurserymen*, op. cit.
70. Robert Davies, 'A Memoir of Sir Thomas Herbert', *Yorkshire Archaeological and Topographical Journal*, Vol. I (1870).
71. Ashmole MS 1131.

Chapter 18

1. Mea Allan, *The Tradescants*, op. cit.
2. B.D. Jackson, *A Catalogue of Plants Cultivated in the Garden of John Gerard 1596–1599* (1876), p. 10.
3. William Turner, *A New Herbal* (1551).
4. William Turner, *The Names of Herbes* (1548), p. 44.
5. R.T. Gunther, *Early British Botanists and Their Gardens* (1922), p. 159.
6. A. Mitchell, *Trees of Britain and Northern Europe* (1974).
7. P.J. Jarvis, 'The Introduced Trees and Shrubs Cultivated by the Tradescants at

South Lambeth, 1629–1679', *Journal of the Society for the Bibliography of Natural History*, Vol. 9, No. 3 (1979).
8. Parkinson, *Paradisus*, op. cit., p. 152.
9. Wilfrid Blunt, *The Art of Botanical Illustration* (1950).
10. Gerard, *Herbal*, ed. Johnson, op. cit., p. 1215.
11. Parkinson, *Theatrum*, op. cit., p. 1058.
12. Parkinson, *Paradisus*, op. cit., p. 388.
13. Ibid., p. 389.
14. Ibid., p. 498.
15. Ibid., p. 506.
16. Ibid., p. 578.
17. Gerard, *Herbal*, ed. Johnson, op. cit., p. 1489.
18. Gerard, *Herbal*, op. cit., p. 1304.
19. Jackson, *A Catalogue of Plants . . .* , op. cit.
20. William Turner, *The First and Seconde Partes of the Herbal of William Turner. . . with the Thirde Parte . . .* (1568).
21. John Dent, *The Quest for Nonsuch* (1970).
22. Gerard, *Herbal*, ed. Johnson, op. cit., p. 1443.
23. Parkinson, *Paradisus*, op. cit., p. 595.
24. Gerard, *Herbal*, ed. Johnson, op. cit., p. 1306.
25. Ibid., p. 1155.
26. Ibid., p. 184.
27. Ibid., p 437.
28. Ibid., p. 731.
29. Ibid., p. 848.
30. Ibid., p. 1427.
31. Gerard, *Herbal*, op. cit., p. 1239.
32. Gerard, *Herbal*, ed. Johnson, op. cit., p. 1043.
33. Ibid., p. 260.
34. Ibid., p. 489.
35. Ibid., p. 948.
36. J.P. Cornut, *Canadensium Plantarum, aliarumque nondum edit arum Historia . . .* (1635).
37. Gerard, *Herbal*, ed. Johnson, op. cit., p. 785.
38. Ibid., p. 135.
39. Parkinson, *Paradisus*, op. cit., p. 102.
40. *The Gardener's Magazine*, 21 November 1874, p. 624.
41. Gerard, *Herbal*, ed. Johnson, op. cit., p. 443.
42. Ibid., p. 412.
43. BM, Arundel MS 42, f. 51v; see also J.H. Harvey, *Medieval Gardens* (1981), p. 125.
44. William Coles, *Adam in Eden* (1657).
45. Gerard, *Herbal*, ed. Johnson, op. cit., p. 1591.
46. Ibid., p. 1492.
47. Jackson, *A Catalogue of Plants . . .* , op. cit., p. 31.
48. Parkinson, *Paradisus*, op. cit., p. 439.
49. Parkinson, *Theatrum*, op. cit., p. 251.
50. Gerard, *Herbal*, op. cit., p. 409.
51. Parkinson, *Theatrum*, op. cit., p. 701.

52. Allan, *The Tradescants*, op. cit., p. 166.
53. Parkinson, *Paradisus*, op. cit., p. 236.
54. Parkinson, *Theatrum*, op. cit., p. 462.
55. Ibid., p. 1427.
56. Ibid., p. 1595.
57. Ibid., p. 1367.
58. Ibid., p. 1163.
59. Ibid., p. 1477.
60. Ibid., p. 1050.
61. Ibid., p. 1417.
62. Ibid., p. 1206.
63. Ibid., p. 1368.
64. Ibid., p. 1235.
65. Ibid., p. 1465.
66. Ibid., p. 1675.
67. Ibid., p. 130.
68. Ibid., p. 1511.
69. Ibid., p. 1109.
70. Parkinson, *Paradisus*, op. cit.
71. Parkinson, *Theatrum*, op. cit., p. 1064.
72. Ibid., p. 1454.
73. Ibid., p. 741.
74. Ibid., p. 1222.
75. Ibid., p. 323.
76. Ibid., p. 1468.
77. Alice M. *Coats, Garden Shrubs and Their Histories* (1963).
78. Parkinson, *Theatrum*, op. cit., p. 534.
79. Ibid., p. 1550.
80. Marjorie F. Warner, 'Jean and Vespasien Robin, "Royal Botanists", and North American Plants, 1601–1635', *National Horticultural Magazine*, Vol. 35 (1956).
81. John Evelyn, *Sylva*, 5th edn (1729).
82. Philip Miller, *The Gardener's Dictionary* (1731).
83. Leonard Plukenet, *Almagestum Botanicum* (1696).
84. Gunther, *Early British Botanists and Their Gardens*, op. cit.
85. Parkinson, *Paradisus*, op. cit., p. 563.
86. Gladys Taylor, *Old London Gardens* (1953).
87. Parkinson, *Paradisus*, op. cit., p. 567.
88. Allan, *The Tradescants*, op. cit., p. 144.
89. John H. Harvey, 'Mid-Georgian Nurseries of the London Region', *Transactions of the London and Middlesex Archaeological Society*, Vol. XXVI (1975), p. 306.
90 T.W.E. Roche, *A Pineapple for the King* (1971).
91. Bodleian Library, MS Eng. Hist. C. 11.
92. John Evelyn, *Diary*, 19 August 1668.
93. Evelyn, *Sylva* (1664), op. cit., p. 57.
94. Parkinson, *Paradisus*, op. cit. p. 608.
95. Allan, *The Tradescants*, op. cit., p. 168.
96. Parkinson, *Theatrum*, op. cit., p. 1617.

The Tradescant Family Tree

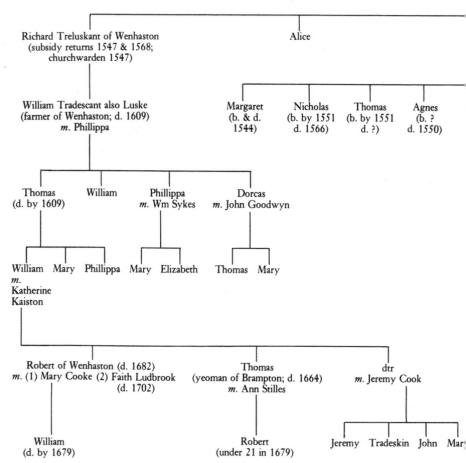

William Treluskant
(farmer of Wenhaston; d. 1536)

Richard Treluskant of Wenhaston
(subsidy returns 1547 & 1568;
churchwarden 1547)

Alice

William Tradescant also Luske
(farmer of Wenhaston; d. 1609)
m. Phillippa

Margaret
(b. & d.
1544)

Nicholas
(b. by 1551
d. 1566)

Thomas
(b. by 1551
d. ?)

Agnes
(b. ?
d. 1550)

Thomas
(d. by 1609)

William

Phillippa
m. Wm Sykes

Dorcas
m. John Goodwyn

William
m.
Katherine
Kaiston

Mary

Phillippa

Mary

Elizabeth

Thomas

Mary

Robert of Wenhaston (d. 1682)
m. (1) Mary Cooke (2) Faith Ludbrook
(d. 1702)

Thomas
(yeoman of Brampton; d. 1664)
m. Ann Stilles

dtr
m. Jeremy Cook

William
(d. by 1679)

Robert
(under 21 in 1679)

Jeremy   Tradeskin   John   Mar

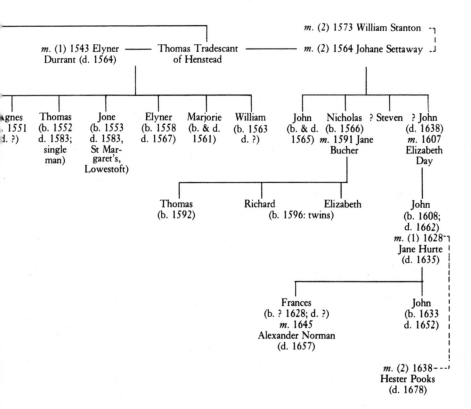

m. Margaret Soper

m. (1) 1543 Elyner ——— Thomas Tradescant ——— *m.* (2) 1564 Johane Settaway
Durrant (d. 1564)   of Henstead

m. (2) 1573 William Stanton

| Agnes (b. 1551 d. ?) | Thomas (b. 1552 d. 1583; single man) | Jone (b. 1553 d. 1583, St Margaret's, Lowestoft) | Elyner (b. 1558 d. 1567) | Marjorie (b. & d. 1561) | William (b. 1563 d. ?) | John (b. & d. 1565) | Nicholas (b. 1566) *m.* 1591 Jane Bucher | ? Steven | ? John (d. 1638) *m.* 1607 Elizabeth Day |

Thomas (b. 1592)   Richard (b. 1596: twins)   Elizabeth

John (b. 1608; d. 1662) *m.* (1) 1628 Jane Hurte (d. 1635)

Frances (b. ? 1628; d. ?) *m.* 1645 Alexander Norman (d. 1657)

John (b. 1633 d. 1652)

m. (2) 1638 Hester Pooks (d. 1678)

Portrait of a seventeenth-century gardener, believed to be the elder
John Tradescant, by an unknown artist. He is holding a mattock-hoe
in his right hand and a basket of red and white pears in his left. The other
baskets contain quinces and grapes: a melon can be seen through
the doorway.

Index

abacus, Russian, 74
Abies sibirica, 73
Acer rubrum, 206–7
Achillea clavennae, 203
Achmouty, Sir John, 182
Actaea alba, 205
Adiantum pedatum, 204
Aeonium arboreum, 203
Aesculus hippocastanum, 149, 197, 198
Agave americana, 203
Aires, John *see* Eyres, John
Albert, Archduke, 38
Algiers, 75, 76
Alicante, 76
Alkenet, 161
Allan, Mea, 24, 25, 73, 115, 197, 204,
    208, 210
Allium, 52, 198
Allspice, 203
aloes, 203
Alston, Sir Edward, 132
Amelanchier ovalis, 203
Amsterdam, 36
Anagyris foetida, 199
Andromeda arborea, 73
anemones, 19, 31, 35, 114, 201
angelica, 69
Annona muricata, 207
Anthyllis barba-jovis, 201
Antwerp, 27, 36, 37, 98
Apothecaries, Society of, 18, 183
apple trees, 34, 70, 101, 102, 195
apricots, 33, 37, 38, 75, 102, 195
Aquilegia canadensis, 204

Arbor Judea, 160
Arborvita, 35, 36
Arbutus unedo, 161, 197
Archangel, 58, 59, 62, 70, 210
Argall, John, 54
Argall, Sir Samuel, 53–5
Aristolachia serpentaria, 199
Ark, *see* Tradescant, John the elder, South
    Lambeth Museum, *and* Tradescant, John
    the Younger, South Lambeth Museum
Artemisia: abrotanum, 73; *maritima*, 94
artichokes, 29, 38
Aruncus dioicus, 199
Arundel, Alathea, Countess of, 176
Arundel, Thomas, Earl of, 133, 167,
    176–8, 181
Arundo donax, 126, 203
Asarum canadense, 203
Ashmole, Elias, 21, 133, 165, 168–9,
    202, 208; correspondence of, 118, 158,
    195; education and career of, 129–30,
    136, 146; Hester T.'s submission to,
    149–50; library of, 145, 157, 160, 171;
    properties of in South Lambeth, 148–9,
    153, 157, 159, 160, 162, 171, 208;
    visitor to S. Lambeth, 129–31,
    146, 147, 148; and Tradescant
    collection: benefactor to, 132; helps to
    catalogue, 131, 137, 141; receives by
    deed of gift, 137–8, 142, 155; lawsuits
    over, 140–3, 154–6; takes possession of,
    149, 153; donates to Oxford University,
    155–8
Ashmole, Mary (*née* Forster), 130–1, 147

329

Hevesson, Dirryk, 34
Heydon, James, 91
Heydon, Sir John, 123
Hoare, Charity, 152
Hoare, Richard, 140, 142, 152
Hobbs, Giles, 72
Hobert, Bertram, 119, 120, 128
Hobert, Sarah, 119
Holborn, 18, 26, 198
Holland House, 36
Hollar, Wenceslaus, 98, 131, 133, 142
honeysuckle, trumpet, 207
Hooke, Dr Robert, 156–7, 173
Hoole, Charles, 100, 163
Hooper, Thomas, 33
horse chestnut tree, 160, 197, 198
Howard, Thomas, 186
Hubert, Robert, 163
Hudson, Jeffrey, 167
humble plant, 210
Hunterian collection, Glasgow, 160, 171
Hurte, Jane, *see* Tradescant, Jane
Hurte, William, 110
Hyll, Thomas, 17, 43
Hymenaea courbaril, 210

Ibiza, 76
Ireland, George, 185
iris, 31, 37

James I, 18, 19, 25, 28, 48, 58, 75, 79, 80, 83, 86, 91–2, 105, 111, 170, 182, 187
James, Richard, 59, 72
Jamestown, 53, 54, 55, 185
Jardin des Plantes, Paris, 39
Jardin Royal des Plantes Médicinales, Paris, 39, 206
Jarvis, Dr P.J., 197
Jasminum: humile, 207; *officinale*, 197
Jennings, Mountain, 29, 170
Johnson, Thomas, 114; botanizing expeditions of, 19, 132, 182; career of, 19; describes Tradescant's plant finds,

26, 77, 94; on Tradescant's plants and museum objects, 100, 101, 198, 199; revised edition of Gerard's *Herbal*, 19, 108, 182, 198 202
Jokket, John, 30, 32
Jones, Inigo, 29, 105, 117, 176
jonquils, 36
Juglans: cinerea, 203; *nigra*, 197
jujube tree, 203
Juniperus sabina, 201
Jupiter's beard, 201

Kalthoff, Caspar, 194
Keighley, Christopher, 50
Kellie, Thomas, Earl of, 81
Killigrew, Lady, 180
King, Katherine, 139, 142, 147. 150, 151, 152, 153, 154–6
King's School, Canterbury, 55–7, 132
Kirby Hall (Northamptonshire), 101, 160, 161
Kirke, Sir David, 179

Laburnum anagyroides, 199
Lambert, William, 194
Lambeth Palace, 99, 177
Lanyon, John, 194
larch trees, 73, 210
Lardner, John, 115
Larix: decidua, 210; *sibirica*, 73, 210
La Rochelle, 92–4, 95
Lascelles, Edmund, 26, 27
Laud, William, 86, 99, 118, 177, 180, 192
laurel, 121
Laurus tinus, 31, 101
Lavendula: latifolia, 203; *stoechas*, 208
Lea (Leigh), Matthew, 153
Lea, William, 128
le Gouche, Steven, 194
Leiden, 35, 183, 209
lettuce, Roman Red, 198
Leveson, Lady Christian, 175
Ligon, Richard, 187

Offley, Robert, 186
Offley, Thomas, 186
Oglander, Sir John, 167
Oldham, John, 99
Olea europea, 202
oleanders, 39
oleaster, 202
onions, 29, 44, 45, 77
Ononis speciosa, 77, 203
orange houses 17, 107
orange trees, 30, 39, 107, 125, 147, 148, 207
orchards, 17, 33, 47, 51, 96, 98, 193
Ornithogalum arabicum, 203; *nutans*, 31
osiers, 42, 43
Owefield, Mr, 194
Owen, Dr John, 182
Oxford Physic Garden, 108–9, 129, 175, 208, 210
Oxford, University of, 58, 109, 126, 129, 137, 140, 142, 143, 150, 155, 156, 157, 158, 159, 183
Oxycoccus palustris, 73

Palmer, Sir Henry, 181
Palmer, Sir Philip, 209

Pancratium illyricum, 31, 32
Paradisea liliastrum, 31, 32
Paris, 21, 38–40, 81, 83, 92, 167, 178, 182, 204, 205, 206
Parkinson, John, 113, 114, 127, 197–200, 202–4; career of, 18; descriptions of plants in *Paradisus*, 32, 34, 36, 37, 38, 43, 77, 196, 197, 210; *Paradisus*, 13–14, 18, 19, 98, 153, 171, 182, 197, 200, 201, 202, 204, 210; references to elder Tradescant in *Paradisus*, 37, 38, 50, 52, 72, 75, 101, 112, 176, 197, 198, 203, 204, 207, 208; in *Theatrum Botanicum*, 112, 118, 204, 205, 206; references to younger Tradescant in *Theatrum Botanicum*, 112, 204–5, 206; *Theatrum*

Botanicum, 18, 73, 94, 118, 204, 205, 210
Parr, Thomas, 153, 167
parsnips, 176, 198
Parthenocissus quinquefolia, 197
Passiflora incarnata, 202
peaches, 37, 40–1, 101, 102, 195
pear trees, 34, 35, 37, 40, 41, 70, 101, 102, 195
Pelargonium triste, 199
Pepys, Samuel, 15, 121, 137, 144
Perkins, Admonisham, 192
Pett, Capt. Phineas, 75, 181–2, 185
Petty, Rev. William, 176–7
Phaseolus coccineus, 198
Philips, Fabian, 193
Physalis pubescens, 204
Physicians, College of, 126, 132, 133, 182, 183
Picea obovata, 73
Pimenta dioica, 203
pineapples, 208–9, 210
pine trees, 73, 121, 160
Pinus sylvestris, 73
Pistacia: lentiscus, 202; *terebinthus*, 77, 204, 208
plane trees, 198, 204, 208; London plane, 208
Plantarum in Horto, see under Tradescant, John the elder
Platanus occidentalis, 160, 204, 208; *orientalis*, 160, 198, 208
Plot, Dr Robert, 157–8
Plukenet, Leonard, 207
Plumleigh, Capt., 185
plums, 40, 44, 45, 101, 102, 121, 195, 198; 'white diapered', 198
Pocahontas, 53–5
poison ivy, 203
pomegranates, 39, 40, 77, 80
Pooks, Hester, see Tradescant, Hester
Pooks, John, 152
Portington, William, 105